Boston

"All you've got to do is decide to go
and the hardest part is over.

So go!"

TONY WHEELER, COFOUNDER – LONELY PLANET

Mara Vorhees

Contents

Plan Your Trip 4

Explore Boston 44

Understand Boston 189

Survival Guide 207

Boston Maps 225

(left) **Charles River and Back Bay p106**

....

(above) **Fenway Park p123** Home of the Boston Red Sox.

....

(right) **Public Garden p72** A 24-acre botanical oasis.

....

Cambridge
p139

Charlestown
p50

West End
& North End
p56

Beacon Hill &
Boston Common p68

Downtown &
Waterfront p80

Back Bay
p106

Kenmore
Square &
Fenway
p117

South End
& Chinatown
p93

Seaport District &
South Boston
p129

Streetcar
Suburbs
p156

Welcome to Boston

Boston's history recalls revolution and transformation, and today the city is still among the country's most forward-thinking and barrier-breaking cities.

Art & Music

The arts have thrived in Boston ever since the 19th century, when this cultural capital was dubbed the Athens of America. Certainly, the intellectual elite appreciated their fine paintings and classical music, but they were also dedicated to spreading the cultural wealth, establishing museums, libraries and symphony orchestras for all to enjoy. Today the lucky residents of (and visitors to) Boston benefit from their largesse. These venerable institutions play an integral role on Boston's cultural stage, which has significantly expanded to include dynamic contemporary art, music and theater scenes.

Sports

'Fanatic' is no idle word here. Boston fans are passionate about sports. And with the five-time world-champion Patriots, the long-overdue World Series–winning Red Sox, the winningest basketball team in history, the Celtics, and the highly successful and historic hockey team, the Bruins, there is a lot to be passionate about. Boston's college teams also inspire fierce loyalties and staunch rivalries. No less spirited is the country's oldest and most celebrated running event, the world-famous Boston Marathon, and the world's largest two-day rowing event, the Head of the Charles Regatta.

Food

A word of advice: when in Boston, eat as much seafood as possible. Local specialties include the 'sacred cod,' fresh steamed lobster, oysters on the half-shell and thick, creamy chowder. You can eat seafood around the city, but especially in the fish-centered Seaport District, where it's accompanied by spectacular harbor views. However, don't miss the chance to devour delectable pasta in the North End or to sample diverse Asian dishes in Chinatown. Trendy fusion restaurants draw on all of these eclectic influences to present contemporary cuisine that is uniquely Boston.

History

For all intents and purposes, Boston is the oldest city in America. And you can hardly walk a step on its cobblestone streets without running into a historic site. The Freedom Trail winds its way through the city, connecting 16 historically significant sites, from the country's oldest public park to a Revolutionary War battle site. These are the very places where history unfolded, especially the events leading to the American fight for independence from Britain. Other sites remember the city's role in the abolition movement, its cultural contributions and more. In effect, Boston is an amazing outdoor history museum.

Why I Love Boston

By Mara Vorhees, Writer

Boston is wicked *smaaht*. I love that my city is motivated not by money or politics, but by learning. The academic institutions are a source of groundbreaking ideas, creative endeavors and renewable energy, which contribute to a dynamic, forward-looking city. But not all Bostonians are innovators: some are also scholars and conservators of history. After all, this is the 'Cradle of Liberty' and all that. So while it looks to the future, Boston also appreciates and celebrates the past, and maybe even learns from the compelling history that happened here.

For more about our writers, see p256

Top: Old State House (p82)

Boston's
Top 10

Freedom Trail *(p28)*

1 For a sampler of Boston's revolutionary sights, follow the red-brick road. It leads 2.5 miles through the center of Boston, from Boston Common to the Bunker Hill Monument, and traces the events leading up to and following the War for Independence. The Freedom Trail is well marked and easy to follow on your own – an ideal strategy if you actually wish to enter some of the historic buildings and museums. Otherwise, there are plenty of tours that follow this trail, including the National Park Service's (NPS) free option.

BELOW LEFT: FANEUIL HALL (P83)

👁 *Walking the Freedom Trail*

Fenway Park *(p123)*

2 There might as well be signs on I-90 reading 'Now entering Red Sox Nation.' The intensity of baseball fandom has only grown since the Boston Red Sox broke their agonizing 86-year losing streak and won the 2004 World Series. The hometown team has since repeated its feat – thrice – which means it continues to sell out every game. Catch the boys at Fenway Park, the iconic old-style ballpark that has hosted the Sox for more than a century.

🏃 *Kenmore Square & Fenway*

3

4

Copley Square (p111)

3 Boston's most exquisite architecture is clustered around this stately Back Bay plaza. The square's centerpiece is Henry Hobson Richardson's celebrated Romanesque masterpiece, Trinity Church. It's lovely in reality and even lovelier as reflected in the mirrored facade of the modern John Hancock Tower. This assemblage faces off against the elegant neo-Renaissance facade of the Boston Public Library. The plaza itself is peppered with whimsical and serious pieces commemorating the city's biggest sporting event, the Boston Marathon, for which Copley Sq is the finish line.

TOP LEFT: TRINITY CHURCH (P110) AND THE JOHN HANCOCK TOWER (P112)

⊙ *Back Bay*

Charles River Esplanade (p111)

4 When we talk about the 'waterfront,' we're usually talking about the Boston Harbor. But there's a second, equally appealing waterfront along Charles River. The Esplanade is a long and narrow riverside park that offers endless opportunities for outdoor recreation, from playgrounds and picnic areas to bike trails and ballparks. There's no swimming in the river, but there is sunbathing, sailing, kayaking and canoeing. The Hatch Memorial Shell is a venue for (free) outdoor entertainment, including the annual July 4 concert by the Boston Pops.

🏃 *Back Bay*

Museum of Fine Arts (p119)

5 The collections at the Museum of Fine Arts span the centuries and span the globe, but it's the Art of the Americas that make this museum shine. It's the Americas – plural – so you might see Maya artifacts and Peruvian textiles alongside the world's largest collection of American Colonial art. Highlights include countless paintings by John Singleton Copley and John Singer Sargent, as well as Paul Revere's famed *Sons of Liberty Bowl*. It's a niche – New World art – but the MFA fills it in a way that few other museums can.

⊙ *Kenmore Square & Fenway*

North End *(p56)*

6 What's so special about eating in the North End? For starters, it actually feels like you're in Italy. As one of Boston's oldest neighborhoods, the narrow streets and brick buildings exude an Old World ambience that is only enhanced by its Italian-American population. It sounds like Italy, too, with local residents carrying on lively conversations in the mother tongue. Most importantly, it tastes like Italy. Packed with romantic restaurants, cozy cafes and aromatic bakeries, the North End will delight the senses and the stomach.

✖ *West End & North End*

Rose Kennedy Greenway *(p85)*

7 This glorious green ribbon winds through Boston's Downtown area, weaving through the city streets with blooming flowers, flowing fountains, art markets, beer gardens, food trucks, whimsical sculpture and one fabulous merry-go-round. It's a green gateway to the big blue, that is the Boston Harbor and all the activities that take place along the waterfront. The fact that the Greenway used to be the site of a hulking overhead highway makes it all the more appealing. A highlight is the fantastic seasonal public art exhibits.

👁 *Downtown & Waterfront*

6

Harvard Square *(p144)*

8 Harvard Sq is overflowing with bookstores and boutiques, coffee shops and record shops, street performers and street dwellers. Although many Cantabridgians rightly complain that the square has lost its edge – shops that were once independently owned are continually gobbled up by national chains – Harvard Sq is still a vibrant, exciting place to hang out. The university is the centerpiece of the square, with ivy-covered architecture and excellent museums. Harvard Sq is also a hotbed of colonial and revolutionary history, from the Cambridge Common to Mt Auburn Cemetery.

⊙ *Cambridge*

Boston Harbor Islands *(p165)*

9 If you're dreaming of an island vacation, you've come to the right place. The Boston Harbor Islands consist of 34 islands, many of which are open for trail-walking, bird-watching, camping, kayaking and swimming. Explore a 19th-century fort at Georges Island, walk the trails and lounge on the beach at Spectacle Island, or climb to the top of Boston's iconic oldest lighthouse (pictured; p167) at Little Brewster. Mostly operated by the NPS, the Harbor Islands offer a unique opportunity for outdoor adventure – and they're a quick boat ride from downtown Boston.

⊙ *Day Trips from Boston*

Beacon Hill *(p68)*

10 With an intriguing history, distinctive architecture and unparalleled neighborhood charm, Beacon Hill is Boston's most prestigious address. It's hard to beat the utter loveliness of the place: the narrow cobblestone streets lit with gas lanterns; the distinguished brick town houses decked with purple windowpanes and blooming flower boxes; and streets such as stately Louisburg Sq that capture the neighborhood's grandeur. The commercial street that traverses the flat of the hill – Charles St – is Boston's most enchanting spot for browsing boutiques and haggling over antiques.

ABOVE: ACORN ST (P74)

🏠 *Beacon Hill & Boston Common*

What's New

Somerville
Somehow, this gritty city that was nick-named 'Slummer-ville' has turned into one of Boston's hippest neighborhoods. There are no historic sights to speak of but you'll find terrific dining, nightlife and entertainment. (p152)

East Boston
Next up is East Boston, where the city's last stretch of undeveloped waterfront offers the best views around. Currently, Reelhouse is perhaps the only place in Boston to watch the sunset over the harbor. Look for more East Boston activity in the coming years. (p54)

Craft Breweries
Boston is awash in beer. Not just Sam Adams and Harpoon IPA, but hundreds of varieties of pilsners, ales, ambers and sours. Nowadays, almost every neighborhood has its own microbrewery. (p36)

Lynch Family Skate Park
After much anticipation, this excellent new skate park is Boston's best place for skateboarders and BMX riders to show off their stuff. (p155)

Underground at Ink Block
Speaking of cool urban parks created in the shadow of a highway, this cool new green space features walking trails, fitness classes and some awesome street art. (p95)

Odyssey Opera
Opera in Boston takes a backseat to the symphony and the ballet. And yet conductor Gil Rose saw fit to start a new company, Odyssey Opera, dedicated to underperformed operatic repertoire. (p37)

Boston Calling
Boston's biggest music festival started in 2013 as a two-day festival on City Hall Plaza. Now the event has gone big league, upgrading to three days in a much larger venue (Harvard Stadium) and attracting the likes of Jack White and Eminem. (p81)

Pod Hotel
Check in at a self-service kiosk. Sleep in a 'cabin' instead of a hotel room. Get served by a robot. Experience the future of hospitality at Yotel. (p186)

Dockless Bike Sharing
Companies such as Lime (www.li.me) are now offering dockless bike sharing in the suburbs. Boston and immediate environs – Brookline, Cambridge and Somerville – are under exclusive agreement with Blue Bikes; nonetheless, the green bikes keep turning up in the oddest of places. (p210)

2018 World Series Banner
That's right, *another* World Series banner hangs outside Fenway Park. Go Sox!

For more recommendations and reviews, see **lonelyplanet. com/boston**

Need to Know

For more information, see Survival Guide (p207)

Currency
US dollar ($)

Language
English

Visas
Citizens of most countries are eligible for the Visa Waiver Program, which requires prior electronic approval via Electronic System for Travel Authorization (ESTA).

Money
ATMs widely available. Credit cards accepted at most hotels, restaurants and shops.

Cell Phones
Most US cell-phone systems work on the GSM 850/1900 standard, as opposed to the GSM 900/1800 standard used throughout Europe, Australia and Asia.

Time
Eastern Standard Time (GMT/UTC minus five hours)

Tourist Information
Boston Common Information Kiosk (GBCVB Visitors Center; Map p236; ☑617-426-3115; www.bostonusa.com; Boston Common; ◎8:30am-5pm Mon-Fri, from 9am Sat & Sun; Ⓣ Park St) provides maps and all kinds of tourist information; starting point for the Freedom Trail and many other walking tours.

Daily Costs

Budget:
Less than $100
➡ Dorm bed: $50
➡ Pizza or dumplings: $5–10
➡ Certain museum nights and walking tours: free
➡ Ride on the T: $2.25–2.75

Midrange:
$100–300
➡ Double room in a midrange hotel: $150–250
➡ Meal at a midrange restaurant: $15–25
➡ Museum admission: $15–25
➡ Short taxi ride: $15–20

Top End:
More than $300
➡ Double room in a top-end hotel: from $250
➡ Meal at a top-end restaurant: from $25
➡ Concerts, events and other activities: from $50

Advance Planning
One month before Reserve a place to stay. Budget travelers, this means you! Make sure to buy your tickets for the Boston Symphony Orchestra, the Boston Red Sox or your favorite Boston band.

One week before Book tours and make reservations for weekend dinners.

One day before Check the weather (again). Pack your umbrella anyway.

Useful Websites
Lonely Planet (www.lonelyplanet.com/usa/boston) Destination information, hotel bookings, traveler forum and more.

My Secret Boston (www.mysecretboston.com) Not *that* secret restaurants, nightlife, cultural and family events.

Blue Mass Group (www.bluemassgroup.com) Left-leaning political junkies report on State House goings-on.

Universal Hub (www.universalhub.com) Round-up of local news, with rich local commentary.

Greater Boston Convention & Visitors Center (www.bostonusa.com) The official guide to what to do and where to stay.

WHEN TO GO

Peak travel times are autumn and spring, with lovely weather and many events. Summer is humid but also busy.

Boston

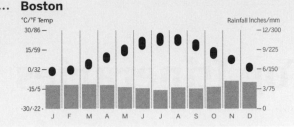

Arriving in Boston

Boston Logan International Airport Take the silver line bus (free) or blue line subway ($2.25 to $2.75) to central Boston from 5:30am to 12:30am, or catch a taxi for $25 to $30.

South Station Located in central Boston on the red line.

Manchester Airport Book in advance for the hourly Flight Line Inc shuttle bus to Logan International Airport, or catch the infrequent Greyhound bus to South Station.

Green Airport Take the commuter rail to South Station ($12).

For much more on **arrival** see p208

Getting Around

➡ **T (Subway)** The quickest and easiest way to get to most destinations. Runs from 5:30am or 6am until 1:30am.

➡ **Blue Bikes** Boston's bike-share program, with 1800 bikes available to borrow at 200 stations.

➡ **MBTA bus** Supplements the subway system.

For much more on **getting around** see p209

Sleeping

Boston offers a wide range of accommodations, from inviting guesthouses in historic quarters to swanky hotels with all the amenities. There is no shortage of stately homes that have been converted into B&Bs, offering an intimate atmosphere and personal service. Considering that this city is filled with students, there are surprisingly few accommodations targeting budget travelers and backpackers.

Useful Websites

➡ **Lonely Planet** (lonelyplanet.com/usa/boston/hotels) Reviews and bookings.

➡ **B&B Agency of Boston** (www.boston-bnbagency.com) Fully furnished vacation rentals.

➡ **Bed & Breakfast Associates Bay Colony** (www.bnbboston.com) Huge database of unhosted, furnished rooms and apartments.

➡ **Inn Boston Reservations** (www.innbostonreservations.com) Studio and apartment rentals in Boston's best neighborhoods.

For much more on **sleeping** see p178

Top Itineraries

Day One

Downtown & Waterfront (p80)

 Spend your first day in Boston following the **Freedom Trail**, which starts on the Boston Common and continues through downtown. There isn't time to go inside every museum, but you can admire the architecture, learn the history and pay your respects at the graves of the history makers. Highlights include the **Granary Burying Ground**, the **Old South Meeting House**, the **Old State House** and **Faneuil Hall**.

 Lunch Grab a bite from Clover DTX (p85) or Spyce (p85).

West End & North End (p56)

In the afternoon, the Freedom Trail continues into the North End, where you can visit the historic **Paul Revere House**, **Old North Church** and **Copp's Hill Burying Ground**. If you have the stamina, cross the Charlestown Bridge to see the **USS Constitution** and the **Bunker Hill Monument**.

Dinner You are perfectly poised for an Italian feast at Pomodoro (p62).

West End & North End (p56)

Move on to the exquisite **Liberty Hotel**, former site of the Charles St Jail. After admiring the impressive architectural transformation in the lobby, head downstairs for a drink in the former drunk tank, which now houses the ultracool club and cocktail bar, **Alibi**.

Day Two

Back Bay (p106)

Spend the morning admiring Boston's most architecturally significant collection of buildings, clustered around **Copley Square**. Admire the art and books at the **Boston Public Library**, ogle the magnificent stained-glass windows at **Trinity Church** and gaze at the clean lines on the **John Hancock Tower**. Perhaps enjoy a spot of shopping on **Newbury Street** on your way to lunch.

 Lunch Snag a spot at Saltie Girl (p113) or Luke's Lobster (p112).

Kenmore Square & Fenway (p117)

Your afternoon is reserved for one of Boston's magnificent art museums. Unfortunately, you'll have to choose between the excellent, encyclopedic collection at the **Museum of Fine Arts** or the smaller but no less extraordinary exhibits at the **Isabella Stewart Gardner Museum**. Either way, you won't be disappointed.

 Dinner Eat oysters and drink craft beer at Island Creek Oyster Bar (p125).

Kenmore Square & Fenway (p117)

There is music in the air this evening. It might be emanating from the acoustically perfect **Symphony Hall**, where you can hear the world-renowned Boston Symphony Orchestra (procure tickets in advance). For a rowdier night on the town, catch a baseball game at **Fenway Park** or go barhopping on **Lansdowne Street**.

Day Three

Cambridge (p139)

 Rent a bicycle and spend the morning cycling along the **Charles River**. Stop for scenic views of scullers and sailboats on the Charles, with the Boston city skyline as the backdrop. Depending where you start, the route passes both Harvard University and MIT campuses. Ambitious riders can return along the **Charles River Esplanade**, continuing through Harvard's Allston campus and ending near Harvard Sq.

 Lunch Slurp a bowl of noodles at Hokkaido Ramen Santouka (p145).

Cambridge (p139)

While away an afternoon in **Harvard Square**, browsing the bookstores and cruising the cafes. Hang out at the **Smith Campus Center**. Catch a free campus tour (or try the unofficial **Hahvahd Tour** for laughs). If you're in the mood for a museum, the university offers several excellent options.

Dinner Go casual at Night Market (p145) or classy at Waypoint (p147).

Cambridge (p139)

See whatever brilliant or bizarre production is playing at the **American Repertory Theater.** Alternatively, catch a band at **Lizard Lounge** or **Club Passim**, or just patronize the buskers in Harvard Sq.

Day Four

Downtown & Waterfront (p80)

 Spend the morning on the water. If the weather is fine, book yourself on a **whale-watching tour** to Stellwagen Bank. Alternatively, get a closer view of the marine life inside the **New England Aquarium**. Afterward, stroll along the **Rose Kennedy Greenway**, stopping to watch the fun at the Rings Fountain and contemplate the public art at Dewey Sq.

 Lunch Try one of Boston's best lobster rolls from James Hook & Co (p86).

Seaport District & South Boston (p129)

Continue along the HarborWalk, admiring the harbor views along the way. Your destination is the **Institute of Contemporary Art** for an afternoon of provocative contemporary art. Don't miss the amazing view from the Founders Gallery.

Dinner Try Coppa Enoteca (p96) or tapas from Barcelona Wine Bar (p96).

South End & Chinatown (p93)

Continue your night on the town in the South End. Hear some down and dirty blues at **Wally's Café** or sip cocktails with the sophisticates at **Beehive**.

If You Like...

Revolutionary History

Freedom Trail The 2.5-mile walking trail includes Boston's most important revolutionary sites. (p28)

Lexington & Concord An easy day trip from Boston, these towns are the sites of the first battles in the War for Independence. (p167)

Boston Tea Party Ships & Museum This excellent museum includes replicas of the merchant ships that hosted the historic tea party. (p132)

Patriots' Day A day of re-enactments and parades commemorating the first battles of the American Revolutionary War. (p21)

Cambridge Common The city green is where George Washington took command of his army in 1775. (p144)

Warren Tavern One of the country's oldest taverns, this historic watering hole is named for Dr Joseph Warren, who died in the Battle of Bunker Hill. (p55)

The Ocean

Boston Harbor Islands Thirty-four islands dot the Boston Harbor, and many are open for hiking, swimming, sea kayaking and camping. (p165)

New England Aquarium Whale Watch Cruise out to Stellwagen Bank to spot some marine life in the wild. (p92)

Carson Beach Want to escape summer in the city? Pick an inviting urban beach in South Boston. (p138)

DENISTANGNEYJR / GETTY IMAGES © NEW WING ARCHITECT RENZO PIANO

Isabella Stewart Gardner Museum (p121)

Liberty Fleet Sail around the Boston Harbor on board the *Liberty Clipper* or the *Liberty Star*. (p92)

Codzilla High speeds and cold water guarantee a splashin' good time. (p211)

Courageous Sailing Learn some sailing skills or just enjoy the cruise around the Boston Harbor. (p55)

Contemporary Art

Institute of Contemporary Art Boston's preeminent venue for contemporary art boasts a dramatic waterside setting. (p131)

Museum of Fine Arts The Linde Family Wing for Contemporary Art tripled the exhibition space for its growing collection. (p119)

Isabella Stewart Gardner Museum A dynamic artist-in-residency program ensures a rich rotation of innovative exhibits and performances. (p121)

SoWa Artists Guild Visit on the first Friday of the month, when artists open their studios to the public. (p95)

Harvard Art Museums Often shows off contemporary art from its collections in its top-floor temporary exhibit space. (p142)

Fort Point Arts Community A long-standing artists' cooperative that organizes gallery exhibits, open studio events and other artsy goings-on. (p132)

Kennedy Family History

John F Kennedy National Historic Site See where the 35th US president was born and raised. (p158)

John F Kennedy Library & Museum Learn about Kennedy's

political legacy at the official presidential library. (p133)

Edward Kennedy Institute for the US Senate Check out the newest Kennedy venue, this one a tribute to JFK's youngest brother. (p133)

Rose Kennedy Greenway Pay your respects to the matriarch of the Kennedy clan. (p85)

Union Oyster House Request the JFK booth and order the lobster bisque. (p87)

Harvard University This was JFK's alma mater, and the university now has a public policy institute and a riverside park that bear his name. (p141)

Literature

Concord Tour the homes and visit the gravesites of Concord's literary masters; take a detour to Walden Pond to experience *Life in the Woods*. (p169)

Longfellow House See where the Fireside Poet composed the *Song of Hiawatha* and *Paul Revere's Ride*. (p144)

Public Garden Don't miss *Make Way for Ducklings*, a whimsical bronze statue based on Robert McCloskey's famous children's book. (p72)

Boston Athenaeum Since its founding in 1807, this esteemed institution has counted many noteworthy writers and thinkers among its members. (p73)

Brookline Booksmith Boston's best bookstore hosts author talks several nights a week. (p162)

Architecture

Copley Square Some of Boston's most stunning signature buildings are clustered around this plaza. (p111)

For more top Boston spots, see the following:
→ Eating (p32)
→ Drinking & Nightlife (p35)
→ Entertainment (p37)
→ Shopping (p40)
→ Sports & Activities (p42)

PLAN YOUR TRIP IF YOU LIKE...

Harvard University Features the best of all eras, including buildings by Henry Hobson Richardson, Walter Gropius and Le Corbusier. (p141)

Massachusetts Institute of Technology The campus contains masterful examples of 20th-century modernism and 21st-century mayhem. (p143)

Institute of Contemporary Art Boston's art museums are housed in buildings that also make impressive architectural statements – a trend that was started when the ICA built this striking edifice. (p131)

City Hall Plaza Love it or hate it, this brutalist landmark is undeniably iconic. (p84)

Design Museum Boston A pop-up museum hosting exhibits and talks all around town. (p91)

Animals

New England Aquarium Whale Watch Sightings of whales, dolphins and other marine life are practically guaranteed. (p92)

New England Aquarium Get to know all kinds of marine life, from seals to penguins to jellyfish. (p83)

Franklin Park Zoo Visit the Serengeti Plain, the Australian outback and the Amazonian rain forest all in one afternoon. (p159)

Museum of Science More than 120 furry, feathered and scaly creatures are featured in daily live animal presentations. (p58)

Harvard Museum of Natural History Hundreds of (stuffed) animals peer out of glass showcases, representing all classes and continents. (p142)

Greenway Carousel Take a ride on one of 36 animals that are native to Massachusetts. (p85)

Gardens

Public Garden The Victorian-era Public Garden is an island of loveliness, always awash in blooms and breezes. (p72)

Arnold Arboretum Flowering trees galore, with special collections of bonsai, lilacs, conifers, roses and fruit-laden Malus. (p158)

Rose Kennedy Greenway The Greenway shows off a variety of landscaping styles, including the delightful Carol Lynch Garden, a European-style perennial garden in the North End Parks. (p85)

Back Bay Fens At the end of June, the Kelleher Rose Garden explodes in fireworks of colors and scents. (p124)

Old North Church Boston's oldest church is surrounded by delightfully secluded gardens, including an 18th-century garden featuring blooms from the days of yore. (p59)

Hidden Gardens of Beacon Hill Once a year, the reserved residents of Beacon Hill open up their perfectly manicured plots to the public. (p74)

Free Stuff

Freedom Trail The National Park Service (NPS) offers a free walking tour; several sites along the route do not charge admission. (p28)

Black Heritage Trail Another free NPS walking tour that explores the history of African American settlement in Beacon Hill. (p79)

Museum of Fine Arts Free on Wednesday evenings. (p119)

Institute of Contemporary Art Free on Thursday evenings. (p131)

Boston Public Library See the BPL's impressive art and architecture on daily free guided tours. (p108)

Massachusetts Institute of Technology Free campus tours. (p143)

Harvard University Free campus tours. (p141)

JFK National Historic Site See the birthplace of the 35th president – for free. (p158)

Hatch Memorial Shell The Esplanade stage is the place for free summertime entertainment. (p111)

Samuel Adams Brewery Free tours of the brewery and free samples. (p161)

Month by Month

January

January represents the deepest, darkest part of winter. Expect cold temperatures and plenty of snow. The weather is often fantastic for sledding, skating and other winter sports.

🎎 Chinese New Year

In January or February, Chinatown lights up with a colorful parade, firecrackers, fireworks and lots of food. The highlight is the traditional lion dances, which fill the streets following the parade.

February

The weather is still cold, but the days are getting longer. Tourists are few and far between, so prices are cheap.

🏃 Beanpot

Since 1952, local college hockey teams face off in the hotly contested Beanpot Tournament (p38). Games take place at TD Garden on the first two Mondays in February.

March

By March, Boston is officially sick of winter. On March 17 the city celebrates Evacuation Day, when the British pulled out of Boston Harbor in 1776.

🎎 St Patrick's Day

The large and vocal South Boston Irish community hosts a parade (www.southbostonparade.org) on West Broadway, complete with participation by gay and lesbian groups (who were famously banned for 20-plus years).

🍴 Dine Out Boston

For the first full week of March, scores of restaurants offer prix-fixe menus: $15 to $25 for lunch, $28 to $38 for dinner (www.dineoutboston.com). The menus are usually excellent value. This event repeats in August.

April

Emerging crocuses and blooming forsythias signal the arrival of spring, and baseball fans await opening day at Fenway Park. Temperatures range from 40°F to 55°F, although the occasional snowstorm can also occur.

☆ Patriots' Day

On the third Monday in April, history buffs commemorate the start of the American Revolution with a reenactment of the battle on Lexington Green (11 miles west of Boston) and a commemoration ceremony at the North Bridge in Concord (17 miles west of Boston).

🏃 Boston Marathon

The world's oldest marathon attracts tens of thousands of ambitious runners to pound the pavement for 26.2 miles. Held on Patriots' Day.

☆ Independent Film Festival of Boston

During the last week in April, venues around the city host screenings of independent films (www.iffboston.org), including shorts, documentaries and drama produced locally and nationally.

May

In May – one of Boston's most beautiful months – the sun comes out on a semipermanent basis and the magnolia trees bloom all along Newbury St and Commonwealth Ave. Memorial Day, on the last Monday in May, officially kicks off the summer season.

Mayfair

When the sun comes out, so do folks in Harvard Sq, for Mayfair (www.harvard square.com). On the first or second Sunday in May, artists, merchants and restaurants set up booths on the streets, while children's events and live entertainment take place on stages around the square.

Lilac Sunday

On the second Sunday in May, the Arnold Arboretum celebrates the arrival of spring on Lilac Sunday (www.arboretum.harvard. edu), when more than 400 varieties of fragrant lilac are in bloom.

Boston Calling

Twice a year, independent-music-lovers take over Harvard Stadium for three days of all-out, rock-out music. The festival (p81) occurs during the last weekend in May.

June

June brings temperatures ranging from 55°F to 70°F, and lots of rain.

Student calendars are packed with end-of-academic-year events and graduation ceremonies. Then students depart the city, causing a noticeable decline in traffic and noise.

Boston Pride Festival

The week-long LGBTQ+ festival (p214) kicks off with the raising of a rainbow flag on City Hall Plaza. Events occur throughout the week, culminating in the Pride Parade and Festival on the second Saturday in June.

Bunker Hill Day

Charlestown historians remember the crucial Battle of Bunker Hill (www.face book.com/bunkerhillday parade) on the second or third Sunday in June. The city celebrates with a road race and a parade.

July

By July the city has emptied, as students vacate for summer and Bostonians head to their summer houses. It's also Boston's hottest month, with temperatures ranging from 70°F to 85°F, and there's always a week or two when the mercury shoots to the high 90s.

Harborfest

The week-long Independence Day festival (www. bostonharborfest.com) starts on the last weekend in June. It includes events such as fireworks, an art market and Chowderfest, where you can sample dozens of chowders prepared by Boston's top chefs.

Independence Day

On July 4, Boston hosts a free concert (www.boston popsjuly4th.org) that culminates with the Boston Pops playing the *1812 Overture,* complete with brass cannon and synchronized fireworks. Half a million people descend on the Esplanade to watch it live.

August

Summer in the city continues in August, with hot, humid temperatures and plenty of tourists. Only at the end of the month will you begin to feel fall coming.

Italian Festivals

Throughout July and August, the North End's religious societies sponsor feasts and processions honoring their patron saints. Major celebrations include the Fisherman's Feast (p59) and St Anthony's Feast (p59), both in late August.

Boston Carnival

On the last weekend in August, Boston's Caribbean community recreates a Trinidad-style Carnival (www.bostoncarnival.org), complete with spectacular costumes, sultry music and spicy cooking. The festival takes place in Franklin Park.

September

By September the humidity disappears, leaving slightly cooler temperatures and a crispness in the air. The students return and the streets are filled with

(Top) Fourth of July fireworks on the Charles River

(Bottom) Patriots' Day reenactment, Concord

JESSE JAMES PHOTOGRAPHY / GETTY IMAGES ©

SPIRANER / GETTY IMAGES ©

U-Hauls during the first week. The first Monday in September is Labor Day, the official end of the summer season.

☆ Boston Film Festival

For four days in mid-September, Bostonians become film critics. The Boston Film Festival (www.bostonfilmfestival.org) screens some 30 films at theaters around the city.

🏃 Hub on Wheels

On the third Sunday in September, the citywide bicycle ride, Hub on Wheels, starts at City Hall Plaza and offers two different scenic routes (12 or 40 miles).

October

October is Boston's best month. The academic year is rolling, the weather is crisp and cool, and the trees take on shades of red, gold and amber.

🔒 Oktoberfest

On the first or second Sunday in October, Harvard Sq artisans and entertainers take to the streets. The street fair (www.harvard square.com) coincides with the crazy-fun Honk! parade (www.honkfest.org).

🏃 Head of the Charles Regatta

Spectators line the banks of the Charles River on a weekend in mid-October to watch the world's largest rowing event, the Head of the Charles.

🎃 Haunted Happenings

Salem (16 miles north of Boston) goes all out for

Halloween (www.haunted happenings.org). The city celebrates for much of October, with parades, concerts, pumpkin carvings, costume parties and trick-or-treating.

November

In November, you can feel winter in the air. You may even see snow flurries. Thanksgiving Day – the third Thursday in November – kicks off the holiday season.

☆ Boston Comedy Festival

This festival is dedicated to the funny guys and gals, who cut up at venues all around town as a part of the Boston Comedy Festival (www.bostoncomedy fest.com).

✨ America's Hometown Thanksgiving Celebration

Plymouth (40 miles south of Boston) is the birthplace of Thanksgiving (www. usathanksgiving.com), so it's appropriate that the town celebrates this heritage with a parade, concerts, crafts and – of course – food, the weekend before the holiday.

December

In early December, the huge Christmas trees at the Prudential Center and the Boston Common are lit, lending the city a festive air that remains throughout the month. There is usually at least one good snow storm.

☆ Boston Tea Party Reenactment

On the Sunday before December 16, costumed actors march from Old South Meeting House to the waterfront and toss crates of tea into the harbor. Nowadays, the ticketed event (www.bostonteapartyship. com/boston-tea-party-reenactment) takes place on the newly rebuilt Griffin's Wharf, where the Tea Party Ships are docked.

✨ First Night

New Year celebrations (www.firstnightboston.org) begin early and continue past midnight, culminating in fireworks over the harbor. The fun continues on New Year's Day, with more activities and exhibitions.

With Kids

Boston is a giant history museum, the setting for many informative field trips. Cobblestone streets and costumed tour guides can bring to life the events that kids have read about, while hands-on experimentation and interactive exhibits fuse education and entertainment.

RYAN MCGURL / SHUTTERSTOCK ©

Boston Children's Museum (p132)

History

USS Constitution & Museum

Aside from exploring the warship (p52), kids can swing in hammocks and experience life as a sailor in the museum (p52).

Boston Tea Party Ships & Museum

Kids can imagine what it was like to take part in the protest, with role-playing and interactive exhibits (p132).

Old South Meeting House

Scavenger hunts and activity kits direct children's exploration of this historic building (p82).

Prudential Center Skywalk Observatory

Assuming your kids are not acrophobes, they will be thrilled to see Boston from above (p111). A special audio tour caters to little ones.

Art

All of Boston's art museums are free for kids (except the MFA during school hours).

Museum of Fine Arts

The museum (p119) offers loads of programs for kids of all ages, including the Art Cart, which teaches children to use art, music and poetry to explore the gallery's collections.

Institute of Contemporary Art

The ICA (p131) offers innovative programs for families, including weekend story hours and monthly 'play dates,' as well as a supercool program organized by teens for teens.

Isabella Stewart Gardner Museum

In addition to scavenger hunts and sketch materials, the Gardner Museum (p121) has drop-in art activities on Saturdays.

Science

Museum of Science

More opportunities to combine fun and learning than anywhere in the city. The Discovery Center (p58) is specially designed for kids aged under eight.

New England Aquarium

Kids can see eye to eye with thousands of sea species in the Giant Ocean Tank (p83).

Boston Children's Museum

Hours of fun climbing, constructing and creating. The museum (p132) is especially good for kids aged three to eight.

Franklin Park Zoo

In addition to the many animal exhibits, the zoo (p159) has a wild and wonderful 10,000-sq-ft playground.

Harvard Museum of Natural History

It's almost as good as the zoo. Sure, the stuffed animals (p142) don't move, but they let the kids get really close and look them in the eye.

Outdoor Adventures

Boston Harbor Islands

Spectacle Island has family-friendly facilities (and beaches), while Georges Island (p166) has Fort Warren, which is fun to explore.

Castle Island & Fort Independence

Plenty of run-around space and a fort (p132) to explore, plus beaches and playground.

New England Aquarium Whale Watch

Whale sightings are practically guaranteed on this boat ride (p92).

Swan Boats

The boat rides (p72) on the Public Garden lagoon are short (15 minutes) and sweet (read: tame). Perfect for little tykes.

Tours

Boston by Foot

'Boston by Little Feet' is the only Freedom Trail walking tour (p212) designed especially for children aged six to 12.

Boston Duck Tours

Kids of all ages are invited to drive the duck on the raging waters of the Charles River (p212). Bonus: quacking loudly is encouraged.

Urban AdvenTours

This bike tour (p210) is great for all ages. Kids' bikes and helmets are available for rent, as are bike trailers for toddlers.

Entertainment

Quincy Market

There are always jugglers, puppeteers, break-dancers and acrobats performing on weekends at Quincy Market (p86).

Boston Symphony Orchestra

The BSO (p127) has a rich 'Youth & Family' program, with weekend concerts that are designed specifically to introduce young people to classical music. Recommended for ages five to 12.

Improv Boston

At Improv Boston (p153), there are two shows on Saturday afternoons that are appropriate for kids aged four and up.

Parks & Playgrounds

Charlesbank Playground

Aka the Esplanade Playground (p111).

Boston Common Playground

Bonus: summertime spray pool on the Frog Pond (p71).

Stoneman Playground

Two gated areas (p111) target different age groups.

Like a Local

For all its worldliness, Boston is a city of neighborhoods, home to local people doing their local things, eating at local joints, drinking local beer and maybe even talking with local accents. Here are some of the city dwellers' favorite places to go and things to do.

Sights & Activities

Charles River

Bostonians love that dirty water (and the Standells even sang about it). You'll know why if you go for a run or ride along the Charles River Bike Path (p155) or just catch some rays on the Esplanade (p111).

Boston Public Library

This is a high-minded city, so it should come as no surprise that Bostonians patronize their public library. You too can plug in your laptop at the BPL (p108). Or, here's a novel concept, read a book there.

Candlepin Bowling

New England's fast disappearing favorite pastime. You can still bowl with the little balls at Sacco's Bowl Haven (p152).

Food & Drink

Some local specialties (besides seafood):

Food Trucks

Boston's best weekday lunch comes from a truck. Find the good ones on the Rose Kennedy Greenway at Dewey Sq, in front of the Science Center at Harvard Sq, on the Boston Common and elsewhere around town (p33).

Pizza

Every Bostonian has a favorite neighborhood pizza joint. It might be Galleria Umberto (p61) in the North End, Picco (p96) in the South End, Area Four (p147) in Cambridge or – the ultimate local joint – Santarpio's (p60) in East Boston.

Dive Bars

The friendliest locals drink at dive bars, such as Sevens (p76) in Beacon Hill, Biddy Early's Pub (p90) downtown or the Southie original Croke Park Whitey's (p137).

Markets

Bostonians love to buy produce and other yummies from their neighborhood farmers markets. But they know to head to Haymarket (p92) for the best bargains on fresh fruit, veggies and fish.

Language

Aside from the notorious local accent, you may need some help with the local lingo.

How ah yah?

Boston's standard friendly greeting.

Wicked

A modifier meaning 'extremely.' So something might be 'wicked expensive' or it could be 'wicked cold' outside. The best compliment a Bostonian can give is to say something is 'wicked pisser.'

Coffee

If you order a 'regular' coffee, you'll get cream and sugar.

Sweets

A soda is a 'tonic.' A milkshake is a 'frappe.' A glazed doughnut is 'honey-dipped.'

Boston Common

It's singular. Please don't refer to America's oldest public park as 'the Commons.'

Walk the Freedom Trail

Summon your inner Paul Revere and follow the red-brick road of the Freedom Trail, from the Boston Common to the Bunker Hill Monument. This 2.5-mile walking trail is the best introduction to revolutionary Boston and its status as the 'Cradle of Liberty.'

Freedom Trail sign

1 Boston Common

The Freedom Trail kicks off at the Boston Common (p70), America's oldest public park and a centerpiece of the city. The 50-acre green is crisscrossed with walking paths and dotted with monuments. Don't miss the powerful memorial to the victims of the Boston Massacre, erected in 1888.

2 Massachusetts State House

Overlooking the Boston Common from the northeast corner, the Massachusetts State House (p73) occupies a proud spot atop the city's last remaining hill – land that was previously part of John Hancock's cow pasture. Other members of the Sons of Liberty (a clandestine network of patriots during the American Revolution) also had a hand in building the new capitol, literally: Samuel Adams and Paul Revere laid the cornerstones on July 4, 1795.

3 Park St Church

Just south of the State House, the soaring spire of Park St Church (p74) has been an unmistakable landmark since 1809. The church earned the moniker 'Brimstone Corner' both for its usage as a gunpowder storage place during the War of 1812 and for its fiery preaching.

4 Granary Burying Ground

Walk north on Tremont St, where you will pass the Egyptian Revival gates of the Granary Burying Ground (p73). Steeped in history, the serene cemetery is the final resting place of many of the Sons of Liberty, as well as the victims of the Boston Massacre and other historical figures.

5 King's Chapel & Burying Ground

Continue north to School St, where the Georgian King's Chapel (p82) overlooks its adjacent burying ground. It is perhaps an odd choice for inclusion since it was founded as an Anglican church in 1688. It does, however, contain a large bell crafted by Paul Revere, and the prestigious Governor's pew, once occupied by George Washington.

lent conflict, in 1770. On March 5, an angry crowd of protesters was throwing snowballs and rocks at the British soldiers, who eventually fired into the crowd, killing five.

6 Site of the First Public School

Turn east on School St, and take note of the bronze statue of Benjamin Franklin outside Old City Hall (p83). A plaque commemorates this spot as the site of the country's first public school. Enter the courtyard to discover some of the school's distinguished alumni and some quirky artwork.

7 Old Corner Bookstore

Continue east to the intersection of School St and Washington St. The little brick building on your left is known as the Old Corner Bookstore (p84), a literary and intellectual hot spot for 75 years. Strangely, it is now a Mexican fast-food joint.

8 Old South Meeting House

Diagonally opposite across Washington St, the Old South Meeting House (p82) saw the beginnings of one of the American Revolution's most vociferous protests, the Boston Tea Party. Come off the street and listen to a reenactment of what went down that day.

9 Old State House

Before the revolution, the seat of the Massachusetts government was the Old State House (p82), a redbrick colonial edifice that is now surrounded by modern buildings. Inside, you can peruse historic artifacts and listen to firsthand accounts of revolutionary events. Outside, gaze up at the balcony, where the Declaration of Independence was first read to Bostonians in 1776.

10 Boston Massacre Site

In front of the Old State House, the cobblestone circle marks the site of the Boston Massacre (p82), the revolution's first vio-

11 Faneuil Hall

Nearly every visitor to Boston stops at Quincy Market to grab a beer or shop for souvenirs, but most bypass historic Faneuil Hall (p83), the original market and public meeting place that was built in 1740. Pause to admire the bronze statue of Samuel Adams, who sits astride his horse in Dock Sq. Then ascend to the 2nd-floor hall, where Adams was one of the many orators to speak out against British rule.

12 Paul Revere House

From Faneuil Hall, cross the Rose Kennedy Greenway and head up Hanover St into the heart of the North End. A zigzag right on to Richmond St and left on North St brings you to charming North Sq, once home to Paul Revere. The weathered clapboard house here – Paul Revere House (p60) – is the oldest example in Boston, as most other wooden construction was destroyed by the fires that ravaged the city. This is likely where Paul Revere commenced his famous midnight ride.

13 Old North Church

Back on Hanover St, walk two blocks north to Paul Revere Mall. Besides a dramatic statue of the patriot himself, this park also provides a lovely vantage point to view your next destination, the Old North Church (p59). Boston's oldest house of worship, the 1723 church played a crucial role in

NEED TO KNOW

Freedom Trail Foundation (www.the freedomtrail.org) Includes extensive information about all 16 sites.

Consider purchasing a **Freedom Trail Ticket** (adult/child $11/1), which covers admission to the Old South Meeting House and Paul Revere House.

Freedom Trail

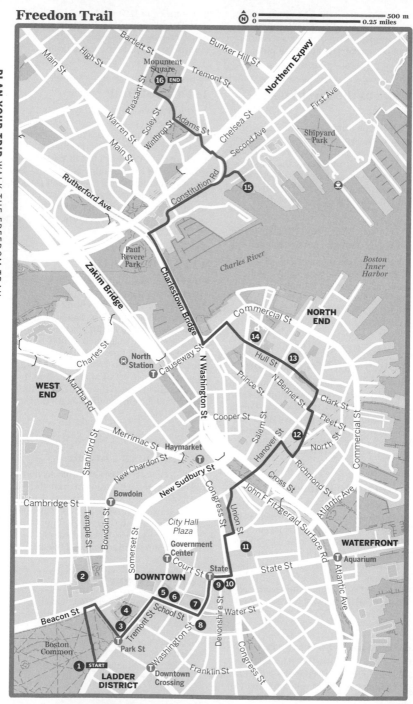

DIEGO GRANDI / SHUTTERSTOCK ©

Bunker Hill Monument (p52)

TIMELINE

➡ **1635** The Puritans establish the first public school in the home of the schoolmaster. Now the Boston Latin School, it still operates in Fenway.

➡ **1688** Amid much wrangling with the local leadership, King's Chapel is founded as an Anglican congregation in Puritan Boston.

➡ **March 5, 1770** The Boston Massacre is the first violent conflict leading up to the War for Independence.

➡ **December 16, 1773** Angry protesters have a Tea Party, storming out of the Old South Meeting House, raiding a merchant ship docked nearby and dumping crates of tea overboard.

➡ **April 18, 1775** The sexton hangs two lanterns in the Old North Church to signal the Redcoats' route to Concord. Paul Revere rides from his home on North Sq to warn the patriots of the Redcoats' approach.

➡ **June 17, 1775** The Battle of Bunker Hill inflicts significant damage to British troops.

➡ **July 18, 1776** The Declaration of Independence is read for the first time in Boston.

➡ **October 21, 1797** The 44-gun USS *Constitution* is launched from a Boston shipyard, just in time for victorious battles in the new nation's first naval wars.

➡ **1798** Symbolic of the new state, the new Massachusetts State House becomes the seat of government for the Commonwealth.

revolutionary events. Take a breather in the delightful gardens behind the church.

14 Copp's Hill Burying Ground

From the church, head west on Hull St to Copp's Hill Burying Ground (p60). This quiet corner contains some of the city's oldest gravestones and offers grand views across the river to Charlestown. Find the headstone of Daniel Malcolm, which is littered with bullet holes from British troops who apparently took offense at his epitaph. Incidentally, little is known about Malcolm's actual role in protests or revolution; historical records only show that he was arrested for failing to pay duty on 60 casks of wine.

15 USS Constitution

Continue west on Hull St to its end. Turn left on Commercial St and walk across the Charlestown Bridge. Turning right on Constitution Rd brings you to the Charlestown Navy Yard, home of the world's oldest commissioned warship, the USS *Constitution* (p52). Board the ship for a tour of the upper decks, where you will learn about its exploits in America's earliest naval battles.

16 Bunker Hill Monument

Walk through the winding cobblestone streets up to the 220ft granite obelisk that is the Bunker Hill Monument (p52). Check out the dioramas in the museum to better understand what transpired on that fateful day in June 1775, when the Battle of Bunker Hill took place. Then climb 294 steps to the top of the monument to enjoy the panorama of the city, the harbor and the North Shore.

James Hook & Co (p86)

Eating

The Boston area is the home of the first Thanksgiving and of bountiful autumnal harvests. It's also America's seafood capital. In this era of creative culinary discovery, many Bostonians are reclaiming their roots in one crucial way: through appreciation of local, seasonal and organic products. This thriving 'locavore' movement highlights the bounty of local waters and rich New England farms.

Beantown

With a nickname like Beantown, you know that Boston is into food. Culinary historians believe that Native Americans cooked beans with fatty bear meat and molasses in earthenware pots. Early settlers likely adapted this recipe by substituting pork for bear meat, resulting in the famed Boston baked beans. Despite the name, you'll have some trouble finding baked beans on a menu in Boston today. Look for it at restaurants specializing in old-fashioned fare, such as Union Oyster House (p87).

Seafood

Evolving from its environment, Boston cuisine has always featured plenty of seafood, especially the 'sacred cod,' halibut and various shellfish. Lobster – once so plentiful that it was served to prisoners – is now a recognized delicacy that appears on most local menus. Many restaurants have 'raw bars' where they serve local oysters and clams on the half-shell. The most traditional preparations of seafood are boiled and fried, but nowadays creative chefs are calling on new techniques and all kinds of international influences to present the seafood in even more delicious ways.

Italian & International Influences

The international influence on Boston cuisine cannot be underestimated. A tight-knit immigrant enclave, the North End is an upholder of old-fashioned Italian-American cooking, with tomato sauces simmering and pasta boiling on every stove. This neighborhood is still packed with ristoranti, *enoteche* (wine bars) and *pasticcerie* (bakeries) – making it one of the city's best eating destinations.

In the 20th century, a new wave of immigrants arrived from South America and Asia, bringing the flavors of Brazil, China, India, Korea and Vietnam. The Asian element is most evident in Chinatown, but the international influences show up on menus all over the city.

Food Trucks

Boston has dozens of food trucks cruising its streets, serving up cheap, filling fare to hungry patrons who are short on time and/or money. There's a full range of meals on offer, from noodles and tacos to burgers, hot dogs, lobster rolls and vegetarian food.

In Boston, you'll find food trucks on the Rose Kennedy Greenway and on the Boston Common, among other places. In Cambridge, look for trucks on the plaza in front of the Harvard Science Center or on Carleton St across from the Kendall Sq T station. And on summer weekends, head for the Food Truck Bazaar at the SoWa Open Market along Harrison Ave. Find out more at the Boston Food Truck Blog (www.boston foodtruckblog.com) or Hub Food Trucks (www.hubfoodtrucks.com).

Eating by Neighborhood

➜ **Charlestown** (p54) A small selection of welcoming restaurants on Main St and City Sq.

➜ **West End & North End** (p60) Harking back to Italy, the North End is Boston's most authentic Old World eating destination.

➜ **Beacon Hill & Boston Common** (p74) A mix of cute cafes, business lunches and gourmet delis, with a few notable swanky spots.

➜ **Downtown & Waterfront** (p84) Sandwich shops and lunch spots catering to the workaday world.

➜ **South End & Chinatown** (p95) Boston's best eating, overflowing with Asian eateries, trendy restaurants and neighborhood cafes.

NEED TO KNOW

Opening Hours

Breakfast is usually 7am to 10am; lunch 11:30am to 2:30pm or 3pm; and dinner starts around 5pm with last service 9pm or 10pm. Exceptions are noted in reviews.

Price Ranges

Prices listed are for main courses.

$ less than $15

$$ $15–25

$$$ more than $25

Booking Tables

Reservations are recommended for most top-end restaurants, especially on Friday and Saturday evenings. Make reservations at www.opentable.com.

Tipping

In restaurants with sit-down service, customers should leave a 15% tip for acceptable service and a 20% tip for good service; tipping at a lower level reflects dissatisfaction with the service.

Food Blogs

Edible Boston (www.edibleboston.net)

Boston Vegetarian Society (www.boston vcg.org)

Boston Foodies (www.boston-foodies.com)

Boston Chefs (www.bostonchefs.com)

➜ **Back Bay** (p112) Classy grills and cozy cafes lined up along Newbury St and Boylston St.

➜ **Kenmore Sq & Fenway** (p124) Cheap eats and burger joints, with a few excellent upscale options.

➜ **Seaport District & South Boston** (p133) Boston's newest dining epicenter, with dozens of trendy eateries, including fantastic seafood options.

➜ **Cambridge** (p144) Coffeehouses, sandwich shops, noodle houses, taquerias and upscale restaurants to suit every taste.

➜ **Streetcar Suburbs** (p159) An eclectic assortment of dining options, including kosher delis and other international eats.

Lonely Planet's Top Choices

Saltie Girl (p113) Big seafood surprises in a small space.

Island Creek Oyster Bar (p125) Slurp oysters in style at this classy Fenway spot.

O Ya (p99) Sushi like you've never seen it done before.

Pomodoro (p62) The most intimate atmosphere in the North End.

Courtyard (p114) A beautiful setting for high tea and books.

jm Curley (p86) Burgers and other A+ bar fare.

Best by Budget

$
El Pelon (p125) Fish tacos. Cheap. Delicious.

Grass Roots Cafe (p84) Korean food with a twist.

Eventide Fenway (p125) Oysters on the cheap.

Blunch (p95) Breakfast for lunch.

Galleria Umberto (p61) A slice of Sicilian and a can of soda.

Soup Shack (p160) Slurp some soup. *Mmmmm.*

$$
Pomodoro (p62) Perfectly romantic North End restaurant.

Row 34 (p133) Top-notch oyster bar in the Seaport District.

Puro Ceviche Bar (p113) Tacos and ceviche with a bit of funk.

Myers & Chang (p96) Small plates with Asian flare.

jm Curley (p86) Pub food at its finest.

Paramount (p75) A Beacon Hill institution.

$$$
Saltie Girl (p113) Intimate setting, amazing seafood.

Island Creek Oyster Bar (p125) The luscious oysters are only the beginning.

O Ya (p99) Who knew that raw fish could be so exciting?

Courtyard (p114) Afternoon tea at the BPL.

Best by Cuisine

Seafood
Saltie Girl (p113) Sample the delicacies at this seafood bar.

James Hook & Co (p86) It doesn't get any fresher than this retail fish market.

Row 34 (p133) Eight kinds of oysters, five kinds of fish; seafood galore.

Daily Catch (p62) It's not fancy, but it sure is fresh.

Italian
Pomodoro (p62) A romantic hole-in-the-wall on Hanover St.

Giulia (p145) Locally sourced delights prepared with modern flair by chef Michael Pagliarini.

Coppa Enoteca (p96) An upscale *enoteca* in the trendy South End.

Chinese
Dumpling House (p146) Chinatown comes to Cambridge.

Gourmet Dumpling House (p98) Often packed, but always worth the wait.

Myers + Chang (p96) Asian-inspired small plates from local celebrity Joanne Chang.

Best for Vegetarians

Veggie Galaxy (p147) Your favorite diner fare – all animal-free.

Whole Heart Provisions (p146) Vegan's delight! Dinner in a bowl.

Life Alive (p147) Smoothies, salads and sandwiches that are good for body and soul.

Clover DTX (p85) Their chickpea fritter is a thing of beauty.

CloverHSQ (p145) Ditto.

Best for Kids

Friendly Toast (p147) No need for a kids' menu, because kids the regular menu has everything that kids love.

Flatbread Co (p152) Pizza, bowling and plenty of love for the little ones.

Life Alive (p147) Smoothies (and other deceptively healthful food) – plus a play area.

Tasty Burger (p125) Burgers on the menu and billiards in the house.

Best Late-Night Grub

Kaze Shabu Shabu (p99) One of many late-night options in Chinatown.

Franklin Café (p96) Delicious full menu every night until 1:30am.

Eastern Standard (p126) Late-night menu available until 1:30am EST.

jm Curley (p86) Irresistible snacks and hefty sandwiches round out the late-night menu.

South Street Diner (p98) Open around the clock for your noshing needs.

Citizen Public House (p126) Dinner menu until 1:30am nightly.

Drinking & Nightlife

Despite the city's Puritan roots, modern-day Bostonians like to drink. While Boston has its fair share of Irish pubs, it also has a dynamic craft-beer movement, with more and more microbreweries opening yearly; a knowledgeable population of wine drinkers (and pourers); and a red-hot cocktail scene, thanks to some talented local bartenders. So pick your poison...and drink up!

Where to Drink

ALCOHOL

Boston's drinking scene is dominated by five categories: dive bars, Irish bars, sports bars and truly hip cocktail bars. Nowadays there are also plenty of beer bars and local breweries, but any of these types might cater to discerning beer drinkers, with local craft brews on tap or a wide selection of imported bottles. Boston also boasts a few sophisticated and semiswanky wine bars, which are delightful for a glass of vino (and usually accompanying food).

COFFEE

Aside from Dunkin' Donuts on every corner, there are scores of cute cafes and cool coffeehouses, many of which serve dynamite sandwiches and pastries. Many also offer free wi-fi – another inducement to linger.

Where to Dance

The main neighborhood in Boston where the dancing goes down is the Theater District. Boylston St is the main drag, but there are venues all over this groovy 'hood. There are also clubs in Back Bay, Fenway, Cambridge and Downtown. Most clubs organize thematic dance parties, often centered on a particular type of music, clientele or DJ. As such, the atmosphere can vary greatly from night to night.

Drinking & Nightlife by Neighborhood

➡ **Charlestown** (p55) An eclectic mix of drinking options, ranging from historic to exotic.

➡ **West End & North End** (p63) Drink beer (West End) or Campari (North End) with your sports on the tube.

➡ **Downtown & Waterfront** (p87) Some perennial favorites are embedded in the streets away from the Freedom Trail.

➡ **South End & Chinatown** (p99) Gay-friendly and ubertrendy places to drink, plus the city's hottest clubbing scene.

➡ **Back Bay** (p114) Divey student haunts at one end, trendy yuppie bars at the other (with plenty in between).

➡ **Kenmore Sq & Fenway** (p126) Overflowing with drinking joints for students and sports-lovers.

➡ **Seaport District & South Boston** (p137) Salty treats in Seaport for the diligent drinker, but head deeper into Southie for a Boston Irish experience.

➡ **Cambridge** (p147) Students and scholars congregate at creative cafes and beloved dives.

➡ **Streetcar Suburbs** (p161) Some of Boston's best beer pubs and music clubs are in these outlying areas.

Lonely Planet's Top Choices

Café Pamplona (p147) Quintessentially Cambridge Euro-style cafe.

Lamplighter Brewing Co (p150) Drink beer, play games, hang out.

Bleacher Bar (p126) Sneak a peek inside Fenway Park at this sweet sports bar.

Drink (p137) Sets the standard for Boston cocktail bars, with the industry's most knowledgeable mixologists.

Trillium Fort Point (p137) Boston's favorite microbrewery, plus a roof deck.

A4cade (p150) Flashback to fun.

Best Beer

Trillium Fort Point (p137) A brand-new beer hall for a Boston original.

Publick House (p161) With 30-plus drafts, including the good stuff from Belgium.

Lamplighter Brewing Co (p150) Hipster hoppy hangout in Cambridge.

Bukowski Tavern (p115) More kinds of beer than we could count, served with plenty of sass.

Tip Tap Room (p76) Classy gastropub with 40 kinds of cool craft beers.

Best Cocktails

Drink (p137) Let the mixologists mix something that suits.

Hawthorne (p126) Custom cocktails served in a sophisticated setting.

Yvonne's (p86) Scrumptious cocktails get lined up on this gorgeous mahogany bar.

Ward 8 (p63) West End bar serving up the namesake cocktail and many others.

Best Wine Bars

Coppa Enoteca (p96) A buzzy Italian wine bar with amazing food.

Barcelona Wine Bar (p96) Order some tapas to accompany your wine.

Bin 26 Enoteca (p76) A sophisticated restaurant with an amazing wine selection.

Best Irish Pubs

Plough & Stars (p150) Tiny pub serving cold beer, folk music and Irish breakfast.

Brendan Behan Pub (p161) A dark and inviting pub, fit for poets and dogs.

Mr Dooley's (p90) Downtown classic, with live music and good craic.

Croke Park Whitey's (p137) The ultimate Southie Irish bar: rough and lovable.

Best Sports Bars

Bleacher Bar (p126) Big sandwiches and Boston beers, with a view into Fenway Park.

West End Johnnies (p63) Upscale sports bar near TD Garden.

Caffè Dello Sport (p66) Here's how they do sports bars in Italy.

Four's (p64) The classic fanatic's Boston sports bar.

Best Dance Scene

Havana Club (p150) Get your Latin groove on, with salsa, socca and more.

Bella Luna Milky Way (p161) A pizza place with weekend dance parties.

Zuzu (p150) It's all about the dance.

6B Lounge (p76) Wildly popular 1990s dance party on Fridays.

Lansdowne Pub (p126) Coverband dance parties on Friday and Saturday nights.

Good Life (p90) Three bars and two dance floors.

Best Gay & Lesbian

Midway Café (p162) Thursday night is dyke night, but queers are cool at any time.

Club Café (p114) The fun never stops with dinner, dancing, karaoke and gay cabaret.

Alley (p90) A friendly bear bar that welcomes all-comers.

Machine (p127) Two clubs in one, keeping gay crowds drinking and dancing all week long.

Best Views

Lookout Rooftop Bar (p137) Fabulous views of the harbor and environs.

Pier Six (p55) Watch the sun drop behind the Boston city skyline.

Top of the Hub (p115) See the whole city from the top floor of the Pru.

Reelhouse (p54) City views from East Boston.

Trillium Fort Point (p137) Take a peek from the rooftop deck.

MICHAEL DWYER / ALAMY STOCK PHOTO ®

Boston Ballet performing at the Hatch Memorial Shell (p111), Charles River Esplanade

 # Entertainment

Welcome to the Athens of America, a city rich with artistic and cultural offerings. We're talking not only about the world-class symphony orchestra and top-notch theater and dance companies, but also rock clubs, poetry slams and avant-garde performance art. Not to mention the championship sports teams that fans live and die by.

Music

Home to the Boston Symphony Orchestra and the New England Conservatory of Music, Boston boasts some of the country's oldest and most prestigious houses for symphonic experiences.

Boston's modern music scene is centered in the student areas of Cambridge and Allston/Brighton. There's also a thriving jazz scene, starting with the students and faculty of the Berklee College of Music. To figure out who's playing where, take a look at the clubs' websites or listings in *Dig Boston* (www.dig boston.com).

Comedy

Boston is a funny place, and we mean funny ha-ha. To cite some famous examples, Conan O'Brian, Jay Leno and Denis Leary are all from Boston. The Wilbur Theatre (p102) is Boston's largest comedy venue, but the local talent is normally found at smaller funny outlets all around town.

Theater

The Theater District is packed with venues showcasing the city's opera, dance and dramatic prowess, while more innovative

NEED TO KNOW

Opening Hours

Classical music, theater and dance performances usually start at 7pm or 8pm, and there may be weekend matinees. Club concerts often start at 9pm or 10pm, though venues might offer an early show at 7pm or 8pm.

Tickets

Tickets for cultural and sporting events are available online or at box offices.

BosTix Deals

ArtsBoston (www.artsboston.org) offers discounted tickets to theater productions through BosTix Deals (up to 25% for advance purchases online, up to 50% for same-day purchase at ArtsBoston kiosks at Quincy Market and Prudential Center).

Useful Websites

Boston Music Intelligencer (www.classical-scene.com)

World Music (www.worldmusic.org)

Jazz Boston! (www.jazzboston.org)

Unscene Comedy (www.unscenecomedy.com)

Boston Opera Calendar (www.bostonopera calendar.org)

experimental theaters are in Cambridge and the South End. The Boston Ballet (www.bostonballet.org) performs at the Boston Opera House (p90), also in the Theater District. Two opera companies – Boston Lyric Opera (www.blo.org) and Odyssey Opera (www.odysseyopera.org) – perform at venues around town.

Spectator Sports

BASEBALL

The intensity of baseball fandom has only grown since the Boston Red Sox broke their 86-year losing streak and won the 2004 World Series. The Red Sox play from April to October at Fenway Park (p123), the nation's oldest and most storied ballpark.

FOOTBALL

With six Super Bowl victories in the new millennium, the New England Patriots are a football dynasty that is much loved at home but detested in other parts of the country.

They play in the state-of-the-art **Gillette Stadium** (New England Patriots; ☎508-543-8200; www.patriots.com; 1 Patriot Pl), 50 minutes south of Boston in Foxborough. The season runs from late August to January.

Part of the competitive Atlantic Coast Conference (ACC), the Boston College Eagles (www.bceagles.com) play in the new Alumni Stadium every second Saturday from September to November. Staunch Ivy League rivalries bring out alumni and fans to see the Harvard Crimson (www.gocrim son.com) play at Harvard Stadium.

HOCKEY

Stanley Cup winners in 2011, the Boston Bruins (www.bostonbruins.com) play ice hockey at TD Garden (p66) from mid-October to mid-April. College hockey is also huge in Boston, as local schools earn the devotion of spirited fans. The local rivalries come out in full force during the annual **Beanpot Tournament** (www.beanpothockey. com; ☉Feb).

BASKETBALL

The Boston Celtics have won more basketball championships than any other NBA team, most recently in 2008. From October to April, they play at TD Garden (p66). The Boston College Eagles (www.bceagles.com) are competitive in the ACC and are usually still standing for March Madness. The Eagles play at Conte Forum.

Entertainment by Neighborhood

➡ **West End & North End** (p66) Aside from big-name concerts at the Garden, there's one comedy venue.

➡ **Downtown & Waterfront** (p90) The spillover from the Theater District includes several Downtown venues.

➡ **South End & Chinatown** (p101) The epicenter of Boston's cultural life, with dozens of theaters.

➡ **Back Bay** (p115) Home to a few music venues associated with the Berklee College of Music.

➡ **Kenmore Sq & Fenway** (p127) Avenue of the Arts includes Symphony Hall and other esteemed venues.

➡ **Seaport District & South Boston** (p138) One outdoor concert venue, plus performances at the ICA and some other small venues.

➡ **Cambridge** (p151) A huge selection of innovative, independent music, theater, dance and comedy.

➡ **Streetcar Suburbs** (p162) Boston's best indie music scene is up the street in Allston/Brighton.

New England Conservatory (p128) Look for free recitals in the impressive Jordan Hall.

Lonely Planet's Top Choices

Boston Symphony Orchestra (p127) The star of the city.

American Repertory Theater (p151) Ground-breaking, award-winning theater.

Club Passim (p151) Legendary club that constitutes the folk scene in Boston.

Comedy Studio (p152) Cutting-edge comedy, every night of the week.

Wally's Café (p101) Low-down blues bar with funky live music.

Red Room @ Cafe 939 (p115) Berklee-student-run venue that showcases up-and-coming stars in an intimate setting.

Best Indie Rock

Lizard Lounge (p151) Dark basement club with groovable local music.

Sinclair (p151) This venue near Harvard Sq books awesome indie bands.

Great Scott (p162) Gritty Allston club; one of the city's best places to hear cool music.

Toad (p151) A closet-sized Cambridge club with free local music every night.

Best Jazz & Blues

Wally's Café (p101) You won't have the blues for long at this legendary club.

Red Room @ Cafe 939 (p115) Not only jazz and blues, but all kinds of experimental and innovative music.

Lily Pad (p152) Jazz (and other oddities) in a stripped-down setting.

Scullers Jazz Club (p162) A soulless club showcasing soulful music.

Regattabar (p152) An intimate space to hear jazzy music.

Best Classical Music

Boston Symphony Orchestra (p127) Boston's world-class philharmonic plays at Symphony Hall.

Best Theater

American Repertory Theater (p151) Racking up Tony awards for its artistic interpretations of classic musicals.

Huntington Theatre Company (p128) Recent winner of the Tony Award for Outstanding Regional Theatre.

Boston Center for the Arts (p102) Home to a slew of independent theater companies, including the radical Company One.

Paramount Center (p90) Emerson College's fabulous art deco performance space.

Club Oberon (p151) Fun and funky black-box theater, where the ART lets loose.

Opera House (p90) Lavish venue for musicals on tour after Broadway.

Best Comedy

Comedy Studio (p152) Nothing but funny stuff at this comedy innovator.

Improv Boston (p153) Laughs for everyone at this Cambridge club.

Great Scott (p162) It's a Gas on Friday nights.

Improv Asylum (p66) Dark humor in a dark basement.

Dick's Beantown Comedy (p91) Dick Doherty and other funny guys keep the laughs coming.

Bill's Bar (p127) Things get funny on Wednesday nights.

Best Poetry

Lizard Lounge (p151) The Sunday-night poetry slam is an unforgettable event melding music and minds.

Grolier Poetry Bookshop (p153) Check the store calendar for poetry readings and other events.

Cantab Lounge (p153) Poets descend on Wednesday nights.

Lily Pad (p152) You never know what you're gonna get but it might be poetry.

 # Shopping

Boston is known for its intellect and its arts, so you can bet it's good for bookstores, art galleries and music shops. The streets are also sprinkled with offbeat boutiques – some carrying vintage treasures and local designers. Besides to-die-for duds, indie shops hawk handmade jewelry, exotic household decorations and arty, quirky gifts. Fun to browse, even if you don't buy.

Fashion

Fashionistas continue to take their cues from New York, but a few local designers are trying to put Boston on the map à la mode. Recognizing Boston's conservative tastes in clothes, the styles tend to be relatively down to earth and decidedly wearable compared to what you might see in *Vogue* magazine. That Boston's most famous names in the fashion industry are Bert and John Jacobs (Life is Good) proves the point.

Recycled Goods

Vintage is hot in Boston. Sure, you can buy 'vintage-inspired' clothing, or you can go for the real deal at one of Boston's many secondhand clothing stores. Other popular recyclables include books, records, jewelry and wicked nice furniture.

Locally Made

Boston's vibrant art scene makes its presence known in local shops, galleries and markets that are dedicated to arts and crafts. High-quality handmade items run the gamut from designer clothes and jewelry to colorful ceramics and housewares. Sometimes quirky and clever, sometimes sophisticated and stylish, these handmade, locally made items are hard to classify, but easy to appreciate.

Food & Drink

Some of Boston's best souvenirs are consumables. Stock up on standard New England favorites such as maple syrup, artisanal cheeses and chocolates, and cranberry anything. (Cardullo's Gourmet Shoppe (p153) has a whole section dedicated to tantalizing local products.) Browse North End specialty shops for all things Italian, or explore Chinatown for hard-to-find Asian ingredients and medicinal herbs. And if all else fails, you can always take home a lobster package from Legal Seafoods.

Shopping by Neighborhood

➡ **West End & North End** (p66) Get some gourmet treats from the Italian grocers in the North End.

➡ **Beacon Hill & Boston Common** (p78) Cutesy boutiques (several featuring local designers) and scads of antiques.

➡ **Downtown & Waterfront** (p91) Plenty of tourist-oriented shops in Quincy Market.

➡ **South End & Chinatown** (p102) Fast becoming Boston's best shopping destination, with trendy boutiques and excellent galleries.

➡ **Back Bay** (p115) The traditional 'shopping and lunch' destination.

➡ **Cambridge** (p153) Long famous for its used bookstores and secondhand record shops.

➡ **Streetcar Suburbs** (p162) Sweet shopping strips with eclectic collections of interesting shops.

Lonely Planet's Top Choices

Ward Maps (p153) Awesome antique and reproduction maps; get one printed on a T-shirt or a tote.

Salmagundi (p163) Hip hats for everyone's heads.

SoWa Open Market (p103) A weekly (seasonal) outdoor extravaganza of arts and crafts and other creations.

Artists for Humanity (p91) Clever T-shirts designed by local teens.

Best Fashion

Paridaez (p78) A local designer shows off innovative styles for modern busy women.

Crush Boutique (p78) Basement boutique packed with unexpected fashion finds.

December Thieves (p78) Showcasing all things unique and beautiful.

In-Jean-ius (p67) Denim to fit everybody, plus cute shirts and sweaters.

Lucy's League (p91) Fashionable duds for Boston sports fans.

Sault New England (p103) Cool clothing and unusual gifts from South End style mavens.

Ball & Buck (p116) All-American jeans and plaid for urban hipsters.

Best Locally Made

SoWa Open Market (p103) The city's biggest and best artists market.

For Now (p138) Retail incubator showcasing cool local stuff.

Cambridge Artists Cooperative (p154) Two-level gallery of exquisite, handcrafted pieces.

North Bennet Street School (p66) Woodwork, jewelry and journals crafted at this century-old trade school.

Best Sportswear

New Balance Factory Store (p155) A great selection of shoes and sportswear at discount prices.

Crane & Lion (p79) Yoga gear and other casual everyday-wear – with super sales.

Converse at Lovejoy Wharf (p66) Iconic sneakers with designs to suit every taste.

Marathon Sports (p116) Buy your sneakers at the Boston Marathon finish line.

Best for Kids

Curious George Store (p154) Featuring the curious little monkey and a whole lot more.

Boing! (p163) Where shopping equals playing.

Eureka Puzzles (p163) Boston's best selection of puzzles, games and other mind-bending fun.

Games People Play (p154) Smart games for smart people.

Red Wagon (p79) Cute clothes for kids, from birth to tween.

Best for Gifts

Good (p78) So, so good, all made right here in New England.

Blackstone's of Beacon Hill (p79) Tiny shop crammed with quirky and clever gifts.

On Centre (p163) Jewelry and other inventive items – much of it made by local creatives.

Black Ink (p79) Packed floor to ceiling with stuff you never knew you needed.

Topdrawer (p115) Gear up for the next trip.

Best Antiques

SoWa Vintage Market (p103) Intriguing indoor flea market, open on Sundays.

Marika's Antique Shop (p79) Beacon Hill classic, hawking antiques for more than 50 years.

Eugene Galleries (p78) Maps, magazines and other old printed matter.

Central Flea (p154) Find some treasures amid the...other stuff.

Best Food & Drink

Cardullo's Gourmet Shoppe (p153) A fabulous selection of specialty foodstuffs.

Boston Public Market (p92) Top spot for local delicacies, including nuts, chocolate, beer and more.

Beacon Hill Chocolates (p78) Divine candies in artistic packaging.

Salumeria Italiana (p66) Shop like your *nonna*.

🏃 Sports & Activities

Considering Boston's large student population and extensive green spaces, it's no surprise to see urban outdoorsy people running along the Esplanade and cycling the Emerald Necklace. For water bugs, the Charles River and the Boston Harbor offer opportunities for kayaking, sailing and even swimming, if you don't mind the frigid temperatures.

Cruises & Whale-Watching

You don't have to commandeer your own boat to experience Boston from the water. Tour boats cruise the Inner Harbor and the Charles River, as well as journey out to the Harbor Islands. These tours generally run from April to October, though the season is shorter for the Harbor Islands.

The most rewarding boat trip from Boston is a whale-watching tour, which cruises out to Stellwagen Bank, a rich feeding ground for marine life. Eagle-eyed passengers usually see several species of whales, including humpback, fin and minke, as well as white-sided dolphins and many kinds of seabirds. There are naturalists on board to help spot and answer questions. Whale-watch cruises run from April to October.

Cycling

Boston is becoming an excellent cycling city, as each year sees more bicycles to rent or share, more bicycle lanes, more bicycle parking and more bicycle safety awareness. For those not comfortable riding on the crowded city streets, there are several scenic off-road cycling trails.

Water Sports

Boston is a city by the sea, and on a river. These two waterfronts offer lots of chances for watery fun, including canoeing, kayaking, sailing and swimming. The season is relatively short (April to October; July to September for swimming) and the water is cold (average

68°F in summer), but the air is salty and the breeze is sweet.

Winter Sports

In Boston, there's plenty of winter to go around. Outdoor ice-skating rinks offer an easy way to embrace winter in the city, and there are also ski facilities (downhill and cross-country) just a few miles from the city center, including the Blue Hills Ski Area (www.ski-bluehills.com) and the Weston Cross-Country Ski Track (www.skiboston.com).

Activities by Neighborhood

* **Charlestown** Set sail on the harbor. (p55)
* **Beacon Hill & Boston Common** Outdoor fun on the Boston Common and the Charles River. (p79)
* **Downtown & Waterfront** The waterfront offers many boating adventures. (p92)
* **South End & Chinatown** Catch a yoga class or check out the nearby cycling trails. (p103)
* **Back Bay** The Charles River Esplanade is prime for running, cycling, sunning and funning. (p111)
* **Seaport District & South Boston** Boston's best city beaches. (p138)
* **Cambridge** Easy access to the city's best cycling and kayaking routes. (p154)
* **Streetcar Suburbs** The Emerald Necklace traverses these leafy 'burbs. (p159)

Lonely Planet's Top Choices

New England Aquarium Whale Watch (p92) Journey out to Stellwagen Bank, a feeding ground for ample marine life.

Charles River Bike Path (p155) A 17-mile circuit that runs on both sides of the Charles River between Boston and Watertown.

Fenway Park (p127) See the Red Sox battle it out at America's oldest ballpark.

Sacco's Bowl Haven (p152) Try your hand at candlepin bowling, a New England oddity.

Best Cycling

Urban AdvenTours (p210) The best way to experience the city is on two wheels. This tour is an excellent introduction.

Charles River Bike Path (p155) The best way to explore the Charles River on two wheels.

Minuteman Bikeway (p154) A 10-mile rails-to-trails bikeway that runs from Cambridge to Bedford, MA.

Emerald Necklace (p159) Frederick Law Olmsted's ribbon of green that cuts across Boston, from the Common to Franklin Park.

Southwest Corridor (p116) An urban bike route, running 5 miles from Back Bay to Jamaica Plain.

Best Swimming

Walden Pond (p169) Famous from literature, this scenic kettle pond is a delightful place for a cooling dip.

Boston Harbor Islands (p165) Ferry out to the islands to lounge on deserted beaches and swim in frigid water.

Carson Beach (p138) Boston's best city beach gets crowded on weekends.

Castle Island (p132) The small swimming beach is only the beginning of the fun.

Best Sailing & Kayaking

Charles River Canoe & Kayak Center (p155) With two convenient locations, you can paddle on the Charles or in the Harbor.

Community Boating (p79) Experienced sailors can take a fixed-keel, four-seat sailboat out on the Charles River Basin.

Courageous Sailing (p55) Sailing rental and instruction available out of Charlestown.

Jamaica Pond (p163) Rent a sailboat or rowboat to explore ultracalm waters.

Best Boat Rides

New England Aquarium Whale Watch (p92) A boat ride and wildlife-watching all in one.

Little Brewster (p167) Cruise out to this distant Harbor Island and tour historic Boston Light.

Codzilla (p212) A wild ride on the Boston Harbor.

Liberty Fleet (p92) Set sail on a schooner for a two-hour scenic adventure.

Swan Boats (p72) These charming boats on the lagoon in the Public Garden are a Boston institution.

Best Winter Sports

Frog Pond (p71) The outdoor rink on the Boston Common gets crowded, but you can't beat it for atmosphere.

Community Ice Skating @ Kendall Square (p155) Off the beaten track in Kendall Sq, this outdoor rink is a great find.

Beanpot Tournament (p38) If you'd rather participate as a spectator, this hockey tournament is one of the city's hottest local sports competitions.

Best Golf

Brookline Golf Club at Putterham (p163) A public golf course in Brookline, right next door to the famous country club.

Fresh Pond Golf Course (p155) Nine holes of golf wrapping around an idyllic reservoir.

Franklin Park (p159) The 18-hole William J Devine is the second-oldest public course in the country.

PLAN YOUR TRIP SPORTS & ACTIVITIES

Explore Boston

BOSTON'S
TOP SIGHTS

Neighborhoods at a Glance

❶ Charlestown p50

The site of the original settlement of the Massachusetts Bay Colony, Charlestown is the terminus for the Freedom Trail. Many tourists tromp across these historic cobblestone sidewalks to admire the USS *Constitution* and climb to the top of the Bunker Hill Monument, which towers above the neighborhood.

❷ West End & North End p56

Although the West End and North End are physically adjacent, they are atmospherically worlds apart. The West End is an institutional area without much zest. By contrast, the North End is delightfully spicy, thanks to the many Italian ristoranti and *salumerie* (delis) that line the streets.

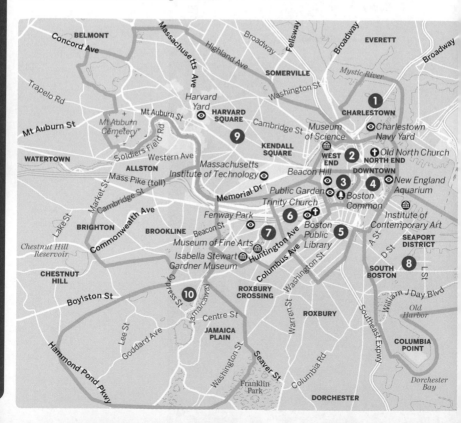

❸ Beacon Hill & Boston Common p68

Abutted by the Boston Common and topped with the gold-domed Massachusetts State House, Beacon Hill is the neighborhood most often featured on Boston postcards.

❹ Downtown & Waterfront p80

Downtown is not the thriving shopping area that it once was, but it is still a bustling district. The Waterfront is home to the Harbor Islands ferries and the New England Aquarium.

❺ South End & Chinatown p93

Chinatown, the Theater District and the Leather District are overlapping areas, filled

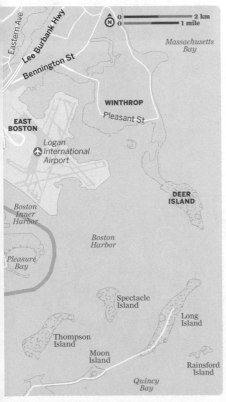

with glitzy theaters, Chinese restaurants and the remnants of Boston's shoe and leather industry. Nearby, the South End has a vibrant restaurant and gallery scene.

❻ Back Bay p106

Back Bay includes the city's most fashionable window-shopping, latte-drinking and people-watching area, on Newbury St, as well as its most elegant architecture, around Copley Sq. Its streets lined with stately brownstones and shaded by magnolia trees, it is among Boston's most prestigious addresses.

❼ Kenmore Square & Fenway p117

Kenmore Sq and Fenway attract club-goers and baseball fans to the streets surrounding Fenway Park. At the other end of the neighborhood, art-lovers and culture-vultures flock to the artistic institutions along Huntington Avenue, including the Museum of Fine Arts and Symphony Hall.

❽ Seaport District & South Boston p129

The Seaport District is a section of South Boston that is fast developing as an attractive destination, thanks to the dynamic contemporary-art museum and the explosion of dining and entertainment options.

❾ Cambridge p139

Stretched out along the north shore of the Charles River, Cambridge is a separate city with two distinguished universities, a host of historic sites, and artistic and cultural attractions galore.

❿ Streetcar Suburbs p156

A chain of parks known as the Emerald Necklace leads south to the Streetcar Suburbs. Brookline was the birthplace of John F Kennedy, while Jamaica Plain is a progressive residential community with gracious Victorian architecture.

NEIGHBORHOODS AT A GLANCE

MARCIO JOSE BASTOS SILVA / SHUTTERSTOCK ©

1. Freedom Trail guide 2. Boston Tea Party Ships & Museum
3. Patriots' Day reenactment, Lexington 4. Minuteman Statue, Concord

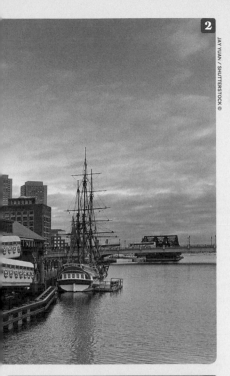

JAY YUAN / SHUTTERSTOCK ©

Revolutionary Boston

There's a good reason why Boston is called the birthplace of the American Revolution. Here, the Sons of Liberty railed against British policies of taxation without representation, the conflict's first blood was shed, and the 'shot heard around the world' launched a war that would spawn a nation.

Freedom Trail

Follow this 2.5-mile walking trail (p28) from the Boston Common to Bunker Hill to see where history unfolded – where protests were staged, battles were fought and heroes were lain to rest.

Boston Tea Party Ships

Protesting an unfair tax on tea, an angry mob of colonists dumped 342 crates of tea into the Boston Harbor in 1773. The Boston Tea Party Ships & Museum (p132) recalls the catalytic event, inviting visitors to participate in the protest and witness its aftermath.

Patriots' Day

On April 19, 1775, rebellious Minutemen stood up to British Regulars and sparked the first battles of the Revolution. Celebrated on the third Monday in April, Patriots' Day commemorates the event with historic re-enactments and parades (not to mention the Boston Marathon).

Lexington & Concord

The Minutemen first faced the Regulars at Lexington Common (now called Battle Green; p168), and then later at the Old North Bridge (p169) in Concord. These sites and the surrounding countryside constitute the Minute Man National Historic Park – still peppered with contemporary buildings and packed with historical significance.

Charlestown

Neighborhood Top Five

1 **Bunker Hill Monument** (p52) Counting the 294 steps as you climb to the top and then catching your breath while you admire the 360-degree view of Boston, Cambridge and beyond.

2 **Warren Tavern** (p55) Sipping an ale at the same bar that propped up the founding fathers.

3 **USS Constitution** (p52) Admiring the craftsmanship and discovering the ship's long and storied history from US Navy sailors.

4 **Pier Six** (p55) Quaffing a beer or a cocktail while watching the sun set behind the city skyline.

5 **USS Constitution Museum** (p52) Learning about the birth of the US Navy, experiencing the life of a sailor and admiring the model ship collection.

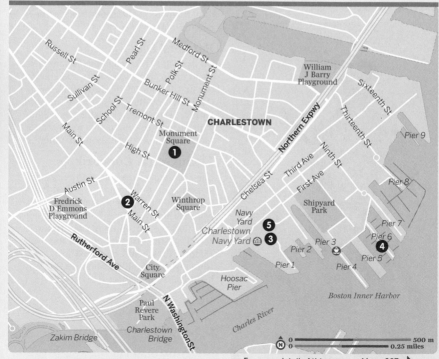

For more detail of this area see Map p227 ➡

Explore Charlestown

Spend a day following the Freedom Trail and you will end up in Charlestown, as the final two sites are located here. Besides seeing the historic USS *Constitution* (p52) and the commemorative Bunker Hill Monument (p52), strolling inland from the Charlestown waterfront provides an opportunity to explore the neighborhood's aged narrow streets, lined with 19th-century Federal and colonial houses. Afterwards, there are a handful of restaurants and cafes surrounding City Sq and lining Main St.

Despite the historic significance, Charlestown retains the distinctive atmosphere of a modern neighborhood, with local people (known as 'Townies') inhabiting the restored town houses and working in the granite buildings. Even the eateries – however recommended – are places to patronize if you happen to be in the area, and do not normally merit a special trip.

Charlestown was incorporated into Boston in 1873, but this neighborhood remains apart, both in terms of geography and atmosphere. On the north shore of the Charles River, it is connected to the rest of the city by the Old Charlestown Bridge. So even though C-town sees its fair share of tourists trudging along the Freedom Trail, the sights and streets will not be as crowded as those in downtown Boston.

Local Life

➡ **Coffee with Kids** Townies of all ages love the coffee and doughnuts at Zume's Coffee House (p55); but it's especially popular among the mommy set, who bring their kids to play with puzzles and eat grilled cheese sandwiches.

➡ **Sundowners** Little known outside of Charlestown, Pier Six (p55) attracts the local after-work crowd with its informal atmosphere and unbeatable city view.

➡ **Historic Hangout** Even though the Warren Tavern (p55) is a historic site of sorts, it's still a favorite place for Townies to drink beers and eat burgers.

Getting There & Away

➡ **Metro** The closest T stations are Community College (orange line) and North Station (junction of orange and green lines), both a 20-minute walk from the Charlestown sights.

➡ **Boat** The MBTA runs the **Inner Harbor Ferry** (Map p227; www.mbta.com; one-way $3.50; ⏱6:30am-8:25pm Mon-Fri, 10am-6:25pm Sat & Sun) every 15 to 30 minutes between the Charlestown Navy Yard (p53) and Long Wharf on the Boston waterfront.

Lonely Planet's Top Tip

For a unique perspective on Charlestown and Boston, walk northeast from the **Navy Yard** (p53), following the shoreline from pier to pier. Crowded with boats, this working waterfront boasts one of the best views of the Boston Harbor and skyline.

✖ Best Places to Eat

➡ Brewer's Fork (p54)

➡ Navy Yard Bistro & Wine Bar (p54)

➡ Monument (p54)

➡ Legal Oysteria (p54)

For reviews, see p54

☕ Best Places to Drink

➡ Warren Tavern (p55)

➡ Pier Six (p55)

➡ Zume's Coffee House (p55)

For reviews, see p55.

☉ Best Boats

➡ USS *Constitution* (p52)

➡ USS *Cassin Young* (p53)

➡ Green Turtle (p181)

For reviews, see p52.➡

◉ SIGHTS

You may be tempted to slough off the Freedom Trail before you complete the whole thing. But the last two stops on the trail are in Charlestown – and they are good ones. It's worth the walk over the old Charlestown Bridge to step on board the USS Constitution and to climb to the top of the Bunker Hill Monument.

★**BUNKER HILL MONUMENT**   MONUMENT
Map p227 (☑617-242-7275; www.nps.gov/bost; Monument Sq; ⊙9am-5pm, to 6pm Jun-Sep; ☑93 from Haymarket, ⊤Community College) FREE This 220ft granite obelisk monument commemorates the turning-point battle that was fought on the surrounding hillside on June 17, 1775. Ultimately, the Redcoats prevailed, but the victory was bittersweet, as they lost more than one-third of their deployed forces, while the colonists suffered relatively few casualties. Climb the 294 steps to the top of the monument to enjoy the panorama of the city, the harbor and the North Shore.

From April to June – due to the seasonal influx of school groups – you'll need a climbing pass, which is available at the Bunker Hill Museum across the street. By the way, the name of the Battle of Bunker Hill is misleading, as most of the fighting took place on Breed's Hill, where the Bunker Hill Monument stands today.

BUNKER HILL MUSEUM   MUSEUM
Map p227 (☑617-242-7275; www.nps.gov/bost; 43 Monument Sq; ⊙9am-5pm, to 6pm Jun-Sep; ☑93 from Haymarket, ⊤Community College)

FREE Opposite the Bunker Hill Monument, this redbrick museum contains two floors of exhibits, including historical dioramas, a few artifacts and an impressive 360-degree mural depicting the battle. If you can find where the artist signed his masterpiece, you win a prize.

★**USS CONSTITUTION**   SHIP
Map p227 (☑617-242-2543; www.navy.mil/local/constitution; Charlestown Navy Yard; ⊙10am-4pm Wed-Sun Jan-Mar, to 6pm Apr, 10am-6pm Tue-Sun May-Sep, to 5pm Oct-Dec; ☒; ☑93 from Haymarket, ☒Inner Harbor Ferry from Long Wharf, ⊤North Station) FREE 'Her sides are made of iron!' cried a crewman upon watching a shot bounce off the thick oak hull of the USS *Constitution* during the War of 1812. This bit of irony earned the legendary ship her nickname. Indeed, she has never gone down in a battle. The USS *Constitution* remains the oldest commissioned US Navy ship, dating to 1797, and she is normally taken out onto Boston Harbor every July 4 in order to maintain her commissioned status.

Make sure you bring a photo ID to go aboard. You'll learn lots, like how the captain's son died on her maiden voyage (an inauspicious start).

USS CONSTITUTION MUSEUM   MUSEUM
Map p227 (☑617-426-1812; www.ussconstitution museum.org; First Ave, Charlestown Navy Yard; suggested donation adult $10-15, child $5-10; ⊙9am-6pm Apr-Oct, 10am-5pm Nov-Mar; ☒; ☑93 from Haymarket, ☒Inner Harbor Ferry from Long Wharf, ⊤North Station) Head indoors to

---

LENNY ZAKIM & BUNKER HILL

Driving north from Boston on the Central Artery, your car emerges from the Tip O'Neill Tunnel into the open air, where you are surrounded on all sides by the Boston city skyline and the crisp white cables of the **Leonard Zakim Bunker Hill Bridge**. Capped with obelisks that mirror its namesake monument, it is the widest cable-stayed bridge in the world. And against the clear blue sky or dark night, it is stunning.

Lenny Zakim (1953–99) was a local human-rights activist who spent years railing against racism. Bunker Hill was the battle where the patriots first proved their potency in the War for Independence. As former Mayor Menino said at the dedication: 'The Leonard P Zakim Bunker Hill Bridge will showcase the diversity and the unity of race, religion and personal background that exist in Boston today, because of the work of community leaders like Lenny Zakim and because patriots fought long ago in Charlestown to make our country independent.' It's a stretch, but he managed to merge these disparate dedicatees.

The name is nonetheless unwieldy, so don't be afraid to take short cuts. The Zakim Bridge will do.

LOCAL KNOWLEDGE

WARREN TAVERN

Eliphalet Newell was an ardent supporter of the revolutionary cause and a supposed participant in the Boston Tea Party. When the War for Independence was over, he opened a tavern and named it after his dear friend General Joseph Warren. Although Warren had died in the Battle of Bunker Hill, he had been an active member of the Sons of Liberty and a respected leader of the Revolution. Indeed, a British commander described him as 'the greatest incendiary in North America.'

So when the Warren Tavern (p55) was opened in 1780 it quickly became a popular meeting place, especially among admirers of General Warren. Over the years Paul Revere was a regular and even George Washington stopped by for a visit when he was in town. Nowadays locals still love to gather here to drink a few pints and engage in debates (perhaps not the heady discussions of building a new nation, but important stuff nonetheless).

this museum for a play-by-play of the USS *Constitution* (p52)'s various battles, as well as her current role as the flagship of the US Navy. The exhibits on the War of 1812 and the Barbary War are especially interesting, and trace the birth of the US Navy during these relatively unknown conflicts. Upstairs, kids can experience what it was like to be a sailor on the USS *Constitution* in 1812.

On the ground floor of the museum, the Model Shipwright Guild operates a workshop, where visitors can see volunteer modelers working on fantastically detailed miniatures of the USS *Constitution* and other ships.

CHARLESTOWN NAVY YARD HISTORIC SITE
Map p227 (617-242-5601; www.nps.gov/bost; visitor center 10am-5pm Wed-Sun Jan-Apr, 9am-5pm May-Sep, 10am-5pm Oct-Dec; 93 from Haymarket, Inner Harbor Ferry from Long Wharf, North Station) FREE Besides the historic ships docked here and the museum dedicated to them, the Charlestown Navy Yard is a living monument to its own history of shipbuilding and naval command. Visit the National Park Service Visitor Center located here for a free film, guided tours and other info about the Navy Yard and Freedom Trail sites.

Although most of the shipyard buildings are not open to the public, you can wander around the dry docks and see how the ships were repaired while resting on wooden blocks. The oldest building in the yard is the imposing Federal-style **Commandant's House**, dating to 1805. Other interesting buildings on the grounds include the 1000ft-long **Ropewalk**, where all the Navy's rope was made for 135 years. Next door, in

the **forge shop**, metal workers hammered out 'die-lock' chains, which eventually put the ropemakers out of business.

USS CASSIN YOUNG SHIP
Map p227 (617-242-5601; Charlestown Navy Yard; 10am-4:30pm May-Dec, to 5:30pm Jun-Sep; 93 from Haymarket, Inner Harbor Ferry from Long Wharf, North Station) FREE This 376ft WWII destroyer is one of 14 Fletcher-class destroyers built at the Charlestown Navy Yard (p53). These were the Navy's fastest, most versatile ships. *Cassin Young* participated in the 1944 Battle of Leyte Gulf, as well as the 1945 invasion of Okinawa, during which the ship sustained two kamikaze hits, leaving 23 crew members dead and many more wounded. Take a free 45-minute tour, or wander around the main deck on your own.

JOHN HARVARD MALL SQUARE
Map p227 (btwn Main & Harvard Sts; dawn-dusk; F4 from Long Wharf, North Station) North of City Sq, this shady, brick plaza leads up Town Hill. Back in the days of the earliest European settlements, a fort crowned Town Hill, which you can read about on the bronze plaques along the mall.

Before the local minister – one John Harvard – died of consumption in 1638, he donated half his £800 estate and all 300 of his books to a young Cambridge college, which saw fit to name its school after him.

GREAT HOUSE SITE ARCHAEOLOGICAL SITE
Map p227 (City Sq; dawn-dusk; Inner Harbor Ferry from Long Wharf, North Station) FREE Besides being an urban plaza, the aptly named City Sq is also an archaeological site. Big Dig construction to reroute I-93

WORTH A DETOUR

REELHOUSE

Of all the reasons to dine at **Reelhouse** (☑617-895-4075; www.realhouseboston.com; 6 New St, East Boston; lunch $15-20, dinner $16-30; ⊘11am-midnight Mon-Wed, to 1am Thu-Sun; ⓉMaverick), the cuisine is near the bottom of the list. The seafood and pub fare is usually pretty good. But you likely won't notice it much, as you'll be relishing the salty air, sea breezes and drop-dead gorgeous views of the Boston city skyline (with a killer sunset if you time it right).

This place is off the beaten track in East Boston. You can drive or take the T, but it's more fun to take a free water taxi from Pier Six (p55) in Charlestown.

unearthed the foundation of a structure called the Great House, widely believed to be the home of Gov John Winthrop and the seat of government in 1630.

Winthrop soon moved across the Charles to the Shawmut Peninsula, and the Great House became the Three Cranes Tavern, as documented in 1635. Informative dioramas demonstrate the remains of the kitchen, the main hall and the wine cellar.

✖ EATING

Charlestown still feels a bit provincial when it comes to its dining scene. But times are changing, and a few innovative spots have opened in recent years. Most restaurants are located along Main St or at City Sq.

★BREWER'S FORK · PIZZA $$

Map p227 (☑617-337-5703; www.brewersfork. com; 7 Moulton St; small plates $8-14, pizzas $14-18; ⊘11:30am-10:30pm, to 11pm Thu-Sat, from 10:30am Sat & Sun; ☑93 from Haymarket, ⓢInner Harbor Ferry from Long Wharf, ⓉNorth Station) This casual hipster hangout is a local favorite thanks to its enticing menu of small plates and pizzas, not to mention the excellent, oft-changing selection of about 30 craft beers. The wood-fired oven is the star of the show, but this place also does amazing things with its cheese and charcuterie boards.

MONUMENT · GASTROPUB $$

Map p227 (☑617-337-5191; www.monument charlestown.com; 251 Main St; lunch $13-17, dinner $15-25; ⊘11:30am-midnight Mon-Fri, from 9am Sat & Sun; ⓉCommunity College) At long last, Charlestown is seeing some intriguing restaurants that cater to its foodie residents and visitors. The latest and greatest is Mon-

ument, with a gorgeous polished wood bar setting the scene. The menu is broad but tasty, ranging from cheeseburger sliders to steamed Thai mussels and seared hanger steak. Brunch is particularly popular. (Lemon poppy-seed pancakes? Yes, please!)

NAVY YARD BISTRO & WINE BAR · FRENCH $$

Map p227 (☑617-242-0036; www.navyyard bistro.com; cnr Second Ave & Sixth St; mains $18-36; ⊘4:30-9pm Sun-Tue, to 9:30pm Wed, to 10pm Thu-Sat; ☑93 from Haymarket, ⓢInner Harbor Ferry from Long Wharf, ⓉNorth Station) Dark and romantic, this hideaway is tucked into an off-street pedestrian walkway, allowing for comfortable outdoor seating in summer months. Inside, the cozy, carved-wood interior is an ideal date destination – perfect for hanger steak, braised short ribs and other old-fashioned favorites. The menu also features seasonal vegetables and excellent wines.

LEGAL OYSTERIA · SEAFOOD $$

Map p227 (☑617-712-1988; www.legalseafoods. com; 10 City Sq; mains $17-25; ⊘11:30am-11pm, to 1am Thu-Sat, from 10am Sun; ☑93 from Haymarket, ⓉNorth Station) Not an *osteria,* but an 'Oysteria.' Get it? This is seafood with an Italian twist, so you'll find dishes like Ligurian fish stew, swordfish *salmoriglio* and even roasted clam pizza. This place has a cool, modern atmosphere for a restaurant that's part of the Legal Sea Foods chain and is a welcome addition to the limited dining options in Charlestown.

FIGS · PIZZA $$

Map p227 (☑617-242-2229; www.toddenglish figs.com; 67 Main St; mains $16-24; ⊘noon-2:30pm & 5-9:30pm Mon-Fri, noon-10pm Sat, noon-9:30pm Sun; ☑; ⓉCommunity College) This creative pizzeria – which also has an outlet in Beacon Hill – is the brainchild of celebrity chef Todd English, who tops whisper-thin crusts with interesting, exotic toppings. Case in point: the namesake fig and prosciutto with Gorgonzola. The menu also includes sandwiches and fresh pasta.

🍷 DRINKING &
🍸 NIGHTLIFE

Charlestown has a long history as a drinking destination (since 1780, to be exact) but the neighborhood today is pretty quiet after dark.

WARREN TAVERN   PUB
Map p227 (☎617-241-8142; www.warrentavern. com; 2 Pleasant St; ⊙11am-1am Mon-Fri, from 10am Sat & Sun; TCommunity College) One of the oldest pubs in Boston, the Warren Tavern has been pouring pints for its customers since George Washington and Paul Revere drank here. It is named for General Joseph Warren, a fallen hero of the Battle of Bunker Hill (shortly after which – in 1780 – this pub was opened). Also recommended as a lunch stop (mains $14 to $20).

PIER SIX   BAR
Map p227 (☎617-337-0054; www.pier6boston. com; 1 Eighth St, Pier 6; ⊙11am-1am; ⬚93 from Haymarket, ⬚Inner Harbor Ferry from Long Wharf, TNorth Station) At the end of the pier behind the Navy Yard, this understated tavern offers one of the loveliest views of the Boston Harbor and city skyline. The food is not that memorable, but it's a fine place to catch some rays on your face and the breeze off the water, and to enjoy an ice-cold one from behind the bar.

You can also catch a free boat to the Pier's sister restaurant in East Boston. The Reelhouse (p54) offers an experience pretty similar to Pier Six, but it's in edgy, up-and-coming East Boston. And, you get to arrive by boat.

TANGIERINO LOUNGE   LOUNGE
Map p227 (☎617-242-6009; www.koullshi.com; 83 Main St; ⊙4pm-1am; TCommunity College) First and foremost, it's a hookah lounge, with plush furniture, ornately carved woodwork, nightly belly-dancing shows

and sophisticated flavors of tobacco. A little bit exotic, a little bit erotic (a little bit expensive). Since people are smoking anyway, they added a cigar bar with a walk-in humidor. Perhaps exotic, but not so erotic.

Alas, there are also the obligatory flatscreen TVs behind the bar, so you can watch sports while you smoke. Not exotic or erotic.

ZUME'S COFFEE HOUSE   CAFE
Map p227 (www.zumescoffeehouse.com; 221 Main St; ⊙6am-4pm Mon-Fri, from 7am Sat & Sun; 🛜🍴; TCommunity College) This is slightly off the beaten path (aka the Freedom Trail), but locals love it for the comfy leather chairs, specialty lattes and housemade English muffins. Also on the menu: soup, sandwiches and lunchy items. Paintings and photographs by local artists adorn the walls; children's books and tot-sized stools keep the kiddies happy.

FIREHOUSE VENDING
MACHINE   VENDING MACHINE
Map p227 (34 Winthrop St; TCommunity College) The kind firefighters at Engine Company 50 work in a 19th-century firehouse with the Freedom Trail passing nearby. On most summer days, they open up a bay so that hot walkers have access to a vending machine that sells cold drinks, embedded in old wooden lockers covered in departmental patches. Sit on the bench out front and admire the streetscape.

🏃 SPORTS &
ACTIVITIES

COURAGEOUS SAILING   BOATING
Map p227 (☎617-242-3821; www.courageous sailing.org; Pier 4; 2hr sail $190; ⊙noon-sunset Mon-Fri, from 10am Sat & Sun May-Oct; 🍴; ⬚93 from Haymarket, ⬚Inner Harbor Ferry from Long Wharf, TNorth Station) Named after a twotime America's Cup winner, Courageous Sailing offers instruction and boat rental for sailors and would-be sailors. A unique public-private partnership, this outfit was established by the City of Boston with the support of private individuals, with the aim of making sailing accessible to kids and adults of all ages, incomes and abilities.

West End & North End

WEST END | NORTH END

Neighborhood Top Five

❶ Pomodoro (p62) Strolling the cobblestone streets, browsing the boutiques and soaking up the Old World atmosphere in the North End and then squeezing into one of the candlelit tables for amazing Italian food and service.

❷ Liberty Hotel (p181) Gawking at the architecture and appreciating the irony that this former jailhouse is now a luxury hotel.

❸ Old North Church (p59) Gazing at the steeple and imagining the lanterns signaling the approach of the British Regulars (soldiers).

❹ Museum of Science (p58) Discovering science at work in your own body in the interactive Hall of Human Life.

❺ Paul Revere House (p60) Exploring the quaint, cramped quarters at Boston's oldest house, once home to one of the celebrated Sons of Liberty.

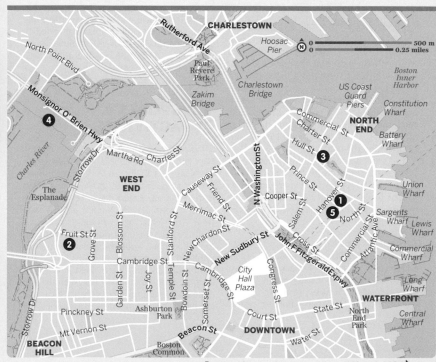

For more detail of this area see Map p228 and p230 ➡

Explore West End & North End

These side-by-side neighborhoods could not be more different from each other. The West End – formerly a multicultural, working-class neighborhood – was razed by 'urban renewal' in the 1950s. Now its streets are dominated by concrete monoliths and institutional buildings, including Mass General Hospital and many government buildings. Most visitors to Boston bypass this bleak district, unless they are catching a train at North Station or attending an event at TD Garden (p66).

That said, the West End borders Beacon Hill and Downtown, putting many sights within walking distance. The West End is actually a convenient, comfortable and relatively affordable place to stay.

By contrast, the North End feels like an Old World enclave. Italian immigrants and their descendants have held court in this warren of narrow streets and alleys since the 1920s. Old-timers still carry on passionate discussions in Italian and play bocce in the park. The neighborhood's main streets are packed with ristoranti and *salumerie* (Italian delis), not to mention bakeries, pizzerias, coffee shops, wine shops and cheesemongers. The North End is a required destination for anyone who likes to eat.

The Freedom Trail winds through the North End, with stops at Paul Revere House (p60), Old North Church (p59) and Copp's Hill Burying Ground (p60). Indeed, this peninsula was an integral part of Boston long before the Italians arrived, and some of these landmarks date back to the 17th century. So come during the day to see the sights and learn the history, but by all means, come back at night for dinner.

Local Life

→ **Drinks** Watch soccer, drink Campari and speak Italian (or just listen) at Caffè dello Sport (p66) or Caffè Paradiso (p64).

→ **Saints** North Enders get lively in August, when they celebrate their favorite saints during the weekend Italian Festivals (p59). If you can't come in August, visit All Saints Way (p65) to see one local's fervor.

Getting There & Away

→ **Metro** For the West End, use the red line Charles/MGH or the Blue Line Bowdoin station to access sites along Cambridge St. At the junction of the green and orange Lines, North Station is more convenient for the northern part of the neighborhood. For the North End, the closest T station is Haymarket, which lies on both the green and orange Lines.

Lonely Planet's Top Tip

Bad news: it's impossible to park in the North End. Good news: **Parcel-7 parking garage** (p59) offers three hours of parking for $3 if you get your ticket validated by a North End establishment.

WEST END & NORTH END

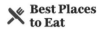 **Best Places to Eat**

→ Pomodoro (p62)
→ Neptune Oyster (p62)
→ Galleria Umberto (p61)
→ Scopa (p62)
→ Carmelina's (p62)

For reviews, see p60.➡

 Best Places to Drink

→ Ward 8 (p63)
→ Caffè Vittoria (p64)
→ Parla (p64)
→ Caffè Paradiso (p64)

For reviews, see p63.➡

 Best Places for Cooks

→ Salumeria Italiana (p66)
→ Polcari's Coffee (p67)
→ Bricco Salumeria (p66)
→ V Cirace & Son, Inc (p67)

For reviews, see p66.➡

◉ SIGHTS

The Freedom Trail runs through the North End, which means there are a cluster of historical sights in this old Boston neighborhood. By contrast, there's not much to see in the West End, although the stellar Museum of Science is here.

◉ West End

★MUSEUM OF SCIENCE   MUSEUM
Map p228 (☑617-723-2500; www.mos.org; Charles River Dam; museum admission adult/child $28/23, planetarium adult/child $10/8, theater adult/child $10/8; ☺9am-7pm Sat-Thu Jul & Aug, to 5pm Sep-Jun, to 9pm Fri year-round; ℗ ♿; ⓣScience Park/West End) This educational playground has more than 600 interactive exhibits. Favorites include the world's largest lightning-bolt generator, a full-scale space capsule, a world population meter and an impressive dinosaur exhibit. Kids go wild exploring computers and technology, maps and models, birds and bees, and human evolution. Don't miss the **Hall of Human Life**, where visitors can witness the hatching of baby chicks. The **Discovery Center** is a hands-on play area for kids under the age of eight.

The **Charles Hayden Planetarium** boasts a state-of-the-art projection system that casts a heavenly star show, as well as programs about black holes and other astronomical mysteries. For total IMAX immersion, check out the space-themed and natural-science-oriented flicks at the **Mugar Omni Theater**. A sweet sound system will have you believing you're actually roving around Mars or being attacked by sharks. There is also a food court–style cafeteria on-site.

OTIS HOUSE   HISTORIC SITE
Map p228 (☑617-227-3956; www.historicnew england.org; 141 Cambridge St; adult/child $10/5; ☺11am-7:30pm Wed, to 4:30pm Thu-Sun Apr-Nov; ⓣCharles/MGH) This stern, Federal brick building was the first of three houses designed by Charles Bulfinch for Mr Harrison Gray Otis at the end of the 18th century. Preservationists have recreated the interior of Otis' day, complete with flashy wallpaper and exquisite period furnishings. Tours take place every half-hour.

A real-estate developer, congressman and mayor of Boston, Otis and his wife Sally were renowned entertainers who hosted many lavish parties here. Since then the house has had quite a history, serving as a women's bath and rooming house. These days it is the headquarters of the preservationist society Historic New England.

WEST END MUSEUM   MUSEUM
Map p228 (☑617-723-2125; www.thewestend museum.org; 150 Staniford St; ☺noon-5pm Tue-Fri, 11am-4pm Sat; ⓣNorth Station) FREE This gem of a neighborhood museum is dedicated to preserving the memory of the West End and educating the public about the ramifications of unchecked urban development. The main exhibit *The Last Tenement* traces the history of the neighborhood from 1850 to 1958, highlighting its immigrant populations, economic evolution and eventual destruction.

Additional space is devoted to temporary exhibits that highlight former residents,

---

GREAT MOLASSES FLOOD OF 1919

For years Boston was a leader in the production and export of rum, made from West Indian sugar cane. Near the water's edge in the North End stood a storage tank for the Purity Distilling Company. On a January morning in 1919, the large tank, filled to the brim with brown molasses, suddenly began shuddering and rumbling as its bindings came undone.

The pressure caused the tank to explode, spewing 2 million gallons of molasses into the city like a volcano. The sweet explosion leveled surrounding tenements, knocked buildings off their foundations and wiped out a loaded freight train. Panic-stricken, people and animals fled the deadly ooze. A molasses wave surged down the streets drowning all in its sticky path. The Great Molasses Flood killed a dozen horses and 21 people, and injured more than 100. The clean up lasted nearly six months. *Dark Tide,* by journalist Stephen Puleo, provides a fascinating account of the causes and controversy surrounding this devastating explosion.

neighborhood architecture and broader issues of historic preservation. The museum also hosts occasional concerts, book talks and guided tours.

NEW ENGLAND
SPORTS MUSEUM
MUSEUM

Map p228 (⏰weekdays 617-624-1232, weekends 617-624-1234; www.sportsmuseum.org; TD Garden, 100 Legends Way; adult/child $15/10; ⏰10am-4pm Mon-Fri, 11am-4pm Sat-Sun, closed on event days; ⓣNorth Station) The New England Sports Museum is not the best place to witness Boston's deep-rooted devotion to sport (try Fenway Park for that), but fans will enjoy the photographs, jerseys and other items from Boston sports history. The highlight is the **Boston Garden Theater**, complete with boards and glass and hard wooden seats from the storied old Boston Garden. Outside of basketball and hockey season, behind-the-scenes arena tours are also available for the same price.

Also on display are Larry Bird's locker, Adam Vinatieri's shoes and Tony Conigliaro's baseball (yes, the one that landed on his left eye and derailed his career). Other interesting exhibits showcase the development of women's basketball, the history of football before the Patriots and – of course – a century in Red Sox nation. The museum is actually in the concourse area of the Garden's box seats, but tours begin in the ProShop on Level Two. The museum often closes for special events at the Garden so check the website and social media before visiting.

ETHER DOME
HISTORIC SITE

Map p228 (☎617-726-2000; www.massgeneral. org/museum/exhibits/etherdome; Mass General Hospital, 55 Fruit St, 4th fl; ⏰9am-5pm; ⓟ; ⓣCharles/MGH) FREE On October 16, 1846, Thomas WG Morton administered ether to the patient Gilbert Abbott, while Dr John Collins Warren cut a tumor from his neck. It was the first use of anesthesia in a surgical procedure and it happened in this domed operating room in Mass General Hospital. The dome is still used today for meetings and lectures, so it is sometimes closed to the public.

The dome looks like a typical, old-fashioned hall used for lectures and medical demonstrations, up to and including the skeleton hanging in the corner. There are a few other items to see, including a painting of the first anesthetized surgery.

ITALIAN FESTIVALS

In July and August, the North End takes on a celebratory air, as old-timer Italians host festivals to honor their patron saints. The streets fill with local residents listening to music, playing games and – of course – eating. The highlight of every festival is the saint's parade, which features local marching bands and social clubs, and the star participant, a statue of the patron saint. The life-size likeness is hoisted onto a wooden platform and carried through the streets, while residents cheer and toss confetti. Banners stream behind the statue so that believers can pin on their dollar bills, thus earning the protection of the saint's watchful eye. While the saints' festivals occur throughout the summer, the biggest events are the **Fisherman's Feast** (www.fishermansfeast.com) and **St Anthony's Feast** (www.stanthonys feast.com), both in late August.

◉ North End

As parking is nigh on impossible here, we suggest **Parcel-7 parking garage** (Map p234, ☎617-973-6954; 136 Blackstone St; 3hr with validation $3).

★OLD NORTH CHURCH
CHURCH

Map p230 (Christ Church; ☎617-858-8231; www. oldnorth.com; 193 Salem St; adult/child $8/4, plus $2 for tour; ⏰10am-4pm Nov-March, 9am-6pm April-Oct; ⓣHaymarket, North Station) Longfellow's poem 'Paul Revere's Ride' has immortalized this graceful church. It was here, on the night of April 18, 1775, that the sexton hung two lanterns from the steeple as a signal that the British would advance on Lexington and Concord via the sea route. Also called Christ Church, this 1723 Anglican place of worship is Boston's oldest church.

The 175ft steeple houses the oldest bells (1744) still rung in the US. Today's steeple is a 1954 replica, since severe weather toppled two prior ones, but the 1740 weather vane is original. All visitors are invited to hear a 10-minute presentation about the history of the Old North Church. For more detailed information, a 30-minute Behind the

WORTH A DETOUR

PIZZA IN EASTIE

People are passionate about pizza in the North End, home to Boston's oldest and most beloved pizzerias. But if you are serious about sampling the city's best slices, you'll have to wander far away from the Freedom Trail to edgy East Boston, fondly known as Eastie.

East Boston is a blue-collar, rough-and-tumble part of town. On the east side of the Boston Harbor, it's the site of Logan Airport, and also the setting for much of the Academy Award–winning movie *Mystic River*. Most importantly, Eastie is the home of the pizza place that constantly tops the lists of Boston's best pizza pies: **Santarpio's** (☑617-567-9871; www.santarpiospizza.com; 111 Chelsea St, East Boston; pizza $10-18; ☺11:30am-11pm; ☑⛟; Ⓣ Airport).

Boston Bruins posters and neon beer signs constitute the decor here. A gruff waitress might offer a menu, but there is really no point. You come here for the thin-crust pizza – unique for its extra-crispy, crunchy texture. This well-done crust is topped with slightly sweet sauce, plenty of pepperoni and not too much cheese.

Divey decor, rough service and delectable pizza. It's all part of the c*haaaahm*.

Scenes tour takes visitors up into the belfry and down into the crypt, while the Bones & Burials tour visits the gallery, the crypt and Copp's Hill Burying Ground (p60).

Behind the church, several hidden brick courtyards offer quiet respite for a moment of peaceful meditation. Heading down the hill, shady **Paul Revere Mall** perfectly frames the Old North Church. Often called 'the Prado' by locals, it is a lively meeting place for North Enders of all generations.

PAUL REVERE HOUSE
HISTORIC SITE

Map p230 (☑617-523-2338; www.paulreverehouse.org; 19 North Sq; adult/child $4.50/1; ☺9:30am-5:15pm mid-Apr–Oct, to 4:15pm Nov–mid-Apr, closed Mon Jan-Mar; Ⓣ Haymarket) When silversmith Paul Revere rode to warn patriots of the British march to Lexington and Concord, he set out from this home on North Sq. This small clapboard house was built in 1680, making it the oldest house in Boston. A self-guided tour through the house and courtyard gives a glimpse of what life was like for the Revere family (which included 16 children!).

Also on display are some examples of his silversmithing and engraving talents, as well as an impressive bell that was forged in his foundry. The Patriot Pass ($11) includes entry to the Paul Revere House and the Old South Meeting House (p82).

The adjacent **Pierce-Hichborn House**, built in 1710, is a fine example of an English Renaissance brick house. Also maintained by the Paul Revere Memorial Association, it can only be visited by guided tour (adult/child $4/1, by appointment).

COPP'S HILL BURYING GROUND
CEMETERY

Map p230 (Hull St; ☺8am-5pm; Ⓣ North Station) The city's second-oldest cemetery – dating to 1660 – is the final resting place for an estimated 10,000 souls. It is named for William Copp, who originally owned this land. While the oldest graves belong to Copp's children, there are several other noteworthy residents.

Near the Charter St gate you'll find the graves of the Mather family – Increase, Cotton and Samuel – all of whom were politically powerful religious leaders in the colonial community. Front and center is the grave of Daniel Malcolm, whose headstone commemorates his rebel activism. British soldiers apparently took offense at this claim and used the headstone for target practice. Also buried on the small plot of land are more than a thousand free African Americans, many of whom lived in the North End.

NARROWEST HOUSE
HISTORIC SITE

Map p230 (44 Hull St; Ⓣ North Station) Across the street from Copp's Hill Burying Ground, this is Boston's narrowest house, measuring a whopping 9½ft wide. Sometimes called a 'spite house,' the four-story, c 1800 edifice was reportedly built to block light from the neighbor's house and to obliterate the view of the house behind it.

 EATING

When it comes to eating options (and just about everything, really), these side-by-side neighborhoods couldn't be more different. Suffice to say, if you're in the area and you're hungry, you'll want to head to the North End *pronto*. The ristoranti are lined up along Hanover St, and at the southern end of Salem St. Keep in mind that many North End establishments do not accept credit cards. By contrast, the West End is suffering from a shortage of eating options, but there are some bars and restaurants in the Bulfinch Triangle, southeast of TD Garden.

✖ West End

CAFE RUSTICO ITALIAN $
Map p228 (☑617-742-8770; www.caferustico boston.com; 85 Canal St; mains $8-12; ☺7am-7pm Mon-Fri; 🐾🍴♿; ⓉNorth Station) This family-run Italian joint is one of Boston's best-kept secrets. But those in the know keep coming back for more – staff seem to know everyone by name, or at least by favorite sandwich. Seating is in short supply, but everything is available for take-out. Excellent choice for breakfast.

SCAMPO ITALIAN $$$
Map p228 (☑617-536-2100; www.scampo boston.com; 215 Charles St; mains $18-48; ☺11:30am-2:30pm daily, 5:30-10pm Sun-Wed, to 11pm Thu-Sat; 🍴; ⓉCharles/MGH) Celeb chef Lydia Shire is the brains and brawn behind this trendy restaurant on the ground floor of the Liberty Hotel. Buzzing with energy, Scampo offers handmade pasta and irresistible thin-crust pizza, as well as a full mozzarella bar. The extensive gluten-free menu is a bonus.

✖ North End

MARIA'S PASTRY BAKERY $
Map p230 (☑617-523-1196; www.mariaspastry. com; 46 Cross St; pastries $3-5; ☺7am-7pm Mon-Sat, to 5pm Sun; 🍴; ⓉHaymarket) Three generations of women from the Merola family are now working to bring you Boston's most authentic Italian pastries. Many claim that Maria makes the best *cannoli* in the North End, but you'll also find more-elaborate concoctions like *sfogliatelle* (layered, shell-shaped pastry filled with ricotta) and *aragosta* (cream-filled 'lobster tail' pastry). Note the early closing time: eat dessert first!

GALLERIA UMBERTO PIZZA $
Map p230 (☑617-227-5709; www.galleriaum bertonorthend.com; 289 Hanover St; mains $2-5; ☺11am-3pm Mon-Sat; 🍴; ⓉHaymarket) Paper plates, cans of soda, Sicilian pizza. This lunchtime legend (and 2018 James Beard Award winner!) closes as soon as the slices are gone. And considering their thick and chewy goodness, that's often before the official 3pm closing time. Loyal patrons line up early so they're sure to get theirs. Other snacking options include calzone, panini and arancini. Cash only.

MODERN PASTRY SHOP BAKERY $
Map p230 (☑617-523-3783; www.modernpastry. com; 257 Hanover St; sweets $2-4; ☺8am-10pm Sun-Thu, to 11pm Fri, to midnight Sat; ⓉHaymarket) The 'Modern' Pastry Shop feels anything but. This family-owned bakery has been making delectable cookies and *cannoli* for some 70 years. Always a contender in the ongoing 'best *cannoli* in Boston' feud. Cash only.

PIZZERIA REGINA PIZZA $
Map p230 (☑617-227-0765; www.pizzeriaregina. com; 11½ Thacher St; pizzas $13-24; ☺11am-11:30pm Sun-Thu, to 12:30am Fri & Sat; 🍴; ⓉHaymarket) The queen of North End pizzerias is the legendary Pizzeria Regina, famous for brusque but endearing waitstaff and crispy, thin-crust pizza. Thanks to the slightly spicy sauce (flavored with aged Romano cheese), Regina repeatedly wins accolades for its pies, including recognition by a certain unmentionable travel website as the best pizza *in the country*. Worth the wait.

PAULI'S SANDWICHES $
Map p230 (☑857-284-7064; www.paulisnorthend. com; 65 Salem St; mains $7-20; ☺8am-9pm Mon-Fri, 10am-9pm Sat, 10am-5pm Sun; 🐾🍴; ⓉHaymarket) If you're in the mood for a 'lobsta roll,' head to Pauli's for 7oz of pink succulent goodness, stuffed into a lightly grilled hot-dog roll – just the way it's meant to be. The menu of sandwiches is extensive and most of them are tasty; the California wrap is popular among the health-conscious.

MIKE'S PASTRY BAKERY $
Map p230 (☑617-742-3050; www.mikespastry. com; 300 Hanover St; pastries $3-5; ☺8am-10pm Sun-Thu, to 11pm Fri & Sat; ⓉHaymarket) A North End staple. Crowds of tourists and suburbanites (and some locals, too) line up at Mike's to sample his diverse selection of

cannoli – not just plain ricotta, but also pistachio, espresso, limoncello and a dozen other flavors. Be assertive if you want to get waited on, but don't try to pay with a credit card.

★ **POMODORO**   ITALIAN $$
Map p230 (617-367-4348; 351 Hanover St; mains $22-26; 5:30-11pm; Haymarket) Seductive Pomodoro offers a super-intimate, romantic setting (reservations are essential). The food is simple but perfectly prepared: fresh pasta, spicy tomato sauce, grilled fish and meats, and wine by the glass. If you're lucky, you might be on the receiving end of a complimentary tiramisu for dessert. Cash only.

SCOPA   ITALIAN $$
Map p230 (857-317-2871; www.scopaboston. com; 319 Hanover St; mains $19-28; 11am-11pm; Haymarket) Every meal at Scopa starts with delectable, warm Italian flatbread, served with a selection of olive oils for dipping. This is just a teaser of the delights to come, which might include Venetian meatballs or porcini mushroom risotto. The atmosphere is intimate and service is consistently excellent.

CARMELINA'S   ITALIAN $$
Map p230 (617-742-0020; www.carmelinas boston.com; 307 Hanover St; mains $18-29; noon-10pm; ; Haymarket) There's a lot to look at when you sit down at Carmelina's, whether you face the busy, open kitchen or the massive windows overlooking Hanover St. This understated, contemporary space serves up Sicilian dishes with a modern American twist – customers are crazy about the Crazy Alfredo and the Sunday Macaroni (which is served every day, in case you're wondering).

DAILY CATCH   SEAFOOD $$
Map p230 (617-523-8567; http://thedaily catch.com; 323 Hanover St; mains $18-25; 11am-10pm; Haymarket) Although owner Paul Freddura long ago added a few tables and an open kitchen, this shoebox fish joint still retains the atmosphere of a retail fish market (complete with chalkboard menu and wine served in plastic cups). Fortunately, it also retains the freshness of the fish. The specialty is *tinta de calamari* (squid-ink pasta). Cash only.

GIACOMO'S RISTORANTE   ITALIAN $$
Map p230 (617-523-9026; 355 Hanover St; mains $15-20; 4:30-10pm Mon-Thu, to 10:30pm Fri & Sat, 4-9:30pm Sun; ; Haymarket) Customers line up before the doors open so they can guarantee themselves a spot in the first round of seating at this North End favorite. Enthusiastic and entertaining waitstaff plus cramped quarters ensure that you get to know your neighbors. The cuisine is no-frills southern Italian fare, served in unbelievable portions. Cash only.

LOCALE   PIZZA $$
Map p230 (617-742-9600; www.localeboston. com; 352 Hanover St; pizzas $10-18; 4-9:15pm Mon-Fri, noon-9:45pm Sat, noon-8:45pm Sun; ; Haymarket) Locale has recently started to appear on lists of Boston's best pizzas. It's a modern affair, with strikingly minimalist decor and some surprising toppings (broccoli rabe, for one). But customers love the bubbly Neapolitan crusts, the specialty combinations and the affordable wines by the glass. The Tartuffo (with mushrooms, caramelized onions, Fontina cheese and truffle oil) is a customer fave.

★ **NEPTUNE OYSTER**   SEAFOOD $$$
Map p230 (617-742-3474; www.neptuneoyster. com; 63 Salem St; mains $19-39; 11:30am-9:30pm Sun-Thu, to 10:30pm Fri & Sat; Haymarket) Neptune's menu hints at Italian, but you'll also find elements of Mexican, French, Southern and old-fashioned New England. The impressive raw bar and daily seafood specials confirm that this is not your traditional North End eatery. Reservations are not accepted so come early and be prepared to wait.

TREMONTE   ITALIAN $$$
Map p230 (617-530-1955; www.tremonte restaurant.com; 76 Salem St; mains $18-32; 4-10pm Mon-Thu, to 11pm Fri, 11:30am-11pm Sat, 11:30am-10pm Sun; Haymarket) Customers are raving about this North End newcomer, which serves classic northern Italian fare in its sophisticated dining room with big windows overlooking Salem St. Indulge in favorites like chicken parmigiana and grilled pork chops, with a nice selection of Italian wines (but no hard liquor). Impeccable service makes the place stand out.

TARANTA   FUSION $$$
Map p230 (617-720-0052; www.tarantarist. com; 210 Hanover St; mains $24-39; 5:30-

10pm; T Haymarket) 🍷 Europe meets South America at this Italian restaurant with a Peruvian twist. So, for example, gnocchi is made from cassava root, salmon fillet is encrusted with macadamia nuts, and beef tenderloin with crushed espresso beans. There's an incredible selection of Italian, Chilean and Argentinean wines, all of which are organic or biodynamic. Taranta is a Certified Green Restaurant.

🍷 DRINKING & NIGHTLIFE

In these side-by-side neighborhoods, most of the drinking and nightlife occurs while watching sport. In the West End, several popular rowdy sports bars are clustered near TD Garden, home of the Bruins and Celtics. Canal St and gritty Friend St are the best bets. Despite the vibrancy of Hanover St, the colorful North End is nearly devoid of proper bars, though you will find a handful of cafes for drinking in Italian-American style. Hipsters take note: gentrification means that there are also a few classy cocktail bars scattered around the neighborhoods.

🍷 West End

WARD 8   COCKTAIL BAR
Map p228 (☎617-823-4478; www.ward8.com; 90 N Washington St; ⏰11:30am-1am Mon-Wed, to 2am Thu & Fri, 10am-2am Sat, 10am-1am Sun; T North Station, Haymarket) The bartenders at this throwback know their stuff, mixing up a slew of specialty cocktails (including the namesake Ward 8) and serving them in clever thematic containers. The menu also features craft beers and tempting New American cuisine (try the sesame chili duck wings). The atmosphere is classy but convivial, and unique in the West End.

ALIBI   COCKTAIL BAR
Map p228 (☎857-241-1144; www.alibiboston. com; 215 Charles St, Liberty Hotel; ⏰5pm-2am; T Charles/MGH) Housed in the former Charles St Jail, this hot-to-trot drinking venue is in the old 'drunk tank' (holding cell for the intoxicated). The prison theme is played up, with mug shots hanging on the brick walls, and iron bars on the doors

MIKE'S VS MODERN

Only slightly less tempestuous than the rivalry between the Red Sox and the Yankees is the rivalry between Mike's Pastry (p61) and Modern Pastry (p61), only a block apart on Hanover St. If you have time to wait in line, you might as well sample both and decide for yourself. If you don't have time to wait in line, go to Maria's (p61) instead.

and windows. Prices are high and service can be lacking, but it's fun to drink in jail. Dress sharp.

EQUAL EXCHANGE CAFE   CAFE
Map p228 (☎617-372-8777; www.equalex changecafe.coop; 226 Causeway St; ⏰7am-7pm Mon-Fri, 8am-5pm Sat, 9am-4pm Sun; 📶; T North Station) 🍷 Just by drinking rich delicious coffee and eating sweet dark chocolate, you are doing a good deed. All the coffees and cocoas are organically grown, fairly traded and locally roasted. The cafe has also received the city's Green Business Award, thanks to its comprehensive recycling program. You should really feel good about yourself.

BOSTON BEER WORKS   BREWERY
Map p228 (☎617-896-2337; www.beerworks.net; 112 Canal St; ⏰11am-11pm Sun-Thu, to 1am Fri & Sat; T North Station) Boston Beer Works is a solid option for beer-lovers and sports-lovers (conveniently located near the city's major sporting venues). The excellent selection of microbrews offers something for everyone, including plenty of seasonal specialties. Fruity brews like blueberry ale get rave reviews, with tasty sour-cream-and-chive fries as the perfect accompaniment.

WEST END JOHNNIES   SPORTS BAR
Map p228 (☎617-227-1588; www.westendjohn nies.com; 138 Portland St; ⏰4pm-2am Tue-Sat, 11am-4pm Sun; T North Station) West End Johnnies is a grown-up sports bar, with black leather furniture and retro sports paraphernalia adorning the walls. On weekend nights, it's also a dance club. And most importantly, on Sundays, its a brunch destination. No matter where you spent your Saturday night, JC's corned-beef hash and eggs and live reggae music make for an excellent way to recover.

FOUR'S SPORTS BAR

Map p228 (617-720-4455; www.thefours.com; 166 Canal St; 11am-midnight; North Station) Boasting all sports, all the time, the Four's makes a great place to appreciate Boston's near-fanatical obsession with sporting events. The large two-level bar was established in 1976 and retains a dash of character from that period. In addition to the game of your choice, admire a jersey collection and loads of pictures depicting legendary events in Boston's sporting past.

North End

CAFFÈ VITTORIA CAFE

Map p230 (617-227-7606; www.caffevittoria. com; 290-296 Hanover St; 7am-midnight Sun-Thu, to 12:30pm Fri & Sat; Haymarket) A delightful destination for dessert or aperitifs, this frilly parlor displays antique espresso machines and black-and-white photos, with a pressed-tin ceiling reminiscent of the Victorian era. Grab a marble-topped table, order a cappuccino and enjoy the romantic setting. Cash only, just like the olden days.

PARLA COCKTAIL BAR

Map p230 (617-367-2824; www.parlaboston. com; 230 Hanover St; 5-11:15pm Mon-Wed, to 12:15am Thu & Fri, 11am-12:15am Sat, 11am-11:15pm Sun; Haymarket) If you have a hankering for something different, duck into this tiny hole-in-the-wall with a retro, Prohibition-era theme. The atmosphere is super-hip and somehow secretive and the talented bartender mixes up inventive cocktails, as you would expect from a speakeasy. Adventurous souls might order the Dungeon Master, then roll the die to get a drink from the secret menu.

CAFFÈ PARADISO BAR

Map p230 (617-742-1768; www.caffeparadiso boston.com; 255 Hanover St; 7am-2am; Haymarket) Some regulars here are so dedicated that they organize their business calendars so they don't miss their spot at the counter. The bartender masterfully minds the espresso machine and pours neat cognacs with efficient and understated finesse. It's a great place to watch Premier League and Serie A football, and the *cannoli* and *cappuccini* are strong contenders for Boston's best.

Local Life
Italian Culture in the North End

The North End's warren of alleyways retains the Old World flavor brought by Italian immigrants, ever since they started settling here in the early 20th century. And when we say 'flavor,' we're not being metaphorical. We mean garlic, basil and oregano, sautéed in extra-virgin olive oil; rich tomato sauces that have simmered for hours; amaretto and anise; and delicious, creamy gelato.

❶ North End Park
Grab a snack from Maria's Pastry (p61), then cross the street to sit in the shade under grape vines in North End Park, designed as the neighborhood's 'front porch.'

❷ Polcari's Coffee
Duck into Polcari's Coffee (p67) and take a deep breath. That is the delightful aroma of imported coffee beans, tea leaves and aromatic spices. Founded in 1932, this old-fashioned dry-goods store hearkens back to the early 20th century, which is when Italian immigration was at its peak.

❸ North End Branch Library
Most Italian immigrants to Boston came from southern Italy and especially Sicily. But the **local library** (Map p230; 617-227-8135; www.bpl.org/branches/north. php; 25 Parmenter St; 10am-6pm Mon, Tue & Thu, noon-8pm Wed, 9am-5pm Fri, 9am-2pm Sat; Haymarket) FREE in the North End contains an unexpected souvenir of northern Italy – a model of the Palazzo Ducale in Venice.

❹ Caffè Paradiso
Stop in at this classic neighborhood cafe (p64) for cappuccino and some of Boston's finest *cannoli* (crisp pastry tubes filled on the spot with creamy sweetened ricotta cheese). Regulars watch Italian football on TV while the bartender masterfully minds the espresso machine and pours neat cognacs with understated finesse.

Polcari's Coffee (p67)

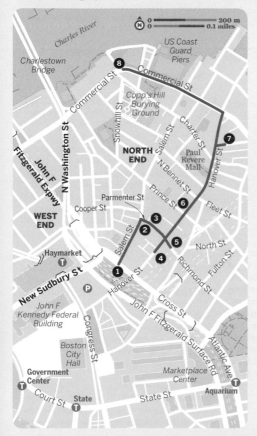

5 Salumeria Italiana

Salumeria Italiana (p66) has been doing its thing for more than 50 years – supplying local *nonne* (Italian grandmothers) with imported products like high-quality balsamic vinegar and extra-virgin olive oil. They also make a mean sandwich.

6 St Leonard's Church

Dating to 1873, **St Leonard's Church** (Map p230; ☎617-523-2110; www.saintleonardchurchboston.org; 320 Hanover St; ⊕9:30am-2:30pm; Ⓣ Haymarket) was founded and built by Italian immigrants. They still hold weekly Mass in Italian, as well as in English. The church sponsors the annual Feast of St Anthony (p59), starring their very own shrine of the beloved saint (the oldest in the city).

7 All Saints Way

Local collector and devout Catholic Peter Baldassari has been collecting holy cards for nearly 80 years. His treasures are on display in this tiny alleyway off Battery St, locally known as **All Saints Way** (Map p230; 4 Battery St; Ⓣ Haymarket). If you're lucky you might catch Mr Baldassari in his sacred space. Otherwise the gate will likely be locked.

8 Langone Park

It was a sad day in North End history when, in 1919, a distillery tank burst and the neighborhood was flooded with molasses (p58), destroying homes and killing and injuring residents. The site of this disaster is now **Langone Park** (Map p230; ☎617-626-1250; Commercial St; Ⓣ North Station), a peaceful place for neighbors to congregate and play bocce. Take in the harbor views and enjoy!

CAFFÈ DELLO SPORT SPORTS BAR

Map p230 (☑617-523-5063; www.caffedello sport.net; 308 Hanover St; ☺6am-11:30pm Mon-Thu, to 12:30pm Fri, 7am-12:30pm Sat & Sun; 🛜; 🔘Haymarket) An informal crowd of thick-accented guys from the 'hood sit at glass-topped tables and drink espresso and Campari. This is a great place to watch a football game (and yes, we mean soccer) – or just to watch the other patrons. They also make a mean *cannoli*. Cash only.

☆ ENTERTAINMENT

IMPROV ASYLUM COMEDY

Map p230 (☑617-263-6887; www.improvasylum. com; 216 Hanover St; tickets $10-28; ☺shows 8pm Sun-Thu, 7:30pm, 10pm & midnight Fri & Sat; 🔘Haymarket) A basement theater is somehow the perfect setting for the dark humor spewing from the mouths of this offbeat crew. No topic is too touchy, no politics too correct. Shows vary from night to night, but the standard Mainstage Show mixes up the improv with comedy sketches that are guaranteed to make you giggle. The Saturday midnight show is aptly named 'Raunchy.'

TD GARDEN STADIUM

Map p228 (☑event info 617-624-1000; www.td garden.com; 150 Causeway St; 🔘North Station) TD Garden is home to the NHL Boston Bruins, who play hockey here from September to June, and the NBA Boston Celtics, who play basketball from October to April. It's the city's largest venue, so big-name musicians perform here, too.

🛍 SHOPPING

Every visitor to Boston goes to the North End to savor the flavors of Italian cooking. These old streets are packed with specialty markets selling imported food products, wine, spices, fresh produce, meats and seafood. The constant flow of foot traffic has started to attract funky boutiques and galleries, too. There's not much in the way of shopping in the West End, so mosey across North End Park to spend your money.

★SALMAGUNDI HATS

Map p230 (☑617-936-4015; www.salmagundi boston.com; 61 Salem St; ☺11am-7pm Tue-Fri, to 8pm Sat, to 6pm Sun & Mon; 🔘Haymarket) While the flagship Salmagundi store in Jamaica Plain has a bigger selection, this second location in the North End still offers some 4000 hats for your head-topping pleasure. From functional caps and protective sun hats to flashy fedoras and gorgeous special-occasion toppers, you'll find something that meets your needs and fits your style. (The passionate, knowledgeable staff guarantee it.)

CONVERSE AT LOVEJOY WHARF SHOES

Map p228 (☑617-377-1000; www.converse.com; 140 N Washington St; ☺10am-7pm Mon-Sat, 11am-6pm Sun; 🔘North Station) Occupying the ground level of the Converse world headquarters, this flagship store has a sweet selection of its classic sneakers, including some true originals. Look for a handful of styles with Boston themes – 'Exclusive at Lovejoy Wharf' as they say. Or, you can customize a pair with your own colors and images.

NORTH BENNET STREET SCHOOL ARTS & CRAFTS

Map p230 (☑617-227-0155; www.nbss.edu; 150 North St; ☺9:30am-5:30pm Mon-Fri; 🔘Haymarket) The North Bennet Street School has been training craftspeople for over 100 years. Established in 1885, the school offers programs in traditional skills like bookbinding, woodworking and locksmithing. The school's on-site gallery sells incredible handcrafted pieces made by students and alumni. Look for unique jewelry, handmade journals, and exquisite wooden furniture and musical instruments.

SALUMERIA ITALIANA FOOD & DRINKS

Map p230 (☑617-523-8743; www.salumeriaitali ana.com; 151 Richmond St; ☺8am-7pm Mon-Sat, 10am-4pm Sun; 🔘Haymarket) Shelves stocked with extra-virgin olive oil and aged balsamic vinegar, cases crammed with cured meats, hard cheeses and olives of all shapes and sizes, boxes of pasta and jars of sauce – this little store is the archetype of North End specialty shops.

BRICCO SALUMERIA FOOD & DRINKS

Map p230 (☑617-248-9629; www.briccosalumer ia.com; 241 Hanover St; ☺10am-7pm Sun-Thu, to 9pm Fri & Sat; 🔘Haymarket) Duck down Board

Alley and into this sense-piquing specialty shop. Sausages and cured meats hang from the ceiling, while the cases are stocked with fresh cheeses, handmade pastas, rich olive oils and spicy sauces. Follow your nose to the lower-level bakery for fresh ciabatta and other Italian breads, straight from the oven.

POLCARI'S COFFEE   FOOD & DRINKS
Map p230 (☏617-227-0786; www.polcariscoffee.com; 105 Salem St; ◷10am-6pm Mon-Fri, from 9am Sat; Ⓣ Haymarket) Since 1932, this corner shop is where North Enders have stocked up on their beans. Look for 40-some kinds of imported coffee, over 150 spices, and an impressive selection of legumes, grains, flours and loose teas.

SEDURRE   CLOTHING
Map p230 (☏617-720-4400; www.sedurrebos ton.com; 28½ Prince St; ◷11am-7pm Mon-Wed, to 8pm Thu & Fri, to 9pm Sat, noon-6pm Sun; Ⓣ Haymarket) If you speak Italian, you'll know that Sedurre's thing is sexy and stylish. (It means 'seduce.') The shop started with fine lingerie – beautiful lacy nightgowns and underthings for special occasions. Sisters Robyn and Daria were so good at that, they created an additional space next door for dresses, evening wear and jewelry (for other kinds of special occasions).

SHAKE THE TREE   FASHION & ACCESSORIES
Map p230 (☏617-742-0484; www.shakethetree boston.com; 67 Salem St; ◷11am-7pm Mon-Fri, 10am-8pm Sat, noon-6pm Sun; Ⓣ Haymarket) You never know what you will find at this sweet boutique, but it's bound to be good. The little shop carries a wonderful, eclectic assortment of jewelry by local artisans, alongside interesting stationery, designer handbags and clothing, and unique housewares.

I AM BOOKS   BOOKS
Map p230 (☏857-263-7665; www.iambooksbos ton.com; 189 North St; ◷10am-6pm Mon-Sat, to 5pm Sun; Ⓣ Haymarket) Calling itself 'an Italian-American cultural hub,' this small independent bookstore is the perfect place to pick up reading materials for an upcoming trip to Italy. Specializing in fiction set in Italy and nonfiction about Italy, there are also children's books, cookbooks, Italian language books, magazines and more. A welcoming place to browse or buy.

IN-JEAN-IUS   CLOTHING
Map p230 (☏617-523-5326; www.injeanius.com; 441 Hanover St; ◷11am-7pm Mon-Sat, noon-6pm Sun; Ⓣ Haymarket) You know what you're getting when you waltz into this denim haven. Offerings from more than 20 designers include tried-and-true favorites and little-known gems, and staff are on hand to help you find the perfect pair. Warning: the surgeon general has determined that it is not healthy to try on jeans after a gigantic plate of pasta, so do come here before dinner.

V CIRACE & SON, INC   FOOD & DRINKS
Map p230 (☏617-227-3193; www.vcirace.com; 127 North St; ◷10am-7pm Mon-Thu, to 8pm Fri & Sat; Ⓣ Haymarket) It's the third generation of the Cirace family that runs this North End institution. Established in 1906, V Cirace & Son carries an impressive selection of Italian wines, grappa and spirits. Other specialties include artisanal pasta and olive oil, Italian sweets and honey, and imported ceramics.

WINE BOTTEGA   FOOD & DRINKS
Map p230 (☏617-227-6607; www.thewinebot tega.com; 341 Hanover St; ◷11am-9pm Tue-Thu, 10am-10pm Fri & Sat, noon-8pm Sun & Mon; Ⓣ Haymarket) With a large choice of wines packed into a small space, this is a delightful place to browse. The owners are enthusiastic about educating their customers, so they will love to help you find something you love too. Free wine tastings on Fridays from 5pm to 8pm.

🏃 SPORTS & ACTIVITIES

NORTH END MARKET TOUR   WALKING
Map p230 (☏617-523-6032; www.bostonfood tours.com; tours $60; ◷tours 10am & 2pm Wed & Sat, 10am & 3pm Fri) A three-hour tour around the North End that includes shopping in a *salumeria* (deli), sampling pastries at the local *pasticceria,* smelling the herbs and spices that flavor Italian cooking, and sampling spirits at an *enoteca* (wine bar). Guests have the opportunity to chat with local shopkeepers and other longtime North End residents to reminisce about living and eating in this food-rich neighborhood.

Beacon Hill & Boston Common

Neighborhood Top Five

1 **Public Garden** (p72) Breathing in the sweet smell of flowering trees and blooming beds as you admire the seasonal display. A ride in a swan boat on the lagoon completes an idyllic outing.

2 **Shakespeare on the Common** (p78) Packing a picnic for an evening of outdoor theater on Boston Common.

3 **Charles Street** (p78) Browsing for trash and treasure in the antique shops and sweet boutiques that line the main shopping street in Beacon Hill.

4 **Black Heritage Trail** (p79) Learning about the early African American settlement on Beacon Hill.

5 **Massachusetts State House** (p73) Searching for the Sacred Cod, the Holy Mackerel and other iconic emblems under the golden dome of the Commonwealth government building.

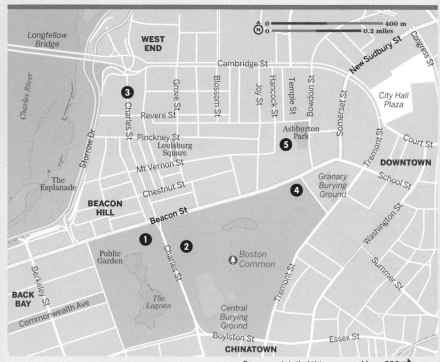

For more detail of this area see Map p236 ➡

Explore Beacon Hill & Boston Common

The Boston Common (p70) is the starting point for the Freedom Trail and, as such, the starting point for many visitors' exploration of Boston. Whether or not it is the first place you visit in Boston, it is a central meeting spot, a jumping-off point for several neighborhoods and an always-enjoyable place for a picnic lunch. You'll likely find yourself passing through more than once.

Besides the Common, several other Freedom Trail sights lie within the borders of Beacon Hill, including the impressive gold-domed Massachusetts State House (p73). This is the focal point of politics in the Commonwealth – the building famously dubbed 'the hub of the solar system' – and the neighborhood buzzes with the business of local politicos and State House staffers.

But the appeal of this neighborhood lies behind the landmarks, along the narrow cobblestone streets that crisscross the hill. Lined with brick town houses and lit by gas lanterns, these streets make a delightful backdrop for an afternoon meander – whether browsing boutiques and haggling for antiques, or just sipping a cappuccino and admiring the quintessentially Bostonian landscape.

Local Life

➜ **Book Nook** Local writers and bibliophiles enjoy the artistic atmosphere and historic setting at the Boston Athenaeum (p73).

➜ **Local Politics** State House staffers hang out across the street at the 21st Amendment (p76) when their working day is through.

➜ **Secret Spot** Escape the crowds on Charles St and retreat to 75 Chestnut (p75) to hobnob with the locals.

Getting There & Away

➜ **Metro** At the junction of the red and green lines, Park St T station services the Boston Common and sights in the southeastern part of Beacon Hill. Also on the red line, Charles/MGH T station is convenient to Beacon Hill's Charles and Cambridge Sts, as well as the Charles River Esplanade. The blue line Bowdoin T station is a less-used stop convenient to the eastern end of Cambridge St.

Lonely Planet's Top Tip

Get a great view of Boston's skyline from the **Longfellow Bridge**, also known as the 'salt and pepper bridge,' which crosses the river at the top of Charles St.

 Best Places to Eat

➜ Paramount (p75)
➜ No 9 Park (p75)
➜ Tatte (p74)
➜ Grotto (p75)
➜ 75 Chestnut (p75)

For reviews, see p74.➜

 Best Places to Drink

➜ Tip Tap Room (p76)
➜ 21st Amendment (p76)
➜ Bin 26 Enoteca (p76)
➜ Pressed (p76)

For reviews, see p76.➜

 Best Shopping

➜ Paridaez (p78)
➜ Eugene Galleries (p78)
➜ Twentieth Century Ltd (p78)
➜ Beacon Hill Chocolates (p78)
➜ Crush Boutique (p78)

For reviews, see p78.➜

BEACON HILL & BOSTON COMMON

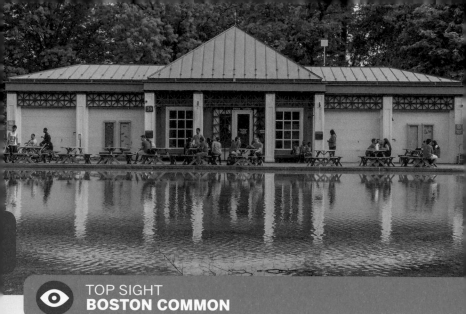

TOP SIGHT
BOSTON COMMON

The 50-acre Boston Common is the country's oldest public park. The Common has served many purposes over the years, including as a campground for British troops during the Revolutionary War and as green grass for cattle grazing until the 1830s. Although there is still a grazing ordinance on the books, the Common today serves picnickers, sunbathers and people-watchers.

Robert Gould Shaw Memorial

It took Augustus St Gaudens nearly 13 years to sculpt this magnificent **bas-relief memorial** honoring the 54th Massachusetts Regiment of the Union Army, the nation's first all-black Civil War regiment (depicted in the 1989 film *Glory*). These soldiers steadfastly refused their monthly stipend for nearly two years, until Congress increased it to match the amount that white regiments received. Shaw and half his men were killed in a battle at Fort Wagner, South Carolina. The National Park Service (NPS) tour of the Black Heritage Trail (p79) departs from here.

Blaxton Plaque

In 1634 William Blaxton sold a piece of land for £30 so the Massachusetts Bay Colony would have a place for the cows to graze. Such was the inglorious beginning of the Boston Common, the country's oldest public park. This **plaque** is emblazoned with the words of the treaty between Governor Winthrop and Mr Blaxton, should you care to know the details.

Brewer Fountain

This bronze beauty dates to 1868, when it was gifted to the city of Boston by the wealthy merchant Gardner Brewer. The lovely **fountain** features four aquatic deities from antiq-

---

DON'T MISS

➡ Blaxton Plaque
➡ Robert Gould Shaw Memorial
➡ Boston Massacre Monument

PRACTICALITIES

➡ Map p236, C5
➡ btwn Tremont, Charles, Beacon & Park Sts
➡ ⏱6am-midnight
➡ P 👬
➡ T Park St

uity: the Roman god of water, Neptune; the Greek sea goddess, Amphitrite; and the spirit Acis and the sea nymph Galatea, both from *Metamorphoses,* by the Roman poet Ovid. The design won a gold medal at the 1855 World's Fair.

Boston Massacre Monument

This 25ft **monument** pays tribute to the five victims of the Boston Massacre, which took place down the street in front of the Old State House. The monument replicates Paul Revere's famous engraving of the tragic event. Revere's effective propaganda depicts the soldiers shooting down defenseless colonists in cold blood, when in reality they were reacting to the aggressive crowd in self-defense.

Soldiers & Sailors Monument

Dedicated in 1877, this massive **monument** atop Flagstaff Hill pays tribute to the namesake soldiers and sailors who died in the Civil War. The four bronze statues represent Peace, the female figure looking to the South; the Sailor, the seaman looking toward the ocean; History, the Greek figure looking to heaven; and the Soldier, an infantryman standing at ease. See if you can recognize the many historical figures in the elaborate bronze reliefs.

Great Elm & the Frog Pond

A plaque marks the spot of the **Great Elm**, a majestic tree that stood here for more than 200 years. History has it that the tree was used for executions in the 17th century, including Ann Hibbens, hanged for witchery in 1656, and Mary Dyer, for religious heresy in 1660. Later, the arbor was popular for picnicking and climbing. The Great Elm eventually became a symbol of endurance and was considered a witness to history. By the mid-19th century, it was more than 70ft tall. Boston's 'oldest inhabitant' was damaged in 1869 in a brutal storm and destroyed for good by another storm in 1876. In winter, the nearby **Frog Pond** (www.bostonfrogpond.com; adult/child $6/ free, skate rental $12/6) attracts ice-skaters.

Central Burying Ground

Dating to 1756, the **Central Burying Ground** (Map p236; Boylston St; ⊗9am-5pm; Ⓣ Boylston) is the least celebrated of the old cemeteries, as it was the burial ground of the down-and-out (according to an account in Edwin Bacon's *Boston Illustrated,* it was used for 'Roman Catholics and strangers dying in the town'). Some reports indicate that it contains an unmarked mass grave for British soldiers who died in the Battle of Bunker Hill.

THE BARD

Every summer the Commonwealth Shakespeare Company hosts the free Shakespeare on the Common (p78) for picnic-packing theater-lovers.

The Boston Common is often called 'the Common' in local parlance, but never 'the Commons.'

PARKING

After 4pm on weekdays and all day on weekends, you can park in the lot under Boston Common for three hours for $14, or overnight for $18. Enter from Charles St.

Boston Common is one of many places in the city that offers Wicked Free wi-fi (free wireless internet connection) for all comers.

WALKING TOURS

Both the Freedom Trail (p28) and the Black Heritage Trail (p79) begin at the Boston Common.

Dating to 1897, Park St station is the oldest subway station in America.

BEACON HILL & BOSTON COMMON BOSTON COMMON

◉ TOP SIGHT
PUBLIC GARDEN

The Public Garden is a 24-acre botanical oasis of Victorian flowerbeds, blooming rose gardens, verdant grass and weeping willow trees shading a tranquil lagoon. Until it was filled in the early 19th century, it was a tidal salt marsh. Now, at any time of the year, it is awash with seasonal blooms, gold-toned leaves or untrammeled snow.

Monuments

At the main entrance (from Arlington St), visitors are greeted by a **statue of George Washington**, looking stately atop his horse.

Other pieces of public art are more whimsical; the most endearing is **Make Way for Ducklings**. The sculpture depicts Mrs Mallard and her eight ducklings, the main characters in the beloved book by Robert McCloskey. As the story goes, Mrs Mallard and her ducklings are stuck at a busy street until a friendly Boston policeman helps them across.

The small-scale fountains also have fun, kid-friendly themes. See if your children can find **Boy and Bird** by Bashka Paeff or **Triton Babies** by Anna Coleman Ladd.

On the northwest side of the lagoon, the **Ether Monument** commemorates the first use of anesthesia for medical purposes, which took place in Boston. Dating to 1868, it is the oldest monument in the garden. The bronze figures tell the story of the Good Samaritan.

Swan Boats

The story of the **swan boats** (www.swanboats.com; adult/child $4/2.50; ⊙10am-4pm Apr-Jun, to 5pm Jul-Aug; ⊤Arlington) goes back to 1877, when Robert Paget developed a catamaran with a pedal-powered paddlewheel. Inspired by the opera *Lohengrin,* in which a heroic knight rides across a river in a swan-drawn boat, Paget designed a graceful swan to hide the boat captain. While today's swan boats are larger than the 1877 original, they still utilize the same technology and they are still managed by Paget's descendants.

DON'T MISS

➡ *Make Way for Duck-lings* statue
➡ Swan Boats

PRACTICALITIES

➡ Map p236, B4
➡ ☏617-723-8144
➡ www.friendsofthepublicgarden.org
➡ Arlington St
➡ ⊙dawn-dusk
➡ ⊤Arlington

⊙ SIGHTS

The neighborhood's most prominent sights – Boston Common, Public Garden and Massachusetts State House – are found in a cluster around Beacon St. However, Beacon Hill's appeal lies not in these star attractions, but in its quiet corners and cobblestone streets, which still evoke 19th-century Boston.

BOSTON COMMON   PARK
See p70.

PUBLIC GARDEN   GARDENS
See p72.

MASSACHUSETTS STATE HOUSE   NOTABLE BUILDING
Map p236 (☑617-727-7030; www.sec.state.ma.us; cnr Beacon & Bowdoin Sts; ☺8:45am-5pm Mon-Fri, tours 10am-3:30pm Mon-Fri; ⊤Park St) FREE
High atop Beacon Hill, Massachusetts' leaders and legislators attempt to turn their ideas into concrete policies and practices within the State House. John Hancock provided the land (previously part of his cow pasture) and Charles Bulfinch designed the commanding state capitol, but it was Oliver Wendell Holmes who called it 'the hub of the solar system' (thus earning Boston the nickname 'the Hub'). Free 40-minute tours cover the history, artwork, architecture and political personalities of the State House.

Tours start in the **Doric Hall**, the columned reception area directly below the dome. Once the main entryway to the State House, these front doors are now used only by a visiting US president or by departing governors taking 'the long walk' on their last day in office.

The nearby **Nurses Hall** is named for the moving statue of a Civil War nurse tending to a fallen soldier. The circular **Memorial Hall**, known as the Hall of Flags, honors Massachusetts soldiers by displaying some of the tattered flags that have been carried to battle over the years. Finally, the impressive marble **Great Hall** is hung with 351 flags, representing all the cities and towns in Massachusetts.

Upstairs, visitors can see both legislative chambers: the House of Representatives, also home of the famous Sacred Cod; and the Senate Chamber, residence of the Holy Mackerel. The massive wooden carving of a codfish (nearly 5ft long) has hung in the State House since the 18th century, as testament to the importance of the fishing industry to the economy and culture of the Commonwealth. The brass casting of a mackerel has hung in the Senate Chamber since 1895.

On the front lawn, statues honor important Massachusetts figures, among them orator Daniel Webster, Civil War general Joseph Hooker, religious martyrs Anne Hutchinson and Mary Dyer, President John F Kennedy and educator Horace Mann. Unfortunately, these lovely grounds are closed to the public, so you'll have to peek through the iron fence to catch a glimpse.

GRANARY BURYING GROUND   CEMETERY
Map p236 (Tremont St; ☺9am-5pm; ⊤Park St)
Dating from 1660, this atmospheric atoll is crammed with historic headstones, many with evocative (and creepy) carvings. This is the final resting place of favorite revolutionary heroes, including Paul Revere, Samuel Adams, John Hancock and James Otis. Benjamin Franklin is buried in Philadelphia, but the Franklin family plot contains his parents.

The five victims of the Boston Massacre (p71) share a common grave, though the only name you are likely to recognize is that of Crispus Attucks, the freed slave who is considered the first person to lose his life in the struggle for American independence. Other noteworthy permanent residents include Peter Faneuil, of Faneuil Hall fame, and Judge Sewall, the only magistrate to denounce the hanging of the so-called Salem witches.

The location of Park St Church was once the site of the town granary; as the burying ground predates the church, it is named after the grain storage facility instead. While it is sometimes called the Old Granary Burying Ground, it's not the oldest; King's Chapel and Copp's Hill date back even further.

BOSTON ATHENAEUM   LIBRARY
Map p236 (☑617-227-0270; www.boston athenaeum.org; 10½ Beacon St; $10, tour $2; ☺noon-8pm Tue & 10am-4pm Wed-Sat; ⊤Park St) Founded in 1807, the Boston Athenaeum is an old and distinguished private library, having hosted the likes of Ralph Waldo Emerson and Nathaniel Hawthorne. Its collection has half a million volumes, including an impressive selection of art, which is showcased in the on-site gallery. The library itself is open to members only, but tourists can visit the gallery. Tours of the library's

HIDDEN BEACON HILL

Take a detour away from Charles St to discover a few Beacon Hill gems.

Louisburg Square (Map p236; ⊤Charles/MGH) There is no more prestigious address than this lane, a cluster of stately brick row houses facing a private park. After she gained literary success, Louisa May Alcott lived at No 10; at the northern corner of the square is the home of former Secretary of State John Kerry and his wife Teresa Heinz.

Acorn Street (Map p236; ⊤Charles/MGH) Boston's narrowest street, this knobbly cobblestone alleyway was once home to artisans and to the service people who worked for the adjacent mansion dwellers. The brick walls on the north side of the street enclose examples of Beacon Hill's hidden gardens , which are opened up to the public once a year.

art and architecture are offered several times a week; reservations recommended.

MUSEUM OF AFRICAN AMERICAN HISTORY   MUSEUM

Map p236 (☎617-725-0022; www.maah.org; 46 Joy St; adult/child $10/free; ⊙10am-4pm Mon-Sat; ⊤Park St, Bowdoin) The Museum of African American History occupies two adjacent historic buildings: the African Meeting House, the country's oldest black church and meeting house; and Abiel Smith School, the country's first school for blacks. The museum offers rotating exhibits about the historic events that took place here, and is also a source of information about the Black Heritage Trail (p79).

Within these walls William Lloyd Garrison began the New England Anti-Slavery Society, which later expanded to become the American Anti-Slavery Society. Here, Maria Stewart became the first American woman – a black woman, no less – to speak before a mixed-gender audience. Frederick Douglass delivered stirring calls to action within this hall, and Robert Gould Shaw recruited black soldiers for the Civil War effort.

NICHOLS HOUSE MUSEUM   MUSEUM

Map p236 (☎617-227-6993; www.nicholshouse museum.org; 55 Mt Vernon St; adult/child $10/

free; ⊙11am-4pm Tue-Sat Apr-Oct, Thu-Sat Nov-Mar; ⊤Park St) This 1804 town house offers the rare opportunity to peek inside one of these classic Beacon Hill beauties. Attributed to Charles Bulfinch, it is unique in its merger of Federal and Greek Revival architectural styles. Equally impressive is the story told inside the museum – that of the day-to-day life of Miss Rose Standish Nichols, who lived here from 1885 to 1960.

Miss Rose was an author, pacifist and suffragette. The museum has reconstructed her home, furnished with art and antiques from all over the world, as well as some impressive examples of her own needlepoint and woodwork.

PARK ST CHURCH   CHURCH

Map p236 (☎617-523-3383; www.parkstreet.org; 1 Park St; ⊙9:30am-3pm Tue-Sat mid-Jun–Aug, Sun year-round; ⊤Park St) Shortly after the construction of Park St Church, powder for the War of 1812 was stored in the basement, earning this location the moniker 'Brimstone Corner.' But that was hardly the most inflammatory event that took place here. Noted for its graceful, 217ft steeple, this Boston landmark has been hosting historic lectures and musical performances since its founding.

In 1829 William Lloyd Garrison railed against slavery from the church's pulpit. And on Independence Day in 1831, Samuel Francis Smith's hymn 'America ('My Country 'Tis of Thee)' was first sung. These days, Park St is a conservative congregational church.

 EATING

Beacon Hill's Old World ambience provides the perfect setting for an afternoon of coffee-drinking and sandwich-munching or a night of swanky dining and sweet nothings. Climbing up Charles St, you'll find a mix of cute cafes, quick bites and gourmet delicatessens, plus a few upscale spots.

★TATTE   BAKERY $

Map p236 (☎617-723-5555; www.tattebakery. com; 70 Charles St; mains $10-14; ⊙7am-8pm Mon-Fri, from 8am Sat, 8am-7pm Sun; ⊤Charles/MGH) The aroma of buttery goodness – and the lines stretching out the door – signal your arrival at this fabulous bakery on the lower floor of the historic Charles St Meeting House. Swoon-worthy pastries (divinely cinnamon-y buns, chocolate-hazelnut twists, avocado and mushroom tartines) from $3 taste even more amazing if you're lucky enough to score a table on the front patio.

PIPERI

MEDITERRANEAN GRILL   MIDDLE EASTERN $

Map p234 (📞617-227-7471; www.piperi.com; 1 Beacon St; mains $7-9; ⊘11am-4pm Mon-Fri, from noon Sat; 🅙 🚻; Ⓣ Government Center) The concept is simple. Decide whether you want a flatbread sandwich, salad or mezze plate. Choose chicken, steak or veggies as a main ingredient. Then add fresh toppings such as hummus, tabouleh, slaw, cheese etc. Hungry Boston workers line up out the door for this quick, healthy, fresh and affordable lunch; service is efficient so you won't wait long.

EARL OF SANDWICH   SANDWICHES $

Map p236 (📞617-426-1395; www.earlofsand wichusa.com; 1b Charles St, Boston Common; sandwiches $6-10; ⊘11am-6pm; Ⓣ Park St, Boylston) Here's a quick and easy lunch spot on the Boston Common, occupying the handsome 'Pink Palace' (formerly a men's toilet, but never mind).

★PARAMOUNT   CAFETERIA $$

Map p236 (📞617-720-1152; www.paramountbos ton.com; 44 Charles St; mains $17-24; ⊘7am-10pm Mon-Fri, from 8am Sat & Sun; 🅙 🚻; Ⓣ Charles/ MGH) This old-fashioned cafeteria is a neighborhood favorite. A-plus diner fare includes pancakes, home fries, burgers and sandwiches, and big, hearty salads. Banana and caramel French toast is an obvious go-to for the brunch crowd. Don't sit down until you get your food! The wait may seem endless, but patrons swear it is worth it.

At dinner, add table service and candlelight, and the place goes upscale without losing its down-home charm.

GROTTO   ITALIAN $$

Map p236 (📞617-227-3434; www.grottorestau rant.com; 37 Bowdoin St; mains $21-27, 3-course prix-fixe dinner $36-42; ⊘11:30am-3pm Mon-Fri, 5-10pm daily; Ⓣ Bowdoin) In a word: romantic. Tucked into a basement on the back side of Beacon Hill, this dark, cave-like place lives up to its name. The funky decor – exposed brick walls decked with rotating art exhibits – reflects the innovative menu. Reservations recommended, as the place is tiny.

75 CHESTNUT   AMERICAN $$

Map p236 (📞617-227-2175; www.75chestnut. com; 75 Chestnut St; mains $18-27; ⊘10:30am-2:30pm Sat & Sun, 5-11pm daily; 🚻; Ⓣ Charles/ MGH) You might not think to take a peek around the corner, away from the well-trod sidewalks of Charles St. But locals know that Chestnut St is the place to go for tried-and-true steaks and seafood, and a genuine warm welcome.

MA MAISON   FRENCH $$

Map p236 (📞617-725-8855; www.mamaison boston.com; 272 Cambridge St; mains $22-30; ⊘11am-10pm; 🚻; Ⓣ Charles/MGH) Cambridge St is lined with restaurants, most of the uninteresting, fast food, greasy spoon variety. Ma Maison is the exception, with its elegant decor and reliably delicious French fare. The onion soup earns rave reviews, as do more exotic options, such as lobster bisque and foie gras, followed by *duck magret à l'orange* or lamb shank with couscous and *merguez* (sausage).

SCOLLAY SQUARE   AMERICAN $$

Map p236 (📞617-742-4900; www.scollaysquare. com; 21 Beacon St; mains $18-24; ⊘noon-9pm Tue-Sat, to 2pm Sun; Ⓣ Park St) This retro restaurant harks back to the glory days of its namesake (an actual city square that used to occupy the site of City Hall Plaza). Old photos and memorabilia adorn the walls, while suits sip martinis to big-band music. The classic American fare is reliably good, with mac 'n' cheese and beef short ribs topping the list of favorites.

FIGS   PIZZA $$

Map p236 (📞617-742-3447; www.toddenglish figs.com; 42 Charles St; mains $18-25; ⊘11:30am-10pm; 🅙 🚻; Ⓣ Charles/MGH) The brainchild of celebrity chef Todd English, Figs rakes 'em in with its innovative whisper-thin pizzas. For a real treat, order the signature fig and prosciutto pizza with Gorgonzola. Equally delish are the sandwiches, salads and pastas.

NO 9 PARK   EUROPEAN $$$

Map p236 (📞617-742-9991; www.no9park.com; 9 Park St; mains $37-47, 6-course tasting menu $125; ⊘5-9pm Mon-Wed, to 10pm Thu-Sat, 4-8pm Sun; Ⓣ Park St) This swanky place has been around since 1998, but it still tops many fine-dining lists. Chef-owner Barbara Lynch has now cast her celebrity-chef spell all around town, but this is the place that made her famous. Delectable French and Italian culinary masterpieces and first-rate wine list. Reservations recommended.

MOOO...   STEAK $$$

Map p236 (☑617-670-2515; www.mooorestau rant.com; 15 Beacon St; lunch $15-30, dinner $40-60; ⊗7am-10pm Mon-Fri, 8am-10:30pm Sat, 10:30am-10pm Sun; ⊤Park St) This super-cool, modern steakhouse presents a challenge: don't fill up on the irresistible rolls before your food arrives. You'll be glad you saved room for the meaty specialties such as beef Wellington and Wagyu beef dumplings. For an extra decadent, carnivorous touch, steaks are served with bone-marrow butter.

🍺 DRINKING & 🍸 NIGHTLIFE

Beacon Hill is not the best destination for a night out on the town, drinking and carousing. But there are a few worthwhile spots for a tipple, if you happen to be in the neighborhood.

PRESSED   JUICE BAR

Map p236 (☑857-350-3103; www.pressedbos ton.com; 120 Charles St; ⊗8am-6pm Mon-Fri, from 9am Sat & Sun; 📶; ⊤Charles/MGH) We'll call it a juice bar, since it does make its own juices (out of every fruit and vegetable imaginable) as well as delicious vegan 'superfood shakes' ($10). But the 'toasts' and 'greens' also deserve mention. Both your body and your taste buds will thank you for eating and drinking this tasty, healthy fare.

TIP TAP ROOM   BAR

Map p236 (☑617-350-3344; www.thetiptap room.com; 138 Cambridge St; ⊗11:30am-2am Mon-Fri, from 10:30am Sat & Sun; 📶; ⊤Bowdoin) The 'tips' are steak, lamb, turkey, chicken or swordfish. The 'taps' are nearly 40 kinds of beer, ranging from local craft brews to international ales of some renown. The food is good (including a daily 'game special' such as braised antelope ribs), and the beer is even better. There's no other place on Beacon Hill with this trendy but friendly vibe.

21ST AMENDMENT   PUB

Map p236 (☑617-227-7100; www.21stboston. com; 150 Bowdoin St; ⊗11:30am-2am; ⊤Park St) Named for one of the US Constitution's most important amendments – the one re-

pealing Prohibition – this quintessential tavern is an ever-popular haunt for State House workers to meet up and talk about the wheels of government. The place feels especially cozy during winter, when you'll feel pretty good about yourself as you drink a stout near the copper-hooded fireplace.

BIN 26 ENOTECA   WINE BAR

Map p236 (☑617-723-5939; www.bin26.com; 26 Charles St; ⊗noon-10pm Mon-Fri, from 10am Sat & Sun; ⊤Charles/MGH, Arlington) If you're into wine, you'll be into Bin. Big windows overlook Charles St and wine bottles line the walls. The extensive wine list spans the globe, including a moderately priced house wine that is bottled in Italy just for the restaurant. Staff will insist you order food (due to licensing requirements), but you won't regret sampling the simple, seasonal menu.

6B LOUNGE   COCKTAIL BAR

Map p236 (☑617-742-0306; www.6blounge andrestaurant.com; 6 Beacon St; cover after 9:30pm Fri $5; ⊗11am-2am; ⊤Park St) Most nights of the week, this is a pleasant but innocuous cocktail bar with forgettable food. But come Friday night, the bar morphs into a wildly popular 1990s dance party (from 10pm), featuring the local spinning legend DJ T-Rex. Saturday nights are fun, too (and free), with all your favorite pop tunes from Madonna, Michael Jackson and Wham!

SEVENS   BAR

Map p236 (☑617-523-9074; www.facebook.com/ SevensAle; 77 Charles St; ⊗11:30am-midnight Sun-Tue, to 1am Wed-Sat; ⊤Charles/MGH) Beacon Hill's long-standing neighborhood dive bar looks old school, with its wooden bar placed under hanging glasses, and a few comfortable booths. Service is brusque but endearing. The place serves only wine and beer, including a house brew from Harpoon. Darts, chess and sports on the tube provide the entertainment.

CHEERS   PUB

Map p236 (☑617-227-9605; www.cheersboston. com; 84 Beacon St; ⊗11am-1am; ⊤Arlington) Be aware that the bar doesn't really look like its famous TV alter ego, unless you sit in the 'set bar,' which is a replica of the set. It's also not really charming or local or 'Boston' in any way. But we understand that this is a mandatory pilgrimage place for fans of the TV show.

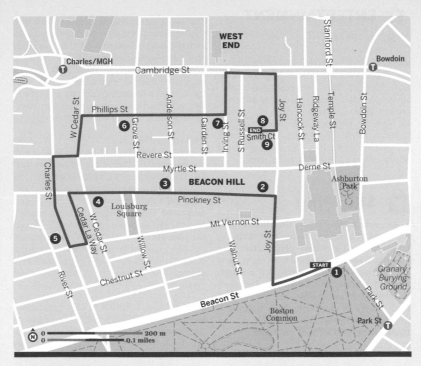

Neighborhood Walk
Black Heritage Trail

START BOSTON COMMON
END MUSEUM OF AFRICAN AMERICAN HISTORY
LENGTH 1.2 MILES; 90 MINUTES

Beacon Hill was never the exclusive domain of blue-blooded Brahmins. In the 19th century, freed African Americans settled on the back side of the hill and the neighborhood became a hive of activity focused on improving housing, establishing schools and creating opportunities for Black residents. NPS rangers lead free tours of the Black Heritage Trail (p79).

If you are heading out solo, start at the **❶ Robert Gould Shaw Memorial** (p70) on Boston Common. Walk north to reach the **❷ George Middleton House**, the oldest existing house that was built by an African American. Middleton was an honorary colonel who led an all-black regiment in the American Revolution. Further west, the **❸ Phillips School** became one of Boston's first interracial schools in 1855.

John J Smith lived in the house at **❹ 86 Pinckney Street** after the Civil War. He had

been a barber, an impassioned abolitionist and a harborer of fugitive slaves. After the war, he became a representative to the Massachusetts State Legislature.

Further west, turn south down Cedar Lane Way, then continue west to Charles St. The **❺ Charles St Meeting House** formerly housed the African Methodist Episcopal Church. Walk north on Charles St, then cut up to Phillips St. The house at **❻ No 66** – which was a station on the Underground Railroad – belonged to Lewis Hayden, an escaped slave and tireless abolitionist.

Further east, at the corner of Irving St, lies the **❼ John Coburn House**. An active member of the New England Freedom Association and the Boston Vigilance Committee, Coburn purportedly harbored fugitives and established a gaming house here.

Heading south on Joy St, the cluster of **❽ residential buildings on Smith Court** is representative of the homes where black Bostonians lived in the 19th century. The tour ends at the **❾ Museum of African American History** (p74).

⭐ ENTERTAINMENT

★ SHAKESPEARE
ON THE COMMON   THEATER
Map p236 (☎617-426-0863; www.commshakes. org; Boston Common; ☺Jul & Aug; ⊤Park St) Each summer, the Commonwealth Shakespeare Company stages a major production on the Boston Common, drawing crowds for (free) Shakespeare under the stars. Productions often appeal to the masses with a populist twist, thus *The Taming of the Shrew*, set in a North End restaurant.

🛍 SHOPPING

There was a time when Charles St was lined with antique shops and nothing else: some historians claim that the country's antique trade began right here on Beacon Hill. There are still enough antique shops to thrill the *Antiques Roadshow*–lover in you, but you'll also find plenty of contemporary galleries, preppy boutiques and practical shops to go along with all that old stuff.

PARIDAEZ   CLOTHING
Map p236 (☎617-835-5396; www.paridaez.com; 127 Charles St; ☺noon-6pm; ⊤Charles/MGH) Boston designer Allison Daroie knows women play many roles, and she believes their clothing should too. That's why her classy, minimalist pieces can transform from daytime to evening, from dressy to casual, from conservative to flirtatious. These styles are so versatile, it's sometimes hard to say exactly what they are (like the ingenious Albatross 3-in-1 skirt+dress+tank).

EUGENE GALLERIES   ANTIQUES
Map p236 (☎617-227-3062; www.eugenegalleries.com; 76 Charles St; ☺11am-6pm Mon-Sat, from noon Sun; ⊤Charles/MGH) This tiny shop has a remarkable selection of antique prints and maps, especially focusing on old Boston. Follow the history of the city's development by examining 18th- and 19th-century maps and witness the filling-in of Back Bay and the greening of the city. Historic prints highlight Boston landmarks, making for excellent old-fashioned gifts.

DECEMBER THIEVES   FASHION & ACCESSORIES
Map p236 (☎857-239-9149; www.december thieves.com; 51 Charles St; ☺11am-7pm Mon-Fri, 10am-6pm Sat, noon-5pm Sun; ⊤Charles/MGH)

The intriguing window dressing will lure you into this artful shop with designer pieces from Boston and abroad. The gorgeous space showcases stylish women's clothing, handbags and jewelry. There's only a few of each item stocked, guaranteeing that your special find will always feel unique. A second shop (88 Charles St) offers an eclectic assortment of finely crafted household goods.

CRUSH BOUTIQUE   CLOTHING
Map p236 (☎617-720-0010; www.shopcrush boutique.com; 131 Charles St; ☺10am-7pm Mon-Sat, 11am-6pm Sun; ⊤Charles/MGH) Fashion mavens rave about this cozy basement boutique on Charles St, which features both well-loved designers and up-and-coming talents. The selection of clothing is excellent, but it's the expert advice that makes this place so popular. Co-owners (and childhood BFFs) Rebecca and Laura would love to help you find something that makes you look fabulous.

BEACON HILL CHOCOLATES   FOOD & DRINKS
Map p236 (☎617-725-1900; www.beacon hillchocolates.com; 91 Charles St; ☺11am-7pm Mon-Sat, to 5:30pm Sun; ⊤Charles/MGH) This artisanal chocolatier puts equal effort into selecting fine chocolates from around the world and designing beautiful boxes to contain them. Using decoupage to affix old postcards, photos and illustrations, the boxes are works of art even before they are filled with truffles. Pick out an image of historic Boston as a souvenir for the sweet tooth in your life.

GOOD   JEWELRY
Map p236 (☎617-982-6777; www.shopatgood. com; 98 Charles St; ☺10am-6pm Tue-Sat; ⊤Charles/MGH) So many lovely things to look at, from exquisite custom-designed jewelry and attractive housewares to quirky baby gifts, chic scarves and handbags. It's hard to ascertain the common theme here, except the items are unique, stylish and supremely classy – and made in New England. Browsing is encouraged.

TWENTIETH CENTURY LTD   JEWELRY
Map p236 (☎617-742-1031; www.boston-vintage-jewelry.com; 73 Charles St; ☺11am-6pm Mon-Sat, noon-5pm Sun; ⊤Charles/MGH) Not just jewelry, but vintage jewelry – especially Bakelite, silver and art deco designs – made by the great designers of yesteryear. The selection is overwhelming, from tiaras to over 1000

pairs of cuff links. There's something for every price range, including the $10 bin for the budget-conscious.

CRANE & LION · CLOTHING

Map p236 (☑857-239-8170; www.craneandlion. com; 40 Charles St; ☉10am-7pm Mon-Fri, 9am-6pm Sat, 10am-5pm Sun; ⓣCharles/MGH) Fitness meets fashion at this sweet boutique (fronting a fitness and wellness center, appropriately). This local company aspires to create clothing that is both functional and beautiful. You'll find a whole line of workout wear, as well as casual but chic sweaters, dresses and tops.

BLACKSTONE'S OF BEACON HILL · GIFTS & SOUVENIRS

Map p236 (☑617-227-4646; www.blackstones beaconhill.com; 46 Charles St; ☉10am-6:30pm Mon-Fri, to 6pm Sat, 11am-5pm Sun; ⓣCharles/ MGH) Here's a guarantee: you will find the perfect gift for that certain someone at Blackstone's. This little place is crammed with classy, clever and otherwise-unusual items. Highlights include the custom-designed stationery, locally made handicrafts, and quirky

MARIKA'S ANTIQUE SHOP · ANTIQUES

Map p236 (☑617-523-4520; 130 Charles St; ☉10am-5pm Tue-Sat; ⓣCharles/MGH) In the mid-20th century, a Hungarian immigrant opened this treasure trove in Boston's antique central. Today it is run by her grandson, Matthew Raisz, who is extremely knowledgeable about his inventory. And the place still holds an excellent selection of fine collectibles – most notably jewelry, silver and porcelain.

UPSTAIRS DOWNSTAIRS ANTIQUES · ANTIQUES

Map p236 (☑617-367-1950; www.upstairsdown stairsboston.com; 93 Charles St; ☉11am-6pm; ⓣCharles/MGH) There's no longer an 'upstairs' to this long-standing antique shop, but there are still five rooms of art, antiques and vintage home decor. The selection is eclectic and the welcome is warm, whether you're buying or just browsing.

BLACK INK · GIFTS & SOUVENIRS

Map p236 (☑617-497-1221; www.blackinkboston. com; 101 Charles St; ☉11am-7pm Mon-Sat, noon-6pm Sun; ⓣCharles/MGH) Black Ink started as a shop for stationery and rubber stamps (thus, the name), but it has developed into

something so much more fun. The tagline – 'unexpected necessities' – conveys the fact that most of this stuff is functional, as well as quirky and clever (if not exactly necessary).

RED WAGON · CHILDREN'S CLOTHING

Map p236 (☑617-523-9402; www.theredwagon. com; 69 Charles St; ☉10am-7pm Mon-Sat, 11am-6pm Sun; ⓣCharles/MGH) The Red Wagon carries adorable, unusual outfits for small tykes, as well as books and toys for kids up to age seven. Upstairs, you'll find sweet and sassy fashions for tweens.

HELEN'S LEATHER · SHOES

Map p236 (☑617-742-2077; www.helensleather. com; 110 Charles St; ☉10am-6pm Mon-Sat, from noon Sun; ⓣCharles/MGH) You probably didn't realize that you would need your cowboy boots in Boston. Never fear, you can pick up a slick pair right here on Beacon Hill. (Indeed, this is the number-one distributor of cowboy boots in New England.) Helen's also carries stylish dress boots and work boots, as well as gorgeous jackets, classy handbags, wallets and belts.

🏃 SPORTS & ACTIVITIES

BLACK HERITAGE TRAIL · WALKING

Map p236 (☑617-742-5415; www.nps.gov/boaf; ☉tours 1pm Mon-Sat, more frequently in summer; ⓣPark St) The NPS conducts excellent, informative 90-minute guided tours exploring the history of the abolitionist movement and African American settlement on Beacon Hill. Tours depart from the Robert Gould Shaw memorial on Boston Common. Alternatively, take a self-guided tour with the NPS Freedom Trail app (www.nps.gov/bost/planyourvisit/app.htm) or grab a route map from the Museum of African American History (p74).

COMMUNITY BOATING · WATER SPORTS

Map p236 (☑617-523-1038; www.community-boating.org; Charles River Esplanade; kayak/SUP/sailboat per day from $45/45/89; ☉1pm-dusk Mon-Fri, 9am-dusk Sat & Sun Apr-Oct; ⓣCharles/MGH) Offers experienced sailors unlimited use of sailboats and kayaks on the Charles River, but you'll have to take a test to demonstrate your ability. A 30-day 'learn to sail' package costs $179, while a 30-day Wicked Basic, No-Frills sailing pass is $99.

Downtown & Waterfront

Neighborhood Top Five

1 **Rose Kennedy Greenway** (p85) Shopping for locally made souvenirs at the Open Market, cooling off in the Rings Fountain, riding whimsical creatures on the carousel or contemplatively walking the labyrinth, all along Boston's linear park.

2 **Whale-Watching** (p92) Taking a boat out to Stellwagen Bank to spy on whales, dolphins and other sea life.

3 **Boston Massacre Site** (p82) Finding the plaque that marks the spot of the first violent confrontation of the American Revolution.

4 **Old State House** (p82) Admiring the colonial architecture and appreciating the historic import amid the Downtown modern bustle.

5 **Democracy Brewing** (p87) Raising a cold one for idealism and activism at this unique, atmospheric drinking establishment.

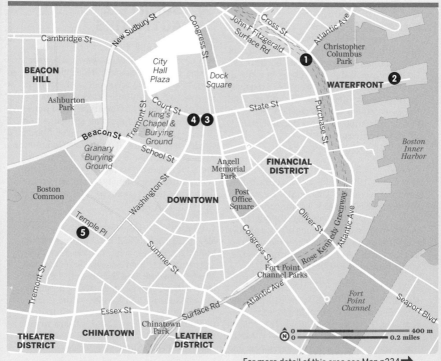

For more detail of this area see Map p234 ➡

Explore Downtown & Waterfront

Almost every visitor will traipse through this neighborhood while following the Freedom Trail to Faneuil Hall (p83) and Quincy Market (p86). Indeed, this marketplace is one of the most visited tourist sites in the country. Even though it's basically a shopping mall (but a *historic* shopping mall!), it's a fun stop to admire the public art, cheer on the street performers and soak up the festive atmosphere.

The area around Faneuil Hall is a contrast to the neighborhood's interior streets around Downtown Crossing and the Financial District. This is the Boston of the work-a-day world – a bustling place, but after hours the streets are eerily empty.

Along the waterfront, the dismantling of the Central Artery has meant that the call of seagulls and the lapping of waves no longer compete with the roar of cars. Instead, pedestrians can stroll across the Rose Kennedy Greenway (p85) parks to the harbor, enjoying the greenery and admiring the Rings Fountain along the way. From Long Wharf, you can catch the ferry out to the Boston Harbor Islands or a whale-watching cruise (p92) to Stellwagen Bank. Harbor cruises and trolley tours also depart from these docks, while seafood restaurants and outdoor cafes line the shore.

It's basically tourist central, and with good reason. With the sun sparkling off the water and the boats bobbing at their moorings, it's hard to resist this city by the sea.

Local Life

→ **Block Party** On Thursday evenings in summer, the Greenway (p85) and **Boston Calling** (www. bostoncalling.com; Harvard Athletic Complex, Allston; ☺May) host a block party on **Dewey Square** (Map p234; www. rosekennedygreenway.org; Atlantic Ave & Summer St), where local workers gather for live music and drinks.

→ **Happy Hour** Mr Dooley's (p90) is the rare downtown bar that feels like a neighborhood bar.

Getting There & Away

→ **Metro** To reach Faneuil Hall and Quincy Market, take the green, orange or blue line to Haymarket, Government Center or State. The blue line Aquarium stop offers the easiest access to the waterfront. Other useful stops downtown include Downtown Crossing (at the junction of the red and orange lines) and Park St (where the red and green lines intersect).

→ **Boat** City Water Taxi stops at Long Wharf on the waterfront, while the MBTA water shuttle runs from Long Wharf to Charlestown Navy Yard.

Lonely Planet's Top Tip

If you are following the red-brick road, consider purchasing the **Freedom Trail Ticket** (adult/child $11/2), which includes admission to the Old South Meeting House and the Paul Revere House.

✖ Best Places to Eat

→ jm Curley (p86)
→ Yvonne's (p86)
→ Grass Roots Cafe (p84)
→ Casa Razdora (p85)
→ Ruka Restobar (p87)

For reviews, see p84.➡

▱ Best Places to Drink

→ Democracy Brewing (p87)
→ Trillium Garden (p87)
→ Thinking Cup (p87)
→ Sip Café (p87)

For reviews, see p87.➡

◉ Best Historic Buildings

→ Old State House (p82)
→ Old South Meeting House (p82)
→ Faneuil Hall (p83)
→ Custom House (p84)

For reviews, see p82.➡

DOWNTOWN & WATERFRONT

⊙ SIGHTS

For all intents and purposes, downtown Boston is 'tourist central,' as hordes of visitors gather at Faneuil Hall and Quincy Market to pick up a tour, shop for souvenirs or grab a bite to eat. These historic buildings served as the center of the city's produce and meat industry for almost 150 years. In the 1970s the old buildings were redeveloped into today's touristy, festive shopping and eating center, so it still serves its original purpose, albeit with all the modern trappings. Other Freedom Trail sites are also in the vicinity.

★ OLD STATE HOUSE   HISTORIC BUILDING
Map p234 (☑617-720-1713; www.bostonhistory.org; 206 Washington St; adult/child $10/free; ⊙9am-6pm Jun-Aug, to 5pm Sep-May; ⓣState) Dating from 1713, the Old State House is Boston's oldest surviving public building, where the Massachusetts Assembly used to debate the issues of the day before the Revolution. The building is best known for its balcony, where the Declaration of Independence was first read to Bostonians in 1776. Inside, the Old State House contains a small museum of revolutionary memorabilia, with videos and multimedia presentations about the Boston Massacre, which took place out front.

BOSTON MASSACRE SITE   MONUMENT
Map p234 (cnr State & Devonshire Sts; ⓣState) Directly in front of the Old State House, encircled by cobblestones, a bronze plaque marks the spot where the first blood was shed for the American independence movement. On March 5, 1770, an angry mob of colonists swarmed the British soldiers guarding the State House, hurling snowballs, rocks and insults. Thus provoked, the soldiers fired into the crowd and killed five townspeople, including Crispus Attucks, a former slave. The incident sparked enormous anti-British sentiment.

Paul Revere helped fan the flames by widely disseminating an engraving that depicted the scene as an unmitigated slaughter. Interestingly, John Adams and Josiah Quincy – both of whom opposed the heavy-handed authoritarian British rule – defended the accused soldiers in court, and seven of the nine were acquitted.

OLD SOUTH
MEETING HOUSE   HISTORIC BUILDING
Map p234 (☑617-482-6439; www.osmh.org; 310 Washington St; adult/child $6/1; ⊙9:30am-5pm Apr-Oct, 10am-4pm Nov-Mar; ▮; ⓣDowntown Crossing, State) 'No tax on tea!' That was the decision on December 16, 1773, when 5000 angry colonists gathered here to protest British taxes, leading to the Boston Tea Party. Download an audio of the historic pre-Tea Party meeting from the museum website, then visit the graceful meeting house to check out the exhibit on the history of the building and the protest.

This brick meeting house, with its soaring steeple, was also used as a church house back in the day. In fact, Ben Franklin was baptized here. Which is why he found it so abhorrent when – after the Tea Party – British soldiers used the building for a stable and riding practice. The Old South congregation moved to a new building in Back Bay in 1875, when Ralph Waldo Emerson and Julia Ward Howe gathered support to convert the church into a museum.

KING'S CHAPEL &
BURYING GROUND   CHURCH, CEMETERY
Map p234 (☑617-523-1749; www.kings-chapel.org; 58 Tremont St; donation $3, tours adult/child $7/3; ⊙church 10am-4:30pm Mon-Sat, 1:30-5pm Sun, hourly tours 10am-3pm; ⓣGovernment Center) Puritan Bostonians were not pleased when the original Anglican church was erected on this site in 1688. The granite chapel standing today – built in 1754 – houses the largest bell ever made by Paul Revere, as well as a historic organ. The adjacent burying ground is the oldest in the city. Besides the biweekly services, recitals are held here every week (12:15pm Tuesday).

The church was built on a corner of the city cemetery because the Puritans refused to allow the Anglicans to use any other land. As a result, these are some of the city's oldest headstones, including one that dates to 1658. Famous graves include John Winthrop, the first governor of the fledgling Massachusetts Bay Colony; William Dawes, who rode with Paul Revere; and Mary Chilton, the first European woman to set foot in Plymouth.

In addition to the self-guided tour, visitors are invited on the **Bells & Bones tour**, which ascends into the bell tower to admire Paul Revere's work and descends into the crypt to wander among 250-year-old remains.

NEW ENGLAND AQUARIUM · AQUARIUM

Map p234 (☑617-973-5200; www.neaq.org; Central Wharf; adult/child $27/19; ⊗9am-5pm Mon-Fri, to 6pm Sat & Sun, 1hr later Jul & Aug; P🚻; T Aquarium) 🐟 Teeming with sea creatures of all sizes, shapes and colors, this giant fishbowl is the centerpiece of downtown Boston's waterfront. The main attraction is the three-story Giant Ocean Tank, which swirls with thousands of creatures great and small, including turtles, sharks and eels. Countless side exhibits explore the lives and habitats of other underwater oddities, as well as penguins and marine mammals.

Harbor seals hang out in an observation tank near the aquarium entrance, while the open-air Marine Mammal Center is home to northern fur seals and California sea lions. Visitors can watch training sessions where the pinnipeds show off their intelligence and athleticism. Note that some animal rights groups make a strong case that marine mammals should not be kept in captivity, no matter how classy their quarters.

The Shark & Ray Touch Tank recreates a mangrove swamp full of Atlantic rays, cownose rays and five species of sharks. Most of the aquarium's 1st floor is dedicated to an enormous penguin exhibit, home to more than 90 birds representing three different species. Upstairs, six different tanks showcase the flora and fauna of the Amazon rain forest, while giant Pacific octopuses stretch their tentacles in the Olympic Coast tank.

The 3D **Simons IMAX Theatre** (adult/child $10/8) features films with aquatic themes, and the aquarium also organizes daily whale-watching cruises (p92). Combination tickets offer modest savings on these supplemental activities.

FANEUIL HALL · HISTORIC BUILDING

Map p234 (☑617-242-5642; www.nps.gov/bost; Congress St; ⊗9am-5pm; T State, Haymarket, Government Center) FREE 'Those who cannot bear free speech had best go home,' said Wendell Phillips. 'Faneuil Hall is no place for slavish hearts.' Indeed, this public meeting place was the site of so much rabble-rousing that it earned the nickname the 'Cradle of Liberty.' After the revolution, Faneuil Hall was a forum for meetings about abolition, women's suffrage and war. You can hear about the building's history from National Park Service (NPS) rangers in the historic hall on the 2nd floor.

The brick colonial building – topped with the beloved grasshopper weather vane – was constructed in 1740 at the urging of Boston benefactor and merchant Peter Faneuil. In 1805 Charles Bulfinch enlarged the building, enclosing the 1st-floor market and designing the 2nd-floor meeting space, where public ceremonies are still held today. On the top floor the Ancient & Honorable Artillery Co of Massachusetts, which was chartered in 1638, maintains a peculiar collection of antique firearms, political mementos and curious artifacts.

NEW ENGLAND HOLOCAUST MEMORIAL · MEMORIAL

Map p234 (www.nehm.org; btwn Union & Congress Sts; T Haymarket) Constructed in 1995, the six luminescent glass columns of the New England Holocaust Memorial are engraved with six million numbers, representing those killed in the Holocaust. Each tower – with smoldering coals sending plumes of steam up through the glass corridors – represents a different Nazi death camp. The memorial sits along the Freedom Trail, a sobering reminder of its larger meaning.

BLACKSTONE BLOCK · HISTORIC SITE

Map p234 (cnr Union & Hanover Sts; T Haymarket) Named after Boston's first settler, this tiny warren of streets dates to the 17th and 18th centuries. Established in 1826, Union Oyster House (p87) is Boston's oldest restaurant. Around the corner in Creek Sq, the c 1767 Ebenezer Hancock House was the home of the brother of founding father John Hancock. At the base of the shop next door, the 1737 **Boston Stone** (Map p234; Marshall St; T Haymarket) served as the terminus for measuring distances to and from the city. (The dome of Beacon Hill's Massachusetts State House (p73) now serves this purpose.)

OLD CITY HALL · HISTORIC SITE

Map p234 (☑617-204-9506; www.oldcityhall.com; 45 School St; T State) This monumental French Second Empire building occupies a historic spot. Out front, a plaque commemorates the site of the country's first public school, Boston Latin, founded in 1635 and still operational in Fenway. The hopscotch sidewalk mosaic, *City Carpet*, marks the site where Benjamin Franklin, Ralph Waldo Emerson and Charles Bulfinch were educated.

Statues of Benjamin Franklin, founding father, and Josiah Quincy, second mayor of Boston, stand inside the courtyard. They are accompanied by a life-size replica of a donkey, symbol of the Democratic Party. ('Why the donkey?' you wonder. Read the plaque to find out.) Two bronze footprints 'stand in opposition.'

CUSTOM HOUSE   HISTORIC BUILDING
Map p234 (☑617-310-6300; www.marriott.com; 3 McKinley Sq; observation deck $5-7.50; ⊙observation deck 2pm & 6pm Sat-Thu; ⊤Aquarium) The lower portion of the Custom House, begun in 1837, resembles a Greek temple, but the federal government wanted something grander, so in 1913 it exempted itself from local height restrictions and financed a 500ft tower. Nowadays there are many taller buildings, but the 22ft illuminated clock makes this gem the most recognizable part of the city skyline. Twice a day (weather permitting), the 26th-floor observation deck opens up for fabulous views.

One of Boston's first skyscrapers, the Custom House now houses a Marriott hotel. But that doesn't mean you have to dole out big bucks to appreciate the building's history and aesthetics. The public is always welcome to the 1st-floor rotunda, a work of art in itself, which houses a small exhibit of maritime art and artifacts from Salem's Peabody Essex Museum (p171).

STEAMING KETTLE   MONUMENT
Map p234 (63-65 Court St) The steaming kettle on Sears Crescent has been a Boston landmark since 1873, when it was hung over the door of the Oriental Tea Co at 57 Court St. The teashop held a contest to determine how much tea the giant kettle might hold. The answer – awarded with a chest of premium tea – was 227 gallons, two quarts, one pint and three gills.

The tea kettle was relocated to its current location on the western tip of the Sears Crescent building in 1967, when 'urban renewal' swept this neighborhood. Tea drinkers are grateful that this icon of old Boston was saved, although many are miffed that it now marks the spot of a Starbucks.

CITY HALL PLAZA   SQUARE
Map p234 (⊤Government Center) City Hall Plaza is a cold, windy, 56-acre concrete plaza, surrounded by government office buildings. Occupying the site of the former Scollay Sq, the plaza was supposed to be a model of innovation and modernization when it was built in the 1960s. But it has been much maligned, topping at least one list of the world's ugliest buildings. The plaza hosts food trucks, public gatherings and occasional summertime performances.

Designed by IM Pei, City Hall Plaza is home to the fortress-like Boston City Hall and the twin towers of the John F Kennedy Federal Building. The plaza's high points are the gracefully curved brick **Sears Crescent**, one of the few buildings that remains from the Scollay Sq days, and the sweeping curve of the modern **Center Plaza**, which mirrors Sears Crescent.

OLD CORNER BOOKSTORE   HISTORIC BUILDING
Map p234 (cnr School & Washington Sts; ⊤Downtown Crossing) In the 19th century, this historic house was leased to a bookseller, Carter & Hendlee. This was the first of nine bookstores and publishing companies that would occupy the spot, making it a breeding ground for literary and philosophical ideas. The most illustrious was Ticknor & Fields, publisher of books by Thoreau, Emerson, Hawthorne, Longfellow and Harriet Beecher Stowe.

In the earliest days of Boston history, this was the site of the home of Anne Hutchinson, the religious dissident who was expelled from the Massachusetts Bay Colony and co-founded the Rhode Island Colony. The current brick building dates to 1718, when it served as a pharmacy and residence. Today the storefront houses a fastfood restaurant, which seems somewhat less lofty than its earlier incarnations.

✖ EATING

Faneuil Hall and its environs are packed with touristy places touting baked beans, live lobsters and other Boston specialties. In the nearby Financial District, local workers lunch on stuffed sandwiches and ethnic eats. It's hard to get off the beaten track, but that doesn't mean you won't find some fun, funky and delicious places to eat.

GRASS ROOTS CAFE   KOREAN $
Map p234 (☑617-951-2124; 101 Arch St; mains $8-10; ⊙6:30am-7pm Mon-Fri; ⊤Downtown Crossing) Here is a surprising hole-in-the-wall Korean gem, where two brothers serve up

ROSE KENNEDY GREENWAY

The gateway to the Boston waterfront is the **Rose Kennedy Greenway** (Map p234; 617-292-0020; www.rosekennedygreenway.org; ; Aquarium, Haymarket). Where once was a hulking overhead highway, now winds a 27-acre strip of landscaped gardens and fountain-lined greens, with an artist market for Saturday shoppers, and food trucks for weekday lunchers.

Walking the Greenway from north to south, here's what you'll find along the way.

North End Park Designed as the North End neighborhood's front yard, the wide lawn is a perfect place for a picnic.

Labyrinth Calm your mind and contemplate the moment as you follow the granite path, winding its way around a serpentine route. The labyrinth represents the journey of life. (The destination is beside the point.)

Greenway Carousel Take a ride on the backs of local sea and woodland creatures, such as American lobsters, harbor seals, monarch butterflies and red-tailed hawks. This one-of-a-kind **carousel** (Map p234; per ride $3; 11am-7pm Apr-Dec; ; Aquarium) was designed by local artist Jeff Briggs with help from local school children.

Boston Harbor Islands Pavilion Want more information about the Boston Harbor Islands? Stop by this seasonal information center (p215). Don't miss the nearby Harbor Fog Sculpture, which immerses passers-by in the sounds and sensations of the harbor.

Rings Fountain This playful fountain is unpredictable and irresistible, especially on a hot day.

Dewey Square Parks With food vendors, farmers markets and block parties, this is a popular lunch spot for the working world. Dewey Sq is also the site of Boston's most prominent street art – usually a mural by an artist of some renown.

Chinatown Park Asian gardens, Chinese chessboards and Falun Gong practitioners populate this plaza, which serves as the gateway to Chinatown.

traditional deliciousness from their ancestral homeland. Favorites include the Triple B (bibimbap) and Porky's Nightmare (spicy marinated pork). For less adventurous palates, the all-American sandwiches are well stuffed and tasty. Fresh ingredients and personable service make this a sure win.

SPYCE INTERNATIONAL $

Map p234 (www.spyce.com; 241 Washington St; bowls $7.50; 10:30am-10pm; ; State) A new concept in dining, Spyce is the brainchild of four hungry MIT grads, who teamed up with a Michelin-starred chef. The food is all prepared in a robotic kitchen – that is, self-rotating woks that are programmed for the optimal temperature and time to create consistently perfect 'bowls' of goodness. It's fast, fresh, healthy and pretty darn delicious.

It's also vegetarian, vegan or gluten-free, if you wish.

CLOVER DTX VEGETARIAN $

Map p234 (www.cloverfoodlab.com; 27 School St; mains $8-12; 7am-9pm Mon-Fri, 8am-8pm Sat-Sun; ; State) Right on the Freedom Trail, the first Downtown branch of this socially conscious local success story serves veggie treats morning, noon and night, from breakfast sandwiches in the morning to platters of BBQ seitan or chickpea fritters the rest of the day.

CASA RAZDORA ITALIAN $

Map p234 (617-338-6700; www.casarazdora. com; 115 Water St; mains $8-14; 11am-4pm Mon-Fri; ; State) The line is often out the door, but it's worth the wait for amazing Italian food, just like *nonna* made. Pick a pasta (all made fresh on the premises) and top it with a delicious sauce of your choosing. Or select one of the chef's mouthwatering daily specials. Seats are limited, so snag one if you can!

GENE'S CHINESE FLATBREAD CHINESE $

Map p234 (617-482-1888; www.genescafe. com; 86 Bedford St; mains $6-11; 11am-6:30am Mon-Sat; Chinatown) It's not often that we recommend leaving Chinatown for Chinese food, but it's only a few blocks away. And it's

BOSTON CREAM PIE

Wondering where to go to sample Boston's namesake dessert? At the Omni Parker House (p183), they could write a book about Boston cream pie, as the hotel's pastry chefs invented this creamy, cakey delight. Literally. Hunker down in the lobby bar, The Last Hurrah, for an individual-sized pie, artfully presented and masterfully paired with a glass of Cava. Delightful!

worth the detour to this unassuming storefront for chewy Xi'an-style noodles. No 9 (cumin lamb hand-pulled noodles) and No 3 (pork flatbread sandwich) are perennial fan favorites. Seating is limited and credit cards are not accepted.

CHACARERO SANDWICHES $
Map p234 (617-542-0392; www.chacarero.com; 101 Arch St; mains $8-12; 11am-6pm Mon-Fri; Downtown Crossing) A *chacarero* is a traditional Chilean sandwich made with grilled chicken or beef, Muenster cheese, fresh tomatoes, guacamole and the surprise ingredient – steamed green beans. Stuffed into homemade bread, the sandwiches are a longtime favorite for lunch around downtown.

FALAFEL KING MIDDLE EASTERN $
Map p234 (617-482-2223; www.falafelkingboston.com; 62 Summer St; mains $9-12; 11am-7:30pm Mon-Fri; Downtown Crossing) Two words: free falafels. That's right, everyone gets a little free sample before ordering. There is no disputing that this is indeed the falafel king of Boston. The sandwiches are fast, delicious and cheap. There's another Downtown location on **Washington St** (Map p234; 617-227-6400; www.falafelkingboston.com; 260 Washington St; mains $9-12; 11am-9pm Mon-Fri, to 8pm Sat & Sun; State).

SAM LA GRASSA'S DELI $
Map p234 (617-357-6861; www.samlagrassas.com; 44 Province St; sandwiches $14; 11am-3:30pm Mon-Fri; Downtown Crossing) Step up to the counter and place your order for one of Sam La Grassa's signature sandwiches, then find a spot at the crowded communal table. You won't be disappointed by the Famous Rumanian Pastrami or the 'Fresh from the Pot' corned beef. The sandwiches are so well stuffed that they are tricky to eat.

QUINCY MARKET FOOD HALL $
Map p234 (617-523-1300; www.faneuilhallmarketplace.com; Congress St; mains $8-20; 10am-9pm Mon-Sat, noon-6pm Sun; Haymarket, Aquarium) Behind Faneuil Hall, this food court offers a variety of places under one roof: the place is packed with about 20 restaurants and 40 food stalls. Choose from chowder, bagels, ice cream, hot dogs etc, and take a seat at one of the tables in the central rotunda. It's usually crowded and mostly overpriced, but it sure is convenient.

★**JM CURLEY** PUB FOOD $$
Map p234 (617-338-5333; www.jmcurleyboston.com; 21 Temple Pl; mains $10-20; 11:30am-1am Mon-Sat, to 10pm Sunday; Downtown Crossing) This dim, inviting bar is a perfect place to settle in for a Dark & Stormy on a dark and stormy night. The fare is bar food like you've never had before: Curley's cracka jack (caramel corn with bacon); mac 'n' cheese (served in a cast-iron skillet); and fried pickles (yes, you read that right). That's why they call it a gastropub.

JAMES HOOK & CO SEAFOOD $$
Map p234 (617-423-5501; www.jameshooklobster.com; 15-17 Northern Ave; lobster rolls $20-24; 10am-5pm Mon-Thu & Sat, to 6pm Fri, to 4pm Sun) For a superlative lobster roll close to Downtown, look no further than this harborside seafood shack near the bridge to the Seaport district. Outdoor tables make it a perfect low-key lunch stop as you make your way between museums on a sunny afternoon.

KOY KOREAN $$
Map p234 (857-991-1483; www.koyboston.com; 16 North St; mains $15-30; 11am-midnight; Haymarket) It's unusual that something so classy, so contemporary and so cosmopolitan should find a home in historic Blackstone Block. But here it is: Korean fusion. There are traditional dishes, including excellent bibimbap, but the 'twists' are what make mouths water, not to mention the original cocktails. Lychee Sangria is where it's at.

YVONNE'S MODERN AMERICAN $$$
Map p234 (617-267-0047; www.yvonnesboston.com; 2 Winter Pl; 5-11pm, bar to 2am; Park) Upon arrival at Yvonne's, staff will usher you discreetly through closed doors into a hidden 'modern supper club.' The spectacular space artfully blends old-school luxury with contemporary eclecticism. The

menu of mostly small plates does the same, with items from tuna crudo to baked oysters to chicken and quinoa meatballs.

RUKA RESTOBAR
FUSION $$$

Map p234 ([✎]617-266-0102; www.rukarestobar. com; 505 Washington St; small plates $13-25; ⊙5-11pm; [T]Downtown Crossing) Ruka Restobar is all about Nikkei – the fusion of Japanese and Peruvian cuisines. Look for intriguing sushi creations, several kinds of ceviche and other inventions featuring Japanese cooking techniques and South American ingredients (or vice versa). Yes, the cocktail menu features the famous pisco sour (and other pisco drinks). It's all very trendy, global and fun.

MARLIAVE
FRENCH $$$

Map p234 ([✎]617-422-0004; www.marliave.com; 10 Bosworth St; mains $18-38; ⊙11am-10pm; [✎]; [T]Park St) Dating to 1885, the Marliave has all of its vintage architectural quirks still intact, from the mosaic floor to the tin ceilings. The wide-ranging menu includes quirky cocktails, a raw bar, delicious egg dishes, homemade pasta and old-fashioned Sunday dinners (eg, Wellington). Best bargain: $1 oysters from 4pm to 6pm and from 9pm to 10pm daily.

UNION OYSTER HOUSE
SEAFOOD $$$

Map p234 ([✎]617-227-2750; www.unionoyster house.com; 41 Union St; mains $24-32; ⊙11am-9:30pm Sun-Thu, to 10pm Fri & Sat; [T]Haymarket) The oldest restaurant in Boston, ye olde Union Oyster House has been serving seafood in this historic redbrick building since 1826. Countless historymakers have propped themselves up at this bar, including Daniel Webster and John F Kennedy (apparently JFK used to order the lobster bisque). Overpriced but atmospheric.

🍷⚓ DRINKING & NIGHTLIFE

After the department store at Downtown Crossing locks up for the night, the street life quiets considerably. There is a cluster of bars around Faneuil Hall and Blackstone Block that actively cater to the tourist crowd, although they have an underwhelming, generic vibe. Embedded nearby are some perennial favorites, some of them quite crowded on weekends.

TRILLIUM GARDEN
BEER GARDEN

Map p234 ([✎]857-449-0083; www.trilliumbrew ing.com; cnr Atlantic Ave & High St; ⊙2-10pm Wed-Fri, from 11am Sat, 1-8pm Sun May-Oct; 🛜; [T]South Station, Aquarium) To say that this seasonal beer garden is a welcome addition to the Rose Kennedy Greenway is an understatement. When the weather is fine, Bostonians are flocking to this shady spot to sample the delicious beers that are brewed just across the canal in Fort Point. No food is served but there are food trucks parked nearby.

DEMOCRACY BREWING
BREWERY

Map p234 ([✎]857-263-8604; www.democracy brewing.com; 35 Temple Pl; ⊙11:30am-11pm Sun-Thu, to 1am Fri & Sat; [T]Downtown Crossing) The beer is fresh, the fries are crispy perfection and the politics are 'woke.' Not only do they brew exceptional beer at Democracy Brewing, they also ferment revolution – by supporting democratic businesses, organizing community events and showcasing the revolutionaries and rabble-rousers from Boston's past and present.

THINKING CUP
CAFE

Map p234 ([✎]617-482-5555; www.thinkingcup. com; 165 Tremont St; ⊙7am-10pm Mon-Wed, to 11pm Thu-Sun; [T]Boylston) 🍴 There are a few things that make the Thinking Cup special. One is the French hot chocolate – *ooh la la*. Another is the Stumptown Coffee, the Portland brew that has earned accolades from coffee drinkers around the country. But the best thing? It's across from the Boston Common, making it a perfect stop for a post–Frog Pond warm-up.

SIP CAFÉ
CAFE

Map p234 ([✎]617-338-3080; www.sipboston.com; 0 Post Office Sq; ⊙6:30am-6pm Mon-Fri Apr-Nov, to 5pm Dec-Mar; ♿; [T]Downtown Crossing) Enclosed by glass and surrounded by the greenery of Post Office Sq, Sip Café is a delightful place to stop for lunch or a caffeinated beverage. There's outdoor seating in warm weather, but even in winter, the high ceilings and streaming sunlight will warm your heart. As will the George Howell coffee, fresh daily-changing soups and yummy sandwiches.

DOWNTOWN & WATERFRONT DRINKING & NIGHTLIFE

Boston by Water

With the expansive Boston Harbor at its front door and the winding River Charles at its back, Boston offers endless opportunities for beach bumming, boat rides, seaside strolls and riverside relaxation. Whatever aquatic activity you choose, don't miss a chance to feel the breeze and soak up the stunning views.

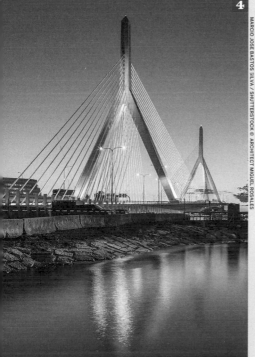

STEVE DUNNWELL / GETTY IMAGES ©

1. Charles River Esplanade (p111)
Three miles of urban escape along the Charles River.

2. Liberty Wharf
The Seaport District's (p129) home of seafood.

3. Stellwagen Bank (p81)
Take a boat out to Stellwagen Bank to go whale-watching.

4. Leonard Zakim Bunker Hill Bridge (p52) Bridge over the Charles River named after the human-rights activist, Lenny Bunker.

MARCIO JOSE BASTOS SILVA / SHUTTERSTOCK © ARCHITECT MIGUEL ROSALES

FABIO LOTTI / SHUTTERSTOCK ©

CAFFE NERO CAFE

Map p234 (✉617-936-3432; http://us.caffenero.com; 560 Washington St; ⊙6:30am-9:30pm; 🛜; Ⓣ Chinatown, Downtown Crossing) Italian coffee. Antique Alsatian bar. Comfy couches and cozy fireplace. Cosmopolitan clientele. This place oozes Old World ambience, and we mean that in the most modern, sophisticated way. Espresso drinks are top-notch, and there's sidewalk seating in warm weather.

ALLEY GAY

Map p234 (✉617-263-1449; www.thealleybar.com; 14 Pi Alley; ⊙2pm-2am; Ⓣ State) Half the fun is trying to find this secret spot, tucked down a pedestrian lane between Washington St and Court Sq, with no sign on the door. This place is known as a 'bear bar,' but most of these big gruff guys are friendly – very friendly. Enjoy the cheap beer and laid-back atmosphere. Cash only.

MR DOOLEY'S IRISH PUB

Map p234 (✉617-338-5656; www.mrdooleys.com; 77 Broad St; ⊙11:30am-2am Mon-Fri, from 9am Sat & Sun; Ⓣ State) With Irish bands playing traditional tunes on Monday and Thursday, and a decent list of appropriate beers, Mr Dooley's is one of the most welcoming joints in the area. Sit in a wooden booth and linger over a copy of the *Irish Immigrant* or *Boston Irish Reporter* to learn about current events on the other side of the Atlantic.

GOOD LIFE CLUB

Map p234 (✉617-451-2622; www.goodlifebar.com; 28 Kingston St; ⊙11am-11pm Mon-Wed, to 2am Thu-Sat; Ⓣ Downtown Crossing) The Good Life means a lot of things to a lot of people – solid lunch option, after-work hangout, trivia-night place etc. But the top reason to come here is to get your groove on. There are three bars and two dance floors, with great DJs spinning tunes Thursday to Saturday (cover $10 to $15).

BIDDY EARLY'S PUB BAR

Map p234 (✉617-654-9944; 141 Pearl St; ⊙10am-2am; Ⓣ South Station) If dive bars are your thing, you'll be happy here. In fact, Biddy's is sometimes called the 'best' dive bar in Boston (a town that has no shortage of them). We're not sure what that means (dirtiest bathrooms? Cheapest beer?), but you'll find a dart board, a jukebox, buckets of beers and friendly faces on both sides of the bar.

 ENTERTAINMENT

BOSTON BALLET DANCE

Map p234 (✉617-695-6955; www.bostonballet.org; Opera House, 539 Washington St; tickets $37-204) Boston's skillful ballet troupe performs modern and classic works at the Opera House (p90). The program varies every year, but at Christmas they always put on a wildly popular performance of the *Nutcracker*. Student and child 'rush' tickets are available for $30 cash two hours before some performances; seniors get the same deal, but only for select Saturday and Sunday matinees.

OPERA HOUSE LIVE PERFORMANCE

Map p234 (✉800-982-2787; www.bostonoperahouse.com; 539 Washington St; Ⓣ Downtown Crossing) This lavish theater has been restored to its 1928 glory, complete with mural-painted ceiling, gilded molding and plush velvet curtains. The glitzy venue regularly hosts productions from the Broadway Across America series, and is also the main performance space for the Boston Ballet (p90).

MODERN THEATRE THEATER

Map p234 (✉866-811-4111; www.suffolk.edu/moderntheatre; 525 Washington St; Ⓣ Downtown Crossing) The Modern Theatre dates to 1876 and showed Boston's first 'talkie' in 1928. Nearly a century later, the building opened its doors again as a venue for Suffolk University, holding an intimate 185-seat theater. Only the facade remains from the original building, but it looks stellar – another step in the revival of a mini theater district on lower Washington St.

PARAMOUNT CENTER THEATER

Map p234 (✉617-824-8400; www.paramountboston.org; 559 Washington St; Ⓣ Chinatown, Downtown Crossing) This art deco masterpiece, restored by Emerson College, reopened in 2010. Originally a 1700-seat, single-screen cinema, it was owned by Paramount Pictures (thus the name). The new facility includes a cinema and a black-box stage, as well as the more traditional but still grand main stage.

DICK'S BEANTOWN COMEDY
COMEDY

Map p234 (☑800-401-2221; www.dickdoherty.
com; 184 High St; $20; ⊙shows 7:30pm Sat,
doors open 6:30pm; ⓣAquarium) In the basement of the nightclub Howl at the Moon,
veteran local comedian Dick Doherty
brings in national acts with Boston roots
as well as up-and-coming local performers,
working the room into painful howls with
surgical precision.

 SHOPPING

**Downtown Crossing is an outdoor
pedestrian mall. Many of the stores are
outlets of national chains, although a
few local shops are still keeping it real.
The Faneuil Hall and Quincy Market area
is possibly Boston's most popular tourist
shopping spot: upward of 15 million
people visit annually. The five buildings
are filled with 100-plus tourist-oriented
shops, pushcart vendors and national
chain stores.**

BRATTLE BOOK SHOP
BOOKS

Map p234 (☑617-542-0210; www.brattlebook
shop.com; 9 West St; ⊙9am-5:30pm Mon-Sat;
ⓣPark St, Downtown Crossing) Since 1825, the
Brattle Book Shop has catered to Boston's
literati: it's a treasure trove crammed with
out-of-print, rare and first edition books.
Ken Gloss – whose family has owned this
gem since 1949 – is an expert on antiquari-
an books, moonlighting as a consultant and
appraiser (see him on *Antiques Roadshow*).
Don't miss the bargains on the outside lot.

GREENWAY OPEN MARKET
ARTS & CRAFTS

Map p234 (☑800-401-6557; www.newengland
openmarkets.com; Rose Kennedy Greenway;
⊙11am-5pm Sat, plus 1st & 3rd Sun May-Oct;
🕏; ⓣAquarium) This weekend artist market brings out dozens of vendors to display
their wares in the open air. Look for unique,
handmade gifts, jewelry, bags, paintings,
ceramics and other arts and crafts – most
of which are locally and ethically made.
Food trucks are always on hand to cater to
the hungry.

ARTISTS FOR HUMANITY
GIFTS & SOUVENIRS

Map p234 (☑617-268-7620; www.afhboston.org;
1 Faneuil Hall; ⊙10am-9pm Mon-Sat & 11am-7pm
Sun Apr-Oct, 10am-7pm Mon-Thu, to 9pm Fri &
Sat, noon-6pm Sun Nov-Mar; ⓣState) Artists
for Humanity is a local charity organiza-

tion that encourages urban youth to get in
touch with their creative sides. That means
you're doing a good deed by shopping here,
as if you needed an excuse to treat yourself
to one of the cute, clever T-shirts or totes
bags. (We're partial to the cycling lobster,
aka 'Lobsta Roll'.)

REVOLUTIONARY
BOSTON MUSEUM STORE
GIFTS & SOUVENIRS

Map p234 (☑617-742-4744; www.revolutionary
boston.org; Quincy Market; ⊙10am-9pm Mon-
Sat, 11am-6pm Sun; ⓣState) Souvenirs with
an Americana theme: woven throws featuring flags, eagles and other all-American
goodness; reproductions of Paul Revere's
depiction of the Boston Massacre; patriotic
coffee mugs etc. The cleverest souvenirs are
in the food aisle: Boston Harbor Tea, Stars
& Stripes pasta and other treats to enliven
your next July 4 cookout.

LUCY'S LEAGUE
CLOTHING

Map p234 (☑617-248-3986; www.rosterstores.
com/lucysleague; North Market, Faneuil Hall;
⊙10am-9pm Mon-Sat, to 7pm Sun; ⓣState) At
Lucy's League, sports fans will find super-
cute styles, flattering shirts, jackets and
other gear designed for women, all sporting
the local team's logos.

JEWELERS
XCHANGE BUILDING
JEWELRY

Map p234 (☑617-367-3461; www.jewelersbuild
ingboston.com; 333 Washington St; ⊙8am-6pm
Mon-Sat; ⓣDowntown Crossing) With over 100
jewelers, this historic building is the first
stop for many would-be grooms. Some jewelers have retail space on the 1st floor, other
less conspicuous artisans work upstairs. If
you're overwhelmed by options, go to Boston Ring and Gem (BRAG) on the 2nd floor.
The Zargarian family has been designing

DOWNTOWN & WATERFRONT SHOPPING

LOCAL KNOWLEDGE

TO MARKET, TO MARKET

Local foodies are buzzing about the long-awaited Boston Public Market, the city's first permanent local farmers market. The location is just a few steps from Haymarket, and a few more steps from Faneuil Hall and Quincy Market, which is the city's historic marketplace. As such, the public market anchors a vibrant 'market district' in downtown Boston.

Boston Public Market (BPM; Map p234; ☑617-973-4909; www.bostonpublicmarket.org; 136 Blackstone St; ◷8am-8pm Mon-Sat, 10am-6pm Sun; ☎; ⊤Haymarket) A locavore's longtime dream-come-true, this daily farmers market – housed in a brick-and-mortar building – gives shoppers access to fresh foodstuffs, grown, harvested and produced right here in New England. Come for seasonal produce, fresh seafood, meats and poultry from local farms, artisan cheeses and dairy products, maple syrup and other sweets. Don't miss the local brews found in Hopsters' Alley. Reserve your spot for a free one-hour tour (10am and 11am, Thursday and Friday).

Haymarket (Map p234; Blackstone & Hanover Sts; ◷7am-5pm Fri & Sat; ⊤Haymarket) Touch the produce at Haymarket and you risk the wrath of the vendors, but nowhere in the city matches these prices on ripe-and-ready fruits and vegetables. Operated by the Haymarket Vendors Association, this outdoor market is an outlet for discount produce that was purchased from wholesalers.

and crafting the sparkly stuff for seven generations.

BOSTON
PEWTER COMPANY
GIFTS & SOUVENIRS

Map p234 (☑617-523-1776; www.bostonpewtercompany.com; 5 South Market, Faneuil Hall; ◷10am-9pm Mon-Sat, noon-6pm Sun; ⊤State) This specialty shop is pretty much what the name says. Think tableware, picture frames and light fixtures, all crafted from the elegant metal. The collection is supplemented with other New England collectibles like scrimshaw, copper weather vanes and hand-blown glass.

GEOCLASSICS
JEWELRY

Map p234 (☑617-523-6112; www.geoclassics.com; 7 North Market, Faneuil Hall; ◷11am-9pm Mon-Sat, to 6pm Sun; ⊤State) Geoclassics sells minerals, fossils and gemstones in jewelry and other decorative settings. The natural beauty of the stones is enhanced by their artistic presentation. The collection of fossils – from dinosaur eggs to dragonflies – is incredible.

🏃 SPORTS & ACTIVITIES

★NEW ENGLAND
AQUARIUM WHALE WATCH
WHALE WATCHING

Map p234 (☑617-227-4321; www.neaq.org/exhibits/whale-watch; Central Wharf; adult/child/infant $53/33/16; ◷times vary late Mar–mid-Nov; ⊤Aquarium) 🚢 Set off from Long Wharf for the journey to Stellwagen Bank, a rich feeding ground for whales, dolphins and marine birds. Keen-eyed boat captains and onboard naturalists can answer all your questions and have been trained by New England Aquarium experts to ensure that the tours do not interfere with the animals or harm them in any way.

LIBERTY FLEET
CRUISE

Map p234 (☑617-742-0333; www.libertyfleet.com; Central Wharf; adult/child from $19/30; ◷times vary Jun-Sep; ⊤Aquarium) The 125ft *Liberty Clipper* and the smaller *Liberty Star* take passengers out for a two-hour, 12-mile cruise around the harbor. The schooners sail several times a day, sometimes offering history re-enactments, brunch or sunsets. Purchase tickets online or from the office on Long Wharf.

South End & Chinatown

SOUTH END | CHINATOWN | THEATER DISTRICT | LEATHER DISTRICT

Neighborhood Top Five

1 **Underground at Ink Block** (p95) Catching a fitness class, having an urban picnic and checking out the fantastic street art at Boston's latest postindustrial playground.

2 **Gourmet Dumpling House** (p98) Hitting Chinatown for pork buns, dumplings or dim sum delights.

3 **SoWa Open Market** (p103) Browsing at the market and splurging on locally made creations, followed by Sunday brunch in the South End.

4 **Wally's Café** (p101) Packing into this cafe for old-time jazz and blues, especially during an early-evening jam session.

5 **SoWa Artists Guild** (p95) Strolling around the SoWa art district on the first Friday of the month, popping into galleries and studios to peruse the art and hobnob with the artists.

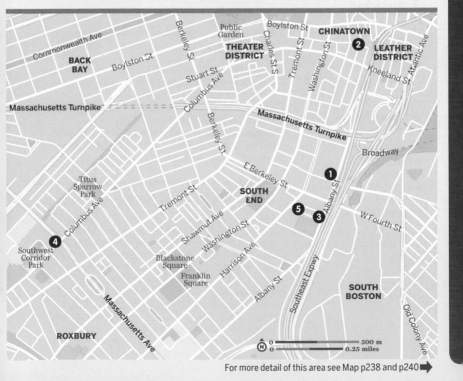

For more detail of this area see Map p238 and p240 ➡

Lonely Planet's Top Tip

Budget travelers will find Boston's best restaurant deals in Chinatown at lunchtime. Go straight to **Kneeland Street** to take advantage of amazing lunch specials. Chow down on soup and a main course for less than $10 – bargain!

Best Places to Eat

➡ O Ya (p99)

➡ Myers + Chang (p96)

➡ Blunch (p95)

➡ Mike & Patty's (p98)

➡ Coppa Enoteca (p96)

➡ Avana Sushi (p98)

For reviews, see p95.➡

Best Places to Drink

➡ Gallows (p99)

➡ Beehive (p99)

➡ Delux Café (p99)

➡ Les Zygomates (p101)

For reviews, see p99.➡

Best Places to Shop

➡ SoWa Open Market (p103)

➡ Ars Libri (p103)

➡ International Poster Gallery (p103)

➡ Sault New England (p103)

For reviews, see p102.➡

Explore South End & Chinatown

Four side-by-side neighborhoods are home to Boston's lively theater scene, its most hip-hop-happening nightclubs, and its best international and contemporary dining.

Once downtrodden, the South End was claimed and cleaned up by the gay community, and now everyone wants to live there. And why not? The neighborhood boasts the country's largest concentration of Victorian row houses, the city's most innovative and exciting options for dining out, and a vibrant art scene.

Although tiny by New York standards, Boston's Theater District has long served as a pre-Broadway staging area. Many landmark theaters have received face-lifts in recent years, and their colorful marquees and posh patrons make for a festive night out on the town. The Theater District is also Boston's club hub.

Nearby, Chinatown is overflowing with ethnic restaurants, live-poultry and fresh-produce markets, teahouses and textile shops. As well as the Chinese, this tight-knit community also includes Cambodians, Vietnamese and Laotians. Chinatown is a popular stop for lunch, a pretheater dinner or a postclubbing munch.

East of Chinatown, the Leather District is a pocket of uniform brick buildings that also shelters some fine restaurants. In all four neighborhoods, there is a dearth of traditional 'sights' to see, but there is a superabundance of eating and entertainment options.

Local Life

➡**First Fridays** On the first Friday of the month, get thee to the open studios at SoWa Artists Guild (p95) to chat with the resident creatives.

➡**Hangouts** Southenders hang out at Delux Café (p99) and Franklin Café (p96).

➡**Chinese Chess** Local residents congregate in the shadow of the Chinatown Gate (p95) for fierce chess competitions and friendly Cantonese chatter.

Getting There & Away

➡ **Metro** For the South End, take the orange line to Back Bay station or Tufts Medical Center station. Chinatown is served by its eponymous station, also on the orange line. The green line Boylston station is handy for the Theater District, while the Leather District is easiest to access from the red line South Station.

➡ **Bus** Good for the South End, the silver line bus runs down Washington St from South Station (SL4) or Downtown Crossing (SL5). If coming from elsewhere in Boston, take the orange line T to Tufts Medical Center, where you can transfer to the SL4 or SL5 southbound.

 SIGHTS

◉ South End

The sights in these neighborhoods are few. The exception is the South End, which is dotted with art galleries and the cool new park, Underground at Ink Block.

★UNDERGROUND
AT INK BLOCK   PUBLIC ART

Map p238 (www.undergroundinkblock.com; 90 Traveler St; ☺24hr; Ⓣ Tufts Medical Center) What used to be an abandoned parking lot beneath the interstate is now an 8-acre playground and art space. The main draw is the fantastic mural project, which turned 150,000 sq ft of concrete wall space into a fabulous outdoor gallery for street art, with bold colorful pieces by a dozen local and national artists. To say the mural brightens the place up is an understatement. There's also a dog park, walking paths and fitness classes to get you moving.

SOWA ARTISTS GUILD   GALLERY

Map p238 (✆857-362-7692; www.sowaartists guild.com; 450 Harrison Ave; ☺5-9pm 1st Fri of month; ⓆSL4, SL5, Ⓣ Tufts Medical Center) **FREE** The brick-and-beam buildings along Harrison Ave were originally used to manufacture goods ranging from canned food to pianos. Now these factories turn out paintings and sculptures instead. Housing about 70 artist studios and more than a dozen galleries, the SoWa Artists Guild is the epicenter of the South End art district. There is a SoWa Open Studios event on the first Friday of every month, while many artists also welcome visitors on Sundays (p103).

Many of the galleries are also open during daytime hours.

CATHEDRAL OF
THE HOLY CROSS   CATHEDRAL

Map p238 (✆617-542-5682; www.holycross boston.com; 1400 Washington St; ☺service 9am Mon-Sat, 8am & 11:30am Sun; ⓆSL4, SL5, Ⓣ Back Bay) When this neo-Gothic cathedral was built in 1875, it was America's largest Catholic cathedral, as big as London's Westminster Abbey. It serves as the main cathedral for the archdiocese of Boston and the seat of the archbishop. The exquisite rose window features King David playing his harp, while the rest of the cross-shaped building

is peppered with stained-glass windows and traditional church art.

◉ Chinatown

CHINATOWN GATE   LANDMARK

Map p240 (Beach St; Ⓣ Chinatown) The official entrance to Chinatown is the decorative gate *(paifong)*, a gift from the city of Taipei. It is symbolic – not only as an entryway for guests visiting Chinatown, but also as an entryway for immigrants who are still settling here, as they come to establish relationships and put down roots in their newly claimed home.

Surrounding the gate and anchoring the southern end of the Rose Kennedy Greenway is **Chinatown Park**. A bamboo-lined walkway runs through the modern gardens. The plaza is often populated by local residents engaged in *Xiangqi* (Chinese chess) and Falun Gong (a Chinese spiritual practice).

✕ EATING

Taken together, the South End and Chinatown certainly represent Boston's hottest spot for dining. The South End is the epicenter of trendy, high-end eateries, with a few old-school neighborhood cafes thrown in to keep it real. Chinatown is overflowing with authentic restaurants (many open late night), bakeries and markets.

✕ South End

The heart of South End dining has always been Tremont St, with a few outliers on Shawmut Ave. In recent years, however, the neighborhood has been expanding south. Nowadays, there are excellent restaurants in the SoWa district (south of Washington) on Washington St and Harrison Ave.

BLUNCH   SANDWICHES $

Map p238 (✆617-247-8100; www.eatblunch.com; 59 E Springfield St; sandwiches $5-10; ☺8am-3pm Mon-Fri, from 9am Sat; ✐; Ⓣ Massachusetts Ave) This is a tiny place with counter service, blackboard menu and a-MAZ-ing chocolate chip cookies. The sandwiches are also delish, especially the eggs-ellent fluffy

LOCAL KNOWLEDGE

SOUTH END RESTAURANT DEALS

Dining in the South End can be pricey, but even hipsters appreciate a bargain.

➡ Gaslight (p97) offers a three-course prix-fixe dinner ($30) every night from 5pm to 6pm.

➡ Gaslight also has a prix-fixe brunch ($12) all day Saturday and from 9am to 11am on Sunday.

➡ On Monday and Tuesday evenings from 5pm to 10pm, head to Myers + Chang (p96) for Cheap Date Night ($45 for two people).

breakfast sandwiches, which are available all day long. If you can't decide what to order, the Bird is the word, at least according to Guy Fieri of the Food Network.

MIKE'S CITY DINER   DINER $
Map p238 (☑617-267-9393; www.mikescitydiner. com; 1714 Washington St; mains $6-12; ☺6am-3pm; 🛗; 🚇SL4, SL5, 🚊Massachusetts Ave) Start the day with a big breakfast of eggs, bacon, toast and other old-fashioned goodness, topped with a bottomless cup of coffee. If you need to refuel at lunchtime, go for classics such as meatloaf and mashed potatoes or fried chicken and biscuits. The service is friendly and fast. Your server will probably call you 'hon.' Cash only.

★COPPA ENOTECA   ITALIAN $$
Map p238 (☑617-391-0902; www.coppaboston. com; 253 Shawmut Ave; small plates $9-17, pizza & pasta $14-25; ☺noon-10pm Mon-Thu, to 11pm Fri, 11am-11pm Sat, to 10pm Sun; 🚇SL4, SL5, 🚊Back Bay) This South End *enoteca* (wine bar) recreates an Italian dining experience with authenticity and innovation, serving up *salumi* (cured meats), antipasti, pasta and other delicious small plates. Wash it all down with an Aperol spritz and you might be tricked into thinking you're in Venice.

★MYERS + CHANG   ASIAN $$
Map p238 (☑617-542-5200; www.myersand chang.com; 1145 Washington St; small plates $7-17, mains $16-25; ☺5-10pm Sun-Thu, to 11pm Fri & Sat; 🚗; 🚇SL4, SL5, 🚊Tufts Medical Center) This super-hip Asian spot blends Thai, Chinese and Vietnamese cuisines, which means delicious dumplings, spicy stir-fries

and oodles of noodles. The kitchen staff do amazing things with a wok, and the menu of small plates allows you to sample a wide selection of dishes. Dim sum for dinner? This is your place.

Food allergies are also no problem, as Myers + Chang has a menu for every dietary restriction.

TORO   TAPAS $$
Map p238 (☑617-536-4300; www.toro-res taurant.com; 1704 Washington St; tapas $9-16; ☺noon-10pm Mon-Thu, to 11pm Fri, 4-11pm Sat, 10:30am-2:30pm & 5-10pm Sun; 🚗; 🚇SL4, SL5, 🚊Massachusetts Ave) 🌿 True to its Spanish spirit, Toro is bursting with energy, from the open kitchen to the communal butcher-block tables. The menu features simple but sublime tapas – seared foie gras with pistachio and sour cherries; grilled corn on the cob dripping with aioli, lime and cheese; and delectable, garlicky shrimp. Wash it down with rioja, sangria or spiced-up mojitos.

BARCELONA WINE BAR   TAPAS $$
Map p238 (☑617-266-2600; www.barcelonawine bar.com; 525 Tremont St; tapas $6.50-10.50; ☺4pm-1am Mon-Fri, from 10am Sat & Sun; 🚊Back Bay) Barcelona calls itself a wine bar (and it does have an impressive wine program, for sure), but most people come for the excellent food and the impeccable customer service. The interior is woody and warm, but still very hip. When the weather is fine, sit outside and sip white sangria and all is right with the world.

FRANKLIN CAFÉ   AMERICAN $$
Map p238 (☑617-350-0010; www.franklincafe. com; 278 Shawmut Ave; mains $16-24; ☺5pm-2am; 🚇SL4, SL5, 🚊Back Bay) The Franklin is probably the South End's longest-standing favorite local joint – and that's saying something in this restaurant-rich neighborhood. It's at once friendly and hip. The menu is New American comfort food prepared by a gourmet chef: surely steak frites with Roquefort butter does a body good.

PICCO   PIZZA $$
Map p238 (☑617-927-0066; www.piccorestau rant.com; 513 Tremont St; pizzas $14-24; ☺11am-10pm Sun-Wed, to 11pm Thu-Sat; 🚗; 🚊Back Bay) The crust of a Picco pizza undergoes a two-day process of cold fermentation before it goes into the oven and then into your mouth. The result is a thin crust with

substantial texture and rich flavor. You can add toppings to create your own pizza, or try the specialty Alsatian (sautéed onions, shallots, garlic, sour cream, bacon and Gruyère cheese).

SOUTH END BUTTERY — CAFE $$

Map p238 (☑617-482-1015; www.southendbuttery.com; 314 Shawmut Ave; mains cafe $5-15, brunch $10-19, dinner $18-23; ⊙cafe 6am-6pm, restaurant 9am-3pm Sat & Sun, 5-10pm Sun-Thu, to 11pm Fri & Sat; ☑; ☐SL4, SL5, ⊤Back Bay) 🍴 The Buttery is a three-in-one affair, featuring a comfy cafe side-by-side with a restaurant and market. The cafe has counter service, outdoor seating and amazing cupcakes. The restaurant has exposed brick walls, sophisticated food and alcohol. And the market has baked goods and prepared foods suitable for taking back to your hotel and eating at midnight. Take your pick!

GASLIGHT — FRENCH $$

Map p238 (☑617-422-0224; www.gaslight560.com; 560 Harrison Ave; mains $22-30; ⊙9am-3pm Sat & Sun, 5-11pm Mon-Wed, 5pm-midnight Thu-Sat; ℗☑; ☐SL4, SL5, ⊤New England Medical Center) Gaslight is the friendly and affordable *brasserie du coin* (brasserie on the corner) that we all wish we had in our own neighborhood. Mosaic tiles, woodbeam ceilings and cozy booths set up the comfortable, convivial atmosphere, which is enhanced by classic French fare and an excellent selection of wines by the glass.

B&G OYSTERS — SEAFOOD $$$

Map p238 (☑617-423-0550; www.bandgoysters.com; 550 Tremont St; oysters $3, mains $19-34; ⊙11:30am-11pm Mon-Sat, noon-10pm Sun; ☎; ⊤Back Bay) Patrons flock to this casually cool oyster bar to get in on the raw delicacies offered by chef Barbara Lynch. Sit at the marble bar or outside on the peaceful terrace, and indulge in the freshest shellfish from local waters. An extensive wine list and a modest menu of mains and appetizers (mostly seafood) are ample accompaniment for the oysters.

BUTCHER SHOP — EUROPEAN $$$

Map p238 (☑617-423-4800; www.thebutchershopboston.com; 552 Tremont St; mains $26-52; ⊙4-10pm Mon-Wed, to 11pm Thu & Fri, 11:30am-11pm Sat & Sun; ⊤Back Bay) Only in the South End does the neighborhood butcher shop double as an elegant eatery and wine bar. The cases filled with tantalizing cuts of meat, fresh foie gras and housemade sausages give a glimpse of the ingredients and

COMBAT ZONE

With the demolition of Scollay Sq in the 1960s, the city's go-go dancers, strippers and prostitutes – as well as their clientele – made their way to the blocks wedged between the Theater District and Chinatown. The city administration supported this move, believing that it could concentrate the city's sleaze into a sort of red-light district (although prostitution was technically illegal), and free the rest of the city of riff-raff.

Washington St – between Boylston and Kneeland Sts – became the center of all skankiness in Boston. Lined with clubs such as the Teddy Bare Lounge and the Naked I, this was the place to come for adult bookstores and X-rated movie theaters. Prostitutes congregated along LaGrange St. Local reporters dubbed it the 'Combat Zone.'

Residents were generally poor immigrants. They had little voice in local government and were unable to change official policy. The Combat Zone flourished.

The heyday of the Combat Zone has passed (although there are still a few strip clubs in this area). Because of rising real-estate values, this area attracted the attention of developers in the 1980s: the Four Seasons Hotel and the State Transportation Building were built on Park Sq, Emerson College moved its campus here, and other development followed suit.

City officials cracked down on street crime, forcing the Combat Zone clientele to stay home and surf the internet. Many of the old theaters – such as the Opera House and the Paramount – were revamped for Broadway shows and upscale nightclubs.

Chinatown residents also engaged in grassroots efforts to shut down the Combat Zone, and for the most part they succeeded. Unfortunately, even as the neighborhood is enjoying revitalization, this community enclave continues to be jeopardized – not by peep shows and porn theaters but by skyrocketing rents.

provide the decoration at this bistro (not a good place for vegetarians). There is a nice selection of artisanal wines.

✕ Chinatown, Theater District & Leather District

Chinatown is not just for Chinese food, but also Vietnamese, Japanese, Korean, Thai, Malaysian and more. This is some of Boston's best budget eating. You'll find it all crammed together between Essex and Kneelands Sts.

★ MIKE & PATTY'S   SANDWICHES $
Map p240 (☑617-423-3447; www.mikeandpattys. com; 12 Church St; sandwiches $9-12; ⊘8am-2pm; 🍴; 🇹Tufts Medical Center, Arlington) Tucked away in Bay Village, this hole-in-the-wall gem of a corner sandwich shop does amazing things between two slices of bread. There are only eight options and they're all pretty perfect, but the hands-down favorite is the Breakfast Grilled Crack (fried egg, bacon and four kinds of cheese on sourdough). There's always a line but it moves quickly. No seating.

GOURMET DUMPLING HOUSE   CHINESE $
Map p240 (☑617-338-6223; www.gourmet dumplinghouse.com; 52 Beach St; dumplings $5-8, mains $9-17; ⊘11am-1am; 🍴; 🇹Chinatown) *Xiao long bao.* That's all the Chinese you need to know to take advantage of the specialty at the Gourmet Dumpling House (or GDH, as it is fondly called). They are Shanghai soup dumplings, and they are fresh, doughy and delicious. The menu offers plenty of other options, including scrumptious crispy scallion pancakes. Come early or be prepared to wait.

AVANA SUSHI   SUSHI $
Map p240 (☑617-818-7782; www.avanasushi. com; 42 Beach St; sushi & sashimi $4-6; ⊘11am-10pm; 🇹Chinatown) This place is essentially unmarked from the street, tucked into a tiny, cramped food court, sharing the space with a few other takeout places. There's only a handful of seats, but the sushi is fresh and affordable, and service is personable. It's hard to beat. We also appreciate the Styrofoam artwork, offering a commentary on our disposable culture, perhaps?

MY THAI VEGAN CAFÉ   THAI $
Map p240 (☑617-451-2395; http://mythaivegan cafe.com; 3 Beach St; lunch specials $8, dinner mains $8-18; ⊘11am-10pm Sun-Thu, to 11pm Fri & Sat; 🍴; 🇹Chinatown) This welcoming cafe is up a sketchy staircase, tucked into a sunlit 2nd-story space. It's an animal-free zone – but good enough that meat eaters will enjoy eating here too. The menu has a Thai twist, offering noodle soups, dumplings, excellent spring rolls and pad Thai. The bubble tea gets raves.

SOUTH STREET DINER   DINER $
Map p240 (☑617-350-0028; www.southstreet diner.com; 178 Kneeland St; mains $10-15; ⊘24hr; 🍴; 🇹South Station) A divey diner that does what a diner is supposed to do – that is, serve bacon and eggs and burgers and fries, at any time of the day or night. Plonk yourself into a vinyl-upholstered booth and let the sass-talking waitstaff satisfy your midnight munchies.

TAIWAN CAFE   TAIWANESE $
Map p240 (☑617-426-8181; www.taiwancafe boston.com; 34 Oxford St; mains $8-18; ⊘11am-1am Wed-Mon; 🍴; 🇹Chinatown) Taiwan Cafe is a few steps off the main drag, so you might not have to wait quite as long for the excellent soup dumplings and other Taiwanese specialties. Regulars rave about the roast beef scallion pancakes. Like most places in Chinatown, the decor is minimal and prices are cheap. Cash only.

BISTRO DU MIDI   FRENCH $$
Map p240 (☑617-426-7878; www.bistrodumidi. com; 272 Boylston St; mains bistro $17-34, dining room $29-48; ⊘bistro 11:30am-10pm, dining room 5-10pm; 🇹Arlington) The upstairs dining room is exquisite, but the downstairs bistro exudes warmth and camaraderie, inviting casual callers to linger over wine and snacks. In either setting, the Provençal fare is artfully presented and delicious. Reservations are required for dinner upstairs, but drop-ins are welcome at the bistro all day.

ℹ NIGHTCLUB GUEST LISTS

If you plan to hit any nightclubs in the Theater District (or anywhere in Boston), definitely go online and get yourself on the guest list. This normally will ensure entry, instead of leaving it to the whims of the bouncer. Sometimes it will get you a reduced cover charge.

Q RESTAURANT ASIAN $$

Map p240 (☑857-350-3968; www.thequsa.com; 660 Washington St; hot pot $13-27; ⊙11:30am-11pm Sun-Thu, to 1am Fri & Sat; 🔝🍴🍺; ⓣChinatown) Hip and hungry patrons flock to this trendy hot-pot spot in Chinatown. Q is unusual for its spacious interior and upscale atmosphere, but it's also a unique, interactive eating experience. Choose your broth, choose your morsels of meat and veggies, cook them in the pot and eat them as you go.

SHŌJŌ FUSION $$

Map p240 (☑617-423-7888; www.shojoboston.com; 9a Tyler St; small plates $6-16; ⊙5-10:30pm Mon-Wed, 11am-10:30pm Thu, 11am-11:30pm Fri & Sat; 🍴; ⓣChinatown) Clean, contemporary and super cool, Shōjō is unique in Chinatown for its trendy vibe (and unfortunately loud music). The menu picks and chooses from all over Asia and beyond, effortlessly blending disparate elements into original, enticing, shareable fare. If you're not afraid for your arteries, the duck fat fries are highly recommended.

KAZE SHABU SHABU ASIAN $$

Map p240 (☑617-338-8283; www.kazeshabu.com; 1 Harrison Ave; lunch specials $9, mains $15-28; ⊙11:30am-1am Sun-Thu, to 2am Fri & Sat; 🍴🍺) Offering a hands-on approach to dinner, 'shabu-shabu' is also known as hot-pot cuisine, where you cook your meal at your table in a big family-style pot. Choose from a variety of seafood, poultry and meats, fresh vegetables and an array of housemade broths, then cook it the way you like it. It's a divine sensory experience in a tranquil setting.

★O YA SUSHI $$$

Map p240 (☑617-654-9900; www.o-ya.restaurant; 9 East St; nigiri & sashimi pieces $14-30; ⊙5-10pm Tue-Sat; 🍴; ⓣSouth Station) Who knew that raw fish could be so exciting? Here, each piece of nigiri or sashimi is dripped with something unexpected but exquisite, from burgundy truffle sauce to ginger kimchee jus. A fried Kumamoto oyster is topped with a Japanese citrus fruit and squid ink bubbles. Foie gras is drizzled in balsamic chocolate *kabayaki* (sweet, soy glaze). And so on.

NAHITA FUSION $$$

Map p240 (☑617-457-8130; www.nahitarestaurant.com; 100 Arlington St; small plates $14-29; ⊙5:30-10:30pm; 🍴; ⓣArlington) The newly revamped space looks terrific, as do the creative concoctions coming out of the kitchen. This is truly global cuisine, focusing on Nikkei (Peruvian-Japanese) dishes – menu categories include ceviche, sashimi, tacos and *perditos* (Peruvian sashimi) – with Turkish highlights all around.

DRINKING & NIGHTLIFE

These overlapping neighborhoods contain some of Boston's hippest bars and clubs. The South End serves as home base for much of Boston's gay community, but the number of spots catering specifically to the fellas has dwindled in recent years. In any case, both gays and lesbians are usually well represented at any place in the 'hood. Drinking establishments are sparse in Chinatown but the nearby Theater District is home to several dance and music clubs.

📍 South End

★GALLOWS PUB

Map p238 (☑617-425-0200; www.thegallowsboston.com; 1395 Washington St; ⊙noon-11pm Mon-Thu, to 1am Fri, 10am-1am Sat, to 11pm Sun; 🚌SL4, SL5, ⓣTufts Medical Center) At this South End favorite, the dark woody interior is inviting and the bartenders are truly talented. The gastropub grub includes such enticing fare as the Scotch egg (a soft-cooked egg wrapped in crispy pork sausage) and the out-of-control *poutine*. Solid beer selection, delectable cocktails.

BEEHIVE COCKTAIL BAR

Map p238 (☑617-423-0069; www.beehiveboston.com; 541 Tremont St; ⊙5pm-midnight Mon-Wed, to 1am Thu, to 2am Fri, 9:30am-2am Sat, to midnight Sun; ⓣBack Bay) The Beehive has transformed the basement of the Boston Center for the Arts into a 1920s Paris jazz club. This place is more about the scene than the music, which is often provided by students from Berklee College of Music. But the food is good and the vibe is definitely hip. Reservations required if you want a table.

DELUX CAFÉ BAR

Map p238 (☑617-338-5258; 100 Chandler St; ⊙5pm-1am; ⓣBack Bay) The South End's

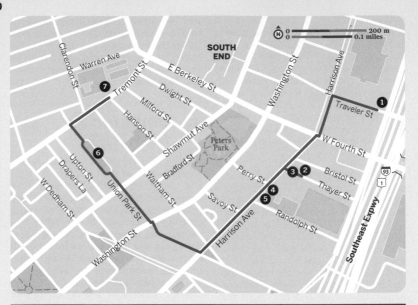

⚡ Local Life
South End Art Stroll

Boston's main art district is the South End. The artistic community has moved into the once-barren area south of Washington St (now known as SoWa), converting old warehouses into studios and galleries. For best results, do this walk on a summer Sunday (May to October) or in the evening on the first Friday of the month (year-round).

❶ Underground at Ink Block
The newest and edgiest art space in SoWa is Underground at Ink Block (p95), a show-case for the city's boldest and brightest street art. Very gritty, very city.

❷ SoWa Artists Guild
This is the epicenter of the South End art scene, where artists have carved out studios and gallery space from the former warehouses and factories on Harrison Ave. The SoWa Artists Guild (p95) hosts an Open Studios event on the first Friday of every month, and in summer the neighborhood streets fill with food trucks, a beer garden and markets selling art, vintage apparel and fresh produce.

❸ Thayer Street
There are dozens of venues lining the pe-destrianized street between the former warehouses at 450 and 460 Harrison

Ave. **Bromfield Art Gallery** (Map p238; ☏617-451-3605; www.bromfieldgallery.com; ◷noon-5pm Wed-Sun; ◻SL4, SL5, Ⓣ Tufts Medical Center) **FREE** for example, is a long-established artist-run gallery that features New England artists. **Alpha Gallery** (Map p238; ☏617-536-4465; www.alphagallery.com; ◷11am-6pm Tue-Sat; ◻SL4, SL5, Ⓣ Tufts Medical Center) **FREE** is a transplant from Newbury St that presents the work of headline-grabbing artists.

❹ Boston Sculpture Gallery
Peek into this unusual cooperative **gallery** (Map p238; ☏617-482-7781; www.bostonsculp tors.com; 486 Harrison Ave; ◷noon-6pm Wed-Sun; ◻SL4, SL5, Ⓣ Tufts Medical Center) **FREE**, which has been going strong for more than 25 years. Three dozen local artists run the innovative gallery, dedicated to three-dimensional art in all media.

best – and perhaps only – hipster dive bar. This long-standing favorite has Christmas-light decor and a totally laid-back atmosphere. The kitchen (open till 11pm nightly) turns out an incredible grilled cheese sandwich. No credit cards.

🍷 Chinatown, Theater District & Leather District

LES ZYGOMATES
WINE BAR

Map p240 (📞617-542-5108; www.winebar129. com; 129 South St; ⏰11:30am-9pm Mon-Fri, 5:30-11pm Sat; 🚇South Station) This late-night Parisian bistro serves up live jazz alongside an excellent selection of wines by the glass and a menu of classic but contemporary French cuisine. The clientele is sophisticated but not stuffy. The tempting selection of starters and cocktails make it a perfect pre- or post-theater spot.

TUNNEL
CLUB

Map p240 (📞617-357-5005; www.tunnelboston. com; 100 Stuart St; cover $10-20; ⏰11pm-2am Tue & Thu-Sat; 🚇Boylston) This is a slick lounge – albeit a tiny one – in the basement of the W hotel. The 'tunnel' is the effect of the LED lights on the ceiling, which lead the way through the chic lounge and back to the dance floor. Tunnel is the rare nightclub where bouncers and bartenders are actually friendly to the patrons.

WHISKY SAIGON
CLUB

Map p240 (📞617-482-7799; www.whiskysaigon. com; 116 Boylston St; cover free-$15; ⏰9pm-2am Fri & Sat; 🚇Boylston) Whisky Saigon is among the hottest dance spots in Boston at the time of writing, and with good reason. Who can resist bubbles and laser lights on the dance floor? It's classy, with upscale decor, good-looking patrons and a top-notch sound system playing mostly electronic dance music. The bottled-water-only policy is a bone of contention, but coat check is free.

First Friday gallery opening, Thayer St

❺ Ars Libri
Ring the doorbell: Ars Libri (p103) is an art bookstore extraordinaire, specializing in rare and out-of-print books. The former warehouse is filled from floor to ceiling with books on all aspects and eras of art, architecture and design. If you love books, and especially books about art, you'll love Ars Libri.

❻ Union Park
Turn up Union Park St to get a glimpse of the neighborhood's charming Victorian rowhouses, clustered around a tree-lined, fountain-filled park. This is South End architecture at its best.

❼ Boston Center for the Arts
Finish your walk at the Boston Center for the Arts, home of the Mills Gallery (p102), which hosts cutting-edge visual arts exhibits, and artist and curator talks. Exhibits feature established and emerging artists from Boston and around the country. Housed in the same complex are several performing arts venues.

☆ ENTERTAINMENT

★ WALLY'S CAFÉ
JAZZ

Map p238 (📞617-424-1408; www.wallyscafe.com; 427 Massachusetts Ave; ⏰5pm-2am; 🚇Massachusetts Ave) When Wally's opened in 1947, Barbadian immigrant Joseph Walcott became the first African American to own

COMPANY ONE

This radical **theater company** (Map p238; ☑617-292-7110; www.companyone. org; 539 Tremont St; Ⓣ Back Bay) strives to be at the 'intersection of art and social change' by offering provocative performances and fostering socially engaged artists. Critics are crazy for C1, which has racked up a slew of awards and nominations for its innovative productions. Most shows are performed in the Boston Center for the Arts (p102) theaters.

a nightclub in New England. Old-school, gritty and small, it still attracts a racially diverse crowd to hear jammin' jazz music 365 days a year. Berklee students love this place, especially the nightly jam sessions (6pm to 9pm).

BOSTON CENTER FOR THE ARTS
THEATER

Map p238 (☑617-426-5000; www.bcaonline.org; 539 Tremont St; Ⓣ Back Bay) There's rarely a dull moment at the BCA, which serves as a nexus for excellent small theater productions. Over 20 companies present more than 45 separate productions annually, from comedies and drama to modern dance and musicals. The BCA complex comprises several buildings, including a cyclorama (1884) built to display panoramic paintings, a former organ factory and the **Mills Gallery** (Map p238; 551 Tremont St; ☻noon-5pm Wed & Sun, to 9pm Thu-Sat; Ⓣ Back Bay) FREE.

JACQUES CABARET
CABARET

Map p240 (☑617-426-8902; www.jacquescabaret.com; 79 Broadway; admission $10-15; ☻11am-midnight, show times vary; Ⓣ Arlington) Head to this dive on a dark side street to experience the gay culture of the South End before gentrification took over. A shaded-lamp and pool-table kind of place, Jacques hosts outstanding low-budget drag shows every night. Reservations are a must on weekends.

CHARLES PLAYHOUSE
THEATER

Map p240 (☑617-426-6912; www.charlesplayhouse.com; 74 Warrenton St; Ⓣ Boylston) Built in 1839, the Charles Playhouse was originally a speakeasy, later a jazz club and finally a theater. With its backstreet location and underground ambience, it has always been

home to offbeat and unusual performances. Nowadays, that means the ever-popular, indefinable **Blue Man Group** (www.blueman. com) and the long-running improv comedy show **Shear Madness** (www.shearmadness.com).

CUTLER MAJESTIC THEATRE
THEATER

Map p240 (☑617-824-8400; www.cutlermajestic.org; 219 Tremont St; Ⓣ Boylston) This beautiful beaux-arts-style opera house dates to 1903. A century after its construction, the theater was sumptuously renovated and reopened by Emerson College. Today, the performances that take place here are incredibly diverse, and include music, dance, comedy, acrobatics and seasonal celebrations like the popular Celtic Christmas Sojourn.

WILBUR THEATRE
COMEDY

Map p240 (☑617-248-9700; www.thewilbur.com; 246 Tremont St; tickets $22-65; Ⓣ Boylston) The colonial-style Wilbur Theatre dates to 1914, and over the years has hosted many prominent theatrical productions. These days it is Boston's premier comedy club. The smallish house hosts nationally known cutups, as well as music acts and other kinds of hard-to-categorize performances. The theater itself could do with a renovation, but the talent is good.

BOCH CENTER
LIVE PERFORMANCE

Map p240 (☑800-982-2787; www.bochcenter.org; 270 Tremont St; Ⓣ Boylston) Boston's biggest music and dance venue, the Boch Center is comprised of two theaters that face off across Tremont St. The main stage is the enormous, opulent **Wang Theatre**, built in 1925. The Wang hosts extravagant musical theater productions, as well as concerts, comedy and occasional giant-screen movies (the center was originally built as a movie palace). The Boch Center also includes the more intimate **Shubert Theatre** (Map p240; ☑866-348-9738) across the street.

🔒 SHOPPING

The South End is the only neighborhood in Boston that has more boutiques for men than women (although this is changing). Still, if you are a straight guy in need of a queer eye (or any guy in need of knock-'em-dead duds), take a walk to the South End. SoWa – the area south of Washington St – is also home to Boston's

edgiest, up-and-coming art scene. There's not much in the way of shopping in Chinatown or the Theater District.

★ SOWA OPEN MARKET   MARKET
Map p238 (☑857-362-7692; www.sowaboston.com; 460 Harrison Ave; ☺10am-4pm Sun May-Oct; ⬛SL4, SL5, ⓣTufts Medical Center) Boston's original art market, this outdoor event is a fabulous opportunity for strolling, shopping and people-watching. More than 100 vendors set up shop under white tents. It's never the same two weeks in a row, but there's always plenty of arts and crafts, as well as edgier art, jewelry, unique homewares, and homemade food and body products.

ARS LIBRI   BOOKS
Map p238 (☑617-357-5212; www.arslibri.com; 500 Harrison Ave; ☺9am-6pm Mon-Fri, 11am-5pm Sat; ⬛SL4, SL5, ⓣTufts Medical Center) Ring the doorbell: it's worth it. Specializing in rare and out-of-print titles, Ars Libri is an art bookstore extraordinaire, filled from floor to ceiling with volumes on all aspects and eras of art, architecture and design. If you love books or art, and especially books about art, you'll love Ars Libri.

INTERNATIONAL
POSTER GALLERY   ART
Map p238 (☑617-375-0076; www.internationalposter.com; 460c Harrison Ave; ☺10am-6pm Mon-Sat, from noon Sun; ⬛SL4, SL5, ⓣTufts Medical Center) This niche gallery stocks thousands of vintage posters from around the world. Thousands. The posters span the globe, with themes ranging from food and drink to travel to political propaganda. They are all there for the browsing, though it's easier to scroll through the online archive, which also offers all kinds of useful information and tips for would-be collectors.

SOWA FARMERS MARKET   MARKET
Map p238 (☑857-362-7692; www.sowaboston.com; 500 Harrison Ave; ☺10am-4pm Sun May-Oct; ⬛SL4, SL5, ⓣTufts Medical Center) With some 60 stands, this is the largest farmers market in New England, and features fresh produce, meats and poultry, dairy products, flowers and more. If all this fresh, local deliciousness is making you hungry, never fear. There are also more than a dozen food trucks serving hot and hearty fare.

SAULT NEW ENGLAND   GIFTS & SOUVENIRS
Map p238 (☑857-239-9434; www.saultne.com; 577 Tremont St; ☺10am-7pm Mon-Sat, to 5pm Sun; ⓣBack Bay) Blending prepster and hipster, rustic and chic, this little basement boutique packs in a lot of intriguing stuff. The eclectic mix of merchandise runs the gamut from new and vintage clothing to coffee-table books and homemade terrariums.

OLIVES & GRACE   GIFTS & SOUVENIRS
Map p238 (☑617-236-4536; www.olivesandgrace.com; 623 Tremont St; ☺10am-8pm Tue-Sat, to 6pm Sun & Mon; ⓣBack Bay) This little shoebox of a store offers an eclectic array of gift items – many from New England – all of them made with love and thoughtfulness by artisans. The most enticing items are the foodstuffs, including chocolate bars, hot sauces, raw honey, saltwater taffy and cocktail mixers. All the good stuff.

SOWA VINTAGE MARKET   MARKET
Map p238 (☑617-286-6750; www.sowavintagemkt.com; 450 Harrison Ave; ☺10am-4pm Sun year-round; ⬛SL4, SL5, ⓣTufts Medical Center) Boston's year-round destination for cool old stuff, the SoWa Vintage Market is like an indoor flea market, with dozens of vendors selling clothes, furniture, posters, homewares, and loads of other trash and treasure.

🏃 **SPORTS & ACTIVITIES**

COMMUNITY BIKE SUPPLY   CYCLING
Map p238 (☑617-542-8623; www.communitybicycle.com; 496 Tremont St; per day $25-35; ☺10am-7pm Mon-Sat year-round, noon-5pm Sun Apr-Sep; ⓣBack Bay) These friendly folks will rent a hybrid so you can explore the area on two wheels. Conveniently located for a ride along the Southwest Corridor.

EXHALE SPA   HEALTH & FITNESS
Map p240 (☑617-532-7000; www.exhalespa.com; 28 Arlington St; ☺6am-9pm Mon-Fri, 7:30am-8pm Sat & Sun; ⓣArlington) If you are waiting to exhale, now you can do it at this spa for mind and body. Offering up to 10 classes a day, Exhale focuses on cardio, barre and yoga basics. Exhale also offers acupuncture, body scrubs and other healing services, in addition to the more traditional spa services. After your workout, treat yourself to a fusion massage.

Boston by Night

As with all things, Boston's nightlife is richer thanks to the huge population of students who keep it real. In Cambridge, Allston and Kenmore Square, you'll find them – cool and casual – drinking, dancing, and rocking out to awesome indie music. The scene goes upscale in the city center, especially in the Theater District.

Theater District

Put on your fancy pants before heading out to the Theater District (p101). This is where you'll find the glamorous set attending a show behind a neon marquee or getting their groove on at a glitzy nightclub like Whisky Saigon or Tunnel. After hours, drinkers and dancers go to Chinatown for late-night noshing.

Central Square, Cambridge

Gritty Central Square (p150 and p152) is the focal point of the Cambridge music scene, with the Middle East and other venues lined up along Mass Ave. Before or after the show, you can grab a drink at low-key bars such as Brick & Mortar and Green Street Grill.

1. Paramount Center (p90), Theater District **2.** Florence & the Machine playing at the House of Blues (p128) **3.** Downtown Boston (p80)

Lansdowne Street

Three words: beer, music and baseball. Fenway Park occupies one side of the street, and the opposite side is lined with fun-filled nighttime venues such as House of Blues (p128), Bill's Bar (p127) and Lansdowne Pub (p126). No matter where you spend the evening, there *will* be a TV showing how the Sox are faring across the street.

Harvard Ave, Allston

West of downtown Boston, Allston (p162) is fondly known as the student ghetto, so it's no surprise that it's home to Boston's best venues for live indie music. See what's on the docket at Great Scott or Brighton Music Hall.

2

Back Bay

Neighborhood Top Five

1 **Copley Square** (p111) Admiring Boston's most evocative and archetypal architecture in this center-piece square, taking time for tours at Trinity Church and the Boston Public Library.

2 **Charles River Esplanade** (p111) Strolling, cycling or running along the water-front, pausing for picnics or photographs.

3 **Newbury St** (p107) Window shopping and gallery hopping, with stops at trendy boutiques, novelty shops and established art venues.

4 **Saltie Girl** (p113) Squeezing into a seat at this fantastic 'seafood bar' to sample the city's most inventive local fare.

5 **Mapparium** (p111) Feeling like you're at the center of the world at this odd but intriguing piece of history.

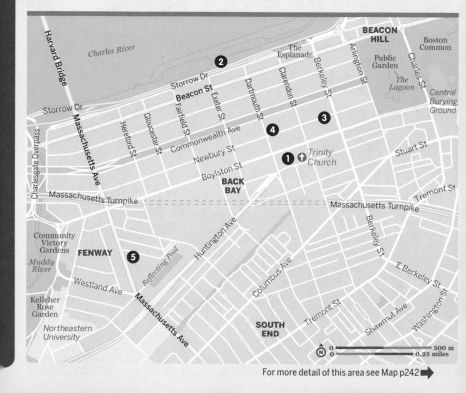

For more detail of this area see Map p242 ➡

Explore Back Bay

Back Bay is not as old as some other Boston neighborhoods, nor is it as historically significant. But thanks to magnificent Victorian brownstones and high-minded civic plazas, it is certainly among the loveliest – and a required destination for all Boston visitors.

Copley Square (p111) represents the best of Back Bay architecture, as it gracefully blends disparate elements such as the Renaissance Revival Boston Public Library (p108), the Richardsonian Romanesque Trinity Church (p110) and the modernist John Hancock Tower (p112). Copley Square should be your first stop in Back Bay, good for whiling away an hour or even a day.

After admiring the architecture and browsing the library books, you are perfectly placed for an afternoon of window shopping or gallery hopping. Swanky Newbury St is famous among fashion mavens, art aficionados and music lovers for its boutiques and galleries (and one legendary music store; p116).

Not surprisingly, this bustling retail and residential center is also a drinking and dining wonderland, with sidewalk cafes, trendy bars and chic restaurants on nearly every block. It's not quite the same slick scene as in the trendsetting South End, but there are still places to see and be seen in Back Bay.

Local Life

→ **Book Nooks** Art and architecture aside, locals come to the Boston Public Library (p108) to, um, read.

→ **Hangouts** It doesn't get more local than the Corner Tavern (p115).

→ **Outdoors** Perfect for picnic lunches and summertime lounging, the Charles River Esplanade (p111) is Boston's backyard.

Getting There & Away

→ **Metro** The main branch of the green line runs the length of Boylston St, with stops at Arlington near the Public Garden, Copley at Copley Square and Hynes at Mass Ave. The orange line is also useful for the Back Bay/South End stop in the southern part of the neighborhood.

Lonely Planet's Top Tip

Visit the **BosTix** (p115) booth run by ArtsBoston on Copley Square for same-day, discounted tickets to local theater, comedy and music events.

 Best Places to Eat

→ Saltie Girl (p113)
→ Courtyard (p114)
→ Puro Ceviche Bar (p113)
→ Luke's Lobster (p112)

For reviews, see p112.➡

 Best Places to Drink

→ Lolita Cocina & Tequila Bar (p114)
→ Club Café (p114)
→ Bukowski Tavern (p115)

For reviews, see p114.➡

 **Best Places to Shop**

→ Topdrawer (p115)
→ Trident Booksellers & Café (p115)
→ Marathon Sports (p116)
→ KitchenWares (p116)
→ Ball & Buck (p116)
→ Newbury Comics (p116)

For reviews, see p115.➡

BACK BAY

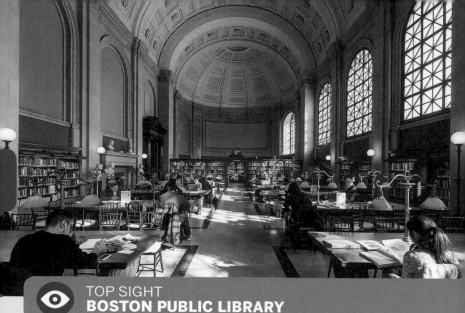

TOP SIGHT
BOSTON PUBLIC LIBRARY

The esteemed Boston Public Library (BPL) was founded in 1852 as a 'shrine of letters.' The old McKim Building is notable for its magnificent facade (inspired by Italian Renaissance *palazzi*) and exquisite interior art. Pick up a free brochure and take a self-guided tour; alternatively, free guided tours depart from the entrance hall (times vary).

Puvis de Chavannes Gallery

From the main entrance, a marble staircase leads past Pierre Puvis de Chavannes' inspirational murals. The artist titled his composition *The Muses of Inspiration Hail the Spirit, the Harbinger of Light*. The mural depicts poetry, philosophy, history and science, which he considered the four great expressions of the human mind.

Don't miss the mighty lions posed on their pedestals, carved by Saint-Gaudens to honor the Massachusetts Civil War infantries.

Upstairs, at the entrance to Bates Hall, there is another Puvis de Chavannes mural, also *The Muses*. Here, the nine muses from Greek mythology are honoring a male figure, the Genius of the Enlightenment.

Bates Hall

The staircase terminates at the splendid Bates Hall Reading Room, where even mundane musings are elevated by the barrel-vaulted, 50ft coffered ceilings.

Bates Hall is named for Joshua Bates, the BPL's original benefactor in 1852. After spending his childhood browsing in bookstores, Bates appreciated the potential for, and importance of, self-education through reading. He donated $50,000 to the city of Boston, with the stipulations that 'the building shall be...an ornament to the city, that there shall be a

DON'T MISS

➡ Mora and Saint-Gaudens' carving of Minerva, goddess of wisdom, on the central keystone on the facade

➡ *Frieze of the Prophets* by John Singer Sargent

➡ Italianate courtyard

PRACTICALITIES

➡ Map p242, E4

➡ ☎617-536-5400

➡ www.bpl.org

➡ 700 Boylston St

➡ admission free

➡ ⊙9am-9pm Mon-Thu, to 5pm Fri & Sat year-round, plus 1-5pm Sun Oct-May

➡ ⓣCopley

room for 100 to 150 persons to sit at reading tables, and that it shall be perfectly free to all.'

Abbey Room

The Abbey Room is among the library's most sumptuous, with its oak wainscoting, checkerboard marble floors, elaborate fireplace and coffered ceiling inspired by the Doge's Palace in Venice. The room is named for the artist responsible for the 1895 murals, which recount Sir Galahad's *Quest and Achievement of the Holy Grail.*

Elliott Room

The two 2nd-floor lobbies borrow their artistic elements from Pompeii and Venice, respectively. Off the Venetian lobby, the relatively plain study room is named for artist John Elliott, who painted the ceiling mural. *The Triumph of Time* depicts 12 angelic figures, representing the 12 hours on the clock, while the male figure in the cart is Father Time. He is flanked on either side by the Hours of Life and Death. The 20 horses represent the centuries that had elapsed since the birth of Christ.

Sargent Gallery

The *pièce de résistance* of the BPL art collection is on the 3rd floor, which features John Singer Sargent's unfinished Judaic and Christian murals entitled *The Triumph of Religion.*

The theme is surprising for an institution of secular learning. The murals trace the history of Western religion from the primitive worship of pagan gods to the foundation of the Law of Israel to the commencement of the Messianic Age with the birth of Christ. Some scholars argue that the sequence depicts a progression toward religious subjectivity and individualist spiritual pursuits. Others have interpreted that the artist portrayed Christianity as being more evolved than Judaism. Most controversial was Sargent's use of a strong and steadfast figure for *Church,* in contrast with the weak and blindfolded figure for *Synagogue.*

A final painting of the Sermon on the Mount was intended for the vacant space above the stairwell; however, the mural was never completed, due in part to the strong reaction from the Jewish community. When the installation was unveiled in 1919, many called it anti-Semitic. Sargent (by all accounts, dismayed) was unable to appease his critics.

The murals were largely (and perhaps intentionally) forgotten for the remainder of the century. They were finally restored in 2003 and unveiled to the public in early 2004.

BPL EVENTS

See the Boston Public Library website for a schedule of free events, which range from author talks to musical performances.

The Boston Public Library was the first free municipal library in the world, as well as the first to allow its guests to borrow books and materials. The BPL was also the first library to establish a branch system, when it opened a branch in East Boston in 1870 (and 20 more in subsequent years). And in 1895, the BPL became the first library with a designated children's area.

TOTS & TEENS & IN-BETWEENS

The BPL offers loads of entertaining and educational resources for kids and teenagers, including homework help, book lists, movie nights and even video games. Of course there is a dedicated Children's Library, but older kids will want to hang out in the media lounge and lab at fun and funky Teen Central.

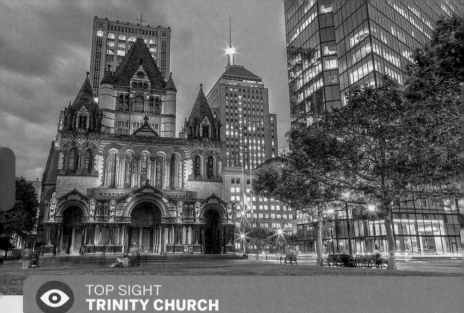

SUSANNE POMMER / SHUTTERSTOCK ©

TOP SIGHT
TRINITY CHURCH

The country's ultimate example of Richardsonian Romanesque, Trinity Church is acclaimed for its integrated composition of shapes, colors and textures, the result of a cooperative effort by artist John LaFarge and architect Henry Hobson Richardson. The granite exterior employs sandstone in colorful patterns, while the interior presents an awe-inspiring array of vibrant murals and stained glass.

The footprint of Trinity Church is a Greek cross, with chancel, nave and transepts surrounding the central square. The wide-open interior was a radical departure from traditional Episcopal architecture, but it embodies the democratic spirit of the congregation in the 1870s.

The walls of the great central tower are covered by two tiers of murals, soaring more than 100ft high. Prior to this commission, LaFarge did not have experience with mural painting on this scale. The result – thousands of square feet of exquisite, jewel-toned encaustic paintings – established his authority as the father of the American mural movement.

The 33 stained-glass windows – mostly executed by different glass workshops – represent diverse styles. The original windows from 1877 and 1878 are the traditional European designs, completed by premier English workshops. Several later examples represent the English arts-and-crafts movement, while the ornate French windows were designed by Parisian artist Achille François Oudinot.

The jewels of the church are the work of LaFarge, distinctive for their use of layered opalescent glass, resulting in an unprecedented richness of shades and dimensions. LaFarge's first commission was *Christ in Majesty*, the spectacular three-panel clerestory window at the western end that is now considered one of the USA's finest examples of stained-glass art.

DON'T MISS

➡ Sunlight streaming through John La-Farge's stained-glass windows

➡ Free pipe-organ concerts on Fridays at 12:15pm from September to early June

PRACTICALITIES

➡ Map p242, F3

➡ ☑617-536-0944 ext 206

➡ www.trinitychurch boston.org

➡ 206 Clarendon St

➡ adult/child $10/free

➡ ⊙10am-4:30pm Tue-Sat, 12:15-4:30pm Sun Easter-Oct, reduced hours rest of year

➡ Ⓣ Copley

◉ SIGHTS

Boston's best architecture – including the Boston Public Library and Trinity Church – is clustered around Copley Square, while the art galleries are lined up along Newbury St. The Charles River Esplanade is not exactly a destination in and of itself, but it's a fantastic place for a bike ride or a stroll.

BOSTON PUBLIC LIBRARY   LIBRARY
See p108.

TRINITY CHURCH   CHURCH
See p110.

★CHARLES RIVER ESPLANADE   PARK
Map p242 (www.esplanadeassociation.org; ⊞; TCharles/MGH, Kenmore) The southern bank of the Charles River Basin is an enticing urban escape, with grassy knolls and cooling waterways, all designed by Frederick Law Olmsted. It stretches almost 3 miles along the Boston shore of the Charles River, from the Museum of Science to Boston University Bridge. The park is dotted with public art, including an oversized bust of Arthur Fiedler, longtime conductor of the Boston Pops. Paths along the river are ideal for bicycling, jogging or walking.

There are several children's playgrounds along the Esplanade, including the **Charlesbank Playground** (Map p228; ⊞; TScience Park/West End), near the Museum of Science, and the **Stoneman Playground** (Map p242; ⊞; THynes), near Massachusetts Ave. The Hatch Memorial Shell often has free shows in summer.

MARY BAKER EDDY LIBRARY
& MAPPARIUM   LIBRARY
Map p242 (☑617-450-7000; www.marybaker eddylibrary.org; 200 Massachusetts Ave; adult/ child $6/4; ◔10am-5pm; ⊞; TSymphony) The Mary Baker Eddy Library houses one of Boston's hidden treasures. The intriguing Mapparium is a room-sized, stained-glass globe that visitors walk through on a glass bridge. It was created in 1935, which is reflected in the globe's geopolitical boundaries. The acoustics, which surprised even the designer, allow everyone in the room to hear even the tiniest whisper.

Besides the Mapparium, the library has an odd amalgam of exhibits related to its full name, the MBE Library for the Betterment of Humanity. The 2nd-floor galleries

deal with the 'search for the meaning of life,' both on a personal and global level. Eddy's papers and transcripts are accessible with permission.

CHRISTIAN SCIENCE CHURCH   CHURCH
Map p242 (☑617-450-2000; www.christian science.com; 210 Massachusetts Ave; ◔10am-5pm Mon, Tue & Thu-Sat, 1-5pm Wed, 11am-3pm Sun, services 10am Sun year-round & 5pm Sun Sep-Jun; TSymphony) Known to adherents as the 'Mother Church,' this is the international home base for the Church of Christ, Scientist (Christian Science), founded by Mary Baker Eddy in 1866. Tour the grand Romanesque basilica, which can seat 3000 worshippers, listen to the 14,000-pipe organ, and linger on the expansive plaza with its 670ft-long reflecting pool.

PRUDENTIAL CENTER
SKYWALK OBSERVATORY   VIEWPOINT
Map p242 (www.skywalkboston.com; 800 Boylston St; adult/child $20/14; ◔10am-10pm Mar-Oct, to 8pm Nov-Feb; ℗⊞; TPrudential) Technically called the Shops at Prudential Center, this landmark Boston building is not much more than a fancy shopping mall. But it does provide a bird's-eye view of Boston from its 50th-floor Skywalk. Completely enclosed by glass, the Skywalk offers spectacular 360-degree views of Boston and Cambridge, accompanied by an entertaining audiotour (with a special version catering to kids). Alternatively, you can enjoy the same view from Top of the Hub (p115) for the price of a drink.

As if these soaring heights weren't enough, you can also watch the fun film called *Wings over Boston* in the multimedia theater (not for acrophobes). Also included in the price of admission is *Dreams of Freedom*, an exhibit that explores the role that immigrants have played in the history of Boston.

KRAKOW WITKIN GALLERY   GALLERY
Map p242 (☑617-262-4490; www.krakowwitkin gallery.com; 10 Newbury St; ◔10am-5:30pm Tue-Sat; TArlington) FREE After years of fruitful cooperation, Barbara Krakow and Andrew Witkin finally renamed their venerable gallery – previously the Barbara Krakow Gallery – to reflect their joint efforts. It continues to be one of Boston's most prominent artistic institutions, with a catalog of artists that reads like something from a major museum. The gallery represents the estates of Sol LeWitt, Fred Sandback and George

LOCAL KNOWLEDGE

WEATHER OR NOT
....

Steady blue, clear view/Flashing blue, clouds due/Steady red, rain ahead/Flashing red, snow instead.

Part of the local lore since 1950, Bostonians have used this simple rhyme and the weather beacon atop the Old Hancock Building (next to the new John Hancock Tower (p112)) to determine if they need to take their umbrella when they leave the house. And yes, the beacon has been known to flash red in midsummer, but that is not a warning of some extremely inclement New England weather, but rather an indication that the Red Sox game has been canceled for the night.

Segal, and shows many others. Look for minimalist, conceptual and reductivist works in all types of media.

JOHN HANCOCK TOWER NOTABLE BUILDING
Map p242 (200 Clarendon St; ⊤Copley) Constructed with more than 10,000 panels of mirrored glass, the 62-story John Hancock Tower was designed in 1976 by Henry Cobb. It is the tallest and most beloved skyscraper on the Boston skyline – despite the precarious falling panes of glass when it was first built. The Hancock offers an amazing perspective on Trinity Church (p110), reflected in its facade.

NEW OLD SOUTH CHURCH CHURCH
Map p242 (www.oldsouth.org; 645 Boylston St; ⊙8am-7pm Sun-Fri, 10am-4pm Sat; ⊤Copley) This magnificent puddingstone Venetian Gothic church on Copley Square (p111) is called the 'new' Old South because up until 1875 the congregation worshiped in the Old South Church on Milk St (now the Old South Meeting House). The Congregational church has an impressive collection of stained-glass windows, all shipped from London, and an organ that was rescued from a Minneapolis church just before demolition.

ARLINGTON STREET CHURCH CHURCH
Map p242 (☑617-536-7050; www.ascboston.org; 351 Boylston St; ⊙10am-3pm Mon & Wed-Sat, 1-4pm Sun; ⊤Arlington) The first public building erected in Back Bay in 1861, this graceful church features extraordinary Tiffany windows and 16 bells in its steeple. The

church's Unitarian Universalist ministry is purely progressive, as it has been since Rev William Ellery Channing preached in the building's predecessor in the early 19th century. (A statue in his honor stands across the street in the Public Garden.)

GIBSON HOUSE MUSEUM HISTORIC BUILDING
Map p242 (☑617-267-6338; www.thegibson house.org; 137 Beacon St; tours adult/child $10/3; ⊙tours 1pm, 2pm & 3pm Wed-Sun; ⊤Arlington) Catherine Hammond Gibson was considered quite the pioneer when she moved to this Italian Renaissance row house in 1860 (that she was a female homeowner in this 'New Land' was even more unusual). The Gibson House remains virtually unchanged since this time, preserving a piece of Victorian-era Boston and showcasing the antique furniture and art collected by the Gibson family.

 **EATING**

You won't find Boston's most innovative dining in this blue-blooded neighborhood, but you will find some fantastic fare, including veggie, seafood, charcuterie and more. Back Bay is also surely the city's top spot for sidewalk seating, so don't miss it if the weather is fine.

★**LUKE'S LOBSTER** SEAFOOD $
Map p242 (☑857-350-4626; www.lukeslobster. com; 75 Exeter St; mains $9-19; ⊙11am-9pm Sun-Wed, to 10pm Thu-Sat; ⊤Copley) ✿ Luke Holden took a Maine seafood shack and put it in the middle of Back Bay (and other places around Boston), so that hungry shoppers could get a classic lobster roll for lunch. The place looks authentic, with weathered wood interior and nautical decor, but more importantly, the lobster rolls are the real deal – and affordable. The only thing lacking is sea breezes.

FLOUR BAKERY $
Map p242 (☑617-437-7700; www.flourbakery. com; 131 Clarendon St; pastries from $3.50, sandwiches $9.50; ⊙6:30am-8pm Mon-Fri, 8am-6pm Sat, 8am-5pm Sun; 🛜☑♿; ⊤Back Bay) Joanne Chang's beloved bakery is taking over Boston. This outlet – on the edge of Back Bay – has the same flaky pastries and rich coffee that we have come to expect, not to men-

tion sandwiches, soups, salads and pizzas. And just to prove there is something for everybody, Flour also sells housemade dog biscuits for your canine friend.

PARISH CAFÉ
SANDWICHES $

Map p242 (☑617-247-4777; www.parishcafe. com; 361 Boylston St; sandwiches $12-20; ⏰11:30am-1am, bar to 2am; ☑; Ⓣarlington) Sample the creations of Boston's most famous chefs without exhausting your expense account. The menu at Parish features a rotating roster of salads and sandwiches, each designed by local celebrity chefs, including Jamie Bissonnette, Barbara Lynch and Tony Maws. The place feels more 'pub' than 'cafe,' with a long bar backed by big TVs and mirrors.

DIRTY WATER DOUGH CO
PIZZA $

Map p242 (☑617-262-0090; www.dirtywater dough.com; 222 Newbury St; slices $3-4, pizzas $11-15; ⏰11am-10pm Sun-Thu, to 11pm Fri & Sat; ☑☑; Ⓣcopley) If there's anything that Bostonians love more than the Standells, it's pizza. That explains why the kids are lining up to get theirs from Dirty Water Dough, where they can get a big slice and a soda for $5. Other perks: locally sourced ingredients, unusual topping combos and gluten-free options, not to mention the Dirty Water IPA.

★PURO CEVICHE BAR
LATIN AMERICAN $$

Map p242 (☑617-266-0707; www.puroceviche bar.com; 264 Newbury St; small plates $10-16; ⏰4-11pm Mon-Thu, 11am-11pm Fri-Sun; Ⓣhynes) Serves up delightfully modern yet still authentic Latin American fare in its funky downstairs digs, where exposed brick walls are covered with bold murals. Choose between six types of *ceviche*, six kinds of tacos and a slew of Latin-inspired small plates. Also on offer are classic cocktails and a nicely curated wine list. Attention, budget-minded travelers: $2 tacos on Tuesdays.

SALTY PIG
ITALIAN $$

Map p242 (☑617-536-6200; www.thesaltypig. com; 130 Dartmouth St; charcuterie $7, mains $12-19; ⏰11:30am-midnight; Ⓣback Bay) With prosciutto, pâté, *rillettes*, *testa* (head cheese), *sanguinaccio* (blood sausage), *porchetta* (pork shoulder) and more, you'll feel like you're in one of those cultures that eats every part of the animal. 'Salty Pig Parts' get paired with stinky cheeses and other accompaniments for amazing charcuterie plates. There's pizza and pasta for the less adventurous, and cocktails and craft beers too.

PIATTINI
ITALIAN $$

Map p242 (☑617-536-2020; www.piattini.com; 226 Newbury St; small plates $9-16, pasta $20-28; ⏰11am-10pm; ☑; Ⓣcopley) If you have trouble deciding what to order, Piattini can help. The name means 'small plates,' so you don't have to choose just one. There's also an enticing array of pasta dishes, as well as an extensive list of wines by the glass. This intimate *enoteca* (wine bar) and its patio are delightful settings to sample the flavors of Italy.

CASA ROMERO
MEXICAN $$

Map p242 (☑617-536-4341; www.casaromero. com; 30 Gloucester St; lunch $10-15, dinner $18-28; ⏰5-10pm Mon-Fri, noon-11pm Sat, 1-9pm Sun; ☑; Ⓣhynes) The entrance to this hidden treasure is in the alley off Gloucester St. Step inside and find yourself in a cozy *casa* – filled with folk art and Talavera tiles – which is wonderful and warm during winter. In pleasant weather, dine under the stars on the delightful patio. This is not your average taqueria – be prepared to pay for the experience.

★SALTIE GIRL
SEAFOOD $$$

Map p242 (☑617-267-0691; www.saltiegirl.com; 281 Dartmouth St; small plates $12-18, mains $18-40; ⏰11:30am-10pm; Ⓣcopley) Here's a new concept in dining: the seafood bar. It's a

BACK BAY EATING

COMMONWEALTH AVENUE

The grandest of Back Bay's grand boulevards is Commonwealth Ave (more commonly Comm Ave). The Champs-Élysées of Boston, the dual carriageway connects the Public Garden with the Back Bay Fens, a green link in Olmsted's Emerald Necklace. The grassy mall is dotted with majestic elms and lined with stately brownstones. The eclectic array of public art honors – among others – a Civil War hero, a First Lady, an abolitionist, a suffragist, a maritime historian, an Argentinian statesman and a Viking explorer.

delightfully intimate place to feast on tantalizing dishes that blow away all preconceived notions about seafood. From your traditional Gloucester lobster roll to tinned fish on toast to the irresistible torched salmon belly, this place is full of delightful surprises.

Reservations are not accepted and the place is tiny, so expect to wait. (It's worth it.)

★COURTYARD
AMERICAN $$$

Map p242 (☑617-859-2251; www.thecateredaffair.com/bpl; 700 Boylston St; tea adult/child $39/19; ⏰11:30am-5pm Mon-Sat, 1-5pm Sun; ⓣCopley) The perfect destination for an elegant afternoon tea is – believe it or not – the Boston Public Library (p108). Overlooking the beautiful Italianate courtyard, this grown-up restaurant serves an artfully prepared selection of sandwiches, scones and sweets, accompanied by a wide range of teas (black, green and herbal). Reserve ahead, especially on weekends.

MOONCUSSER FISH HOUSE
SEAFOOD $$$

Map p242 (☑617-917-5193; www.mooncusserfishhouse.com; 304 Stuart St; mains $32-45, 3-course prix-fixe $49; ⏰5-10pm Mon-Sat; ⓣArlington) This elegant spot pairs an old-fashioned concept (the 'fish house') with thoroughly modern presentations of local seafood, from bluefish to swordfish and everything in between. The dishes are understated, showing off local flavors, but not lacking sophisticated embellishments. The menu is short but sweet, including a few divine appetizers and to-die-for desserts.

SELECT OYSTER BAR
SEAFOOD $$$

Map p242 (☑857-233-0376; www.selectboston.com; 50 Gloucester St; mains $30-42; ⏰11:30am-9:30pm Sun-Thu, to 10:30pm Fri & Sat; ⓣHynes) New England seafood meets Mediterranean flavors at this trendy little oyster bar off Newbury St. The space is delightfully compact and the menu is innovative and amazing. Unfortunately, it's too expensive to be the 'neighborhood spot' that Chef Michael Serpa is going for, but it's still a charmer. Note the 20% gratuity included on all tabs.

ATLANTIC FISH CO
SEAFOOD $$$

Map p242 (☑617-267-4000; www.atlanticfish.com; 761 Boylston St; mains lunch $16-28, dinner $22-44; ⏰11:30am-11pm; ⓣCopley) New England clam chowder in a bread bowl: for a perfect lunch here, that's all you need to know. For nonbelievers, we'll add seafood

fra diavolo, lobster ravioli and local Jonah crab cakes. There's more, of course, and the menu is printed daily to showcase the freshest ingredients. Enjoy eating in the dining room or on the flower-filled sidewalk patio.

DRINKING & NIGHTLIFE

Two words: sidewalk cafes. Newbury St is lined with them, which makes it the perfect place to combine coffee-drinking and people-watching. For Drinking with a capital D, there are great restaurants with bustling bar scenes and a few long-standing dive bar favorites.

LOLITA COCINA & TEQUILA BAR
COCKTAIL BAR

Map p242 (www.lolitamexican.com; 271 Dartmouth St; ⏰4pm-midnight, bar to 2am; ⓣCopley) This spicy little Mexican number is full of surprises (which we won't ruin for you). We will reveal that there are no less than ten different margaritas on offer, including the eye-popping Diablo. The menu is packed with unusual and enticing Mexican fare that does not disappoint. Oh, and there's all-you-can-eat tacos for $9 on (most) Monday nights.

CLUB CAFÉ
GAY

Map p242 (☑617-536-0966; www.clubcafe.com; 209 Columbus Ave; ⏰11am-2am; ⓣBack Bay) It's a club! It's a cafe! It's a cabaret! Anything goes at this glossy, gay nightlife extravaganza. There is live cabaret in the Napoleon Room six nights a week, while the main dance and lounge area has tea parties, salsa dancing, trivia competitions, karaoke, drag bingo and good old-fashioned dance parties.

BARRINGTON COFFEE ROASTING CO
COFFEE

Map p242 (☑857-250-2780; www.barringtoncoffee.com; 303 Newbury St; ⏰7am-7:30pm; 🛜; ⓣHynes) Barrington's 'thing' is their high-tech steampunk machine that uses programmable controls and steam power to brew coffee (sort of like a French press with more buttons and more bubbles). No comment on the technology, but the espresso drinks and cold-brew coffee are top-notch. Seating is limited inside but there are tables on the small patio.

BUKOWSKI TAVERN · BAR

Map p242 (📞617-437-9999; www.bukowski
tavern.net; 50 Dalton St; ⏱11:30am-2am Mon-
Sat, from noon Sun; Ⓣ Hynes) This sweet bar
lies inside a parking garage next to the can-
yon of the Mass Pike. Expect sticky wooden
tables, loud rock music, black hoodies, cuss-
ing, a dozen different burgers and dogs,
and more than 100 kinds of beer. In God we
trust, all others pay cash.

CORNER TAVERN · PUB

Map p242 (📞617-262-5555; www.facebook.com/
thecornerboston; 421 Marlborough St; ⏱11:30am-
2am; Ⓣ Hynes) A true neighborhood bar, the
Corner Tavern has a decent beer selection,
satisfying food and a laid-back atmosphere.
It's convivial, but not overly crowded. The
Sox are on the TVs (lots of TVs), but the volume is down. What more do you want from
your local watering hole?

BRAHMIN · LOUNGE

Map p242 (📞617-723-3131; www.thebrahmin.
com; 33 Stanhope St; ⏱4:30pm-2am Tue-Sat;
Ⓣ Back Bay) You may have never heard of
Nightclub & Bar Magazine, but they once
named this Back Bay original the best
lounge in the country! That seems like a
stretch, but we do love the elegant atmosphere, the chandeliers and leather couches,
the handcrafted cocktails and the seamless
transition to dance club as the evening pro-
gresses. Note the weekend dress code.

TOP OF THE HUB · BAR

Map p242 (📞617-536-1775; www.topofthehub.
net; 800 Boylston St; ⏱11:30am-1am; 🍴; Ⓣ Prudential) Yes, it's touristy. And overpriced.
And the food is not too inspiring. But the
head-spinning city view makes it worthwhile to ride the elevator up to the 52nd
floor of the **Prudential Center** (Map p242;
📞800-746-7778; www.prudentialcenter.com;
800 Boylston St; ⏱10am-9pm Mon-Sat, 11am-
7pm Sun; 🍴; Ⓣ Prudential). Come for spectacular sunset drinks and stay for free live
jazz. Beware the $24 per-person minimum
after 8pm.

⭐ ENTERTAINMENT

**Visit the BosTix (www.artsboston.org)
booth at ArtsBoston on Copley Square
for same-day discounted tickets. There
is also a branch at Faneuil Hall.**

⭐ RED ROOM @ CAFE 939 · LIVE MUSIC

Map p242 (📞617-747-2261; www.berklee.edu/
cafe939; 939 Boylston St; tickets free-$20; ⏱ box
office 10am-6pm Mon-Sat; Ⓣ Hynes) Run by
Berklee students, the Red Room @ Cafe
939 has emerged as one of Boston's least
predictable and most enjoyable music venues. It has an excellent sound system and
a baby grand piano; most importantly, it
books interesting, eclectic up-and-coming
musicians. Buy tickets in advance at the
Berklee Performance Center (p115).

BERKLEE PERFORMANCE CENTER · CONCERT VENUE

Map p242 (📞617-747-2261; www.berklee.edu/
bpc; 136 Massachusetts Ave; tickets $10-65;
⏱ box office 10am-6pm Mon-Sat; Ⓣ Hynes) The
performance hall at this notable music college hosts a wide variety of performances,
from high-energy jazz recitals and songs by
smoky-throated vocalists to oddball sets by
keyboard-tapping guys who look like their
day job is dungeon master.

🛍 SHOPPING

**Newbury St is a magnet for Boston
shoppers, who love the high-end
boutiques, quirky shops and encyclopedic
malls – all within an eight-block strip.**

TOPDRAWER · GIFTS & SOUVENIRS

Map p242 (📞857-305-3934; www.kolo.com; 273
Newbury St; ⏱11am-7pm; Ⓣ Hynes) Travelers! Here is a store full of things you need,
even if you didn't realize you needed them.
Everything from plush fold-up slippers
(perfect for the chilly airplane) to fabulous,
functional daypacks and travel pouches.
The aesthetic is modern and minimalist,
but you'll also find an appealingly old-
fashioned selection of pen sets and travel
journals to record all your memories.

TRIDENT BOOKSELLERS & CAFÉ · BOOKS

Map p242 (📞617-267-8688; www.tridentbooks
cafe.com; 338 Newbury St; ⏱8am-midnight; 🍴;
Ⓣ Hynes) Pick out a pile of books and retreat to a quiet corner of the cafe to decide
which ones you really want to buy. There's
a little bit of everything here, and the 'hip-
pie turned back-to-the-lander, turned Buddhist, turned entrepreneur' owners really
know how to keep their customers happy.

LOCAL KNOWLEDGE

BOSTON FASHION

Ball & Buck (Map p242; ☑617-242-1776; www.ballandbuck.com; 144b Newbury St; ☺10am-7pm; ⊤Copley) The hunter logo is indicative of Ball & Buck's target audience – manly men who are not afraid to wear camouflage and look good in it, too. These attractive, durable duds are meant to be worn for work or play, trekking through the woods or strolling city streets. Every item in the shop is made in the US of A.

Daniela Corte (Map p242; ☑617-262-2100; www.danielacorte.com; 211 Newbury St, 2nd fl; ☺by appointment Mon-Fri; ⊤Copley) Born and raised in Buenos Aires, Daniela Corte attended the Boston School of Fashion Design before launching her own line and opening this understated boutique on Newbury St. The silky tops, fun-loving dresses and skin-hugging leggings may be prohibitively expensive but the swimwear is worth every penny.

MARATHON SPORTS   SPORTS & OUTDOORS

Map p242 (☑617-267-4774; www.marathonsports.com; 671 Boylston St; ☺10am-7:30pm Mon-Wed & Fri, to 8pm Thu & Sat, 11am-6pm Sun; ⊤Copley) Specializing in running gear, this place could not have a better location: it overlooks the finish line of the Boston Marathon. It's known for attentive customer service, as staff work hard to make sure you get a shoe that fits. They also work hard to support the running community, with a weekly running club and a calendar of other events.

KITCHENWARES   HOMEWARES

Map p242 (☑857-366-4237; www.kitchenwaresboston.com; 215 Newbury St; ☺10am-7pm Mon-Sat, noon-5pm Sun; ⊤Copley) KitchenWares is popular for its selection of cutlery, as well as its all-important knife sharpening service. Less known, it's also an excellent spot for unusual gifts and souvenirs, such as lobster-shaped cookie cutters, Fenway Park coasters and beautiful, copper Boston-style cocktail shakers.

HEMPEST   CONCEPT STORE

Map p242 (☑617-421-9944; www.hempest.com; 207 Newbury St; ☺11am-7pm Mon-Sat, noon-6pm Sun; ⊤Copley) ✐ The Hempest is not a well-stocked smoke shop, though there is a small selection of pipes and bongs. It's more about stylish clothing, organic soaps and lotions, and fun home-furnishing items. Most of the products are made from cannabis hemp, the botanical cousin of marijuana.

NEWBURY COMICS   MUSIC

Map p242 (☑617-236-4930; www.newburycomics.com; 332 Newbury St; ☺10am-10pm Mon-Sat, 11am-8pm Sun; ⊤Hynes) How does a music store remain relevant in the digital world? One word: vinyl. In addition to the many cheap CDs and DVDs, there's a solid selection of new-release vinyl. Incidentally, it does sell comic books, as well as T-shirts, action figures and silly gags. No wonder everyone is having such a wicked good time.

🏃 SPORTS & ACTIVITIES

SOUTHWEST CORRIDOR   CYCLING

Map p242 (www.swcpc.org; ⊤Back Bay/South End) Extending for almost 5 miles, the Southwest Corridor is a paved walkway running between and parallel to Columbus and Huntington Aves. It's an ideal urban cycling route, leading from Back Bay, through the South End and Roxbury, to Forest Hills in Jamaica Plain. Borrow a bike from Blue Bikes or rent one at Community Bicycle Supply (p103) or **Papa Wheelies** (Back Bay Bicycles; ☑617-247-2336; www.papa-wheelies.com; 362 Commonwealth Ave; rental per day $55-65; ☺10am-7pm Mon-Fri, to 6pm Sat, noon-5pm Sun; ⊤Hynes).

KINGS   BOWLING

Map p242 (☑617-266-2695; www.kings-de.com; 50 Dalton St; per person per game $7-9, shoe rental $4.50; ☺3pm-1am Mon-Wed, noon-1am Thu-Sat, noon-11pm Sun; ♿; ⊤Hynes) For an over-the-top tenpin experience, roll a few at Kings, where high-tech lanes are lined with neon lights and surrounded by trippy graphics. The enormous cocktail lounge is done up in a style reminiscent of *The Jetsons*. If bowling is not your game, you might prefer the billiards, shuffleboard or skee-ball.

Kenmore Square & Fenway

Neighborhood Top Five

❶ Museum of Fine Arts (MFA; p119) Spending a morning immersing yourself in the Art of the Americas, then dedicating the afternoon to exploring the Impressionist and Postimpressionist paintings.

❷ Fenway Park (p123) Watching the Red Sox whip their opponents at America's oldest ballpark.

❸ Isabella Stewart Gardner Museum (p121) Venerating the artistic, and cultural legacy of Isabella Stewart Gardner at her namesake museum, allowing plenty of time to ponder the *Rape of Europa*.

❹ Symphony Hall (p124) Hearing the world-renowned Boston Symphony Orchestra play in this acoustically perfect hall.

❺ Lansdowne St (p126) Heading out for a night of drinking, music and merry-making on one of Boston's best clubbing strips.

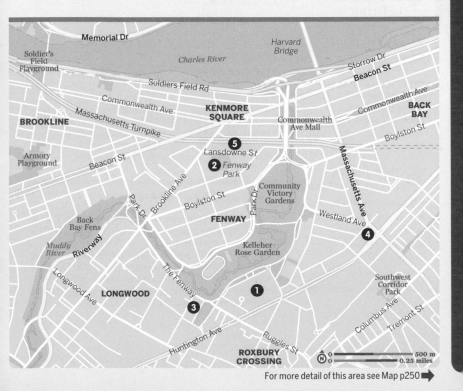

For more detail of this area see Map p250 ➡

Lonely Planet's Top Tip

If you can't score tickets to the baseball game, you can still watch the action and soak up the atmosphere at one of the bars on Lansdowne St (they all definitely have TVs). You can even hear the gasps and the cheers from the fans inside the ballpark.

✕ Best Places to Eat

➡ Island Creek Oyster Bar (p125)

➡ Eventide Fenway (p125)

➡ El Pelon (p125)

➡ Gyro City (p125)

For reviews, see p124. ➡

🍷 Best Places to Drink

➡ Bleacher Bar (p126)

➡ Hawthorne (p126)

➡ Pavement Coffeehouse (p127)

➡ Lower Depths Tap Room (p126)

➡ Cheeky Monkey Brewing (p126)

For reviews, see p126. ➡

◉ Best Places to Catch a Game

➡ Fenway Park (p123)

➡ Bleacher Bar (p126)

➡ Tasty Burger (p125)

➡ Cheeky Monkey Brewing (p126)

➡ Lansdowne Pub (p126)

For reviews, see p123. ➡

Explore Kenmore Square & Fenway

Kenmore Sq is the epicenter of student life in Boston. In addition to the Boston University (BU) behemoth, there are more than a half dozen colleges in the area. As such, Kenmore Sq has a disproportionate share of nightlife, inexpensive places to eat and dormitories disguised as brownstones.

Come to Kenmore Sq to cavort at cool clubs and to devour cheap food. If you get the timing right, you can do so before or after the Red Sox game. Watch the boys battle it out from your perch at one of the local sports bars or, if you're lucky, at Fenway Park (p123).

While Kenmore Sq is best for baseball and beer, the southern part of this neighborhood is dedicated to more high-minded pursuits. Dubbed 'Avenue of the Arts,' Huntington Ave represents a concentrated area of major and minor artistic and cultural venues, including Symphony Hall (p124), two universities and two museums. Art lovers should devote a day to exploring one of Boston's celebrated art venues (although deciding which one will be a challenge).

Local Life

➡ **Cheap Grub** Hidden away in the midst of residential Fenway, Peterborough St is popular among the local student population for its informal, international and affordable restaurants.

➡ **Hit the Pavement** There are two outlets of Pavement Coffeehouse (p127) in the Kenmore Sq & Fenway neighborhood, but the one at 1096 Boylston is where the cool students and musicians hang out, due to its proximity to the Berklee College of Music.

➡ **Urban escape** Escape the city with a stroll through the Back Bay Fens (p124). Locals come here to soak up some rays, exercise or flex their green thumbs.

Getting There & Away

➡ **Metro** West of the center, the green line of the T forks into four branches, so you have to pay attention not only to the color of your train, but also its letter (B, C, D or E). To reach Kenmore Sq or Fenway Park, take any of the green line trains except the E branch to Kenmore T station. Sights along Huntington Ave in Fenway are accessible from the E-branch Museum of Fine Arts stop or the orange-line Ruggles station.

APHOTOSTORY / SHUTTERSTOCK ©

TOP SIGHT
MUSEUM OF FINE ARTS

Since 1876, the Museum of Fine Arts (MFA) has been Boston's premier venue for showcasing art by local, national and international artists. Nowadays, the museum's holdings encompass all eras, making it truly encyclopedic in scope. Gorgeous modern wings dedicated to the Art of the Americas and to contemporary art have contributed to Boston's emergence as an art center in the 21st century.

Art of the Americas

The centerpiece of the MFA is the four-story Americas wing, which includes 53 galleries exhibiting art from the pre-Columbian era up through the 20th century. Some of the newest, most intriguing acquisitions are on the lower level, which houses the pre-Columbian and Native American artwork. There are also a few rooms dedicated to colonial America and the maritime trade, with a wonderful collection of model ships.

Level one showcases 18th- and 19th-century art, with several rooms dedicated to neoclassicism and revolutionary Boston. Thomas Sully's depiction of George Washington's *Passage of the Delaware* is a highlight. The MFA has the world's largest holding of John Singleton Copley paintings. Don't miss the alarming *Watson and the Shark*.

The second level is, perhaps, the richest part of the wing. An entire gallery is dedicated to John Singer Sargent, including his intriguing painting *The Daughters of Edward Darley Boit*. Highlights in the American Impressionism galleries include pieces by Mary Cassat and the perennial local favorite, *Boston Common at Twilight* by Childe Hassam.

DON'T MISS

➡ *The Daughters of Edward Darley Boit* by John Singer Sargent

➡ *Boston Common at Twilight* by Childe Hassam

➡ *Where Do We Come From?* by Paul Gauguin

➡ Buddhist Temple room

PRACTICALITIES

➡ MFA

➡ Map p250, E5

➡ ☎617-267-9300

➡ www.mfa.org

➡ 465 Huntington Ave

➡ adult/child $25/free

➡ ⊙10am-5pm Sat-Tue, to 10pm Wed-Fri

➡ Ⓣ Museum of Fine Arts; Ruggles

FOR KIDS

Children under the age of 17 are admitted free after 3pm on weekdays and all day on weekends – a fantastic family bargain.

The murals in the rotunda and above the main staircase were painted by John Singer Sargent in the 1920s. The main rotunda painting depicts the Greek goddess of wisdom, Athena, turning back Time.

GET A GUIDE

You can rent a guided multimedia tour (adult/child $6/4) in one of 10 languages, which uses video, audio and animation to provide extra insight on the museum's highlights. Live guided tours are also available throughout the day.

Since the 2017 donation of the Van Otterloo and Weatherbie collections, the MFA now holds one of the country's foremost collections of Dutch and Flemish Golden Age paintings, with a new Center for Netherlandish Art opening in 2020.

The top floor is devoted to modernism, with wonderful work by Alexander Calder, Frank Stella and Georgia O'Keefe. There are also impressive additions by Latin American artists.

Art of Europe

Located in the museum's northern wing, the MFA's collection of European art spans the Middle Ages to the 20th century. The Italian Renaissance is well represented, with gilded icons and paintings by Botticelli, Titian and Tintoretto. Also on display is the Dutch Golden Age, with five paintings by Rembrandt. The highlights of the European exhibit are no doubt the Impressionists and Postimpressionists, with masterpieces by Degas, Gauguin, Renoir and van Gogh, and a sizable collection of Monets (one of the largest outside Paris).

Art of Asia, Oceania & Africa

One of the MFA's strongest areas, the collection of Asian art is located in the southwestern wing, along with art from the South Pacific and Africa. The centerpiece is the peaceful Buddhist Temple room on the 2nd floor, which is just one exhibit in a vast array of Japanese art, including prints and metalworks. There is also an extensive display of Chinese paintings, calligraphy and ceramics.

Art of the Ancient World

In the southeastern part of the museum, the MFA's collection of ancient art dates from 6000 BC to AD 600 and covers a huge geographic spectrum. The highlight is certainly the Egyptian galleries, especially the two rooms of mummies. The Etruscan painted tombs are also impressive. Greek, Roman and Nubian pieces occupy the second level, with plenty of perfectly sculpted Greek gods and Roman emperors.

Linde Family Wing for Contemporary Art

The renovation of the MFA's west wing – originally designed by IM Pei and opened in 2011 – nearly tripled the exhibition space for contemporary art. There are galleries dedicated to video, multimedia art and decorative arts, in addition to the more traditional media.

The darling of museum patrons is *Black River,* a fantastic woven tapestry of discarded bottle caps, by Ghanaian artist El Anatsui. But the most compelling piece is perhaps the blue neon sign by Maurizio Nannucci, which spells out 'All Art Has Been Contemporary.'

TOP SIGHT
ISABELLA STEWART GARDNER MUSEUM

The magnificent Venetian-style palazzo that houses this museum was home to Isabella Stewart Gardner herself until her death in 1924. A monument to one woman's taste for acquiring exquisite art, the Gardner is filled with some 2500 priceless objects, primarily European. The four-story greenhouse courtyard is a tranquil oasis that alone is worth the price of admission.

Courtyard

The centerpiece of the Gardner Museum is the delightful courtyard, filled with lush greenery, vibrant blooms and evocative sculpture. Almost every room gives a different perspective on this masterpiece of landscape design. The plantings change seasonally; come in early spring to see the courtyard draped in stunning nasturtium blooms (reportedly Isabella's favorite).

Cloisters

On the 1st floor, the Spanish Cloister is paved with striking Islamic tiles. At one end, a Moorish arch frames John Singer Sargent's painting *El Jaleo*. At the other end, a wrought-iron gate leads into the Spanish Chapel, hung with Spanish religious art. Other cloisters encircle the courtyard, dotted with sculptures and stonework.

Several smaller rooms are stuffed with paintings, including work by James McNeill Whistler, Henri Matisse, Edgar Degas and Anders Zorn. Isabella was a patron of John Singer Sargent, and many of his paintings hang in these rooms.

DON'T MISS
....

➜ Ancient art and seasonal landscaping in the courtyard
➜ *Portrait of Isabella Stewart Gardner* by John Singer Sargent
➜ *Rape of Europa* by Titian
➜ The rich decor of the Tapestry Room

PRACTICALITIES
....

➜ Map p250, D5
➜ ☎617-566-1401
➜ www.gardnermuseum.org
➜ 25 Evans Way
➜ adult/child $15/free
➜ ◷11am-5pm Wed-Mon, to 9pm Thu
➜ ⓣMuseum of Fine Arts

ART HEIST

On March 18, 1990, two thieves disguised as police officers broke into the Isabella Stewart Gardner Museum. They left with nearly $200 million worth of artworks. The most famous painting stolen was Vermeer's *The Concert*, but the loot also included three works by Rembrandt, and others by Manet and Degas, not to mention French and Chinese artifacts. The crime was never solved. Since Isabella's will stipulated that the exhibit should never be altered, the empty frames still hang on the walls.

Free tours and public talks are offered, including the 45-minute 'Collection Conversations' on weekdays at 2pm.

MUSEUM CONCERTS

Elegant Calderwood Hall is the setting for concerts – from classical to contemporary – on Sunday afternoons (1:30pm) and occasional Thursdays (7pm).

Admission to the Gardner is free on your birthday! If your name is Isabella, admission is free every day.

The 2nd Floor

On the 2nd floor, the Dutch room contains Isabella's small collection of Dutch and Flemish art, including a self-portrait by Rembrandt and another portrait by Rubens. Note the empty frames, where stolen paintings once hung.

The majestic Tapestry Room evokes a castle hall, hung with 10 allegorical tapestries. One series depicts scenes from the Life of Cyrus the Great, while the other recounts the Life of Abraham.

The Raphael Room shows off two paintings by the namesake Renaissance painter, as well as two gorgeous *cassoni* (Italian wedding chests).

The 3rd Floor

The 3rd floor contains the highlights of this rich collection. The sumptuous Veronese Room is so named for the stunning ceiling painting, but this room is filled with treasures, including pastels by James McNeill Whistler.

The museum's most celebrated gallery is the Titian Room, where Isabella displayed her passion for all things Venetian. The gallery is centered on Titian's famous rendition of *Europa,* which was much loved by the collector.

Your final stop is the Gothic Room, featuring Sargent's remarkable (and rather controversial) portrait of Isabella herself. This room was never open to the public when Isabella was alive, but she did allow Sargent to use it as a studio.

Piano Building

In 2012 the Gardner Museum opened the doors of a greatly anticipated, hotly contested new building, designed by architect Renzo Piano. Isabella's will stipulated that her art-filled palazzo never be altered, so the project required much negotiation (including special permission from the Massachusetts Supreme Court). The end result allows the palazzo to better serve its originally intended purpose, which is to share Isabella's love for art and culture with the community. The space includes a lovely concert hall, a vibrant art-in-residency program and a 'Living Room' where visitors can peruse art books, seated on comfy couches and serenaded by Whistler, the museum's chirping yellow canary.

TOP SIGHT
FENWAY PARK

What is it that makes Fenway Park 'America's Most Beloved Ballpark'? It's not just that it's the home of the Boston Red Sox. Open since 1912, it's the oldest operating baseball park in the country. To learn more, take the hour-long tour of this beloved Boston landmark. Bonus: see the ballpark from atop the legendary Green Monster!

Green Monster

As all Red Sox fans know, 'the wall giveth and the wall taketh away.' The 37ft-high left-field wall is only 310ft away from home plate (compared to the standard 325ft), so it's popular among right-handed hitters, who can score an easy home run with a high hit to left. However, batters can just as easily be deprived of a home run when a powerful but low line drive bounces off the Monster for an off-the-wall double.

The Green Monster was painted green in 1947 and since then, it has become part of the Fenway experience.

Other Features

Scoreboard At the base of the Green Monster is the original scoreboard, still updated manually from behind the wall.

Pesky Pole Fenway's right-field foul pole is named for former shortstop Johnny Pesky.

The Triangle Many a double has turned into a triple when the ball has flown into the deepest, darkest corner of center field (where the walls form a triangle).

Red Seat The bleachers at Fenway Park are green, except for one lone red seat: seat 21 at section 42, row 37. This is supposedly the longest home run ever hit at Fenway Park – officially 502ft, hit by Red Sox left fielder Ted Williams in 1946.

DON'T MISS

➡ Sitting atop the Green Monster

➡ Fenway's beloved manual scoreboard

➡ The nine World Series banners hanging on Jersey St

PRACTICALITIES

➡ Map p250, D3

➡ ☏617-226-6666

➡ www.redsox.com

➡ 4 Jersey St

➡ tours adult/child $20/14, pre-game $35-45

➡ ⏱9am-5pm Apr-Oct, special schedule game days, 10am-5pm Nov-Mar

➡ Ⓣ Kenmore

⊙ SIGHTS

Art lovers should make a beeline for Kenmore Sq & Fenway, a neighborhood that's home to two fabulous art museums. (You'll need more than one day if you intend to see them both.) Sports fans, plan ahead if you are hoping to catch a Red Sox game or to take a tour of the baseball park, as the Hometown Team is Boston's hottest ticket.

⊙ Kenmore Square

FENWAY PARK STADIUM
See p123.

MUGAR MEMORIAL LIBRARY LIBRARY
Map p250 (Howard Gotleib Archival Research Center; ☑617-353-3696; www.bu.edu/archives; 771 Commonwealth Ave; ⊙9am-4pm Mon-Fri; ⊤BU Central) **FREE** The special collections of BU's Mugar Memorial Library are housed in the Howard Gotlieb Archival Research Center, an outstanding 20th-century archive that balances pop culture and scholarly appeal. Rotating exhibits showcase the holdings, including papers from Arthur Fiedler's collection, the personal correspondence of Julius and Ethel Rosenberg, or the correspondence of BU alumnus Dr Martin Luther King, Jr. Hours posted are for the archives; exhibit hours may vary depending on their exact location in the library.

⊙ Fenway

MUSEUM OF FINE ARTS MUSEUM
See p119.

ISABELLA STEWART GARDNER MUSEUM MUSEUM
See p121.

SYMPHONY HALL HISTORIC BUILDING
Map p250 (☑617-266-1492; www.bso.org; 301 Massachusetts Ave; ⊙hours vary; ⊤Symphony) This majestic building has been the home of the Boston Symphony Orchestra since 1900, when it was built by McKim, Mead & White (of Boston Public Library fame). See the hall's public spaces and go behind the scenes on a free, one-hour tour. Tour dates vary and advance bookings are required; visit the website for a current schedule.

Symphony Hall is often lauded for its perfect acoustics, and the architects did in fact engage a Harvard physics professor to achieve this. To truly appreciate the physics, you'll have to come for a concert.

BACK BAY FENS PARK
Map p250 (Park Dr; ⊙dawn-dusk; ⊤Museum of Fine Arts) The Back Bay Fens, or the Fenway, follows the Muddy River, an aptly named creek that is choked with tall reeds. The Fens features well-cared-for community gardens, the elegant Kelleher Rose Garden, and plenty of space to toss a Frisbee, play pick-up basketball or lie in the sun.

MASSART BAKALAR & PAINE GALLERIES GALLERY
Map p250 (Massachusetts College of Art and Design; ☑617-879-7000; www.massart.edu; 621 Huntington Ave, South Bldg; ⊙noon-6pm Mon-Sat, to 8pm Wed; ⊤Longwood Medical Area) **FREE** MassArt is the country's first and only four-year independent public art college. There's always some thought-provoking or sense-stimulating exhibits to see at one of the seven galleries on campus. In the South Building, the Bakalar and Paine galleries host nationally and internationally known artists – as well as emerging talents – as a complement to the school's curricula. Closed at the time of writing for renovation, the galleries are scheduled to reopen in 2020.

✕ EATING

Kenmore Sq & Fenway have always enjoyed a disproportionate share of budget restaurants, due to the large student population. Ethnic eats and divey sandwich shops abound. One of the quiet roads between the Back Bay Fens and Fenway Park, Peterborough St is lined with international cafes and take-out joints, making it a sort of urban food court. In recent years, the neighborhood has also seen the opening of more upscale restaurants, especially with the development along Boylston St.

✕ Kenmore Square

INDIA QUALITY INDIAN $
Map p250 (☑617-267-4499; www.indiaquality. com; 484 Commonwealth Ave; mains lunch $9,

dinner $14-17; ⊘11:30am-11pm; ✐; ⊤Kenmore) India Quality has been serving chicken curry and lamb *saag* to hungry students, daytime professionals and baseball fans since 1983 – and it repeatedly tops the lists of Boston's best Indian food. The place is rather nondescript, but the food is anything but, especially considering the reasonable prices (look for lunch specials under $10). Service is reliably fast and friendly.

UBURGER   BURGERS $

Map p250 (✐617-536-0448; www.uburger.com; 636 Beacon St; burgers $5-7; ⊘11am-11pm; ⊤Kenmore) The way burgers were meant to be: beef is ground fresh daily on the premises and burgers are made to order, with fancy (grilled mushrooms, bacon and Pepper Jack cheese) or basic (American cheese and pickles) toppings. French fries and onion rings are hand-cut and crispy-crunchy good. Also available: chicken sandwiches, hot dogs and salads, but burgers get top billing.

AUDUBON BOSTON   PUB FOOD $$

Map p250 (✐617-421-1910; www.audubonbos ton.com; 838 Beacon St; sandwiches $10-13, mains $16-19; ⊘11:30am-midnight, bar to 1am; ✐; ⊤St Mary's Street) Audubon is a long-standing Fenway favorite, which mixes minimalist decor with a friendly neighborhood vibe. Stop in to sample the intriguing cocktail menu and interesting dishes like crispy salt and pepper shrimp and fantastic veggie burgers. Highly recommended for grabbing a bite before the Sox game.

★ISLAND CREEK
OYSTER BAR   SEAFOOD $$$

Map p250 (✐617-532-5300; www.islandcreek oysterbar.com; 500 Commonwealth Ave; oysters $3, mains lunch $13-21, dinner $24-36; ⊘4-11pm Mon-Fri, 11:30am-11:30pm Sat, 10:30am-11pm Sun; ⊤Kenmore) Island Creek claims to unite farmer, chef and diner in one space – and what a space it is. It serves up the region's finest oysters, along with other local seafood, in an ethereal new-age setting. The specialty – lobster-roe noodles topped with braised short ribs and grilled lobster – lives up to the hype.

✕ Fenway

★EVENTIDE FENWAY   SEAFOOD $

Map p250 (✐617-545-1060; www.eventide oysterco.com; 1321 Boylston St; mains $9-16;

⊘11am-11pm; ☎; ⊤Fenway) James Beard award winners Mike Wiley and Andrew Taylor opened this counter-service version of their beloved Maine seafood restaurant. Fast, fresh and fabulous, the menu features just-shucked oysters and brown-butter lobster rolls, along with some pretty sophisticated seafood specials. Wash it down with a craft beer or a glass of rosé and the whole experience feels (and tastes) gourmet.

EL PELON   MEXICAN $

Map p250 (✐617-262-9090; www.elpelon.com; 92 Peterborough St; mains $6-9; ⊘11am-11pm; ✐; ⊤Fenway) If your budget is tight, don't miss this chance to fill up on Boston's best burritos, tacos and tortas, made with the freshest ingredients. The *tacos de la casa* are highly recommended, especially the *pescado,* made with crispy cod and topped with chili mayo. Plates are paper and cutlery is plastic.

TASTY BURGER   BURGERS $

Map p250 (✐617-425-4444; www.tastyburger. com; 1301 Boylston St; burgers $5-6; ⊘11am-2am; ⊤Fenway) Once a Mobil gas station, this place is now a retro burger joint, with picnic tables outside and a pool table inside. The name is a nod to *Pulp Fiction,* as is the wall-mounted poster of Samuel L Jackson, whose character would surely agree that 'this is a tasty burger.'

GYRO CITY   GREEK $

Map p250 (✐617-266-4976; www.gyrocity boston.com; 88 Peterborough St; mains $9-10; ⊘11am-11pm Mon-Sat, to 9pm Sun; ✐; ⊤Fenway) This authentic *gyrotico* fits right in on Peterborough St, with cheap, scrumptious, filling food. There are a variety of gyros, each with a delightful twist (eg french fries on the traditional pork gyro) – as well as baklava made by a real live Greek mama. Counter seating inside, patio seating outside.

TAPESTRY   PIZZA $$

Map p250 (✐617-421-4470; www.tapestry.res taurant; 69 Kilmarnock St; mains brunch $12-14, dinner $15-23, pizzas $14-17; ⊘5:30-10pm Tue-Thu & Sun, to 11pm Fri & Sat, plus 10:30am-2:30pm Sat & Sun; ⊤Fenway) At this dual-concept restaurant, chefs toss pizzas and shuck oysters in the sharp but casual setting of the Expo Kitchen. The adjacent Club Room is a higher-end lounge where diners sample innovative New American dishes – you may need help identifying some of the unfamiliar ingredients. On weekends, brunch is served on the front patio.

CITIZEN PUBLIC HOUSE   AMERICAN $$
Map p250 (☑617-450-9000; www.citizenpub.com; 1310 Boylston St; mains $16-24; ⊙11am-1:30am; ⊤Fenway) This is a dark, urban gastropub with food and drinks for a refined palate. There is an eye-catching and daily-changing raw bar, while the short list of main dishes focuses on roasts and grills. It's all complemented by an extensive bar menu, featuring over 200 varieties of whiskey.

DRINKING & NIGHTLIFE

Most bars in the vicinity of Fenway Park unsurprisingly cater to sports fans. While many are forgettable, a few complement and enhance the hysteria.

Kenmore Square

★BLEACHER BAR   SPORTS BAR
Map p250 (☑617-262-2424; www.bleacherbarboston.com; 82a Lansdowne St; ⊙11am-1am Sun-Wed, to 2am Thu-Sat; ⊤Kenmore) Tucked under the bleachers at Fenway Park, this classy bar offers a view onto center field. It's not the best place to watch the game, as it gets packed, but it's a fun way to experience America's oldest ballpark, even when the Sox are not playing.

If you want a seat in front of the window, get your name on the waiting list an hour or two before game time; once seated, diners have 45 minutes in the hot seat.

HAWTHORNE   COCKTAIL BAR
Map p250 (☑617-532-9150; www.thehawthornebar.com; 500a Commonwealth Ave; ⊙4pm-1am; ⊤Kenmore) Located in the basement of the Hotel Commonwealth, this is a living-room-style cocktail lounge that attracts the city's sophisticates. Sink into the plush furniture and sip a custom cocktail.

EASTERN STANDARD   COCKTAIL BAR
Map p250 (☑617-532-9100; www.easternstandardboston.com; 528 Commonwealth Ave; ⊙7am-2am; ⊤Kenmore) Whether sitting in the swish, brasserie-style interior or on the heated patio (open year-round), you're sure to enjoy the upscale atmosphere at this Kenmore Sq favorite. French bistro fare, with a hint of New American panache (mains $15 to $30), caters to a pregame crowd that prefers wine and cheese to peanuts and popcorn. Great people-watching on game nights.

CHEEKY MONKEY BREWING   BREWERY
Map p250 (☑617-859-0030; www.cheekymonkeyboston.com; 3 Lansdowne St; ⊙5pm-2am Mon-Fri, from noon Sat & Sun; ☎; ⊤Kenmore) A big brewing and drinking complex with plenty of potential. The service and food are variable, but the space is sweet and everybody loves the beer, which includes a couple of different IPAs, a stout, a fruity wheat beer, and other seasonal choices. Besides the Cheeky Monkey brews, there are pool and ping-pong tables and shuffleboard courts.

LOWER DEPTHS TAP ROOM   BAR
Map p250 (☑617-266-6662; www.thelowerdepths.com; 476 Commonwealth Ave; ⊙4pm-1am Mon-Thu, from 11:30am Fri-Sun; ⊤Kenmore) This subterranean space is a beer lover's paradise, with all the atmosphere (and beer knowledge) of its sister establishment, Bukowski Tavern (p115). Besides the impressive beer selection, the kitchen – under the direction of beloved Boston chef Brian Poe – turns out a tasty array of tacos and tater tots. Cash only.

CORNWALL'S   PUB
Map p250 (☑617-262-3749; www.cornwalls.com; 654 Beacon St; ⊙noon-2am Mon-Fri, 4pm-2am Sat, open Sun during home games only; ⊤Kenmore) It's not a sports bar, or a dive bar, or a cocktail bar. It's a pub. An English pub – there's a clue in the extensive list of English beers, both draft and bottled. Friendly and family-run, Cornwall's has board games, darts and pool tables to keep the drinkers entertained.

LANSDOWNE PUB   IRISH PUB
Map p250 (☑617-247-1222; www.lansdownepubboston.com; 9 Lansdowne St; cover $5; ⊙4pm-2am Mon-Fri, from 10am Sat & Sun; ⊤Kenmore) Disclaimer: this place gets packed with college kids on weekends and on game nights. If you can stand the happy, sweaty people, it's a great vibe, especially if the Sox are winning. But if you're not into baseball, maybe you'll like the trivia (Wednesday), live-band karaoke (Thursday) or cover band dance parties (Friday and Saturday).

BILL'S BAR
CLUB

Map p250 (☎617-247-1222; www.billsbarboston. com; 5 Lansdowne St; ⊙5pm-2am; ⓉKenmore) Once the unofficial 'Dirty Rock Club' of this strip, Bill's Bar is still an obligatory stop if you're clubbing on Lansdowne St. Not your first stop, though, as the scene only starts to pick up around 11pm. This scrubby joint is reminiscent of the Lansdowne St of bygone days – a contrast to the glossier venues on this stretch.

🍸 Fenway

PAVEMENT COFFEEHOUSE
CAFE

Map p250 (☎617-236-1500; www.pavement coffeehouse.com; 1096 Boylston St; ⊙7am-8pm; 🛜; ⓉHynes) Exposed brick walls hung with art create a bohemian atmosphere at this coffee lovers' dream. Berklee students and other creative types congregate for fair-trade coffee, bagel sandwiches, including many veg-friendly options (such as vegan cream cheese).

MACHINE
GAY

Map p250 (Ramrod; ☎617-266-2986; www.ma chineboston.club; 1256 Boylston St; ⊙noon-2am; ⓉKenmore) This long-standing gay favorite practically guarantees a fun night out, partially because it's two clubs in one, upstairs and downstairs. So there are two different entertainment options nearly every night of the week, including All Star Drag Mondays, Latin Fridays, Hip Hop Saturdays, Sunday Pajama Parties and much more. Cash only.

☆ ENTERTAINMENT

Fenway is an obvious destination for live music, either classical or contemporary pop and rock. But there are other entertainment options as well. If you packed your thinking cap, check out the MFA's highbrow film events and film festivals.

★BOSTON RED SOX
BASEBALL

Map p250 (☎617-226-6666; www.redsox.com; 4 Jersey St; bleachers $10-45, grandstand $23-87, box $38-189; ⓉKenmore) From April to September you can watch the Red Sox play at Fenway Park, the nation's oldest and most storied ballpark. Unfortunately it is also the most expensive – not that this stops the

---

❶ CLASSIC ON THE CHEAP

The Boston Symphony Orchestra often offers various discounted ticket schemes, which might allow you to hear classical music on the cheap:

➡ Same-day 'rush' tickets ($10) are available for Tuesday and Thursday evening performances (on sale from 5pm) as well as Friday afternoon performances (on sale from 10am).

➡ Check the schedule for occasional Open Rehearsals, which usually take place in the afternoon midweek. General admission tickets are $18 to $30.

➡ Discounted tickets are offered for certain segments of the population (eg under 40=$20).

➡ Tomorrow's BSO musicians are today's New England Conservatory musicians. NEC concerts and recitals are often free!

Fenway faithful from scooping up the tickets. There are sometimes game-day tickets on sale, starting 90 minutes before the opening pitch.

Head to Gate E on Lansdowne St; arrive early (but no earlier than five hours before game time) and be prepared to enter the ballpark as soon as you purchase your tickets. Otherwise, you can always get tickets in advance from online vendors or on game-day from scalpers around Kenmore Sq. If the Sox are doing well, expect to pay two times the face value (less if you wait until after the game starts).

★BOSTON SYMPHONY ORCHESTRA
CLASSICAL MUSIC

Map p250 (BSO; ☎617-266-1200, 617-266-1492; www.bso.org; 301 Massachusetts Ave; tickets $30-145; ⓉSymphony) Flawless acoustics match the ambitious programs of the world-renowned Boston Symphony Orchestra. From September to April, the BSO performs in the beauteous Symphony Hall (p124), featuring an ornamental high-relief ceiling and attracting a well-dressed crowd. In summer months the BSO retreats to Tanglewood in Western Massachusetts.

BOSTON POPS
CLASSICAL MUSIC

Map p250 (☎617-266-1200; www.bostonpops. org; 301 Massachusetts Ave; tickets $40-175; ⓉSymphony) Playing out of the delightful

WHAT'S IN A NAME?

For more than four decades, the road on the west side of Fenway Park was called Yawkey Way, named for the former owner of the Red Sox. In 2018, with the blessing of current Red Sox ownership, city officials changed it back to its original Jersey St.

Namesake Tom Yawkey – Red Sox owner from 1933 until his death in 1976 – was revered for the good work of his family foundation. But during Yawkey's tenure, while society and baseball changed, the team and the city did not, sparking allegations of racism. Red Sox management resisted efforts to integrate, and Yawkey passed on the chance to sign baseball greats Jackie Robinson and Willie Mays. The Red Sox were the last all-white team in the major leagues, holding out until 1959 to sign their first African American player.

The racist legacy of the organization, as well as the city, plagued the franchise well after Yawkey's death. Even now, this seemingly progressive city has a reputation for overtly racist displays, especially by sports fans. *The Boston Globe* documented that athletes reported more incidents of being targeted by racial slurs in Boston than in any other city in the past 25 years (including one highly publicized incident in 2017).

In an attempt to make Fenway Park more welcoming to all, current Red Sox owner John Henry led the push to revert the street name, telling local newspapers that he was 'haunted' by the club's history. The Red Sox are also involved in the Take the Lead Campaign (www.taketheleadboston.org), an initiative to end hate speech and to promote diversity and inclusion on the fields.

Symphony Hall, the Boston Pops arranges crowd-pleasers for the orchestra to tackle, including Christmas carols, movie scores and thematic mischief. Conductor Keith Lockhart has been making Boston hearts swoon since 1995. Real live pop stars, such as Ben Folds, Amy Mann and Elvis Costello, have also been known to front the Pops.

HUNTINGTON
THEATRE COMPANY   THEATER
Map p250 (Boston University Theatre; 617-266-7900; www.huntingtontheatre.org; 264 Huntington Ave; Symphony) Boston's leading theater company, the award-winning Huntington specializes in developing new plays, staging many shows before they're transferred to Broadway (several of which have won Tony Awards). The company's credentials include over 50 world premieres of works by playwrights such as Tom Stoppard and Christopher Durang.

NEW ENGLAND
CONSERVATORY   CLASSICAL MUSIC
Map p250 (NEC; Jordan Hall; 617-585-1100; www.necmusic.edu; Jordan Hall, 30 Gainsborough St; Northeastern; Symphony) Founded in 1867, the NEC is the country's oldest music school. The conservatory hosts professional and student chamber and orchestral concerts in the acoustically superlative Jordan

Hall, which dates from 1904. Admission is often free.

HOUSE OF BLUES   LIVE MUSIC
Map p250 (888-693-2583; www.hob.com/boston; 15 Lansdowne St; Kenmore) This legendary place was originally founded by Dan Aykroyd and Isaac Tigrett in a historic house in Harvard Square. Now the slick Fenway venue is bigger and better than ever (well, bigger), attracting national acts and some indie bands. The balcony seating offers an excellent view of the stage, while fighting the crowds on the mezzanine can be brutal.

🏃 SPORTS & ACTIVITIES

JILLIAN'S & LUCKY STRIKE   BOWLING
Map p250 (www.jilliansboston.com; 145 Ipswich St; 11am-2am Mon-Sat, from noon Sun; Kenmore) Bowling, billiards, and gettin' jiggy with it. That's what you can do at this enormous (but usually packed), three-story entertainment complex, which also has seven bars and a full-service menu. On the 2nd floor, the 24 pool tables are in pristine condition. Upstairs, the high-tech bowling alley has only 16 flashy lanes, so it's often a long wait.

Seaport District & South Boston

Neighborhood Top Five

1 **Institute of Contemporary Art** (ICA; p131) Spending an afternoon at the striking waterfront site, contemplating the artistic curiosities on display and admiring the stunning harbor and city views.

2 **Boston Tea Party Ships** (p132) Brushing up on Revolutionary War history by boarding replicas of the historic ships and tossing crates of tea into the harbor.

3 **Row 34** (p133) Slurping down seafood delicacies and sipping craft beers at this beloved oyster bar.

4 **Drink** (p137) Sidling up to the bar for some serious swilling at Boston's coolest cocktail bar.

5 **Edward M Kennedy Institute for the United States Senate** (p133) Witnessing (and participating in) the workings of the legislative process in the replica Senate chamber.

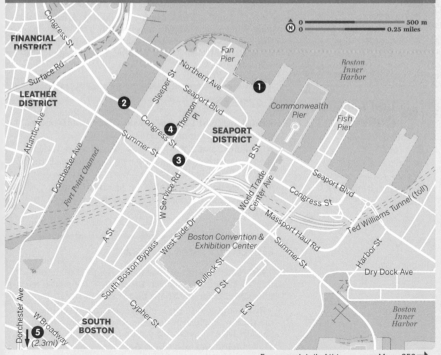

For more detail of this area see Map p252 ➡

Lonely Planet's Top Tip

Thursday nights are free at the **Institute of Contemporary Art**, while Friday nights at the **Boston Children's Museum** (p132) are only $1. The reduced admission is from 5pm to 9pm in both cases.

Best Places to Eat

➡ Row 34 (p133)

➡ Yankee Lobster Co (p133)

➡ Sportello (p136)

➡ Legal Harborside (p136)

For reviews, see p133.➡

Best Places to Drink

➡ Drink (p137)

➡ Trillium Fort Point (p137)

➡ Lucky's Lounge (p137)

➡ Croke Park Whitey's (p137)

➡ Lookout Rooftop Bar (p137)

For reviews, see p137.➡

◎ Best Lookout Points

➡ Founders Gallery, ICA (p131)

➡ Castle Island (p132)

➡ John F Kennedy Presidential Library & Museum (p133)

For reviews, see p131.➡

Explore Seaport District & South Boston

Separated from Boston proper by the Fort Point Channel, the Seaport District has always afforded a spectacular vista of the Boston Harbor and downtown Boston. Now this hot district offers all kinds of opportunities to see and savor it. Follow the HarborWalk around the Moakley Federal Courthouse to enjoy the landscaped parks and fantastic views from Fan Pier, eventually ending up at the Institute of Contemporary Art (p131). Further east, the wharves were once dominated by fish-processing facilities and a marine industrial center. Now, restaurants, bars and retail outlets are opening in the new buildings. The hot dining and drinking scene means that this area is super lively at night. Rooftop bars and restaurants take advantage of the amazing harbor views, while chefs old and new offer their most innovative cooking.

Meanwhile, the rest of South Boston remains well off the beaten path. Former stomping ground of Whitey Bulger and preferred setting for Boston-based mafia movies, 'Southie' lives large in local and national lore. Despite its reputation, South Boston has its own charm. The waterside community offers great harbor views, as well as Boston's best city beaches. On a hot summer day, Castle Island (p132) is a windy, welcoming waterside playscape for families and outdoorsy types. The 'hood is packed with Irish pubs, but there are also a few notable New American restaurants, should you care to drink something other than Guinness or PBR. This area is getting a glimpse of the gentrification that has transformed other parts of the city, but Southie is still unapologetically old-school.

Local Life

➡ **Drinking Joint 1** Boston's favorite local beer is brewed right here at Trillium Fort Point (p137).

➡ **Drinking Joint 2** You know it's a local hangout when they don't bother to put a proper sign outside, as is the case at Lucky's Lounge (p137).

➡ **Drinking Joint 3** For a singular picture of South Boston, chat up the regulars at Croke Park Whitey's (p137).

Getting There & Away

➡ **Metro** It's a 10-minute walk from South Station (red line) to the Seaport District; Broadway Station (also red line) sits at the top of South Boston's main street.

➡ **Bus** Connected to the metro system, the silver-line bus (SL1 or SL2) travels from South Station through the Seaport District, with stops at Courthouse, the World Trade Center and Silver Line Way.

TOP SIGHT
INSTITUTE OF CONTEMPORARY ART

Boston has become a focal point for contemporary art in the 21st century, as hundreds of thousands of visitors flock to the dramatic quarters of the Institute of Contemporary Art. In addition to its innovative collections, the spacious, light-filled interior hosts multimedia presentations, educational programs and studio space.

Founders Gallery

Arguably, the ICA building and setting are as much of an attraction as the art. Opened in 2006, the structure skillfully incorporates its surroundings into the architecture. In the Founders Gallery, which spans the entire width of the building, a glass wall virtually eliminates any barrier between viewer and seascape.

Permanent Collection

In addition to dynamic temporary exhibits, the ICA showcases national and international artists in its permanent collection. You'll find the likes of graffiti artist Shepard Fairey, conceptual artist Gillian Wearing, video artist Christian Jankowski, photographer Boris Mikhailov and sculptor Sarah Sze. Look for all manner of art, from painting to video to multidimensional mixed-media mash-ups.

Mediatheque

The museum's digital media center, where visitors learn more about featured art and artists. The terraced room has a wall of windows at the front, but the room's unique downward-slanting perspective shows only the dancing and rippling of water, with no horizon in sight.

DON'T MISS

➡ Fineberg Art Wall in the lobby

➡ *Peace Goddess* and other powerful pieces by Shepard Fairey

➡ *Hanging Fire (Suspected Arson)* by Cornelia Parker

➡ View from the Founders Gallery

PRACTICALITIES

➡ ICA

➡ Map p252, C1

➡ ☏617-478-3100

➡ www.icaboston.org

➡ 25 Harbor Shore Dr

➡ adult/child $15/free, Thu 5-9pm free

➡ ⊗10am-5pm Tue, Wed, Sat & Sun, to 9pm Thu & Fri

➡ 🚻

➡ 🚌SL1, SL2, Ⓣ South Station

⊙ SIGHTS

For all its ongoing development, the Seaport District is not really a sightseeing destination, with only a handful of museums and galleries. That said, several of the museums are truly excellent, including the Institute of Contemporary Art and the Boston Tea Party Ships & Museum.

⊙ Seaport District & South Boston

INSTITUTE OF CONTEMPORARY ART
MUSEUM

See p131.

BOSTON TEA PARTY
SHIPS & MUSEUM   MUSEUM

Map p252 (☎866-955-0667; www.bostontea partyship.com; Congress St Bridge; adult/child $30/18; ⊙10am-5pm; ⛟; TSouth Station) 'Boston Harbor a teapot tonight!' To protest against unfair taxes, a gang of rebellious colonists dumped 342 chests of tea into the water. The 1773 protest – the Boston Tea Party – set into motion the events leading to the Revolutionary War. Nowadays, replica Tea Party Ships are moored at Griffin's Wharf, alongside an excellent experiential museum dedicated to the catalytic event. Using re-enactments, multimedia and fun exhibits, the museum addresses all aspects of the Boston Tea Party and subsequent events.

Visitors can board the fully rigged *Eleanor* and the whaler *Beaver* to experience life aboard an 18th-century vessel. Would-be rebels can throw crates of tea into the harbor, in solidarity with their fiery forebears. To hear both sides of the story, visitors can witness a virtual debate between Sam Adams and King George III (though in reality they never met). The museum's one actual artifact – a tea crate known as the Robinson Half Chest – is highlighted with an audio presentation.

Tickets are expensive, considering it's a small museum. Save a couple of dollars by purchasing tickets online.

BOSTON CHILDREN'S MUSEUM   MUSEUM

Map p252 (☎617-426-6500; www.bostonchild rensmuseum.org; 308 Congress St; $17, Fri 5-9pm $1; ⊙10am-5pm Sat-Thu, to 9pm Fri; ⛟; TSouth Station) ✿ The interactive, educational exhibits at the delightful Boston Children's Museum keep kids entertained for hours. Highlights include a bubble exhibit, rock-climbing walls, a hands-on construction site and intercultural immersion experiences. The light-filled atrium features an amazing three-story climbing maze. In nice weather kids can enjoy outdoor eating and playing in the waterside park. Look for the iconic Hood Milk Bottle (p136) on Fort Point Channel.

FORT POINT ARTS COMMUNITY   GALLERY

Map p252 (FPAC; ☎617-423-4299; www.fort pointarts.org; 300 Summer St; ⊙variable; TSouth Station) FREE This refurbished big-windowed warehouse is the hub of the Fort Point Arts Community, and contains a gallery featuring work from the talented collective. See huge psychedelic oils, prints inspired by 14th-century Venetian laces, lampshades made from birch, and mixed-media films. Several times a year, FPAC hosts popular open-studio events that allow you to see the artists' working spaces as well as their creations.

⊙ South Boston

CASTLE ISLAND
& FORT INDEPENDENCE   PARK

Map p252 (Marine Park; ⊙dawn-dusk May-Sep; ⛟; ☐11, TBroadway) FREE The 19th-century Fort Independence sits on 22 acres of parkland called Castle Island (a misnomer, as it's connected to the mainland). A paved pathway follows the perimeter of the peninsula – good for strolling or cycling – and there is a small swimming beach. Kids get a kick out of watching the low-flying planes heading in and out of Logan Airport.

From the Seaport District, walk south on Summer St for about a half-mile, then turn left on East 1st St and continue to the waterfront.

DORCHESTER HEIGHTS   MONUMENT

Map p252 (btwn G & Old Harbor Sts; ⊙dawn-dusk; ☐11, TBroadway) High above Boston Harbor, this strategic spot played a crucial role in overcoming the British occupation. The Georgian Revival tower that stands today was built in 1898 but it is not open to the public. To reach the monument, walk southeast along West Broadway from the T station, turn right onto Dorchester St and head up any of the little streets.

COLUMBIA POINT

Columbia Point juts into the harbor south of the city center in Dorchester, one of Boston's poorer neighborhoods. The location is unexpected, but it does offer dramatic views of the sea. It's a four-mile stroll or ride along the HarborWalk from Castle Island to Columbia Point. Otherwise, take the red line to JFK/UMass and catch a free shuttle bus (departures every 20 minutes).

John F Kennedy Presidential Library & Museum (Map p252; ☑617-514-1600; www. jfklibrary.org; adult/child $14/10; ☺9am-5pm; T JFK/UMass) The legacy of JFK is ubiquitous in Boston, but the official memorial to the 35th president is the presidential library and museum – a striking, modern, marble building designed by IM Pei. The architectural centerpiece is the glass pavilion, with soaring 115ft ceilings and floor-to-ceiling windows overlooking Boston Harbor. The museum is a fitting tribute to JFK's life and legacy. The effective use of video re-creates history for visitors who may or may not remember the early 1960s.

Edward M Kennedy Institute for the United States Senate (EMK Institute; Map p252; ☑617-740-7000; www.emkinstitute.org; adult/child $16/8; ☺10am-5pm Tue-Sun; T JKF/UMass) Ted Kennedy served in the US Senate for nearly half a century. It is fitting, therefore, that his legacy should include an institute and museum designed to teach the public about the inner workings of democracy. Opened in 2015, this state-of-the-art facility uses advanced technology, multimedia exhibits and interactive designs to engage visitors and demonstrate the functioning (and sometimes non-functioning) of the legislative process. The museum centerpiece is a full-scale replica of the Senate chamber.

In the winter of 1776, rebel troops dragged 59 heavy cannons to Boston from Fort Ticonderoga in upstate New York. On the night of March 4, they perched them high atop Dorchester Heights, from where the British warships in the Harbor were at their mercy. The move caught the British completely by surprise, and ultimately convinced them to abandon Boston.

✗ EATING

The Seaport District isn't just for seafood anymore. You'll do well if you wish to feast on seafood near the former fishing wharf, but you can also enjoy's Boston's most creative cooking, sampling world cuisines with many modern touches. Deeper into South Boston, the options are more limited, but even the pickiest palates can find something satisfying.

✗ Seaport District

FLOUR   CAFE $
Map p252 (☑617-338-4333; www.flourbakery. com; 12 Farnsworth St; pastries $2.25-5, salads & sandwiches $9.50-10.50; ☺6:30am-8pm Mon-Fri, 8am-6pm Sat, to 5pm Sun; ☎⏚♿; T South Station) ✔ Flour implores patrons to 'make life sweeter...eat dessert first!' It's hard to resist at this pastry-lover's paradise. If you can't decide – and it can be a challenge – go for the melt-in-your-mouth brioche sticky buns. But dessert is not all: delicious sandwiches, salads and grain bowls are also available. Flour is a Certified Green Restaurant.

YANKEE LOBSTER CO   SEAFOOD $
Map p252 (☑617-345-9799; www.yankeelobster company.com; 300 Northern Ave; mains $11-26; ☺10am-9pm Mon-Sat, 11am-6pm Sun; ☒SL1, SL2, T South Station) The Zanti family has been fishing for three generations, so they definitely know their stuff. A relatively recent addition is this retail fish market, scattered with a few tables in case you want to dine in. And you do. Order something simple like clam chowder or a lobster roll, accompany it with a cold beer, and you won't be disappointed.

★ROW 34   SEAFOOD $$
Map p252 (☑617-553-5900; www.row34.com; 383 Congress St; oysters $2-3, mains $14-32; ☺11:30am-10pm Sun-Thu, to 11pm Fri & Sat; T South Station) In the heart of the new Seaport District, set in a sharp, postindustrial

1. Lobster is a Boston favorite **2.** Barking Crab (p136)
3. Lobster roll **4.** Clam chowder

TORRESIGNER / GETTY IMAGES ©

2

Seafood Capital

What's so special about seafood in Boston? As one local restaurant used to boast, 'the fish is so fresh it jumps out of the water and onto your plate.'

Chowder

Ask 10 locals for Boston's best chowder and you'll get 10 different answers. This thick, cream-based soup is chock-full of clams or fish, although clam chowder, using the meaty insides of giant surf clams, is more prevalent.

Clams & Oysters

Many seafood restaurants showcase their shellfish at a raw bar. Any self-respecting raw bar will have a selection of hard-shelled clams. The most famous type of oysters are Wellfleet oysters from Cape Cod; they're eaten raw, with a dollop of cocktail sauce and a few drops of lemon juice. For a raw-bar experience, head to Row 34 (p133) or Neptune Oyster (p62).

You can also get clams deep-fried or steamed (aka 'steamers').

4

Lobster

Traditionally, lobsters are steamed or boiled, then it's up to the patron to crack the shell to get the succulent meat out. A less labor-intensive choice is a lobster roll, where the lobster meat is dressed with a little mayonnaise and stuffed into a grilled, buttered hot-dog roll. Either way, you can't go wrong at Yankee Lobster Co (p133).

Fish

Atlantic codfish has played such an important role in the region's culture and economy that it is known as the 'sacred cod,' and a carved wooden effigy hangs in the Massachusetts State House.

BEST PLACES FOR CLAM CHOWDER

➡ Legal Harborside (p136)

➡ Island Creek Oyster Bar (p125)

➡ Neptune Oyster (p62)

➡ Atlantic Fish Co (p114)

➡ Barking Crab (p136)

HOOD MILK BOTTLE

Towering 40ft over Fort Point Channel, the giant **Hood Milk Bottle** (Map p252) would hold 50,000 gallons of milk if it could hold a drop (that's 800,000 glasses of milk, if anybody's counting). This unlikely landmark was built in 1934 to house an ice-cream stand, which it did for 30-odd years. The milk bottle was finally purchased by Hood Milk, New England's largest and oldest dairy, and moved to its current location. Open for sandwiches and snacks during summer months.

space, this place offers a dozen types of raw oysters and clams, alongside an amazing selection of craft beers. There's also a full menu of cooked seafood, ranging from the traditional to the trendy.

LEGAL HARBORSIDE
SEAFOOD $$
Map p252 (617-477-2900; www.legalseafoods.com; 270 Northern Ave; mains $18-30; 11am-10pm Sun-Thu, to 11pm Fri & Sat; SL1, SL2, South Station) This vast glass-fronted waterfront complex offers three different restaurant concepts on three floors. Our favorite is the 1st floor – a casual restaurant and fish market that is a throwback to Legal's original outlet from 1904. The updated menu includes a raw bar, small plates, seafood grills and plenty of international influences. There is outdoor seating in the summer months.

BARKING CRAB
SEAFOOD $$
Map p252 (617-426-2722; www.barkingcrab.com; 88 Sleeper St; sandwiches $14-18, mains $18-36; 11:30am-10pm Sun-Wed, to 11pm Thu-Sat; SL1, SL2, South Station) Big buckets of crabs (snow, king, Dungeness etc), steamers dripping in lemon and butter, paper plates piled high with all things fried, pitchers of ice-cold beer... Devour your feast at communal picnic tables overlooking the water. Service is slack, noise levels are high, but the atmosphere is jovial. Prepare to wait for a table if the weather is warm.

COMMITTEE
GREEK $$
Map p252 (617-737-5051; www.committeeboston.com; 50 Northern Ave; lunch mains $10-20, dinner meze $10-18; 11:30am-11pm Sun-Wed, to midnight Thu-Sat; ; SL1, SL2, South

Station) This trendy spot serves small plates, it's true, but they're not talking about pita bread and hummus. These are Greek meze, featuring irresistible dishes like lamb souvlaki, artichoke moussaka and grilled octopus. Drinks include craft beers, Greek wine, unique cocktails and ouzo.

SPORTELLO
ITALIAN $$$
Map p252 (617-737-1234; www.sportelloboston.com; 348 Congress St; mains $24-29, 2-course lunch prix fixe $32; 11:30am-11pm; South Station) Modern and minimalist, this brainchild of Barbara Lynch fits right in to this up-and-coming urban 'hood. At the *sportello*, or lunch counter, suited yuppies indulge in sophisticated soups and salads and decadent polenta and pasta dishes. It's a popular spot, which means it's usually a tight squeeze, but the attentive waitstaff ensure that everybody is comfortable and content.

MENTON
EUROPEAN $$$
Map p252 (617-737-0099; www.mentonboston.com; 354 Congress St; lunch mains $24-30, dinner mains $26-45, dinner tasting menus $165; 11:30am-2pm Mon-Fri, 5:30-10pm Tue-Sat, 5:30-9pm Sun & Mon; South Station) Boston's favorite celebrity chef Barbara Lynch has outdone herself at this high-class conglomeration of classic European cuisine and modern American innovation, set in a revamped warehouse in the edgy, eclectic Seaport District. The setting and the cooking are sophisticated and wholly satisfying – sure ingredients for a stylish business lunch or a memorable night out.

🍴 South Boston

South Boston is not a dining destination. But if you happen to be in the neighborhood, you'll find a decent variety of restaurants along West Broadway (near the Broadway T station).

SULLIVAN'S
FAST FOOD $
Map p252 (617-268-5685; www.sullivanscastleisland.com; 1080 Day Blvd; mains $3-10; 8:30am-5pm Mar-Nov, to 10pm in summer; ; 11, Broadway) A Southie tradition since 1951, Sullivan's is beloved for hot dogs in the casing, known as 'Sully's snappers.' In 60-plus years, the price of those dogs has increased by more than 10 times – making them a whopping $2.10. Fried seafood,

burgers and soft-serve ice cream round out the menu. You can't miss Sullivan's at the entrance to Castle Island.

LOCAL 149 GASTROPUB $$

Map p252 (☑617-269-0900; www.local149.com; 149 P St; mains $16-22; ☺4-10pm Mon-Thu, 11am-11pm Fri-Sun, bar to 1am; ☐11, ⊤Broadway) Southie's first gastropub puts a curious, local-with-a-twist on things, which might catch you off guard. But why wouldn't you want a lobster scramble for brunch or tuna tartare sandwich with fried oysters for dinner? Besides the interesting menu, there is a great beer list, including nearly 20 selections on draft, many of which are brewed nearby.

Walk about one mile south from Castle Island along the shoreline.

⬤ DRINKING & ⬥ NIGHTLIFE

The Seaport has transformed into one of Boston's hottest spots for drinking and nightlife, thanks to a proliferation of rooftop bars, vast entertainment complexes, local breweries and trendy cocktail bars. Head further into South Boston for an authentic Boston Irish experience. Pubs galore line East and West Broadway.

⬤ Seaport District

★DRINK COCKTAIL BAR

Map p252 (☑617-695-1806; www.drinkfortpoint. com; 348 Congress St; ☺4pm-1am; ☐SL1, SL2, ⊤South Station) There is no cocktail menu at Drink. Instead you have a chat with the bartender, and he or she will whip something up according to your mood and taste. It takes seriously the art of mixology – and you will too, after you sample one of its concoctions. The subterranean space, with its low-lit, sexy ambience, makes a great date destination.

TRILLIUM FORT POINT MICROBREWERY

Map p252 (☑857-449-0083; www.trilliumbrew ing.com; 50 Thompson Pl; ☺11am-11pm; ⊤South Station) Trillium has been brewing beer in the Fort Point area for years. But it was only in 2018 that they opened this fantastic new

tap room, complete with bar, dining room and rooftop deck. Enjoy the full range of Trillium favorites – not only India pale ales, but also American pale ales, gose ales, wild ales and stouts.

LOOKOUT ROOFTOP BAR BAR

Map p252 (☑617-338-3030; www.theenvoy hotel.com; Envoy Hotel, 70 Sleeper St; ☺4-11pm Mon-Thu, to midnight Fri & Sat, from noon Sun; ☐SL1, SL2, ⊤South Station) This trendy bar starts filling up almost as soon as it opens, as hotel guests and local workers ascend to the rooftop to take in potent drinks and spectacular views. When temperatures drop, there are heaters and igloos to keep you warm. Note the dress code.

LUCKY'S LOUNGE COCKTAIL BAR

Map p252 (☑617-357-5825; www.luckyslounge. com; 355 Congress St; ☺11:30am-2am Mon-Fri, from 10am Sat & Sun; ☐SL1, SL2, ⊤South Station) Keep alert or you'll miss the hidden entrance into this subterranean space, home to a delightful lounge that looks straight out of 1959. Enjoy well-priced drinks, excellent martinis and cover bands playing tunes, though there's not much room for dancing. Sinatra Sunday Brunch remains a perpetual favorite.

HARPOON BREWERY
& BEER HALL BREWERY

Map p252 (☑617-456-2322; www.harpoonbrew ery.com; 306 Northern Ave; ☺beer hall 11am-7pm Sun-Wed, to 11pm Thu-Sat, tours noon-5pm Mon-Wed, to 6pm Thu-Sun; ☐SL1, SL2, ⊤South Station) Take an hour-long tour ($5) to see how the beer is made and to sample some of the goods. Or just take a seat at the bar in the beer hall and watch the action from above.

⬤ South Boston

CROKE PARK WHITEY'S BAR

Map p252 (☑617-606-5971; www.crokepark whiteys.com; 268 W Broadway; ☺noon-2am; ⊤Broadway) Whitey's is everything a dive bar is supposed to be, with cheap beer, free pool, free popcorn and a cast of colorful local characters propping up the bar. This is old-school Southie, and it's not nearly as scary as it's made out to be in the movies. Potent mixed drinks are served in pint glasses, as are Guinness and PBRs.

Walk a half-mile south from Broadway station.

☆ ENTERTAINMENT

Visitors to the Seaport District are amply entertained, with live music, comedy and cutting-edge performing arts.

BARBARA LEE FAMILY FOUNDATION THEATER
THEATER

Map p252 (☑617-478-3100; www.icaboston.org; 25 Harbor Shore Dr; ⬚SL1, SL2, ⓣSouth Station) Against a gorgeous, blue-water backdrop, the glass theater at the ICA (p131) is one of its coolest features and a venue for dance, music and other performance art. The ICA also hosts occasional film festivals and screenings of offbeat and arty cinema.

LAUGH BOSTON
COMEDY

Map p252 (☑617-725-2844; www.laughboston.com; 425 Summer St; $20-30; ⊙times vary Wed-Sun; ⬚SL1, SL2, ⓣSouth Station) The funny guys over at Improv Asylum decided that Boston needed a few more laughs, so they opened this premier, stand-up comedy club in the Westin Hotel. The place has a swanky, happy atmosphere, and there's pro-gramming five nights a week. In addition to local and national acts, look out for The Moth, the legendary true-story slam.

BLUE HILLS BANK PAVILION
LIVE MUSIC

Map p252 (☑617-728-1600; www.bostonpavilion.net; 290 Northern Ave; ⬚SL1, SL2, ⓣSouth Station) A white sail-like tent with sweeping harbor views, this is a great venue for sum-mer concerts. It seats about 5000 people, so you can actually see the smiling faces of the performers on stage.

🛍 SHOPPING

You wouldn't come to the Seaport District to shop. But if you happen to be in the neighborhood, you'll be delighted by the scattering of galleries and artsy-craftsy shops among the bars and restaurants.

★FOR NOW
CONCEPT STORE

Map p252 (☑857-233-4639; www.itsfornow.com; 68 Seaport Blvd; ⊙10am-7pm Mon-Fri, 10am-6pm Sat, 11am-5pm Sun; ⓣSouth Station) Calling itself a 'retail incubator' and a 'pop-up col-lective,' For Now showcases a constantly changing and growing collection of local and regional designers and brands. Come in to browse and you'll likely find fashion-

forward clothing, shoes, jewelry, handbags, stationery, body-care products and home-wares. Or something else completely unex-pected, but totally unique.

SOCIETY OF ARTS & CRAFTS
ARTS & CRAFTS

Map p252 (SAC; ☑617-266-1810; www.societyofcrafts.org; 100 Pier 4, Suite 200; ⊙10am-6pm Tue, Wed, Fri & Sat, to 9pm Thu, 11am-5pm Sun; ⬚SL1, SL2, ⓣSouth Station) After 120 years, this prestigious nonprofit gallery is still fulfilling its mission to promote emerging and established artists and to encourage innovative handicrafts. In a spacious locale on the Boston waterfront, the SAC offers a craft library, lectures and workshops, in ad-dition to retail and exhibit space.

🏃 SPORTS & ACTIVITIES

THE LAWN ON D
PLAYGROUND

Map p252 (☑877-393-3393; www.signatureboston.com/lawn-on-d; 420 D St; ⊙7am-10pm; ⬚SL1, SL2) This open-air 'adult playground' is a fun summer destination. At the heart of the experience is SwingTime, a set of glow-in-the-dark swings (yes, for adults), lit by multicolored, solar-powered LEDs. The vast lawn and adjacent tented area host a variety of special events each summer, fea-turing food, drink, movie nights, games and live music.

CARSON BEACH
SWIMMING

Map p252 (☑617-727-8865; Day Blvd; ⊙dawn-dusk; 🚻; ⬚11, ⓣBroadway) Heading west from Castle Island (p132), 3 miles of beach-es offer opportunities for swimming in an urban setting. L and M St beaches are ad-jacent to each other along Day Blvd, while Carson Beach is further west. They all have smooth sand, nice harbor views, decent fa-cilities and frigid water.

KINGS
BOWLING

Map p252 (☑617-401-0025; www.kings-de.com; 60 Seaport Blvd; ⊙noon-1:30am Mon-Sat, 11am-midnight Sun; ⬚SL1, SL2, ⓣSouth Station) This is a massive entertainment complex offer-ing all types of indoor recreation (starting at the bar). In addition to the 16 bowling lanes, there are pool tables, air hockey, shuffleboard and foosball, as well as an old-fashioned 'retro' arcade. Yes, they have PacMan.

Cambridge

HARVARD SQUARE | CENTRAL & KENDALL SQUARES

Neighborhood Top Five

❶ Harvard Square (p144) Browsing the bookstores, rifling through the records and trying on vintage clothing, then camping out in a local cafe to watch the world go by.

❷ Minuteman Bikeway (p155) Cycling from urban Cambridge to idyllic Bedford on this car-free bike trail, taking in scenery and history along the way.

❸ Harvard Art Museums (p142) Checking out the varied collections (European, Asian and more) and superb architecture at this university gem.

❹ Massachusetts Institute of Technology (p143) Exploring the riverside campus and discovering its fantastic, eclectic collection of public art.

❺ Mt Auburn Cemetery (p144) Strolling around in search of famous gravestones, impressive artwork and elusive birds in this gorgeous garden cemetery.

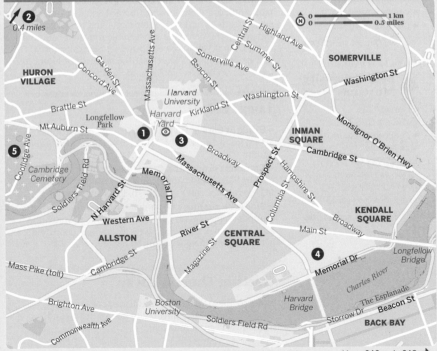

For more detail of this area see Map p246 and p248 ➡

Lonely Planet's Top Tip

The **Harvard Book Store** (p153) hosts lectures, author talks and book readings almost every night, Monday to Friday, presenting a cool opportunity to hobnob with local writers and scholars.

Best Places to Eat

➡ Area Four (p147)

➡ Waypoint (p147)

➡ Toscanini's (p146)

➡ Giulia (p145)

For reviews, see p144. ➡

Best Places to Drink

➡ Café Pamplona (p147)

➡ Lamplighter Brewing Co (p150)

➡ A4cade (p150)

➡ Green Street (p150)

➡ LA Burdick (p149)

For reviews, see p147. ➡

Best University Museums

➡ Harvard Art Museums (p142)

➡ Peabody Museum of Archaeology & Ethnology (p142)

➡ Harvard Museum of Natural History (p142)

➡ MIT Museum (p143)

For reviews, see p142. ➡

Explore Cambridge

Here, we count Cambridge as one among many 'neighborhoods' in Boston. But truth be told, this independent town has the historical and cultural offerings to rival many major cities. Certainly, it matches Boston for quality (if not quantity) and diversity of drinking, dining and entertainment options. Exploring museums, historic sites and university landmarks, you could just as easily spend a day as spend a year.

Much of life in Cambridge is centered on the universities – Harvard (p141) and MIT (p143) – each of which occupies its respective corner of town, with restaurants, shops and clubs clustered around each campus. If you have limited time, you'll probably want to choose one or the other. (Harvard or MIT...? MIT or Harvard...? Now you can appreciate the dilemma prospective students face).

Both universities provide excellent, free campus tours – Harvard is packed with history, while MIT has a wealth of public art and innovative architecture. Both universities have interesting and unusual museums showcasing cutting-edge art and science. Both universities have excellent dining and entertainment options in their vicinities. So, take your pick.

All that said, only Harvard has Harvard Square. Brimming with coffee houses and pubs, bookstores and record stores, street musicians and sidewalk artists, panhandlers and professors, Harvard Square exudes energy, creativity and nonconformity – and it's all packed into a handful of streets between the university and the river. Even if you have your heart set on exploring MIT and its environs, it's worth setting aside a few hours to hang out up the road in Harvard Square.

Local Life

➡ **Student bars** Local life is student life. To see it in action go to Shays Pub & Wine Bar (p149) in Harvard Square.

➡ **Campus corners** JFK Park is a favorite local spot for picnics, dogs and Frisbee, while the area outside the MIT Stratton Center attracts students and pigeons.

➡ **Sidewalk seating** The outdoor plazas at the Smith Campus Center (p142) give front-row seats to watch the buskers, homeless, chess-players, good-deed-doers and general Harvard Square hullabaloo.

Getting There & Away

➡ **Metro** Take the red line to Harvard station for Harvard Square, Central station for Central Sq and Kendall/MIT for Kendall Sq.

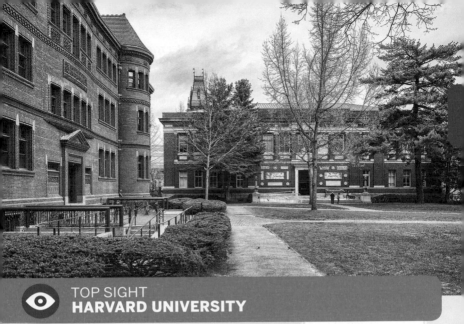

Founded in 1636 to educate men for the ministry, Harvard is America's oldest college. While the university now occupies vast areas in Cambridge, Allston and further afield, its geographic and historic heart remains at Harvard Yard. This is where red-brick buildings and leaf-covered lawns exude academia, where students congregate to study and socialize, and where graduates proudly receive their degrees.

DON'T MISS

→ John Harvard Statue
→ Memorial Hall

PRACTICALITIES

→ Map p246, E6
→ ☎617-495-1000
→ www.harvard.edu
→ Massachusetts Ave
→ tours free
→ ⓣHarvard

Harvard Yard

Flanking Johnston Gate are the two oldest buildings on campus. South of the gate, **Massachusetts Hall** (1720) houses the offices of the President of the University. It is the oldest building at Harvard and one of the oldest academic buildings in the country. North is **Harvard Hall** (1766), which originally housed the library.

The focal point of the **yard** is the **John Harvard Statue**, where every Harvard hopeful has a photo taken (and touches the statue's shiny shoe for good luck). Daniel Chester French's sculpture, inscribed 'John Harvard, Founder of Harvard College, 1638,' is known as the 'statue of three lies': it does not actually depict Harvard (since no image of him exists), but a random student; John Harvard was not the founder of the college, but its first benefactor in 1638; and the college was actually founded two years earlier in 1636. The Harvard symbol hardly lives up to the university's motto, *Veritas,* or 'truth.'

Memorial Hall

North of Harvard Yard, just outside Bradstreet Gates and across the Plaza, this massive Victorian Gothic building was built to honor Harvard's Civil War heroes. The impressive Memorial Transept is usually open for visitors to admire the stained-glass windows and stenciled walls. Most of the building's artistic treasures are contained in Annenburg Hall, which is not open to the public.

THE PLAZA

Just outside Bradstreet Gate on the north side of Harvard Yard, the Plaza is a lively outdoor space, replete with food trucks, farmers markets, ping-pong tables and other seasonal recreation.

Free historical tours of Harvard Yard depart from the Smith Campus Center; self-guided tours also available.

HARVARD BY NUMBERS

The original Ivy League school educates 6500 undergraduates and 12,000 graduate students yearly in 10 professional schools. Its alumni include eight US Presidents and dozens of Nobel Laureates and Pulitzer Prize winners.

Climb the steps of Robinson Hall for a perfectly framed photo of Memorial Hall.

WIDENER LIBRARY

The Harvard library was built in memory of rare-book collector Harry Elkins Widener, who perished on the *Titanic*. Apparently Harry gave up his seat in a lifeboat to retrieve his favorite book from his stateroom.

Smith Campus Center

After a massive overhaul, the **Smith Campus Center** (617-495-6916; www.commonspaces.harvard.edu/smith-campus-center/about; 30 Dunster St; 7am-midnight Sun-Fri, to 1am Sat) has been transformed into a fabulous 'living room' for students and visitors to congregate, study, socialize, eat and drink. The two-story lobby is abloom with 12,000 plants, growing on the living walls and irrigated by rainwater collected on the roof.

Harvard Art Museums

The 2014 renovation and expansion of Harvard's art museums allowed the university's massive 250,000-piece collection to come together under one very stylish **roof** (617-495-9400; www.harvardartmuseums.org; 32 Quincy St; adult/child/student $15/free/free; 10am-5pm), designed by architect extraordinaire Renzo Piano. The artwork spans the globe, with separate collections devoted to Asian and Islamic cultures, northern European and Germanic cultures and other Western art.

Harvard Science Museums

The centerpiece of the **Peabody Museum of Archaeology & Ethnology** (617-496-1027; www.peabody.harvard.edu; 11 Divinity Ave; adult/child/student $15/10/10; 9am-5pm; 86, Harvard) is the impressive Hall of the North American Indian, which traces how these peoples responded to the arrival of Europeans from the 15th to 18th centuries. Other exhibits examine indigenous cultures throughout the Americas, including a fantastic comparison of cave paintings and murals of the Awatovi (New Mexico), the Maya (Guatemala) and the Moche (Peru).

The **Harvard Museum of Natural History** (617-495-3045; www.hmnh.harvard.edu; 26 Oxford St; adult/child/student $15/10/10; 9am-5pm; 86, Harvard) is famed for its botanical galleries, featuring some 3000 pieces of handblown, intricately crafted glass flowers and plants. Nearby, the zoological galleries house an enormous number of stuffed animals and skeletons, as well as an impressive fossil collection.

Collection of Scientific Instruments

Science-lovers can geek out at this small but fascinating **museum** (617-495-2779; www.chsi.harvard.edu; 1 Oxford St; 11am-4pm Sun-Fri) FREE. Located inside the Harvard Science Center, it showcases a selection of the 20,000 items in the university collection, some of which date to the 15th century. Look for the geometric sector designed by Galileo, and the clocks illustrating the development of modern timekeeping. The collection was actually compiled by one Benjamin Franklin, so add that to his résumé.

TOP SIGHT
MASSACHUSETTS INSTITUTE OF TECHNOLOGY

The **Massachusetts Institute of Technology (MIT)** offers a completely novel perspective on Cambridge academia: proudly nerdy, but not quite as tweedy as Harvard. A recent frenzy of building has resulted in some of the most architecturally intriguing structures you'll find on either side of the river. Also noteworthy: the fantastic (and growing) collection of public art and a couple of unusual museums.

Leave it to the brainiacs at MIT to come up with the city's quirkiest museum – the **MIT Museum** (☏617-253-5927; http://mitmuseum.mit.edu; 265 Massachusetts Ave; adult/child $10/5; ☉10am-6pm Jul & Aug, to 5pm Sep-Jun; P; TCentral). Exhibits explore questions about art, technology and everything in between, focusing on subjects as diverse as robotics, holograms, model ships and interactive sculpture. Expect great things from the MIT Museum in the coming years, as it is due to move into a larger facility in Kendall Square in 2021.

Of all the eye-catching buildings on the MIT campus, none has received more attention than the **Stata Center** (CSAIL; ☏617-253-5851; www.csail.mit.edu; 32 Vassar St) . The avant-garde edifice was designed by architectural legend Frank Gehry.

Small but subversive, the **List Visual Arts Center** (☏617-253-4680; http://listart.mit.edu; 20 Ames St, Weisner Bldg; donation $5; ☉noon-6pm Tue, Wed & Fri-Sun, to 8pm Thu) is a venue for art in its broadest forms, staging exhibits that ask probing questions about culture, society and science. This is also where you can pick up a map of MIT's magnificent collection of public art, including pieces by Alexander Calder, Sol LeWit and Henry Moore scattered around campus.

DON'T MISS

→ MIT's signature sculpture, *La Grande Voile*, by Alexander Calder
→ Henry Moore's bronze reclining figures
→ Stata Center

PRACTICALITIES

→ MIT
→ Map p248, D5
→ ☏617-253-1000
→ www.mit.edu
→ 77 Massachusetts Ave
→ ☉info session incl campus tour 10am & 2:30pm Mon-Fri
→ TKendall/MIT

◉ SIGHTS

Cambridge is an epicenter of student life, thanks to the presence of two powerhouse universities, Harvard and Massachusetts Institute for Technology (MIT). These renowned academic institutions are worth visiting for their leafy campuses, striking architecture and unique museums. Boston's neighbor to the north is also rich in colonial and postcolonial history, with most of the historic sights clustered around Harvard Square.

◉ Harvard Square

HARVARD UNIVERSITY UNIVERSITY
See p141.

★ MT AUBURN CEMETERY CEMETERY
(📞617-547-7105; www.mountauburn.org; 580 Mt Auburn St; ⊙8am-8pm May-Sep, to 5pm Oct-Apr; 🚇71, 73, Ⓣ Harvard) This delightful spot at the end of Brattle St is worth the 30-minute walk west from Harvard Square. Developed in 1831, it was the first 'garden cemetery' in the US. Maps pinpoint the rare botanical specimens and notable burial plots. Famous long-term residents include Mary Baker Eddy (founder of the Christian Science Church) and Henry Wadsworth Longfellow (19th-century writer).

Other noteworthy residents include Isabella Stewart Gardner (socialite and art collector), Oliver Wendell Holmes (US supreme court justice) and Winslow Homer (19th-century American painter). For more guidance, rent an audio tour at the gatehouse or download the Mt Auburn app.

TORY ROW STREET
Map p246 (Brattle St; Ⓣ Harvard) Heading west out of Harvard Square, Brattle St is the epitome of colonial posh. Lined with mansions that were once home to royal sympathizers, the street earned the nickname Tory Row. Nowadays, it's a delightful place for a stroll to admire the gracious homes and glean some history from the environs.

LONGFELLOW HOUSE HISTORIC BUILDING
Map p246 (📞617-876-4491; www.nps.gov/long; 105 Brattle St; ⊙tours 9:30am-5pm Wed-Sun late May-Oct, grounds dawn-dusk year-round; 🚇71, 73, Ⓣ Harvard) FREE Brattle St's most famous resident was Henry Wadsworth Longfellow,

whose stately manor is now a National Historic Site. The poet lived here from 1837 to 1882, writing many of his most famous poems, including 'Evangeline' and 'The Song of Hiawatha.' Accessible by guided tour, the Georgian mansion contains many of Longfellow's belongings and is surrounded by lush period gardens.

Incidentally, one reason Longfellow was so taken with this house was its historical significance. During the Revolutionary War, General Washington appropriated this beauty from its absent Loyalist owner and used it as his headquarters.

CAMBRIDGE COMMON PARK
Map p246 (cnr Massachusetts Ave & Garden St; Ⓣ Harvard) Opposite the main entrance to Harvard Yard, Cambridge Common is the village green where General Washington took command of the Continental Army on July 3, 1775. Dawes Island at the south end pays tribute to William Dawes, the 'other rider', who on April 18, 1775 warned that the British were coming (look for the bronze hoofprints embedded in the sidewalk).

Parents take note: there's an excellent playground at the northern end.

CHRIST CHURCH CHURCH
Map p246 (📞617-876-0200; www.cccambridge.org; 0 Garden St; ⊙services 7:45am & 10:15am Sun, 12:10pm Wed; Ⓣ Harvard) Cambridge's oldest church was designed in 1761 by America's first formally trained architect, Peter Harrison (who also designed King's Chapel in Boston). Washington's troops used it as a barracks after its Tory congregation fled. Adjacent to the church, the Old Burying Ground is a tranquil Revolutionary-era cemetery, where Harvard's first eight presidents are buried.

◉ Central & Kendall Squares

MASSACHUSETTS INSTITUTE OF TECHNOLOGY UNIVERSITY
See p143.

EATING

From cheap eats to fine dining, Cambridge has it all, offering some of the best eating experiences in the Boston

area. **Vegetarians are particularly well cattered for on this side of the river.**

✖ Harvard Square

INSIDE SCOOP ON HAHVAHD

This company was founded by a couple of Harvard students who shared the inside scoop on history and student life at the university. Now **Hahvahd Tour** (Trademark Tours; Map p245; ☑855-455-8747; www.harvardtour.com; adult/child $12/10.50; Ⓣ Harvard) offers a whole menu of Boston tours, but the funny, offbeat Hahvahd Tour is the trademark. Tour guides are students who are not afraid to ask for tips.

HOKKAIDO RAMEN
SANTOUKA JAPANESE $
Map p246 (☑617-945-1460; www.santouka.co.jp/en; 1 Bow St; mains $11-17; ⊙11am-9:30pm Mon-Thu, to 10:30pm Fri & Sat, to 9pm Sun; Ⓣ Harvard) This worldwide chain is bringing a bit of Japanese simplicity and subtlety to Harvard Square. Service is pleasant and fast, while the noodles are perfectly satisfying.

DARWIN'S LTD SANDWICHES $
Map p246 (☑617-354-5233; www.darwinsltd.com; 148 Mt Auburn St; sandwiches $9-12; ⊙6:30am-8pm Mon-Sat, from 7:30am Sun; 🛜✍; Ⓣ Harvard) Punky staff serve fat sandwiches, fresh soup and salads, and delicious coffee and pastries, all with a generous helping of attitude. The limited seating is often occupied by students who are in for the long haul (thanks to wi-fi access). So unless you need to get online, take your lunch to enjoy at JFK Park or Radcliffe Yard.

MR BARTLEY'S
BURGER COTTAGE BURGERS $
Map p246 (☑617-354-6559; www.mrbartley.com; 1246 Massachusetts Ave; burgers $14-21; ⊙11am-9pm Tue-Sat; Ⓣ Harvard) Packed with small tables and hungry college students, this burger joint has been a Harvard Square institution for more than 50 years. Bartley's offers two dozen different burgers, including topical newcomers with names like Trump Tower and Tom Brady Triumphant; sweet-potato fries, onion rings, thick frappés and raspberry-lime rickeys complete the classic American meal.

Be aware that credit cards not accepted; no bathroom on-site.

NIGHT MARKET ASIAN $
Map p246 (☑857-285-6948; www.nightmkt.com; 75 Winthrop St; plates $8-18; ⊙5-10pm Sun & Tue-Thu, to 11pm Fri & Sat; ✍; Ⓣ Harvard) This super-hip, seemingly 'secret,' subterranean spot dishes up skewers, noodles and other smallish servings that fuse Asian and other international cuisines (think carnitas tacos with Thai green curry). There's an interesting beer selection, along with irresistible sake slushies. The combos are fun but not mind-blowing; the clever concept, graffiti-covered walls and spot-on service earn the A+.

CLOVERHSQ VEGETARIAN $
Map p246 (www.cloverfoodlab.com; 1326 Massachusetts Ave; mains $8-11; ⊙11am-11pm Mon-Sat, to 10pm Sun; 🛜✍♿; Ⓣ Harvard) 🖉 Clover is on the cutting edge. It's all high-tech with its 'live' menu updates and electronic ordering system. But it's really about the food – local, seasonal, vegetarian – which is cheap, tasty and fast. How fast? Check the menu.

CAMBRIDGE, 1 PIZZA $$
Map p246 (☑617-576-1111; www.cambridge1.us; 27 Church St; pizzas $22-30; ⊙11:30am-11pm; ✍; Ⓣ Harvard) This pizzeria is located in an old fire station – its name comes from the sign chiseled into the stonework out front. The interior is sleek, sparse and industrial, with big windows at the back overlooking the Old Burying Ground. The menu is equally simple: pizza, soup, salad, dessert. The oddly shaped pizzas are delectable, with crispy crusts and creative toppings.

RED HOUSE MODERN AMERICAN $$
Map p246 (☑617-576-0605; www.theredhouse.com; 98 Winthrop St; lunch $11-22, dinner $19-37; ⊙noon-11pm; ✍; Ⓣ Harvard) Formerly known as the Cox-Hicks House, this quaint clapboard house dates to 1802. Reminiscent of an old-fashioned inn, it retains its historic charm with wide-plank wood floors, cozy layout and functioning fireplace. The patio overlooks a quiet corner of Harvard Square – a good summertime spot. Seafood and pasta dominate the menu.

★ GIULIA ITALIAN $$$
Map p246 (☑617-441-2800; www.giuliarestaurant.com; 1682 Massachusetts Ave; mains $21-31;

CAMBRIDGE EATING

COOKING COURSES

Patron food-saint Julia Child, longtime Cambridge resident and star of many cooking shows, spent four decades teaching people to cook before she died in 2004. If you want to embody Julia's *bon vivant* spirit, take a cooking class at **Cambridge School of Culinary Arts** (☑617-354-2020; www.cambridgeculinary. com; 2020 Massachusetts Ave; TPorter). The recreation division of this professional school offers one-time courses focusing on seasonal meals such as 'An American Gathering' or on crucial cooking skills such as the 'Art of Grilling' or 'Fish Cookery'. Several times a week there are special 'Cooking Couples' classes, focusing on tapas, sushi, wine pairing and more. Located two blocks north of the Porter Sq T station.

⊙5:30-10pm Mon-Thu, to 11pm Fri & Sat; THarvard, Porter) A half-mile north of Harvard Square, this intimate Italian restaurant opened in 2012 to universal acclaim. Chef Michael Pagliarini's sophisticated, locally sourced creations range from grilled veal with asparagus and wild greens to homemade tortelli stuffed with lamb, sorrel and pecorino cheese. Larger parties can sit family-style at the long oak table.

ALDEN & HARLOW
AMERICAN $$$

Map p246 (☑617-864-2100; www.aldenharlow. com; 40 Brattle St; small plates $15-18; ⊙10:30am-2pm Sat & Sun, 5pm-midnight Sun-Wed, to 1am Thu-Sat; ☑; THarvard) This subterranean space is offering a fresh take on American cooking. The small plates are made for sharing, so everyone in your party gets to sample the goodness. It's no secret that the 'Secret Burger' is amazing. Service sometimes suffers when the place get busy, which is often. Reservations recommended.

✕ Central & Kendall Squares

★TOSCANINI'S
ICE CREAM $

Map p248 (☑617-491-5877; www.tosci.com; 899 Main St; ice cream from $4; ☎; TCentral) People come from miles around for Tosci's burnt-caramel ice cream, which apparently was invented as the result of an accident (you can imagine). Besides the dozens of delicious ice-cream flavors, there is also excellent coffee.

ROXY'S GRILLED CHEESE
SANDWICHES $

Map p248 (☑617-945-7244; www.roxysgrilled cheese.com; 292 Massachusetts Ave; sandwiches $5-9; ⊙11am-11pm Sun-Thu, to midnight Fri & Sat; ☑⬛; TCentral) What started as a food truck is now an actual restaurant, specializing in exotic combinations of bread and cheese (plus some other ingredients). There are still some food trucks roaming around town, but none of them have an arcade in the back room (p150).

DUMPLING HOUSE
CHINESE $

Map p248 (☑617-661-8066; www.dumpling housecambridgema.com; 950 Massachusetts Ave; lunch specials $9, mains $8-18; ⊙11am-10pm; TCentral) Midway between Central and Harvard, this bustling spot is the sister restaurant to the Chinatown favorite Gourmet Dumpling House (p98). If you're a fan of soup dumplings, you'll love it here. There are more than a dozen variants of dumplings to try, in addition to many specialties from both northern and southern Chinese cuisine. Service is fast and furious.

WHOLE HEART PROVISIONS
VEGAN $

Map p248 (☑617-945-8991; www.wholeheart provisions.com; 298 Massachusetts Ave; mains $9-11; ⊙10:30am-10pm; ☑; TCentral) Appealing to health-conscious and earth-conscious eaters, this convivial place serves up lunch (or dinner) in a bowl. Choose one of the signature specialties or create your own, then take a seat at the communal tables and dig in. Regulars also love the Sunday brunch, featuring 'huevos' rancheros and yummy pancakes.

BON ME
VIETNAMESE $

Map p248 (☑617-945-2615; www.bonmetruck. com; 1 Kendall Sq; mains $7-10.50; ⊙11am-8pm; TKendall/MIT) Bon Me started as a food truck that catered to the Kendall Sq crowd, and you'll still see the trucks tooling around town. This little storefront sells the same, simple, fresh, insanely good Vietnamese fare. Choose your dish (sandwich, rice or noodles), filling (chicken, pork or tofu), and extras (edamame, papaya, greens or deviled eggs), eat up and enjoy.

LIFE ALIVE
VEGETARIAN $

Map p248 (☑617-354-5433; www.lifealive.com; 765 Massachusetts Ave; mains $7-10; ⊗8am-11pm Mon-Sat, 10am-10pm Sun; ☑♿; Ⓣcentral) 🌿 Life Alive offers a joyful, healthful, purposeful approach to fast food. The unusual combinations of animal-free ingredients yield delicious results, most of which come in a bowl (like a salad) or in a wrap. There are also soups, sides and smoothies, all served in a colorful, light-filled space.

VEGGIE GALAXY
DINER $

Map p248 (☑617-497-1513; www.veggiegalaxy.com; 450 Massachusetts Ave; mains $8-14; ⊗9am-10pm Sun-Thu, to 11pm Fri & Sat; ☑; Ⓣcentral) What does the word 'diner' mean to you? All-day breakfasts? Check. Burgers and milkshakes? Check. Counter seating and comfy booths? Got those, too. A circular glass display case showing off desserts? Yes, complete with tangy lemon-meringue pie. In short, Veggie Galaxy does everything that a diner is supposed to do, but it does it without meat.

FRIENDLY TOAST
DINER $

Map p248 (☑617-621-1200; www.thefriendlytoast.com; 1 Kendall Sq; mains $9-16; ⊗8am-9pm Sun-Thu, to 10pm Fri & Sat; ☑; Ⓣkendall/MIT) Some people think that this retro diner is one of the best places to eat breakfast *in the country*. Decadent delights such as coconut pancakes, six kinds of eggs Benedict, and loads of vegetarian and vegan options have hungry folks lining up out the door for weekend brunch. (Use the NoWait app to avoid the weekend lines.)

MIRACLE OF SCIENCE
BAR & GRILL
AMERICAN $

Map p248 (☑617-868-2866; www.miracleofscience.us; 321 Massachusetts Ave; mains $10-15; ⊗11am-midnight, bar to 1am; Ⓣcentral) With all the decor of your high-school science lab, this bar and grill was a pioneer of geek chic. The menu takes the form of the periodic table posted on the wall, so you get the idea. Join the MIT wannabes for burgers, kebabs and other grilled fare, as well as a choice selection of beers on tap.

★WAYPOINT
GASTRONOMY $$

Map p246 (☑617-864-2300; www.waypointharvard.com; 1030 Massachusetts Ave; mains $16-25; ⊗10am-2:30pm Sun, 5pm-1am daily; Ⓣharvard) After his success at Alden & Harlow, chef Michael Scelfo turned his attention to seafood and other 'coastally inspired fare'. The wide-ranging menu includes a raw bar, original pizzas, decadent pasta dishes and whole roasts for the table. There is some pretty daring stuff here, so come with an open mind as well as an empty stomach.

★AREA FOUR
CAFE, PIZZA $$

Map p248 (☑617-758-4444; www.areafour.com; 500 Technology Sq; pizza $18-28; ⊗11:30am-10pm Mon-Fri, 10:30am-10pm Sat & Sun, cafe from 7am daily; 🛜☑; Ⓣkendall/MIT) The post-industrial vibe at Area Four is perfect for the high-tech block where it's located (and for which it's named). Doubling as a cool cafe and modern pizzeria, Area Four offers strong coffee and pastries by day, and local brews, sustainable wines and wood-fired pizzas by night. Eat and drink your way around the clock.

LITTLE DONKEY
TAPAS $$

Map p248 (☑617-945-1008; www.littledonkeybos.com; 505 Massachusetts Ave; small plates $10-20; ⊗11am-11pm Mon-Fri, 10am-11:30pm Sat, 10am-11pm Sun; Ⓣcentral) Ken Oringer and Jamie Bissonnette's latest culinary venture, this high-ceilinged but cozy brick-walled bistro serves tapas with an international twist. Take raw bar offerings like oysters and ceviche to great heights (literally) on the showy triple-decker Donkey Platter ($135), or order à la carte items like *manti* (Turkish-inspired meat ravioli), halibut biryani, or black pepper popovers with wagyu steak tartare.

🍷 DRINKING & NIGHTLIFE

There are plenty of students in Cambridge, which means there are loads of places to drink. Beyond the dirty dives and student hangouts (of which there are many), you'll also find coffee shops, local breweries, cocktail lounges and wine bars.

🍷 Harvard Square

★CAFÉ PAMPLONA
CAFE

Map p246 (☑617-492-0392; www.cafepamplona.weebly.com; 12 Bow St; ⊗11am-10pm; 🛜; Ⓣharvard) Located in a snug cellar on a backstreet, this no-frills European cafe is the

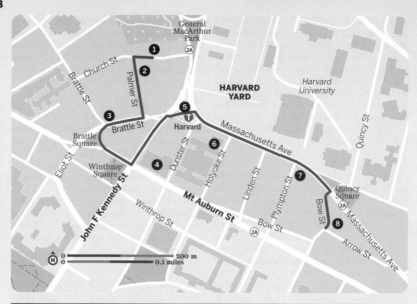

🏃 Local Life
Offbeat Harvard Square

Harvard Square is overflowing with cafes, bookstores, record shops and street musicians. Although many Cantabrigians rightly complain that the area has lost its edge, Harvard Square still has a thriving counterculture, if you know where to look. This route takes in some of the square's offbeat spots, both old and new.

❶ Raven Used Books
Beloved by scholars, dilettantes and anyone who likes to browse, this used-bookshop (p153) is a trove of nonfiction treasures, especially on history, art and culture. Pop in for a quick look, but don't be surprised when you're still there an hour later.

❷ Club Passim
Back in the day, Club 47 hosted the likes of Joan Baez, Bob Dylan and Joni Mitchell on its storied stage. Now known as Club Passim (p151), the basement joint still hosts top folk music acts.

❸ Brattle Square
Close to the historic Brattle Theatre (p151), this intersection is a main stage for street performers. Tracy Chapman played here in the 1980s and Amanda Palmer busked as a living statue in the 1990s. Puppeteer Igor Fokin performed here until his unexpected death in 1996. Look for the tiny memorial

sculpture erected to honor him – and by extension, all street performers.

❹ The Garage
You can feel the grit at this parking garage turned **mini-mall** (Map p246; ☑617-354-5096; 36 John F Kennedy St; ☉10am-10pm Mon-Sat, 11am to 8pm Sun; ☩Harvard). Some of the shops change frequently but a few long-standing institutions – especially Newbury Comics and Chameleon Tattoo & Body Piercing – attract a steady stream of goths, punks and other loyal shoppers.

❺ The Pit
In the center of Harvard Square, **Out of Town News** (Map p246; ☑617-354-1441; Harvard Sq; ☉6am-10pm Sun-Thu, to 11pm Fri & Sat; ☩Harvard) has been selling newspapers and magazines from around the world since 1955. The sunken area nearby, aka 'the Pit,' is a popular spot for street artists,

Harvard Book Store (p153)

skateboarders and counterculture youth to congregate.

⑥ Smith Campus Center

The plaza in front of the Smith Campus Center (p142) has hosted an ongoing chess tournament for 30 years and counting – look for the 'Play the Chessmaster' sign. It's also a top spot to take in the buskers, beggars and other Harvard Square goings-on.

⑦ Harvard Book Store

The Harvard Book Store (p153) is not just a bookstore, but a reading community. Come in to browse the stacks and check out discounted 'seconds' in the basement. Next door, Grolier Poetry Bookshop (p153) is a one of the country's most esteemed poetry bookstores, having hosted many famous poets since its founding in 1927.

⑧ Café Pamplona

For sustenance, make your way to this atmospheric Spanish-style cafe (p147) in a cozy backstreet cellar, which has been serving coffee and tea to Cantabrigian bohemians since 1959.

top choice among old-time Cantabrigians. In addition to tea and coffee, Pamplona serves up snacks such as soup, sandwiches and biscotti. The tiny outdoor terrace is a delight in summer; when the weather cools down, order *sopa de ajo* (garlic soup) to warm your soul.

LA BURDICK   CAFE
Map p246 (☎617-491-4340; www.burdickchocolate.com; 52 Brattle St; ⊗8am-9pm Sun-Wed, to 10pm Thu-Sat; ⊤Harvard) This boutique chocolatier doubles as a cafe, usually packed full of happy patrons drinking hot cocoa. Whether you choose dark or milk, it's sure to be some of the best chocolate you'll drink in your lifetime. There are only a handful of tables, so it's hard to score a seat when temperatures are chilly.

SHAYS PUB & WINE BAR   PUB
Map p246 (☎617-864-9161; www.shayspubwinebar.com; 58 John F Kennedy St; ⊗11am-1am Mon-Sat, noon-1am Sun; ⊤Harvard) A charming basement-level bar, Shays is an enduring favorite among Harvard students – definitely more 'pub' and less 'wine bar.' Inside, it's an intimate space that's often crammed with friendly folks noshing on excellent burgers and appetizers. Out front is a small brick patio full of sun-seekers jockeying for a table and watching the sidewalk goings-on.

BEAT BREW HALL   BEER HALL
Map p246 (☎617-499-0001; www.beatbrewhall.com; 13 Brattle St; ⊗4pm-midnight Mon-Wed, to 1am Thu, to 2am Fri, 10am-2am Sat, 10am-midnight Sun; ⊤Harvard) This vast, underground nightspot, formerly the Beat Brasserie, has morphed into the Beat Brew Hall (not a bad shtick, but it's a shame to bid farewell to the brasserie). It has about two dozen craft brews on tap that you can quaff at communal tables. For fun, there's billiards, shuffleboard and lots of televisions.

CHARLIE'S KITCHEN   BAR
Map p246 (☎617-492-9646; www.charlieskitchen.com; 10 Eliot St; ⊗11am-1am Sun-Wed, to 2am Thu-Sat; ⊤Harvard) Charlie's is a three-in-one. Downstairs is a lovable greasy spoon serving burgers and bargain-price lobster rolls late into the night; upstairs is a much beloved dive bar blasting The Cars from the jukebox. And outside, there's a rocking, year-round beer garden with 22 taps. The kids love this place – just as they have for 40 years and counting.

⚲ Central & Kendall Squares

★LAMPLIGHTER BREWING CO   BREWERY
Map p248 (☑617-945-0450; www.lamplighter brewing.com; 284 Broadway; ⊘11am-midnight Tue-Sat, to 10pm Sun; ⓉCentral) This East Cambridge brewery and taproom is a favorite Boston hangout. In addition to the flights and pints of frothy goodness, there are free beer snacks and board games, plus a front-row view of the beer-brewing process.

A4CADE   BAR
Map p248 (☑617-714-3960; www.areafour.com; 292 Massachusetts Ave; ⊘5pm-1am Mon-Fri, noon-1:30am Sat & noon-midnight Sun; ⓉCentral) Slipping through a barely marked door inside Roxy's Grilled Cheese, you know it's gonna be good. And it is... This retro bar will whisk you back to 1980 with pinball, Pacman and other old-timey arcade games. They're made all the more fun thanks to the menu of local brews and creative cocktails (and, of course, grilled cheese sandwiches).

HAVANA CLUB   CLUB
Map p248 (☑617-312-5550; www.havana clubsalsa.com; 288 Green St; admission $5-12; ⊘8pm-midnight Mon & Thu, 9pm-2am Fri & Sat; ⓉCentral) Five nights a week, this old social club on a backstreet in Central Sq transforms into the Boston area's most happening salsa and *bachata* dance party. It's an international crowd – not just Latino – and the first hour is devoted to lessons.

GREEN STREET   COCKTAIL BAR
Map p248 (☑617-876-1655; www.greenstreet grill.com; 280 Green St; ⊘5:30pm-1am; ⓉCentral) Gritty on the outside, cozy on the inside, Green Street is a long-standing neighborhood joint that still manages to be thoroughly up-to-date – thanks in part to bartenders in flannel and killer cocktails. The urban bar and grill hints at upscale, but keeps it real with affordable prices (all cocktails under $10), tried-and-true American fare and no snoot.

LORD HOBO   CRAFT BEER
Map p248 (☑617-250-8454; www.lordhobo.com; 92 Hampshire St; ⊘4pm-1am Mon-Wed, 4pm-2am Thu & Fri, 11am-2am Sat, 11am-1am Sun; ⓉCentral) If high-caliber craft IPAs are your idea of beer-drinking bliss, make a beeline for this unassuming corner brewpub north of Central Sq. What started as a local secret has exploded in popularity, with distribution of the trademark beers Hobo Life, Boom Sauce and Consolation Prize stretching clear to Colorado.

BRICK & MORTAR   COCKTAIL BAR
Map p248 (☑617-491-5599; www.brickmortar ltd.com; 567 Massachusetts Ave; ⊘5pm-1am Sun-Wed, to 2am Thu-Sat; ⓉCentral) Enter through the unmarked door (next to Central Kitchen) and climb the dark stairs to cool cocktail heaven. No pretenses here – just a pared-down setting and a choice list of craft cocktails and beers. The staff are attentive and friendly. If you're hungry, go for the duck fries.

PLOUGH & STARS   IRISH PUB
Map p248 (☑617-576-0032; www.ploughand stars.com; 912 Massachusetts Ave; ⊘11:30am-1am Mon-Wed, 11:30am-2am Thu-Fri, 10am-2am Sat, 10am-1am Sun; 🛜; ⓉCentral) The Plough & Stars is real-deal Irish, serving up bangers, eggs and gastropub fare in a cozy wooden room with stout on tap and in bottles. Weekend soccer matches are on the telly and stringed bands play Irish tunes. Actually, there's music every night of the week – not only Irish, but also jazz, blues, rockabilly, funk and other indefinable genres.

ZUZU   CLUB
Map p248 (☑617-864-3278; www.mideastof fers.com; 474 Massachusetts Ave; cover free-$10; ⊘9pm-2am; ⓉCentral) This is a no-pretense, all-comers, dance-your-booty-off club, wedged in between (and managed by) the Middle East (p153). From Grassfed Disco to 'soulful dance music', there's some sort of dance party four nights a week. No dress code and no games at the door, which is refreshing.

CAFÉ ARTSCIENCE   COCKTAIL BAR
Map p248 (☑857-999-2193; www.cafeart science.com; 650 E Kendall St; ⊘11:30am-10pm Mon-Fri, 5-10pm Sat, bar to midnight; 🛜; ⓉKendall) Before David Edwards was a restaurateur, he was a Harvard professor and an inventor, dreaming up novelties such as Wikipearl (edible food wrapper) and oPhone (an aroma gadget). Now he's channeling his energies into the 'artscience' of food and drink. It's not as gimmicky as it sounds, though there are futuristic touches (cocktails involving vaporized alcohol, for instance).

 ENTERTAINMENT

Cambridge has unlimited options for a night out on the town, from top-notch music and theater to polished jazz and gritty rock 'n' roll; and from comedy, poetry, dancing to all manner of performance art.

☆ Harvard Square

★CLUB PASSIM   LIVE MUSIC

Map p246 (☑617-492-7679; www.clubpassim. org; 47 Palmer St; tickets $10-32; TℾHarvard) The legendary Club Passim is a holdout from the days when folk music was a staple in Cambridge (and around the country). The club continues to book top-notch acts, single-handedly sustaining the city's folk scene. The colorful, intimate room is hidden off a side street in Harvard Square, just as it has been since 1969.

AMERICAN REPERTORY THEATER   PERFORMING ARTS

Map p246 (ART; ☑617-547-8300; www.american repertorytheater.org; 64 Brattle St; tickets from $45; TℾHarvard) There isn't a bad seat in the house at the Loeb Drama Theater, where the prestigious ART stages new plays and experimental interpretations of classics. Artistic Director Diane Paulus encourages a broad interpretation of 'theater,' staging interactive murder mysteries, readings of novels in their entirety and robot operas. The ART's musical productions, in particular, have been racking up Tony awards.

SANDERS THEATRE AT MEMORIAL HALL   CONCERT VENUE

Map p246 (☑617-495-8676; www.ofa.fas. harvard.edu; 45 Quincy St; TℾHarvard) Set inside the magnificent Memorial Hall, this beautiful, 1166-seat, wood-paneled theater is known for its acoustics. It is frequently used for classical musical performances by local chorales and ensembles, as well as occasional concerts by jazz and world musicians. Buy tickets at the booth inside the Smith Campus Center (p142).

BRATTLE THEATRE   CINEMA

Map p246 (☑617-876-6837; www.brattlefilm. org; 40 Brattle St; TℾHarvard) The Brattle is a film lover's *cinema paradiso*. Film noir, independent films and series that celebrate directors or periods are shown regularly in this renovated 1890 repertory theater. Some famous (or infamous) special events include the annual Valentine's Day screening of *Casablanca* and occasional cartoon marathons.

TOAD   LIVE MUSIC

(☑617-497-4950; www.toadcambridge.com; 1912 Massachusetts Ave; ⊗5pm-1am Mon-Wed, 5pm-2am Thu-Sat, 3pm-1am Sun; TℾPorter) This tiny, laid-back place is beloved for its excellent lineup of music (seven nights a week) and its no-cover-charge policy. (Ever. At all.) Among the booze on offer there are a dozen beers on tap. You wouldn't make a special trip for the food, but there are burgers and tater tots to be had.

Located about a mile north of Harvard Square, across from the Porter Sq shopping plaza.

SINCLAIR   LIVE MUSIC

Map p246 (☑617-547-5200; www.sinclaircam bridge.com; 52 Church St; tickets $15-35; ⊗5pm-1am Mon-Wed, 5pm-2am Thu & Fri, 11am-2am Sat, 11am-1am Sun; TℾHarvard) First-rate small venue to hear live music. The acoustics are excellent and the mezzanine level allows you to escape the crowds on the floor. The club attracts a good range of local and regional bands and DJs.

LIZARD LOUNGE   LIVE MUSIC

Map p246 (☑617-547-0759; www.lizardlounge club.com; 1667 Massachusetts Ave; cover $5-15; ⊗7:30pm-late Sun & Mon, 8:30pm-late Tue-Sat; TℾHarvard) The underground Lizard Lounge doubles as a rock and jazz venue. The big drawcard is the Sunday-night poetry slam. Also popular are the Monday open-mike challenge and regular appearances by local favorite Club d'Elf. The bar stocks an excellent list of New England beers, which are complemented by the sweet-potato fries.

Located a quarter-mile north of Cambridge Common (the park), below Cambridge Common (the restaurant).

CLUB OBERON   PERFORMING ARTS

Map p246 (☑617-495-2668; www.cluboberon. com; 2 Arrow St; TℾHarvard) The second stage of the American Repertory Theater, this black box is ideally suited for flashy song and dance performances and interactive, acrobatic theater. The long-running favorite is the Shakespearean disco, *The Donkey Show,* but you might also see *The Moth* story slams, variations on burlesque

CAMBRIDGE ENTERTAINMENT

SOMERVILLE

North of Cambridge is Somerville, a gritty urban 'burb that is home to artists, students and assorted creative cats. Here, rents are cheaper (slightly), people are cooler and nightlife is hotter. Did we say 'hotter'? We meant odder. A night out in the 'Ville is anything but boring. Here are a few of our top picks:

Flatbread Co & Sacco's Bowl Haven (☑617-776-0552; www.flatbreadcompany.com; 45 Day St, Somerville; per lane per hour $30, shoe rental $3; ⊘9am-midnight Mon-Sat, to 10:30pm Sun; ♠; ⊤Davis) Founded in 1939, Sacco's Bowl Haven is a Somerville institution – old-time candlepin bowling lanes that managed to survive into the 21st century. When Flatbread Company took over they brightened the space and added clay ovens, but preserved most of the lanes and the good-time atmosphere. Now you can enjoy delicious organic pizzas and cold craft beers with your candlepins.

Aeronaut Brewing Co (☑617-987-4236; www.aeronautbrewing.com; 14 Tyler St, Somerville; ⊘6-11pm Mon, 5pm-midnight Tue-Fri, noon-12:30am Sat, noon-9:30pm Sun; ⊒86 from Harvard, ⊒87 from Lechmere) Aeronaut Brewery is a bold experiment in beer, founded by a couple of MIT grads with a passion for local ingredients and scientific methods. Down a dark alley and tucked inside a courtyard, the hidden facility is usually filled with in-the-know and high-tech types, quaffing the seasonal creations and playing Jenga.

Comedy Studio (☑617-661-6507; www.thecomedystudio.com; 1 Bow Market Way #23, Somerville; shows $10-20; ⊘show 8pm; ⊒86 from Harvard or Sullivan) This low-budget, cutting-edge comedy gem moved out of its Harvard Square noodle house digs in 2018 and settled into happening Union Sq, Somerville. Mondays are reserved for the Mystery Lounge, a weird (and hilarious) magic show. Tuesdays are called Comedy Hell (aka open mike night); and Wednesdays are for Fresh Faces.

Somerville Theatre (☑617-625-5700; www.somervilletheatreonline.com; 55 Davis Sq, Somerville; ⊤Davis) This classic neighborhood movie house dates from 1914 and features plenty of well-preserved gilding and pastel murals of muses. On offer are first-and second-run Hollywood hits, live performances by local and world musicians, and the Independent Film Festival of Boston screenings. The main theater is the biggest, best and oldest, and has the added treat of a balcony.

This gem is in Davis Sq, just a hop and a skip north from Cambridge. Don't miss the amusing Museum of Bad Art in the basement (free with your movie ticket).

theater, or some sort of politically woke performance art.

HARVARD FILM ARCHIVE CINEMATHEQUE

CINEMA

Map p246 (☑617-495-4700; https://library.harvard.edu/film/index.html; 24 Quincy St; tickets $9-12; ⊘screenings Fri-Mon; ⊤Harvard) Five nights a week, the Cinematheque presents retrospectives of distinguished actors, screenings of rare films, thematic groupings and special events featuring the filmmakers themselves. The screenings – which often sell out – take place in the 200-seat theater in the esteemed Carpenter Center for the Arts (designed by Le Corbusier). Tickets go on sale 45 minutes ahead of show times.

REGATTABAR

JAZZ

Map p246 (☑617-395-7757; www.regattabarjazz.com; 1 Bennett St; tickets $20-30; ♠; ⊤Harvard) Why does Boston have such clean jazz clubs? Regattabar looks just like a conference room in a hotel – in this case the Charles Hotel. Despite the uninspiring ambience, the sound system is excellent, it gets big enough names (James Montgomery, Mike Doughty) to transcend the mediocre space, and with only 225 seats, you're guaranteed a good view.

☆ Central & Kendall Squares

★LILY PAD

PERFORMING ARTS

Map p248 (www.lilypadinman.com; 1353 Cambridge St; tickets $5-15; ⊒91, ⊤Central) Lily

Pad is a tiny space that fills up with music and performance art, whether it's tango dancing or narrated jazz storytelling. You might also hear indie, avant-garde, folk and even chamber music. The space is stripped down – basically benches in a room – which adds to the underground ambience. There's not much here, but there is beer and wine!

IMPROV BOSTON COMEDY
Map p248 (☑617-576-1253; www.improvboston. com; 40 Prospect St; tickets $10-20; ☺Wed-Sat; ♿; ⓣCentral) This group has been making things up and making people laugh for more than a quarter of a century. Nowadays, the troupe's funny shows feature not just improv, but also comedy competitions, musical comedy and nude stand-up. The early Saturday show (4pm) is family oriented. There's free stand-up every Friday at 11:30pm for night owls.

MIDDLE EAST LIVE MUSIC
Map p248 (☑617-864-3278; www.mideastoffers. com; 472-480 Massachusetts Ave; cover $10-30; ⓣCentral) The Middle East is as good as the bands it books, which means it varies wildly. This is the preferred venue for local garage bands (hit or miss, by definition), as well as 1980s rockers and fun Euro-pop artists.

CANTAB LOUNGE LIVE MUSIC
Map p248 (☑617-354 -2685; www.cantab-lounge.com; 738 Massachusetts Ave; cover free-$10, ⓣCentral) The Cantab is one of the neighborhood's divier dives (and that's saying something in Central Sq). But the eclectic music lineup attracts an awesome mixed crowd. Tuesday night is the area's best bluegrass night, Wednesday is the poetry slam, and Thursday is the famous Chickenslacks. Friday is a get-down, old-timer sweaty dance party. Cash only.

🛍 SHOPPING

Harvard Square is home to upwards of 150 shops, all within a few blocks of the university campus. The area used to boast an avant-garde sensibility and dozens of independent stores, and vestiges of this free spirit remain. Certainly, there are still more bookstores in Harvard Square than anywhere else in the Boston area. However, many of the edgier shops have been replaced by chains, leading critics to complain that the square has become an outdoor shopping mall.

🛍 Harvard Square

★WARD MAPS MAPS
Map p246 (☑617-497-0737; www.wardmaps.com; 1735 Massachusetts Ave; ☺10am-6pm Mon-Fri, noon-5pm Sat & Sun; ⓣPorter) If you're into maps, you'll be into Ward Maps. It has an incredible collection of original antique and reproduction maps, with a special focus on Boston, Cambridge and Somerville. What's more, maps are printed on coffee mugs, mouse pads, journals and greeting cards, making unique gifts. There's also an awesome selection of T-station signs and other vintage MBTA paraphernalia.

HARVARD BOOK STORE BOOKS
Map p246 (☑617-661-1515; www.harvard.com; 1256 Massachusetts Ave; ☺9am-11pm Mon-Sat, 10am-10pm Sun; ⓣHarvard) Family-owned and operated since 1932, the Harvard Book Store is not officially affiliated with Harvard University, but it is the university community's favorite place to come to browse. While the shop maintains an academic focus, there is plenty of fiction for less lofty reading, as well as used books and bargain books in the basement.

GROLIER POETRY BOOKSHOP BOOKS
Map p246 (☑617-547-4648; www.grolierpoetry bookshop.org; 6 Plympton St; ☺11am-7pm Tue & Wed, to 6pm Thu-Sat; ⓣHarvard) Founded in 1927, Grolier is the oldest – and perhaps the most famous – poetry bookstore in the US. Over the years, TS Eliot, ee cummings, Marianne Moore and Allen Ginsberg have all passed through these doors. Today Grolier continues to foster young poets and poetry readers. The store also hosts readings.

RAVEN USED BOOKS BOOKS
Map p246 (☑617-441-6999; www.ravencam bridge.com; 23 Church St; ☺10am-9pm Mon-Sat, 11am-8pm Sun; ⓣHarvard) This cherished shop is one of the last used-books holdouts in Harvard Square. Its huge collection focuses on scholarly titles, especially in the liberal arts.

CARDULLO'S GOURMET SHOPPE FOOD & DRINKS
Map p246 (☑617-491-8888; www.cardullos.com; 6 Brattle St; ☺9am-9pm Mon-Sat, 10am-7pm Sun;

TｾHarvard) So many goodies packed into such a small space – you'll find every sort of imported edible your heart desires here, from caviar to chocolate. The excellent selection of New England products is a good source of souvenirs. Take home some Cranberry Bog Frogs (candy) from Cape Cod, maple sugar candy from Vermont and even clam chowder from Maine.

CURIOUS GEORGE STORE   BOOKS, TOYS

Map p246 (⌂617-547-4500; www.thecurious georgestore.com; 1 John F Kennedy St; ⊙10am-6pm Sun-Thu, to 8pm Fri & Sat; TｾHarvard) You can find the much-loved tales about the mischievous monkey, Curious George, in this store, but there are also thousands of other books and toys to choose from. *Curious George* authors HA and Margret Rey lived for more than 30 years on nearby Brattle St.

CAMBRIDGE ARTISTS
COOPERATIVE   ARTS & CRAFTS

Map p246 (⌂617-868-4434; www.cambridgeart istscoop.com; 59a Church St; ⊙10am-6pm Mon-Wed & Sat, 10am-7pm Wed & Thu, noon-6pm Sun; TｾHarvard) Owned and operated by Cambridge artists, this two-level gallery displays an ever-changing exhibit of their work. The pieces are crafty: handmade jewelry, woven scarves, leather products and pottery. The craftspeople double as sales staff, so you may get to meet the creative force behind your souvenir.

GAMES PEOPLE PLAY   TOYS

Map p246 (⌂617-492-0711; www.thegames peopleplaycambridge.com; 1100 Massachusetts Ave; ⊙10am-6pm Mon-Sat, to 8pm Thu, noon-5pm Sun; TｾHarvard) A lovely little store run by folks who are passionate about playing games. The well-curated selection includes many unique toys and games that are imported from Europe and beyond. Be sure to ask for recommendations.

FORTY WINKS   CLOTHING

Map p246 (⌂617-492-9100; www.shopforty winks.com; 56 John F Kennedy St; ⊙10am-7pm Mon-Sat, noon-6pm Sun; TｾHarvard) Forty Winks is a little slice of luxurious lingerie heaven. The items are pricey, but they are also soft, silky and oh-so-sexy. And the staff are graciously determined to help you find the perfect fit for body and soul. So if you're looking to treat yourself – or your significant other – this is an excellent place to start.

🔒 Central & Kendall Squares

CENTRAL FLEA   ARTS & CRAFTS

Map p248 (⌂800-401-6557; www.newengland openmarkets.com; 91 Sidney St; ⊙11am-5pm Sun May-Oct; TｾCentral) Part garage sale, part art market, part street fair, Central Flea is a diverse urban market. There's less art but more grit than at the other New England Open Markets, which means it caters to locals, scavengers and treasure-hunters, in addition to yuppies and visitors.

PLANET RECORDS   MUSIC

Map p246 (⌂617-492-0693; www.planet-records. com; 144 Mt Auburn St; ⊙11am-8pm Mon-Fri, 10am-9pm Sat, noon-8pm Sun; TｾHarvard) Harvard Square is still a great place to get your vinyl fix and your first stop should probably be Planet Records. It's a small space with an impressive selection, especially of jazz and classical music. Blues, bluegrass, folk, country, R&B and, of course, rock are also well represented.

RODNEY'S BOOKSTORE   BOOKS

Map p248 (⌂617-876-6467; www.rodneysbook store.com; 698 Massachusetts Ave; ⊙10am-9pm Mon-Sat, noon-8pm Sun; TｾCentral) Mainly, Rodney sells bookcases and books (including some 45,000 used and discounted books in all genres). It's a quirky place, though, as it also carries an eclectic collection of vintage posters, an odd assortment of furniture and miscellaneous other stuff.

CHEAPO RECORDS   MUSIC

Map p248 (⌂617-354-4455; www.cheap orecords.com; 538 Massachusetts Ave; ⊙11am-7pm Mon-Wed & Sat, to 8pm Thu & Fri, to 5pm Sun; TｾCentral) With tunes blasting out onto the sidewalk, Cheapo Records lures in music lovers to browse through its huge selection of vinyl and decent selection of CDs. The staff know their stuff, and the collection spans all genres, with a fun box of new arrivals for the regulars.

🏃 SPORTS & ACTIVITIES

★MINUTEMAN BIKEWAY   CYCLING

(www.minutemanbikeway.org; TｾAlewife, Davis) The best of Boston's bicycle trails starts

NEW BALANCE FACTORY STORE

Run like the wind...to the **New Balance Factory Store** ([🖉]617-779-7429; www.nbfactory stores.com; 173 Market St; ⊙9am-8pm Mon-Sat, 11am-6pm Sun; [🚍]64, 70) store for comfortable, supportive running shoes at discounted prices. Runners rejoice over these shoes, but regular people wear them too. This gymnasium-sized store also carries plenty of other athletic gear. The New Balance Factory store is in Brighton: take the bus from Central Sq or Kenmore Sq.

near Alewife station and leads 5 miles to historic Lexington Center, then traverses an additional 4 miles of idyllic scenery and terminates in the rural suburb of Bedford. The wide, straight, paved path gets crowded on weekends. Rent a bike at the **Bicycle Exchange** ([🖉]617-864-1300; www.cambridge bicyclecxchange.com; 2067 Massachusetts Ave; rental 1 day $25, additional days $10; ⊙hours vary; [T]Porter).

CHARLES RIVER BIKE PATH   CYCLING

(Storrow Dr & Memorial Dr; [🚲]; [T]Harvard, Kendall/MIT, Charles/MGH, Science Park) A popular cycling circuit runs along both sides of the Charles River between the Museum of Science and the Mt Auburn St Bridge in Watertown center (5 miles west of Cambridge). The round trip is 17 miles, but 10 bridges in between offer ample opportunities to shorten the trip. Rent a bike at **Cambridge Bicycle** ([🖉]617-876-6555; www.cambridgebicy cle.com; 259 Massachusetts Ave; per 24hr $35; ⊙10am-7pm Mon-Sat, noon-6pm Sun; [T]Central) or Back Bay Bicycles (p210).

LYNCH FAMILY SKATE PARK   SKATING

(Education St, Cambridge; ⊙dawn-9pm; [T]Science Park) [FREE] Local sculptor Nancy Schön had the brilliant idea of turning an underhighway urban wasteland into a playground for Boston's BMX riders, skateboarders and anybody that rolls. It's under the access ramp to the Zakim Bridge. Access the park from North Point Park in Cambridge or Paul Revere Park in Charlestown.

CHARLES RIVER CANOE
& KAYAK CENTER   CANOEING, KAYAKING

Map p248 ([🖉]617-965-5110; www.paddleboston. com; 500 Broad Canal Way; per hour canoe $21, kayak $16-21, per hour SUP $19-22; ⊙noon-8pm Mon-Fri, 9am-8pm Sat & Sun Jun-Sep, to 5:30pm May & Oct; [🚲]; [T]Kendall/MIT) Besides canoe and kayak rental, Charles River Canoe & Kayak offers classes and organized outings. Experienced kayakers can venture

out to the harbor, but the river and basin are lovely for skyline views and fall foliage. There is another outlet in **Allston** (Soldier's Field Rd; ⊙10am-8pm Mon-Fri, from 9am Sat & Sun May-Oct; [T]Harvard Sq), near Harvard Square, which allows for an excellent one-way 5-mile trip between the two rental centers.

FLAT TOP JOHNNY'S   BILLIARDS

Map p248 ([🖉]617-494-9565; www.flattopjohn nys.com; 1 Kendall Sq; pool per hour $12; ⊙noon-1am; [T]Kendall/MIT) Twelve red-felt tournament tables are set in a tall-ceilinged space surrounded by brick walls and comic-book murals. There are 16 beers on tap, plus darts and pinball for while you're waiting on a table. Fun for all. Pool is half-price before 6pm.

FRESH POND GOLF COURSE   GOLF

([🖉]617-349-6282; www.freshpondgolf.com; 691 Huron Ave; 9 holes $24-27; ⊙6am-sunset Apr-Sep, opens later Oct-Dec; [🚍]71, 73 or 78) About 2 miles west of Harvard Square, the Fresh Pond is a nine-hole public course that wraps around the city's reservoir. It's easily accessible, but the setting is suburban. Drive west on Mt Auburn St and turn right on the Fresh Pond Parkway and left on Huron Ave.

COMMUNITY ICE SKATING
KENDALL SQUARE   ICE SKATING

Map p248 ([🖉]617-492-0941; www.skatekendall. com; 300 Athenaeum St; adult/child $5/1, rental $8/5; ⊙noon-8pm Mon-Thu, 11am-9pm Fri & Sat, to 6pm Sun Dec-Mar; [🚲]; [T]Kendall/MIT) Kendall Sq may not have the same charm as the Boston Common, but this smallish rink has many other benefits. There are usually fewer people, for a start, which means more room for your pirouettes (or whatever you do on the ice). The rental skates are in excellent condition and the staff are helpful if you're not an experienced skater.

Streetcar Suburbs

BROOKLINE | JAMAICA PLAIN

Neighborhood Top Five

1 John F Kennedy National Historic Site (p158) Taking a pilgrimage to the birthplace of JFK, touring the home, and then following the NPS walking tour to see the schools, churches and other places from Kennedy lore.

2 Coolidge Corner Theatre (p162) Sitting in the balcony and catching an art-house flick.

3 Tres Gatos (p160) Enjoying an evening of delightful food, music and camaraderie, as if you were a personal guest of the three cats.

4 Brookline Booksmith (p162) Browsing the stacks, listening to a lecture or finding a bargain at the Boston area's favorite bookstore.

5 Emerald Necklace (p159) Cycling or strolling along this Olmsted-designed string of parks, from downtown Boston to Franklin Park.

For more detail of this area see Map p254 and p255 ➡

Explore Streetcar Suburbs

Brookline and Jamaica Plain (among others) are Streetcar Suburbs, residential areas that developed around Boston in the late 19th century. They are geographically isolated from other parts of Boston, though transitionally connected, yes, by streetcar (or metro now). Both JP and Brookline maintain distinct identities and unique 'neighborhood' atmospheres that make them attractive, off-the-beaten-path destinations.

Brookline was built as a modest, middle-income neighborhood, suitable for young families, which explains the draw to Joseph and Rose Kennedy, who moved here in 1914. Today, JFK admirers and history buffs make the pilgrimage to Beals St near Coolidge Corner to see the birthplace of the 35th president of the United States. While away the rest of the afternoon lunching at local Jewish delis and browsing the boutiques and bookstores. After dark, things quiet down, although the local cinema – a retro movie house – draws crowds for its arty international films and balcony seating. For a more raucous good time, check out the music clubs up the street in Allston and Brighton.

Further south, Jamaica Plain was a summertime retreat for wealthy Bostonians who built stately homes overlooking the quaint glacial pond, and its open spaces are still part of this outer neighborhood's appeal. If you want to enjoy the great outdoors, but you can't leave the city, head to Jamaica Plain instead. Downtown JP is Centre St – that's where you'll find an eclectic assortment of eateries and delightful neighborhood shopping, as well as some drinking options if you are in the mood for Guinness.

Local Life

➤ **Brookline Local** Eat breakfast at Kupel's Bakery (p159) or lunch at Michael's Deli (p160).
➤ **JP Local** Go jogging around Jamaica Pond (p163) or take your dog for a drink at Brendan Behan Pub (p161).

Getting There & Away

➤ **Metro** Two branches of the green line traverse Brookline. Take the C-line to Coolidge Corner or the D-line to Brookline Village. Traveling to Jamaica Plain, orange-line stations such as Green St and Stony Brook provide the easiest access to Centre St and Jamaica Pond. Use Forest Hills station to reach JP's major sights, which are further out.

Lonely Planet's Top Tip

The **Coolidge Corner Theatre** (p162) is not just a cinema. It offers a wide variety of programming for all segments of the population, including @fter Midnite (horror and comedy for the late-night set), Opera at the Cinema (high-def screenings straight from the world's best opera houses), Off the Couch (film accompanied by psychoanalytic discussion), Sounds of Silents (silent-film classics accompanied by live music) and more.

✖ Best Places to Eat

➤ Tres Gatos (p160)
➤ Soup Shack (p160)
➤ JP Licks (p160)
➤ Ten Tables (p161)
➤ Michael's Deli (p160)

For reviews, see p159.➡

🍺 Best Places to Drink

➤ Publick House (p161)
➤ Haven (p161)
➤ Brendan Behan Pub (p161)

For reviews, see p161.➡

⊙ Best Urban Oases

➤ Arnold Arboretum (p158)
➤ Larz Anderson Auto Museum & Park (p158)
➤ Franklin Park (p159)

For reviews, see p158.➡

⊙ SIGHTS

The Streetcar Suburbs' sights are mostly parks and green spaces, many of them linked together in a long chain known as the Emerald Necklace. There are also a few National Historic Sights that are worth your attention.

⊙ Brookline

JOHN F KENNEDY
NATIONAL HISTORIC SITE   HISTORIC SITE

Map p254 (☑617-566-7937; www.nps.gov/jofi; 83 Beals St, Brookline; ⊙9:30am-5pm daily mid-May–Aug, Wed-Sun Sep & Oct; ⓉCoolidge Corner) **FREE** Four of the nine Kennedy children were born and raised in this modest house, including Jack, who was born in the master bedroom in 1917. Matriarch Rose Kennedy oversaw the restoration of the house in the late 1960s; today her narrative sheds light on the Kennedy's family life. Guided tours allow visitors to see furnishings, photographs and mementos that have been preserved from the time the family lived here.

A self-guided walking tour of the surrounding neighborhood sets the scene for the Kennedy family's day-to-day life, including church, school and shopping.

FREDERICK LAW
OLMSTED NATIONAL
HISTORIC SITE   HISTORIC SITE

(☑617-566-1689; www.nps.gov/frla; 99 Warren St, Brookline; ⊙grounds dawn-dusk year-round, exhibits 10am-4pm Wed-Sun Jun-Sep, shorter hours Apr, May & Oct; ☒60 from Kenmore, ⓉBrookline Hills) **FREE** Widely considered the father of landscape design, Frederick Law Olmsted ran his operation from his home 'Fairsted,' which is now a National Historic Site. The grounds are open to casual callers. Take a tour to visit Olmsted's home and office, which remain as they were a century ago. You can peruse his designs for the country's most beloved green spaces, which include the Emerald Necklace in Boston, Central Park in New York City, many national parks and more.

From Brookline Hills, walk two blocks south on Cypress St and a long three blocks west on Walnut St, then turn south on Warren.

LARZ ANDERSON AUTO
MUSEUM & PARK   MUSEUM

(☑617-522-6547; www.larzanderson.org; 15 Newton St, Brookline; adult/child $10/5; ⊙10am-4pm Tue-Sun; ☒51, ⓉForest Hills, Reservoir) Larz and Isabel Anderson, a high-society couple, bought their first automobile in 1899: a Winton Runabout. It was the first of 32 autos that they would purchase over the next 50 years. 'America's oldest motorcar collection' is now on display in the carriage house on the grounds of the estate (now Larz Anderson Park). Take bus 51 from Forest Hills (orange) or Reservoir (green D-line).

⊙ Jamaica Plain

FOREST HILLS CEMETERY   CEMETERY

(☑617-524-0128; www.foresthillstrust.org; 95 Forest Hills Ave; ⊙8:30am-dusk; ℗; ⓉForest Hills) Dating to 1848, Forest Hills is a gorgeous, green cemetery that is filled with art and whimsy. It is still an active burial ground, but it also plays the role of open-air museum. The walking paths are lined with sculptures paying tribute to individuals and causes from times past, while a contemporary sculpture path winds its way around the historic gravestones, connecting then and now.

Gravestones are dedicated to such famous figures as Revolutionary War heroes William Dawes and Joseph Warren, abolitionist William Lloyd Garrison and suffragette Lucy Stone, poets ee cummings and Anne Sexton, sculptors Daniel Chester French and Martin Milmore, and playwright Eugene O'Neill. The on-site Forsyth Chapel, in the midst of the greenery, is a spot for peaceful contemplation surrounded by vaulted wood ceilings and stained-glass windows. Concerts, poetry readings and other events are often held in this exquisite space. Walk east along the Arborway a half-mile from Forest Hills station.

ARNOLD ARBORETUM   PARK

(☑617-524-1718; www.arboretum.harvard.edu; 125 Arborway; ⊙dawn-dusk; ☷; ⓉForest Hills) **FREE** Under a public/private partnership with Harvard University, the 265-acre Arnold Arboretum is planted with over 15,000 exotic trees and flowering shrubs. This gem is pleasant year-round, but it's particularly beautiful in the bloom of spring. Dog walking, Frisbee throwing, bicycling, sledding and general contemplation are encouraged (but picnicking is not allowed). The southern Forest Hills gate is located on the Arborway just west of the metro station.

A **visitor center** (⊙10am-5pm Thu-Tue) is located at the main gate, just south of the rotary at Rte 1 and Rte 203. Free one-hour walking tours are offered several times a week from April to November.

FRANKLIN PARK ZOO   ZOO

(☑617-541-5466; www.zoonewengland.com; 1 Franklin Park Rd; adult/child $20/14; ⊙10am-5pm Mon-Fri, to 6pm Sat & Sun Apr-Sep, 10am-4pm daily Oct-Mar; P🐾; T Ruggles) Tucked into Franklin Park (p159), the zoo features a half-dozen different habitats, as well as special exhibits devoted to birds and butterflies. The highlight is the well-designed Tropical Forest pavilion, complete with lush vegetation, waterfalls, lowland gorillas and over 30 species of free-flight birds. The Australian Outback Trail allows visitors to walk among red kangaroos and wallabies.

Several exhibits are devoted to life on the savannah, showcasing an African lion, as well as giraffes, zebras and wildebeests. The Franklin Farm lets kids get up close and personal with sheep and goats. Take bus 22 or 28 from Ruggles station.

🍴 EATING

You probably won't go out of your way to dine in the Streetcar Suburbs. But if you did, you probably wouldn't be disappointed, as both Brookline and Jamaica Plain are home to an eclectic array of restaurants. You'll find food from all parts of the world in these diverse neighborhoods, as well as some modern American culinary options.

🍴 Brookline

Brookline enjoys an eclectic assortment of dining options, including kosher delis and many other ethnic eats. Coolidge Corner, which is around the intersection of Harvard and Beacon Sts, is the hub for the Brookline dining scene.

KUPEL'S BAKERY   BAKERY **$**

Map p254 (☑617-566-9528; www.kupelsbakery. com; 421 Harvard St, Brookline; mains $3-8; ⊙6am-6pm Sun-Fri; ☑; T Coolidge Corner) Kupel's has 24 kinds of chewy bagels and 24 kinds of decadent cream cheese. We're not good at math, but that's a lot of breakfast goodness. Lines are out the door on Sunday mornings, but it's worth the wait for a

STREETCAR SUBURBS EATING

EMERALD NECKLACE

The Emerald Necklace (www.emeraldnecklace.org) is an evocative name for a series of parks and green spaces that weave some 7 miles through Boston, from the Boston Common to Franklin Park. Designed by Frederick Law Olmsted in the late 19th century, the Emerald Necklace treats city residents to fresh air, green grass and flowing water, right within the city limits. It's well suited for cycling, so hop on a bike and go for the green.

At its northern end, the **Boston Common** (p70) and the **Public Garden** (p72) anchor the green chain. From here, the **Commonwealth Ave mall** stretches west to Fenway. The **Back Bay Fens** (p124) follows the muddy river as it winds its way south. The Fens features well-cared-for community gardens, the elegant Kelleher Rose Garden, and plenty of space to toss a Frisbee, play pick-up basketball or lie in the sun.

Olmsted Park (Map p255; Jamaica Plain; T Riverway) features a paved path that hugs the banks of Leverett Pond and Ward's Pond in Jamaica Plain. The idyllic spring-fed **Jamaica Pond** (p163), on the west side of the Jamaicaway, is more than 50ft deep and great for boating, fishing, jogging and picnicking. Beautifully landscaped and wonderfully serene, the **Arnold Arboretum** will appeal not only to green thumbs and plant lovers, but also to anyone who can take time to smell the roses. Check the website to see what's blooming when you're visiting.

Franklin Park (Map p255; T Stony Brook, Green St, Forest Hills), at 500-plus acres, is an underutilized resource, partly because it is so huge. Still, on weekend afternoons the park is full of families from the nearby neighborhoods of Jamaica Plain, Dorchester and Roxbury. Take the orange line to Stony Brook, Green St or Forest Hills and walk about a half-mile east to the park's edge. **Franklin Park Zoo** is also contained within the park.

sesame, toasted, with chive cream cheese and lox. Not only is this place kosher, it's also vegan friendly.

★ MICHAEL'S DELI
DELI $

Map p254 (☑617-738-3354; www.michaelsdeli brookline.com; 256 Harvard St, Brookline; sandwiches $8-12; ☺9am-5:30pm Mon-Sat, to 3pm Sun; Ⓣ Coolidge Corner) There are two menu listings you need to know: corned-beef Reuben; and sour pickle. That said, there are dozens of sandwiches on the menu and you really can't go wrong (but don't forget the pickle). The sammies are generously stuffed and the service is super friendly. On the downside, there's limited seating and they don't accept credit cards.

ZAFTIGS DELICATESSEN
JEWISH $

Map p254 (☑617-975-0075; www.zaftigs.com; 335 Harvard St, Brookline; mains $10-15; ☺8am-9pm Sun-Thu, to 10pm Fri & Sat; 🖽; Ⓣ Coolidge Corner) 'Let us be your Jewish mother,' Zaftigs implores. And on weekend mornings, patrons craving potato pancakes with smoked salmon, challah French toast and cheese blintzes line up out the door to oblige. Fortunately, breakfast is served all day, so nobody has to miss it. Otherwise, the deli turns out a huge selection of sandwiches, including classics like Reubens and pastrami.

JERUSALEM PITA & GRILL
ISRAELI $

Map p254 (☑617-739-2400; www.jerusalempita. com; 10 Pleasant St, Brookline; lunch specials $7-11, mains $13-23; ☺10am-10pm Sun-Thu, to 3pm Fri; Ⓣ Coolidge Corner) There's nothing fancy going on at this popular lunchtime spot, but it sure is tasty. Settle in for delicious falafel, assorted kebabs, or the all-time favorite Meorav Yerushalmi, with grilled beef, chicken and lamb on a plate or in a pita. Service is friendly and the kitchen is kosher.

FUGAKYU
SUSHI $$$

Map p254 (☑617-734-1268; www.fugakyu.net; 1280 Beacon St, Brookline; lunch $12-21, sushi $6-16, mains $20-26; ☺11:30am-1:30am; 🍴; Ⓣ Coolidge Corner) The name aptly translates as 'house of elegance.' Upscale and over-the-top, Fugakyu offers a gorgeous array of sushi and sashimi, served by staff dressed in kimonos. The food is beautiful to look at and delicious to eat, especially the expertly plated sushi boats. Don't fall in the koi pond.

✗ Jamaica Plain

Funky, progressive Jamaica Plain hosts an ever-growing restaurant scene along Centre St. The neighborhood's diverse population enjoys a variety of spunky cafes and international eateries, with many veg-friendly options.

★ JP LICKS
ICE CREAM $

Map p255 (☑617-524-6740; www.jplicks.com; 659 Centre St, Jamaica Plain; ice cream from $4; ☺6am-midnight; 🛜; Ⓣ Green St) 'JP' stands for Jamaica Plain: this is the flagship location of the ice-creamery that's now all over Boston. You can't miss the happy Holstein head looking down over Centre St. And you shouldn't miss the white-coffee ice cream, either. Expensive, but worth it.

★ SOUP SHACK
ASIAN $

Map p255 (☑617-477-9805; www.soupshackjp. com; 779 Centre St, Jamaica Plain; mains $11-13; 🍴; Ⓣ Green St) Soup does a body good, and it doesn't matter if it's Vietnamese pho, Japanese ramen or Thai *tom yum*. The Soup Shack serves up all of the above – steaming hot bowls of deliciousness. The space is snug and service is accommodating.

EL ORIENTAL DE CUBA
CUBAN $

Map p255 (☑617-524-6464; www.elorientalde cuba.net; 416 Centre St, Jamaica Plain; sandwiches $7-10, plates $13-20; ☺8am-9pm Mon-Thu, to 10pm Fri & Sat, to 8pm Sun; Ⓣ Stony Brook) Lunchtime lines often run out the door as hungry patrons wait patiently for the specialty Cuban sandwich. Roast pork, Swiss cheese and ham are stuffed into a roll, and served with a side of *maduros*, or fried plantains. Wash it down with a tropical shake or a sugar-cane juice, and you'll think you're in Havana. Or at least Miami.

★ TRES GATOS
TAPAS $$

Map p255 (☑617-477-4851; www.tresgatosjp. com; 470 Centre St, Jamaica Plain; brunch $8-16, tapas $8-20; ☺5:30-10pm Mon-Wed, to 11pm Thu & Fri,10am-11pm Sat & Sun; 🍴; 🚌39, Ⓣ Stony Brook) This small space is not only a tapas bar, but also a bookstore and music store. It all feels like you are eating, browsing books and listening to music in somebody's living room, but that somebody is a gracious, fun host, and somehow it works. The menu features charcuterie, cheeses and a selection of authentic Spanish tapas and wine.

BELLA LUNA MILKY WAY PIZZA $$

Map p255 (☑617-524-6060; www.milkywayjp.
com; 284 Amory St, Jamaica Plain; mains $12-20;
☺5-11pm Sun-Wed, to 1am Thu & Fri, noon-1am
Sat; ☑⬛; ⓉStony Brook) Now housed in an
old brewery building, Bella Luna Milky
Way is a neighborhood haunt that has long
enticed JP residents with its colorfully
painted walls and sci-fi decor. Regulars
keep coming back, year after year, for crispy
thin-crust pizza pies with interesting com-
binations of toppings, such as the all-time
favorite Gypsy King, with spinach, ricotta
and caramelized onions.

While waiting for pizza, regulars keep
themselves entertained with pool, Connect
Four and vintage video games. After 9pm,
there's trivia (Monday), line dancing (Tues-
day) and jazz music (Wednesday) in addi-
tion to DJs and dance parties (Thursday to
Saturday).

★**TEN TABLES** INTERNATIONAL $$$

Map p255 (☑617-524-8810; www.tentables.
net; 597 Centre St, Jamaica Plain; mains $28-32;
☺5:30-10pm Mon-Sat, 5-9pm Sun; ☑; ⓉGreen
St) ☑ True to its name, this gem has only
10 tables (you'll need to reserve one of
them). The emphasis here is on simplicity –
appropriate for a restaurant that specializes in traditional cooking techniques. The
menu is short, but changes frequently to
highlight local, organic produce, handmade pasta, fresh seafood and housemade
sausages.

Ten Tables offers a few fantastic opportunities to save money while savoring your
meal. Stop by for Sunday Supper (a three-
course prix fixe for $39), Pasta Thursday
(plate of pasta and glass of wine for $15)
and a monthly wine dinner ($59 for four
courses and four wines).

VEE VEE INTERNATIONAL $$$

Map p255 (☑617-522-0145; www.veeveejp.com;
763 Centre St, Jamaica Plain; mains $22-29;
☺5:30-10pm daily, plus 10:30am-3pm Sun; ☑;
ⓉGreen St) Vee Vee stands for Valachovic,
the last name of the two creative genii be-
hind this sweet spot on Centre St. The decor
is minimalist and modern, but nothing too
trendy for granola-loving Jamaica Plain.
The menu focuses on seafood and vegetar-
ian items, with the occasional meat and
poultry dishes, but the focus is always on
seasonal and local.

♟ DRINKING & NIGHTLIFE

**The Streetcar Suburbs are not exactly
drinking destinations, but there are
several inviting neighborhood watering
holes which are more than adequate
when you're in the area. In fact, you may
walk away wishing you lived here, so one
of these places could become your local.**

HAVEN PUB

Map p255 (☑617-524-2836; www.thehavenjp.
com; 2 Perkins St, Jamaica Plain; ☺noon-1am
Mon-Fri, from 10:30am Sat & Sun; ☞; ⓉStony
Brook) If you can't stand to drink in another
Irish pub, this is your Haven: a Scottish
pub. There are more than a dozen Scottish
craft beers, a full menu of Scotch whiskies,
haggis, and men in kilts. Special events re-
volve around soccer matches and whisky
tastings. The food also gets rave reviews,
especially the burgers and the Scotch egg.

PUBLICK HOUSE BAR

(☑617-277-2880; www.publickhousebrookline.
com; 1648 Beacon St, Brookline; ☺5pm-2am
Mon-Fri, from noon Sat & Sun; ☞; ⓉWashington
Square) This friendly, award-winning pub
is buzzing with good vibes, thanks to the
superb selection of brews (30-plus rotating
drafts). The specialty is pints from Belgium,
most of which seem to have a high alcohol
content. The place gets crowded on week-
ends, so be prepared to wait if you want to
sample the mussels and *frites* or mac 'n'
cheese.

SAMUEL ADAMS BREWERY BREWERY

Map p255 (☑617-368-5080; www.samueladams.
com; 30 Germania St, Jamaica Plain; donation $2;
☺tap room 11am-8pm Mon-Sat, tours 10am-3pm
Mon-Thu & Sat, to 5:30pm Fri; ⓉStony Brook) To
sample Sam Adams ales and lagers straight
from the barrel, pay a visit to the flagship
brewery, with taproom on site. If you wish
to learn more about Sam Adams (the pa-
triot and the beer), come early in the day
and tour the operation. Tours last about one
hour and end at the bar.

BRENDAN BEHAN PUB IRISH PUB

Map p255 (☑617-522-5386; www.facebook.
com/the-behan-223737580265; 378 Centre St,
Jamaica Plain; ☺noon-1am; ☒; ⓉStony Brook)
Candlelit tables, stained glass and old liq-
uor cabinets make this dark den an attrac-
tive destination for regulars of all ages and

WORTH A DETOUR

MUSIC THEORY 101: ALLSTON/BRIGHTON

If you care to sample the Boston music scene, venture west to Allston/Brighton, the gritty 'student ghetto.' Some of Boston's best music clubs are located in these innocuous alleys and subterranean spaces.

Great Scott (Map p254; ☑617-566-9014; www.greatscottboston.com; 1222 Commonwealth Ave; cover $5-20; ⊡66, ⊤Harvard Ave) A music palace for rock and indie. Get up close and personal with the bands, hang out with them after sets and buy them some beers. The sound system is not perfect, but this is where you can hear the future of music. On Friday nights, the place turns into a popular comedy club known as the Gas (7pm). Cash only.

Brighton Music Hall (Map p254; ☑617-779-0140; www.crossroadspresents.com; 158 Brighton Ave; tickets $10-20; ⊤Harvard Ave) A great smaller venue, owned and operated by Crossroads (the force behind the Paradise Rock Club and House of Blues). Attracts great local bands, some cool world-music acts and touring national bands. Fans appreciate the quick service at the bar, the excellent sound system and the pool tables in the back.

Paradise Rock Club (Map p254; ☑617-562-8800; www.crossroadspresents.com; 967 Commonwealth Ave; tickets $20-40; ⊤Pleasant St) Top bands rock at this landmark club – like U2, whose first gig in the USA was on this stage. Nowadays, you're more likely to hear the likes of Lucinda Williams, The Floozies and plenty of Boston bands that made good, but still come home to play the 'Dise.

Scullers Jazz Club (☑866-777-8932; www.scullersjazz.com; 400 Soldiers Field Rd; tickets $25-75; ⊡47, 70, ⊤Central) A more mature music experience, this club books big names (David Sanborn, Dr John, Michael Franks) in a small room. That said, it lacks the grit you might hanker for in a jazz club. It feels like it's inside a Doubletree Hotel (which it is). Book in advance.

origins (including dogs). The beer list is not massive, but it's thoughtful and diverse. There are a few things that make this place unique: no food (but you can bring it in), no TVs, no credit cards.

punk bar books some of Boston's finest independent music. Inside, find Pabst beer signs of antique vintage, some longhorn skulls, pinball and a genuinely friendly atmosphere. Cash only.

ENTERTAINMENT

COOLIDGE
CORNER THEATRE
CINEMA

Map p254 (☑617-734-2500; www.coolidge.org; 290 Harvard St, Brookline; tickets $9-13; ⊤Coolidge Corner) An art deco neighborhood palace, this old theater blazes with exterior neon. Inside, view select Hollywood hits, cult flicks, popular independent fare and special events. Fifty cents of every ticket sale goes to the upkeep of the building.

MIDWAY CAFÉ
LIVE MUSIC

(☑617-524-9038; www.midwaycafe.com; 3496 Washington St, Jamaica Plain; cover $5-10; ☺4pm-2am; ⊤Green St) In addition to hosting a kick-ass 'Queeraoke' party (Thursday), a Grateful Dead–themed 'hippie hour' (Friday), and a regular open mic (Sunday), this queer-friendly rock and

SHOPPING

Centre St (JP) is edgy and urban, while Coolidge Corner (Brookline) is sophisticated and suburban.

⌂ Brookline

★BROOKLINE BOOKSMITH
BOOKS

Map p254 (☑617-566-6660; www.brooklinebooksmith.com; 279 Harvard St, Brookline; ☺8:30am-10pm Mon-Thu, to 11pm Fri & Sat, 9am-9pm Sun; ⌨; ⊤Coolidge Corner) Year after year, this independent bookstore wins 'Best Bookstore in Boston.' Customers love the lineup of author talks and poetry readings, the emphasis on local writers and the Used Book Cellar in the basement. Extra-long hours are also a perk.

GOOD VIBRATIONS
ADULT

Map p254 (☑617-487-4992; www.goodvibes.com; 308a Harvard St; ⊙10am-9pm Sun-Thu, to 10pm Fri & Sat; ⓣCoolidge Corner) Down a narrow alley and marked by a discreet sign, this woman-focused sex shop is worth seeking out. The tasteful and tantalizing boutique offers sex-positive products, not to mention newsletters, workshops and pleasure parties. No question is too probing for the women at Good Vibes. And it would seem that no product is either.

EUREKA PUZZLES
TOYS

Map p254 (☑617-738-7352; www.eurekapuzzles. com; 1349 Beacon St, Brookline; ⊙10am-8pm Mon-Sat, 11am-6pm Sun; ⓕ; ⓣCoolidge Corner) Puzzles, of course. But even better, this place has board games. And card games. And many other kinds of games. The folks at Eureka know and love games so much that they will scour their shop to find one that you will love, too. Cool souvenir ideas include the 4D Boston Cityscape and the Eureka exclusive Boston wooden packing puzzle.

⬡ Jamaica Plain

★ SALMAGUNDI
FASHION & ACCESSORIES

Map p255 (☑617-522-5047; www.salmagundi boston.com; 765 Centre St; ⊙11am-7pm Tue-Fri, to 8pm Sat, to 6pm Sun & Mon; ⓣGreen St) In our humble opinion, every man should own at least one fedora. And if not a fedora, some other fun and functional head-topper. If you are intrigued by this idea, head to Salmagundi, where style mavens Jessen and Andria can help you find a hat just made for your head, no matter what your gender identification.

BOING!
TOYS

Map p255 (☑617-522-7800; www.boingtoys.com; 667 Centre St, Jamaica Plain; ⊙10am-6pm Mon-Sat, to 5pm Sun; ⓕ; ⓣGreen St) Boing! is fun. It's fun that they have an exclamation point at the end of their name and crazy colorful creatures adorning their facade. And it's really fun inside, where kids and parents can find educational, age-appropriate toys, games and activities with the help of knowledgeable, caring staff. Favorite aunts/uncles love this place.

ON CENTRE
GIFTS & SOUVENIRS

Map p255 (☑617-522-2255; www.oncentrejp. com; 676 Centre St; ⊙11am-7pm Mon-Fri, 10am-6pm Sat, noon-5pm Sun; ⓣGreen St) The friendly folks at this little boutique can help you find the perfect gift. The jewelry is inexpensive and highly original; much of it is designed by local artists. But if your special person is not into origami earrings, never fear, there are funky reusable shopping bags and silly socks, as well as colorful ceramics, nifty gadgets and other homewares.

HATCHED
CHILDREN'S CLOTHING

Map p255 (☑617-524-5402; www.hatched boston.com; 668 Centre St; ⊙10am-6pm Mon-Sat, to 3pm Sun; ⓕ; ⓣGreen St) ⬥ A baby is surely one of nature's most incredible creations, so why muff it up with synthetic fabrics and toxic toys? If you prefer to dress your little bundle of natural goodness in unbleached cloth diapers and adorable organic clothing, you'll find an excellent selection at 'Boston's first ecobaby store' (but you can't buy an ecobaby here).

🏃 SPORTS & ACTIVITIES

JAMAICA POND
BOATING

Map p255 (☑617-522-5061; www.jamaicapond. com; 507 Jamaica Way, Jamaica Plain; boat rental per hour $15-20; ⊙boathouse noon-sunset Mon-Thu, from 10am Fri-Sun Apr-Oct; ⓕ; ⓣGreen St) Once a summer destination for city residents, Jamaica Pond is now a tranquil urban oasis, perfect for paddling or rather tame sailing. A 1.4-mile paved path circles the glacial kettlehole. Rowboats and sailboats are available for rental at the 1913 Tudor boathouse. The pond is even stocked with fish, though you'll need your own equipment and a MA fishing license.

BROOKLINE GOLF CLUB AT PUTTERHAM
GOLF

(☑617-730-2078; www.brooklinegolf.com; 1281 West Roxbury Pkwy, Brookline; 18 holes weekday/weekend $35/45) You probably can't play golf on the famous Brookline Country Club green, but you can at Putterham, a less famed but pleasant public course. Wide fairways and a lack of water hazards make it suitable for all levels. Take Huntington Ave west to Boylston St (Rte 9); turn left on Hammond St, then turn onto Newton St at the rotary.

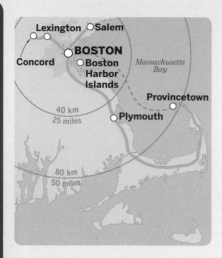

Day Trips from Boston

Boston Harbor Islands p165

These offshore islands are inviting for walking trails, rocky beaches, wild berries and one highly explorable abandoned fort.

Lexington & Concord p167

Now serene suburbs, these twin towns were the site of the dramatic kickoff to the War for Independence in April 19, 1775.

Salem p170

In addition to the many witchy sites in 'Witch City,' Salem showcases a proud maritime history and unique artistic legacy.

Plymouth p172

Settled by the Pilgrims in 1620, Plymouth is now home to *Mayflower II*, a replica of their ship, and Plimoth Plantation, a replica of their settlement.

Provincetown p175

Provincetown is a perfect summertime destination, with vast stretches of sandy beaches, miles of seaside bicycle trails and an eclectic strip of art galleries and seafood restaurants.

Boston Harbor Islands

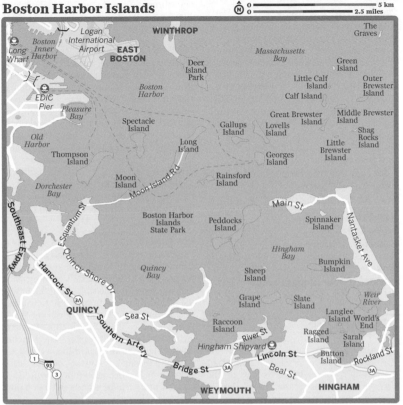

Boston Harbor Islands

Explore

Boston Harbor is sprinkled with 34 islands, many of which are open for trail walking, bird-watching, fishing, swimming and camping. You can't visit them all in one day, so consider the activities on offer and plan accordingly.

Hop on the first ferry to Georges Island, where you can spend the morning exploring Fort Warren. After lunch, take the shuttle to one of the other islands. Hit Spectacle Island for good walking trails and marvelous city views. Head to Lovells to catch some rays on the otherwise empty beach and cool off in the refreshing Atlantic wa-

ters. Or venture to Grape Island to hunt for wild berries.

Catch a shuttle (if necessary) and ferry back to the mainland from Spectacle or Georges Islands.

The Best...

→ **Sight** Fort Warren (p166)
→ **Place to Hike** Spectacle Island (p166)
→ **Place to Swim** Lovells Island (p166)

Top Tips

Don't try to visit more than two islands in one day: you'll end up spending all your time riding on or waiting for boats.

Check the website (www.bostonharbor islands.org) for special events, such as live music, outdoor activities and other family programs, especially on Georges and Spectacle Islands.

Getting There & Away

➡ **Boat** To reach most of the islands, Boston Harbor Cruises (p208) offers seasonal ferry services from Long Wharf and from Hingham, a coastal town 15 miles south of Boston. Purchase a round-trip ticket to Georges Island or Spectacle Island (adult/child $20/13), where you catch other boats to the smaller islands. Make sure you check the schedule in advance and plan your day accordingly. The exception is Thompson Island, which has a dedicated ferry that runs from EDIC Pier.

➡ **Car** Deer Island and World's End are accessible only by car.

Need to Know

➡ **Area Code** ☎617

➡ **Location** Scattered around Boston Harbor, 20 to 40 minutes from downtown Boston

➡ **Boston Harbor Islands Pavilion** (p215)

SIGHTS

GEORGES ISLAND — ISLAND, FORT

(⏲early May–mid-Oct; 👪; ⛴from Long Wharf or Hingham) Georges Island is one of the transportation hubs for the Boston Harbor Islands. It is also the site of **Fort Warren**, a 19th-century fort and Civil War prison. While National Park Service (NPS) rangers give guided tours of the fort and there is a small museum, it is largely abandoned, with many dark tunnels, creepy corners and magnificent lookouts to discover. Weekends on Georges are packed with kids programs, Civil War–era baseball games and jazz concerts.

This is one of the only islands with facilities such as a snack bar and restrooms.

SPECTACLE ISLAND — ISLAND

(⏲dawn-dusk early May–mid-Sep; 👪; ⛴from Long Wharf) 🍃 A Harbor Islands hub, Spectacle Island has a large marina, a solar-powered visitor center, a healthy snack bar and sandy, supervised beaches. Five miles of walking trails provide access to a 157ft peak overlooking the harbor. Special events include Saturday morning yoga classes, Sunday afternoon jazz concerts and Thursday evening clam bakes. Spectacle Island is relatively close to the city and a ferry runs here directly from Long Wharf (hourly in July and August, less frequently in June and September).

LOVELLS ISLAND — ISLAND

(⏲late Jun-early Sep; ⛴from Long Wharf or Georges) With camping and picnicking facilities, Lovells is one of the most popular Harbor Islands destinations. Two deadly shipwrecks may bode badly for seafarers, but that doesn't seem to stop recreational boaters, swimmers and sunbathers from lounging on Lovells' long rocky beach. Some of the former uses of Lovells are evident: European settlers used the island as a rabbit run, and until recently descendant bunnies were still running this place; Fort Standish dates from WWI and is ripe for exploration.

BUMPKIN ISLAND — ISLAND

(⏲late June–early Sep; ⛴from Georges or Hingham) This small island has served many purposes over the years, first farming, then fish drying and smelting. In 1900 it was the site of a children's hospital, but it was taken over for navy training during WWI. You can still explore the remains of a stone farmhouse and the hospital. The beaches are not the best for swimming, as they are slate and seashell. A network of trails leads through fields overgrown with wildflowers. It's one of four islands with camping facilities.

GRAPE ISLAND — ISLAND

(⏲late Jun-early Sep; ⛴from Georges or Hingham) Grape Island is rich with fruity goodness. An arbor decked with cultivated grapes greets you opposite the boat dock, while the wild raspberries, bayberries and elderberries growing along the island's scrubby wooded trails attract abundant birdlife. Unlike many of the Harbor Islands, Grape Island has no remains of forts or military prisons, although during the Revolutionary War it was the site of a skirmish over hay, known as the Battle of Grape Island. The island also offers a few campsites.

PEDDOCKS ISLAND — ISLAND

(⏲late Jun-early Sep; ⛴from Long Wharf or Georges) One of the largest Harbor Islands, Peddocks consists of four headlands connected by sandbars. Hiking trails wander through marsh, pond and coastal environs, and there are campsites and yurts if you wish to spend the night. Meanwhile, the dominant feature of Peddocks Island is the remains of Fort Andrews, a large facility with more than 20 buildings. Peddocks' proximity to the mainland ensured its use as a military stronghold, from the Revolutionary War right through to WWII.

LITTLE BREWSTER
ISLAND
ISLAND, LIGHTHOUSE

(☑617-223-8666; www.bostonharborislands. org/bostonlight; adult/child $35/25; ⊙9:30am & 1pm Fri-Sun Jun-Sep; ☒from Long Wharf) Little Brewster is the country's oldest light station and site of the iconic **Boston Light**, dating from 1783. To visit Little Brewster, you must take an organized tour (reservations required). Learn about Boston's maritime history during a narrated sail around the harbor, passing Graves Light, Long Island Light and Boston Light.

Tours depart from the Boston Harbor Islands Pavilion on the Rose Kennedy Greenway. At the time of research, public access to Little Brewster Island was cut off due to storm damage. Check the website to discover whether travelers can once again climb the 76 steps to the top of the lighthouse for a close-up view of the rotating light and a far-off view of the city skyline.

THOMPSON ISLAND
ISLAND

(☑617-328-3900; www.thompsonisland.org; adult/child $17/10; ⊙8am-4:30pm Sat & Sun Jun-Aug, ☒from EDIC Pier) Thompson Island was settled as early as 1626 by a Scotsman, David Thompson, who set up a trading post to do business with the Neponset Indians. Today this island is privately owned by Thompson Island Outward Bound, a nonprofit organization that develops fun and challenging physical adventures, especially for training and developing leadership skills. As such, the public can explore its 200-plus acres only on weekends when it's wonderful for walking, fishing and birding.

A dedicated ferry leaves from EDIC Pier in the Seaport District; see the website for details.

WORLD'S END
PARK

(www.thetrustees.org; 250 Martin's Lane, Hingham; adult/child $8/free; ⊙8am-dusk) This 251-acre peninsula was designed by Frederick Law Olmsted for residential development in 1889. Carriage paths were laid out and trees were planted, but the houses were never built. Instead, wide, grassy meadows attract butterflies and grass-nesting birds. Today, management by the Trustees of Reservations guarantees continued serenity and beauty. The 4 miles of tree-lined paths are perfect for walking, mountain biking or cross-country skiing – download a map from the website. World's End is accessible by car from Hingham.

✖ EATING & DRINKING

On Georges and Spectacle Islands, there are surprisingly good grills run by Salty's. There is no food or water on the other islands, so pack a picnic.

SALTY'S
GRILL $

(www.saltwaterboston.com/saltys; mains $7-10; ⊙variable) The food service on Spectacle and Georges Islands is a delightful surprise. Sure, it's a fast-food grill, but the salads and sandwiches are fresh and tasty. Salty's also oversees the Thursday-night clam bake ($99) and Sunday-evening luau ($75) on Spectacle Island.

Lexington & Concord

••

Explore

Students of history and lovers of liberty can trace the events of the fateful day that started a revolution – April 19, 1775. Follow in the footsteps of British troops and colonial Minutemen, who tromped out to Lexington to face off on the town green, then continued on to Concord for the battle at the Old North Bridge. Concord is the bigger town with many more sights to see, so don't dally in Lexington.

The day trip is an excellent bicycle outing: the paved Minuteman Bikeway covers the route from Cambridge to Lexington, while the more rugged Battle Rd (within the Minute Man National Historic Park) continues from Lexington to Concord. If you don't feel like pedaling back, you can take your bicycle on the commuter rail.

Otherwise, you will probably need a car (or the Liberty Ride) to see both towns in one day.

The Best...

➡ **Sight** Walden Pond
➡ **Place to Eat** Concord Cheese Shop (p170)
➡ **Place to Drink** Haute Coffee (p170)

Top Tip

If you don't have your own wheels, consider catching the **Liberty Ride** (www.libertyride.us; adult/child $28/12; ⊘10am-4pm daily Jun-Oct, 10am-4pm Sat & Sun Apr & May), a hop-on, hop-off trolley, which includes all of the major sites in both Lexington and Concord. Buy tickets at the Lexington Visitors Center.

Getting There & Away

➡ **Bicycle** The Minuteman Bikeway runs for 6 miles from Alewife in Cambridge to Lexington. From Lexington you can follow the Battle Rd Trail to Concord.

➡ **Bus** MBTA buses 62 and 76 run from the Red Line subway terminus at Alewife to Lexington at least hourly on weekdays, less frequently on Saturday; there are no buses on Sunday.

➡ **Car** Take MA 2 west from Boston or Cambridge to Waltham St (exit 54) for Lexington or Walden St (Rte 126) for Concord.

➡ **Train** MBTA commuter rail trains run between Boston's North Station and the Concord Depot ($9.25, 40 minutes, 12 daily) on the Fitchburg/South Acton line.

Need to Know

➡ **Area Code** ☑978
➡ **Location** 12 miles west of Boston (Lexington), 18 miles west of Boston (Concord)
➡ **Lexington Visitors Center** (Lexington Chamber of Commerce; www.lexingtonchamber.org; 1875 Massachusetts Ave; ⊘9am-5pm)
➡ **Concord Chamber of Commerce** (☑978-369-3120; www.concordchamberofcommerce.org; 58 Main St; ⊘10am-4pm Apr-Oct)

◉ SIGHTS

◉ Lexington

BATTLE GREEN HISTORIC SITE

(Lexington Common; Massachusetts Ave) The historic Battle Green is where the skirmish between patriots and British troops jump-started the War of Independence. The **Lexington Minuteman Statue** (crafted by Henry Hudson Kitson in 1900) stands guard at the southeastern end of Battle Green, honoring the bravery of the 77 minutemen who met the British here in 1775, and the eight who died.

The **Parker Boulder**, named for their commander, marks the spot where the minutemen faced a force almost 10 times their strength. It is inscribed with Parker's instructions to his troops: 'Stand your ground. Don't fire unless fired upon. But if they mean to have a war, let it begin here.' Across the street, history buffs built a replica of the **Old Belfry** that sounded the alarm signaling the start of the revolution.

BUCKMAN TAVERN MUSEUM

(www.lexingtonhistory.org; 1 Bedford Rd; adult/child $8/5; ⊘9:30am-4pm mid-Mar–Nov) Facing the Battle Green, the 1709 Buckman Tavern was the headquarters of the minutemen. Here, they spent the tense hours between the midnight call to arms and the dawn arrival of the Redcoats. Today, the tavern has been restored to its 18th-century appearance, complete with bar, fireplace and bullet holes resulting from British musket fire.

★**MINUTE MAN NATIONAL HISTORIC PARK** PARK

(www.nps.gov/mima; 3113 Marrett Rd; ⊘9am-5pm Apr-Oct; 🖟) FREE The route that British troops followed to Concord has been designated the Minute Man National Historic Park. The visitor center at the eastern end of the park shows an informative multimedia presentation depicting Paul Revere's ride and the ensuing battles. Within the park, Battle Rd is a 5-mile wooded trail that connects the historic sites related to the battles – from Meriam's Corner, where gunfire erupted while British soldiers were retreating, to the Paul Revere capture site.

Minute Man National Historic Park is about 2 miles west of Lexington center on Rte 2A.

◉ Concord

★**OLD NORTH BRIDGE**   HISTORIC SITE

(www.nps.gov/mima; Monument St; ⊘dawn-dusk) A half-mile north of Monument Sq in Concord center, the wooden span of Old North Bridge is the site of the 'shot heard around the world' (as Emerson wrote in his poem *Concord Hymn*). This is where enraged minutemen fired on British troops, forcing them to retreat to Boston. Daniel Chester French's first statue, *Minute Man,* presides over the park from the opposite side of the bridge.

On the far side of the bridge, the Buttrick mansion contains the **visitor center** (174 Liberty St; ⊘9am-5pm Apr-Oct), where you can see a video about the battle and admire the Revolutionary War brass cannon, the Hancock.

OLD MANSE   HISTORIC SITE

(www.thetrustees.org; 269 Monument St; adult/child $10/5; ⊘noon-4pm Wed-Sun Apr-Jun, 11am-5pm Wed-Mon Jul-Oct, Sat & Sun only Nov-Mar) Right next to Old North Bridge, the Old Manse was built in 1769 by Ralph Waldo's grandfather, Reverend William Emerson. Today it's filled with mementos, including those of Nathaniel and Sophia Hawthorne, who lived here for a few years. The highlight of Old Manse is the gorgeously maintained grounds – the fabulous organic garden was planted by Henry David Thoreau as a wedding gift to the Hawthornes.

★**SLEEPY HOLLOW**
CEMETERY   CEMETERY

(www.friendsofsleepyhollow.org; Bedford St; ⊘7am-6pm) This is the final resting place for the most famous Concordians. Though the entrance is only a block east of Monument Sq, the most interesting part, **Authors' Ridge**, is a 15-minute walk along Bedford St. Henry David Thoreau and his family are buried here, as are the Alcotts and the Hawthornes. Ralph Waldo Emerson's tombstone is a large, uncarved rose-quartz boulder, an appropriate transcendentalist symbol.

CONCORD MUSEUM   MUSEUM

(www.concordmuseum.org; 200 Lexington Rd; adult/child $10/5; ♿) Southeast of Monument Sq, Concord Museum brings the town's diverse history under one roof. The museum's prized possession is one of the 'two if by sea' lanterns that hung in the steeple of the Old

---

DECORDOVA SCULPTURE PARK & MUSEUM

The magical **DeCordova Sculpture Park** (www.decordova.org; 51 Sandy Pond Rd, Lincoln; adult/child $14/free; ⊘10am-5pm daily Jun-Aug, closed Mon & Tue Sep-May; ♿) encompasses 35 acres of green hills, providing a spectacular natural environment for a constantly changing exhibit of outdoor artwork. As many as 75 pieces are on display at any given time. Inside the complex, a museum hosts rotating exhibits of sculpture, painting, photography and mixed media.

North Church in Boston as a signal to Paul Revere. It also has the world's largest collection of Henry David Thoreau artifacts, including his writing desk from Walden Pond.

ORCHARD HOUSE   HISTORIC SITE

(www.louisamayalcott.org; 399 Lexington Rd; adult/child $10/5; ⊘10am-4:30pm Mon-Sat, from 11am Sun Apr-Oct, 11am-3pm Mon-Fri, 10am-4:30pm Sat & 1-4:30pm Sun Nov-Mar) Louisa May Alcott (1832–88) was a junior member of Concord's august literary crowd, but her work proved to be durable: *Little Women* is among the most popular young-adult books ever written. The mostly autobiographical novel is set in Concord. Take a tour of Alcott's childhood home, Orchard House, to see how the Alcotts lived and where the novel was actually written.

RALPH WALDO EMERSON
MEMORIAL HOUSE   HISTORIC SITE

(☏978-369-2236; www.facebook.com/emersonhouseconcord; 28 Cambridge Turnpike; adult/child $10/7; ⊘10am-4:30pm Thu-Sat, from 1pm Sun mid-Apr–Oct) This house is where the philosopher lived for almost 50 years until 1882. Emerson was the paterfamilias of literary Concord, one of the great literary figures of his age and the founding thinker of the transcendentalist movement. The house often hosted his renowned circle of friends and still contains many original furnishings.

WALDEN POND   STATE PARK

(☏978-369-3254; www.mass.gov/dcr; 915 Walden St; parking $15; ⊘dawn-dusk) **FREE** Henry

WORTH A DETOUR

PUNTO URBAN ART MUSEUM

If you walk south on Lafayette from Derby St, you'll find yourself on the other side of the tracks (or river, in this case). Welcome to **Punto Urban Art Museum** (www.puntourbanartmuseum. org; Lafayette, Peabody & Ward Sts), or 'The Point,' a rough and tumble Dominican neighborhood that has been transformed into a vibrant, open-air art museum. A group of local and nationally renowned artists painted 50 murals on the brick walls and buildings, all within a three-block radius, creating a fantastical colorful cityscape.

David Thoreau took the naturalist beliefs of transcendentalism out of the realm of theory and into practice when he left the comforts of the town and built himself a rustic cabin on the shores of the pond. His famous memoir of his time spent there, *Walden; or, Life in the Woods* (1854), was full of praise for nature and disapproval of the stresses of civilized life – sentiments that have found an eager audience ever since. The glacial pond is now a state park, surrounded by acres of forest preserved by the Walden Woods project, a nonprofit organization.

Walden Pond lies about 1.7 miles south of Monument Sq, along Walden St (MA 126) south of MA 2. There's a swimming beach and facilities on the southern side, and a footpath that circles the large pond (about a 1.5-mile stroll). The **site of Thoreau's cabin** is on the northeastern side, marked by a cairn and signs.

The park gets packed when the weather is warm; the number of visitors is restricted, so arrive early in summer.

✖ EATING & DRINKING

BEDFORD FARMS   ICE CREAM **$**
(www.bedfordfarmsicecream.com; 68 Thoreau St; ice cream from $4; ⊙11am-9:30pm Mar-Nov, noon-7pm Dec-Feb; ⊛) Dating to the 19th century, this local dairy specializes in delectable ice cream, and frozen yogurt that tastes like delectable ice cream. If prices seem a tad high, it's because the scoops are gigantic. Its trademark flavor is Moosetracks

(vanilla ice cream, chocolate swirl, peanut-butter cups). Conveniently located next to the train depot.

HAUTE COFFEE   CAFE **$**
(www.myhautecoffee.com; 12 Walden St; mains $6-10; ⊙7am-5pm Mon-Fri, from 8am Sat & Sun; ☎☏) Here's a sweet coffee shop serving rich Counter Culture coffee, ground and brewed to order. If you're hungry, there are simple, delicious soups, sandwiches and tartines. The baked goods and pastries are made in-house and they're pretty irresistible.

CONCORD CHEESE SHOP   DELI **$**
(www.concordcheeseshop.com; 29 Walden St; sandwiches $8-12; ⊙10am-5:30pm Tue-Sat; ☏) This is a cheese shop, as it claims, with an excellent selection of imported and local cheese, as well as wine and other specialty food items. But the folks behind the counter can whip those ingredients into an amazing sandwich (or soup or salad) – perfect for a picnic on Memorial Sq. Want something fabulous? Try the Thursday/Saturday special sandwich.

VIA LAGO CAFÉ   CAFE **$**
(www.vialagocatering.com; 1845 Massachusetts Ave; mains $6-10; ⊙7am-8pm Mon-Sat; ☏⊛) This cafe has high ceilings, intimate tables, a scent of fresh-roasted coffee and a great deli case. It's a perfect stop for breakfast or lunch, but the on-site dining room is also popular for dinner.

Salem

Explore

A lot of history is packed into this gritty city. There is much more than a day's worth of sights and activities, so be selective when planning your time here.

Your starting point should be the Salem Maritime National Historic Site, which includes a smattering of historic buildings and the impressive ship *Friendship*. This overview of the city's maritime exploits is the perfect introduction to the Peabody Essex Museum, which is Salem's unrivaled highlight.

Dubbed 'Witch City,' Salem is also infamous as the site of the witch trials in 1692, when 19 people were hanged as a result of witch-hunt hysteria. There are dozens of witch-themed sights, as well as an excellent trial re-enactment. Most of these destinations are more about fun than authenticity.

The Best...
→ **Sight** Peabody Essex Museum
→ **Place to Eat** New England Soup Factory (p172)
→ **Place to Drink** Gulu-Gulu Café (p172)

Top Tip
During the month of October, **Haunted Happenings** (www.hauntedhappenings.org; ☺Oct) is a Halloween festival that includes parades, concerts, pumpkin carvings, costume parties and trick-or-treating.

Getting There & Away
→ **Boat** Departing four or five times daily, **Boston Harbor Cruises** (p208) makes the scenic, one-hour trip between Salem Ferry Center and Long Wharf in Boston.
→ **Car** From MA 128, take MA 114 east into Salem center.
→ **Train** The Rockport/Newburyport line of the MBTA commuter rail runs from Boston's North Station to Salem Depot ($7.50, 30 minutes).

Need to Know
→ **Area Code** ☎978
→ **Location** 20 miles north of Boston
→ **NPS Regional Visitor Center** (☎978-740-1650; www.nps.gov/sama; 2 New Liberty St; ☺9am-5pm May-Oct, from 10am Wed-Sun Nov-Apr)

⊙ SIGHTS

SALEM MARITIME NATIONAL HISTORIC SITE
HISTORIC SITE

(www.nps.gov/sama; 160 Derby St; ☺9am-5pm May-Oct, 10am-4pm Wed-Sun Nov-Apr) **FREE** This National Historic Site comprises the Custom House, the wharves and other buildings along Derby St that are remnants of the shipping industry that once thrived along this stretch of Salem. Of the 50 wharves that once lined Salem Harbor, only three remain, the longest of which is Derby

Wharf. Check the website for a schedule of guided tours of the various buildings, or download an audio walking tour of the whole area.

The most prominent building along Derby St is the Custom House, where permits and certificates were issued and, of course, taxes paid. Other buildings at the site include warehouses, the middle-class Norbonne House and the fancier Elias Hasket Derby house. If you're lucky and the ship is at dock, you can climb aboard the tall ship *Friendship*. All are open by guided tour only.

★PEABODY ESSEX MUSEUM
MUSEUM

(☎978-745-9500; www.pem.org; 161 Essex St; adult/child $20/free; ☺10am-5pm Tue-Sun; ♠) All of the art, artifacts and curiosities that Salem merchants brought back from the Far East were the foundation for this museum. Founded in 1799, it is the country's oldest museum in continuous operation. The building itself is impressive, with a light-filled atrium, and it's a wonderful setting for the vast collections, which focus on New England decorative arts and maritime history.

HOUSE OF THE SEVEN GABLES
HISTORIC SITE

(www.7gables.org; 54 Turner St; adult/child $16/11; ☺10am-7pm Jul-Oct, to 5pm Nov-Jun) 'Halfway down a by-street of one of our New England towns stands a rusty wooden house, with seven acutely peaked gables facing towards various points of the compass, and a huge clustered chimney in their midst.' So wrote Nathaniel Hawthorne in his 1851 novel *The House of Seven Gables*. The house brings to life the gloomy Puritan atmosphere of early New England. Look for wonderful seaside gardens, many original furnishings and a mysterious secret staircase.

WITCH HOUSE
HISTORIC SITE

(Jonathan Corwin House; ☎978-744-8815; www.thewitchhouse.org; 310 Essex St; adult/child $8.25/4.25, guided tour $2; ☺10am-5pm mid-Mar–mid-Nov, noon-4pm Thu-Sun mid-Nov–mid-Mar) Of more than a score of witchy attractions in town, this is the only actual historic site. The house was once the home of Jonathan Corwin, a local magistrate who was called on to investigate witchcraft claims. He examined several accused witches, possibly in the 1st-floor rooms of this house.

The house demonstrates the family's daily life at the time of the witch hysteria, providing historical context for the episode. Open longer hours in October.

✕ EATING & DRINKING

NEW ENGLAND SOUP FACTORY
SOUP **$**
(www.nesoupfactorysalem.com; 140 Washington St; soup $6.50-7.50, sandwiches $5-9; ⏰11am-8pm Mon-Fri, noon-7pm Sat & Sun; 🅿🚹) When there's a chill in the air, nothing warms body and soul like a bowl of hot soup. It's not much to look at, but the New England Soup Factory offers 10 amazing, rotating options every day. Favorites include chicken-pot-pie soup (topped with puff pastry) and pumpkin lobster bisque. In summer, it serves cold soups, of course.

DERBY JOE
SANDWICHES **$**
(www.derbyjoe.co; 142 Derby St; sandwiches $9; ⏰6am-4pm Mon-Fri, 7:30am-5pm Sat & Sun; 🛜🚶) Derby Joe has quickly become beloved in Salem for its friendly owners, strong coffee, tasty sandwiches and nonstop chess tournament in the house. Now on offer: picnic baskets packed with your favorite sandwiches.

★GULU-GULU CAFÉ
CAFE
(www.gulugulucafe.com; 247 Essex St; ⏰8am-1am Tue-Sat, to 11pm Sun & Mon; 🛜) *Gulu-gulu* means 'gulp, gulp' in French, and this place is named after a now-defunct cafe in Prague. That's an indication of how eclectic it is, featuring (in no particular order) delicious coffee, art-adorned walls, live music, exotic liqueurs and board games.

★MERCY TAVERN
BAR
(www.mercysalem.com; 148 Derby St; ⏰11:30am-1am Mon-Sat, to 11pm Sun) A dark and cozy pub with exposed brick walls, this is the perfect place to sip a pint and listen to the blues. This happens every Friday (4pm to 7pm), with other live music acts throughout the week. The 'pub fare' here includes the typical burgers and tacos, but it's locally sourced and made with love.

Plymouth

Explore

Neatly contained and historically significant, Plymouth is the perfect day trip. Start the day at *Mayflower II* to experience life aboard the 17th-century sailing vessel. Make the obligatory stop at Plymouth Rock to see where the Pilgrims (might have) first stepped ashore. Then climb the hill into town, which is lined up along Main St. This is an opportunity to stop for lunch, before moving on to spend the afternoon at Plimoth Plantation to experience what life was like for the Pilgrims once they were settled here.

Not surprisingly, Plymouth has a handful of historic houses and other micromuseums that are also open for visitors. The best is Pilgrim Hall (America's oldest museum!), which contains some cool artifacts and excellent educational exhibits.

The Best...
➡ **Sight** Plimoth Plantation
➡ **Place to Eat** KKatie's Burger Bar (p174)
➡ **Place to Drink** Blue Blinds Bakery

Top Tip
Native Plymouth Tours (☎774-454-7792; www.facebook.com/nativeplymouthtours; adult/child $15/10) offers a walking tour with a Native American guide. You'll see many typical sights, but your guide Timothy Turner will debunk myths, give unusual insights and share a completely different perspective on Plymouth (and American) history.

Getting There & Away
➡ **Boat** The **Plymouth-to-Provincetown Express Ferry** (☎508-746-2643; www.captjohn.com; State Pier, 77 Water St; ⏰round-trip adult/child $53/32) deposits you on the tip of Cape Cod faster than a car would. From late June to early September, the 90-minute journey departs Plymouth at 10am and leaves Provincetown at 4:30pm.
➡ **Bus** Buses operated by Plymouth & Brockton (www.p-b.com) travel hourly from South Station ($16, 50 minutes) in Boston. From the Plymouth P&B terminal, hop on a GATRA bus into Plymouth center.

➜ **Car** Plymouth is 41 miles south of Boston via MA 3; it takes an hour with some traffic.

➜ **Train** You can reach Plymouth from Boston by MBTA commuter rail trains, which depart from South Station three or four times a day ($11.50, 90 minutes). From the station at Cordage Park, GATRA buses connect to Plymouth center.

Need to Know
➜ **Area Code** 508
➜ **Location** 41 miles south of Boston
➜ **Destination Plymouth** (www.seeplymouth.com; 130 Water St; ⊗9am-5pm Apr-Oct, to 8pm Jun-Aug)

⊙ SIGHTS

★**PLIMOTH PLANTATION**   MUSEUM
(508-746-1622; www.plimoth.org; 137 Warren Ave; adult/child $28/16; ⊗9am-5pm Apr-Nov;
) Three miles south of Plymouth center, Plimoth Plantation authentically re-creates the Pilgrims' settlement in its primary exhibit, entitled **1627 English Village**. Everything in the village – costumes, implements, vocabulary, artistry, recipes and crops – has been painstakingly researched and remade. Costumed interpreters, acting in character, explain the details of daily life and answer your questions as you watch them work and play.

During the winter of 1620–21, half of the Pilgrims died of disease, privation and exposure to the elements. But new arrivals joined the survivors the following year, and by 1627 – just before an additional influx of settlers founded the colony of Massachusetts Bay – Plymouth Colony was on the road to prosperity. Plimoth Plantation provides excellent educational and entertaining insight into what was happening in Plymouth during that period.

In the **crafts center**, you can help artisans as they weave baskets and cloth, throw pottery and build fine furniture using the techniques and tools of the early 17th century. Exhibits explain how these manufactured goods were shipped across the Atlantic in exchange for Colonial necessities.

The **Wampanoag Homesite** replicates the life of a Native American community in the same area during that time. Homesite huts are made of wattle and daub (a framework of woven rods and twigs covered and plastered with clay); inhabitants engage in crafts while wearing traditional garb. Unlike the actors at the English Village, these individuals are not acting as historic characters but are indigenous people speaking from a modern perspective.

★**MAYFLOWER II**   SHIP
(www.plimoth.org/what-see-do/mayflower-ii; State Pier, Water St;) If Plymouth Rock tells us little about the Pilgrims, *Mayflower II* speaks volumes. Climb aboard this replica of the small ship in which the Pilgrims made the fateful voyage, where 102 people lived together for 66 days as the ship passed through stormy North Atlantic waters. Actors in period costume are on board, recounting harrowing tales from the journey.

PLYMOUTH ROCK   MONUMENT
(Water St) Thousands of visitors come each year to look at this weathered granite ball and consider what it was like for the Pilgrims who stepped ashore on a foreign land in the autumn of 1620. In firsthand accounts of the fledgling colony there's no mention of a granite rock, but the story gained popularity during colonial times.

★**PILGRIM HALL MUSEUM**   MUSEUM
(www.pilgrimhall.org; 75 Court St; adult/child $12/8; ⊗9:30am-4:30pm Feb-Dec;) Claiming to be the oldest continually operating public museum in the country, Pilgrim Hall Museum was founded in 1824. Its exhibits are not reproductions but real objects that the Pilgrims and their Wampanoag neighbors used in their daily lives – from Governor Bradford's chair to Constance Hopkins' beaver hat.

✖ EATING & DRINKING

★**BLUE BLINDS BAKERY**   BAKERY $
(www.blueblindsbakery.com; 7 North St; mains $5-9; ⊗6am-9pm Sun-Thu, 7am-3pm Fri;) Blue Blinds is a cozy house – it feels like a home, really – with plants in the windows and a fire in the fireplace and folks sipping coffee on the shady front porch. The baked goods are out of this world, including fresh-baked organic breads, muffins and pastries. Breakfast is served all day, but the sandwiches and homemade soups are also divine.

Provincetown

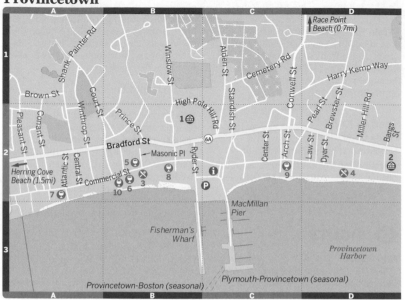

DAY TRIPS FROM BOSTON PLYMOUTH

Provincetown

◎ Sights
1 Pilgrim Monument &
   Provincetown Museum....................B2
2 Provincetown Art Association &
   Museum D2

⊗ Eating
3 Canteen...B2
4 Mews Restaurant & Cafe....................D2

◎ Drinking & Nightlife
5 A-House B2
6 Aqua Bar B2
7 Boatslip Beach Club A2
8 Crown & Anchor.................................B2
9 Harbor Lounge.....................................C2
10 Pied Bar...B2

KKATIE'S BURGER BAR   BURGERS $
(www.kkaties.com; 38 Main St Extension; burgers
$11-13; ⊙11:30am-12:30am; ⊕) Legend has it
that when the Pilgrims landed at Plymouth
Rock, they were dying for a burger. Finally,
after 400 years, KKatie is fulfilling this
wish. And apparently the Pilgrims all wanted different kinds of burger, because she's
got about 20 varieties on offer. Accompaniments are sweet-potato fries, truffle fries,
green fries (fried green beans) and more.

TASTY   GASTROPUB $$
(www.thetastyplymouth.com; 42 Court St; lunch
$8-16, dinner $18-27; ⊙5-9pm Tue, 11:30am-9pm
Wed & Thu, 11:30am-10pm Fri & Sat, 4-8pm Sun)
Plymouth is loving this gastropub, located
on the main drag. The space is modern yet
cozy, while the food is locally sourced and
inventively prepared. Look for delightfully
surprising combinations, such as fried ca-
lamari in a pea shoot and snap pea salad
or cod risotto with braised greens or cran-
berry bread pudding for dessert. Tuesday is
noodle night.

LOCAL YOLK   BREAKFAST $
(www.localyolkcompany.com; 186 Water St; mains
$4-10; ⊙6am-2pm Thu-Tue) The name says it
all. Everything on the menu is made from
scratch using the freshest local ingredients.
Look for amazing breakfast sandwiches,
sweet and savory crepes and to-die-for
fluffy ricotta pancakes. It's a tiny place with
counter service and only a few tables.

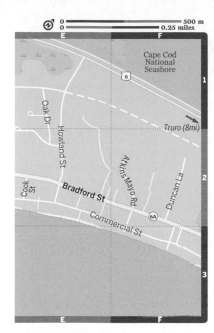

Cape Cod
National
Seashore

Truro (8mi)

Oak Dr
Howland St
Cook St
Bradford St
Atkins Mayo Rd
Duncan La
Commercial St

→ **Place to Eat** Mews Restaurant & Cafe (p177)

→ **Place to Drink** Aqua Bar (p177)

Top Tip

The best way to get around Provincetown is by bicycle (free parking everywhere!). Bring a bicycle on the ferry from Boston for only $6 or rent one from **Ptown Bikes** (www.ptownbikes.com; $24 per day).

Getting There & Away

→ **Air** The closest airport is northwest of town and connected year-round to Boston (25 minutes) via frequent flights with Cape Air (www.capeair.com).

→ **Boat** Both **Bay State Cruise Co** (☑617-748-1428; www.boston ptown.com; round-trip adult/child $95/72) and **Boston Harbor Cruises** (p208) operate a fast-ferry service (1½ hours) from Long Wharf in Boston up to three times daily.

→ **Bus** The **Plymouth & Brockton** (☑508-746-0378; www.p-b.com) bus service from Boston runs several times daily (one way $38, three to 3½ hours) and services other Cape towns. To get all the way to Provincetown you must switch buses in Hyannis.

→ **Car** Allow 2½ ours to make the drive from Boston; weekend traffic can be brutal and will surely slow you down.

Need to Know

→ **Area Code** ☑508 & 774

→ **Location** 115 miles southeast of Boston

→ **Provincetown Chamber of Commerce** (☑508-487-3424; www.ptownchamber.com; 307 Commercial St; ☺9am-5pm)

Provincetown

Explore

Provincetown is far out. We're not just talking geographically (though it does occupy the outermost point on Cape Cod), we're also talking about the flamboyant street scenes, brilliant art galleries and unbridled nightlife. Once an outpost for fringe writers and artists, Provincetown has morphed into the hottest gay and lesbian destination in the Northeast.

Even if you're only in town for a day, you'll want to spend part of it admiring the art and watching the street life on Commercial St. If you are lucky enough to be here at night, you can also partake in some diverse dining, singing and dancing until dawn.

But that's only half the show. As part of the Cape Cod National seashore, Provincetown's untamed coastline and vast beaches beg exploring. A network of bicycle trails wind through picturesque sand dunes and a beach backed by sea and sky (and a lighthouse or two).

The Best...

→ **Sight** Race Point Beach (p176)

DAY TRIPS FROM BOSTON PROVINCETOWN

⊙ SIGHTS & ACTIVITIES

Province Lands Bike Trail (www.nps.gov/caco), an exhilarating 7.5 miles of paved bike trails, crisscrosses the forest and undulating dunes of the **Cape Cod National Seashore** (☑508-255-3421; www.nps.gov/caco; pedestrian/cyclist/motorcycle/car per day $3/3/10/20). As a bonus, you can cool off with a swim: the main 5.5-mile loop trail has spur trails leading to Herring Cove Beach and Race Point Beach.

LGBTQ+ PROVINCETOWN

As you would expect, Provincetown is overflowing with bars and clubs catering to LGBT+ locals and visitors. Keep your ears to the ground – there are parties, drag shows and theme nights regularly, even in the off-season.

A-House (Atlantic House; ☑508-487-3169; www.ahouse.com; 4 Masonic Pl; ⊘Little Bar noon-1am, Macho Bar & club 10pm-1am) P-town's gay scene got its start here and it's still the leading bar in town. Includes an intimate pub and the town's hottest DJ dance club.

Boatslip Beach Club (☑508-487-1669; www.boatslipresort.com; 161 Commercial St; ⊘tea dances daily from 4pm Jun-early Sep, Fri-Sun mid-Sep–May) Hosts wildly popular afternoon tea dances (4pm to 7pm), often packed with gorgeous guys.

Pied Bar (☑508-487-1527; www.piedbar.net; 193 Commercial St; ⊘noon-1am May-Oct) This woman-owned waterfront lounge is a popular dance spot for all genders, especially around sunset.

Crown & Anchor (☑508-487-1430; www.onlyatthecrown.com; 247 Commercial St; ⊘hours vary) The queen of the scene, this multiwing complex has a nightclub, a video bar, a leather bar and a fun, steamy cabaret that takes it to the limit.

There are plenty of bike-rental places in central P-town.

HERRING COVE BEACH   BEACH
(Province Lands Rd) Swimmers favor the relatively calm (though certainly brisk) waters of Herring Cove Beach, part of the Cape Cod National Seashore (p175). The long, sandy beach is popular with everyone. Though technically illegal, nude sunbathers head left to the south section of the beach; families usually break out the picnic baskets closer to the parking lot. The entire beach faces west, making it a spectacular place to be at sunset. Parking costs $20 in summer (the National Seashore fee).

RACE POINT BEACH   BEACH
(Race Point Rd) On the wild tip of the Cape, this Cape Cod National Seashore (p175) beach is a breathtaking stretch of sand, crashing surf and undulating dunes as far as the eye can see. Kick off your sandals, kids – the soft, grainy sand makes for a fun run. This is the kind of beach where you could walk for miles and see no one but the occasional angler casting for bluefish. Parking costs $20 in summer (the National Seashore fee).

★**PROVINCETOWN ART ASSOCIATION & MUSEUM**   MUSEUM
(PAAM; ☑508-487-1750; www.paam.org; 460 Commercial St; adult/child $10/free; ⊘11am-5pm Sat-Thu, to 10pm Fri Jun & Sep, to 8pm Mon-Thu, to 10pm Fri, to 5pm Sat & Sun Jul & Aug, noon-5pm Thu-Sun Oct-May) Founded in 1914 to celebrate the town's thriving art community, this vibrant museum showcases the works of hundreds of artists who have found their inspiration on the Lower Cape. Chief among them are Charles Hawthorne, who led the early Provincetown art movement, and Edward Hopper, who had a home and gallery in the Truro dunes.

★**PILGRIM MONUMENT & PROVINCETOWN MUSEUM**   MUSEUM
(☑508-487-1310; www.pilgrim-monument.org; 1 High Pole Hill Rd; adult/child $12/4; ⊘9am-5pm Apr, May & Sep-Jan, to 7pm Jun-Aug) Climb to the top of the country's tallest all-granite structure (253ft) for a sweeping view of town, the beaches and the spine of the Lower Cape. The climb is 116 steps plus 60 ramps and takes about 10 minutes at a leisurely pace. At the base of the c 1910 tower is an evocative, but quite Eurocentric, museum depicting the landing of the *Mayflower* Pilgrims and other Provincetown history.

 EATING & DRINKING

★CANTEEN
MODERN AMERICAN $

(☑508-487-3800; www.thecanteenptown.com; 225 Commercial St; mains $10-16; ⊙11am-9pm Sun-Thu, to 10pm Fri & Sat; ☑📶) Cool and casual, but unmistakably gourmet – this is your optimal P-town lunch stop. Choose from classics like lobster rolls and barbecued pulled-pork sandwiches, or innovations like cod *bahn mi* and shrimp sliders. We strongly recommend you add crispy Brussels sprouts and a cold beer to your order and then take a seat at the communal picnic table on the sand.

★MEWS RESTAURANT
& CAFE
MODERN AMERICAN $$$

(☑508-487-1500; www.mews.com; 429 Commercial St; mains $19-44; ⊙5-10pm, also 10am-2pm Sun mid-May–Sep) A fantastic water view, the hottest martini bar in town and scrumptious food add up to Provincetown's finest dining scene. There are two sections: opt to dine gourmet on lobster risotto and filet mignon downstairs, where you're right on the sand, or go casual with a juicy Angus burger from the bistro menu upstairs. Reservations recommended.

AQUA BAR
BAR

(☑774-593-5106; www.facebook.com/aquabar ptown; 207 Commercial St; ⊙10:30am-10pm Sun-Thu, to midnight Fri & Sat May-Oct) Imagine a food court where the options include a raw bar, sushi, gelato and other international delights. Add a fully stocked bar with generous bartenders pouring the drinks. Now put the whole place in a gorgeous seaside setting, overlooking a little beach and a beautiful harbor. Now imagine this whole scene at sunset. That's Aqua Bar.

HARBOR LOUNGE
COCKTAIL BAR

(☑508-413-9527; www.theharborlounge.com; 359 Commercial St; ⊙noon-11pm Apr-Dec) The Harbor Lounge takes full advantage of its seaside setting, with floor-to-ceiling windows and a boardwalk stretching out into the bay. Candlelit tables and black leather sofas constitute the decor – nothing else is needed. The cocktails are surprisingly affordable, with many martini concoctions to sample.

🛏 Sleeping

Boston offers a wide range of accommodations, from inviting guesthouses in historic quarters to swanky hotels. There's no shortage of stately homes that have been converted into B&Bs, offering an intimate atmosphere and personal service. Considering that this city is filled with students, there are surprisingly few accommodations targeting budget travelers.

Rates

Boston is a relatively expensive place to stay, due to its busy conference and academic calendars and popular tourist appeal. Book in advance online for the best prices. Budget travelers, especially, will find there is a shortage of affordable options, so book your beds as early as possible. A few welcoming guesthouses and smaller hotels welcome midrange travelers, while many hotels of all sizes cater to high-enders. Prices increase dramatically during peak travel times.

Most hotels, particularly chains, have no set rates. Instead, rates fluctuate seasonally, if not daily. High season is roughly defined as April through October, although prices are more accurately driven by occupancy and high-profile events. Holidays, university graduations, baseball games and pride parades all affect hotel prices. Often the most expensive period is from mid-September to mid-October.

Boutique Hotels

In recent years, Boston has become a hot spot for boutique hotels – small, stylish hotels, usually with personalized service and contemporary flair. The classiest boutique hotels are not cheap, but most offer competitive rates to attract tourists and businesspeople.

Budget Lodgings

Inexpensive accommodations are rare, but the savvy traveler should have no problem locating an acceptable option. Boston has only one hostel catering to traditional backpacking travelers, but some guesthouses also offer simple accommodations and personal service at budget prices. There are also myriad options for staying in private homes, booked through services such as Airbnb and Couchsurfing.

B&Bs

Many B&Bs and inns are housed in historic or architecturally significant buildings. Contact B&Bs directly, or better yet, contact an agency that will try to match your neighborhood desires with the thickness of your wallet.

Apartment Rentals

With hordes of students and other transients moving around town, Boston, Brookline and Cambridge are full of summer sublets and longer-term apartments available to rent. Signs are often posted at coffee shops, bookstores and other student hangouts. University housing offices are also good sources of information.

➡ **Boston Apartments** (www.bostonapartments.com) Includes listings for long- and short-term, furnished and unfurnished, and a search by neighborhood.

➡ **Rental Beast** (www.rentalbeast.com) Rental properties all over town. Search by neighborhood or requirements.

Lonely Planet's Top Choices

Liberty Hotel (p181) Swanky hotel in a former jail.

Verb Hotel (p185) Trendy, retro, rock-n-roll hotel.

Harding House (p186) Affordable and hospitable in Central Sq.

No 284 (p184) A gorgeous guesthouse in a Back Bay brownstone.

HI-Boston (p183) Classy hostel with many perks for budget travelers.

Gryphon House (p185) Luxurious suites overlooking the Charles River.

Best By Budget

$
Revolution Hotel (p183) Small but snazzy.

HI-Boston (p183) A bright shiny hostel in the heart of Chinatown.

Bertram Inn (p188) A charming Brookline B&B.

$$
Gryphon House (p185) Luxurious Fenway brownstone.

Harding House (p186) Homey haven in Cambridge.

College Club (p184) Cozy quarters in the Back Bay.

$$$
Liberty Hotel (p181) Riverside luxury in a former jailhouse.

Verb Hotel (p185) Verb is all about the vibe.

No 284 (p184) A boutique sleep in an opulent brownstone.

Best Green Hotels

InterContinental Hotel (p183) Green Key and Restaurant Certified.

Hotel Marlowe (p187) Green Key certified.

HI-Boston (p183) LEED certified.

Irving House (p187) EPA Energy Star award.

Seaport Boston (p186) Hotel Good Earthkeeping award.

Best For Families

Constitution Inn (p181) Attached to a giant play area (aka YMCA).

Colonnade (p184) Rubber duckies and a rooftop pool, plus a cool Kids See & Do package.

Hotel Commonwealth (p185) 'Voluntourism' package for families who want to do good.

Best For Baseball Fans

Verb Hotel (p185) Behind Fenway Park.

Hotel Commonwealth (p185) Baseball packages available.

Hotel Buckminster (p185) Some ballpark views.

Gryphon House (p185) Discounts for Sox ticket holders.

Best B&Bs

Gryphon House (p185) Beautiful riverside brownstone.

Clarendon Square Inn (p183) Victorian beauty.

Taylor House (p188) Sitting pretty pond-side.

Best Unique Sleeps

Green Turtle (p181) Drift off on a boat.

Liberty Hotel (p181) Spend the night in jail.

Verb Hotel (p185) Rock out.

NEED TO KNOW

Price Ranges
Prices quoted are for a double room in high season. Unless otherwise noted, rates include private bathroom, but exclude breakfast and tax.

$ less than $200

$$ $200–$350

$$$ more than $350

Useful Websites
➜ **Lonely Planet** (lonelyplanet.com/usa/boston/hotels) Reviews and bookings.

➜ **B&B Agency of Boston** (www.boston-bnbagency.com) Fully furnished vacation rentals.

➜ **Bed & Breakfast Associates Bay Colony** (www.bnbboston.com) Huge database of unhosted, furnished rooms and apartments.

➜ **Inn Boston Reservations** (www.innboston reservations.com) Studio and apartment rentals in Boston's best neighborhoods.

➜ **Boston Green Tourism** (www.bostongreen tourism.org) Up-to-date listings of ecofriendly hotels.

➜ **Boston Luxury Hotels** (www.bostonluxury hotels.com) Individualized service for upscale travelers.

Tipping
It's customary to tip housekeeping $3 to $5 for one or two nights, more for longer stays.

Where to Stay

Neighborhood	For	Against
Charlestown	Relatively affordable. Neighborhood charm. Great skyline views. Close to some sights.	Removed from city center. Limited transportation options.
West End & North End	Relatively affordable. Close to major sights. Convenient transportation to other neighborhoods. Great dining and shopping in North End.	Few sleeping options in North End. Desolate atmosphere in West End.
Beacon Hill & Boston Common	Neighborhood charm. Close to major sights. Great dining and shopping.	Few affordable options.
Downtown & Waterfront	Close to major sights and waterfront. Convenient transportation to other neighborhoods. Hustle-and-bustle city atmosphere.	Few affordable options. Hustle-and-bustle city atmosphere (noisy, no neighborhood charm).
South End & Chinatown	Neighborhood charm. Close to major sights. Convenient transportation to other neighborhoods. Great dining, shopping and nightlife. Hustle-and-bustle city atmosphere.	Some areas can be dangerous for solo travelers and late-night revelers who are not cautious. Hustle-and-bustle city atmosphere (noisy).
Back Bay	Neighborhood charm. Close to major sights. Convenient transportation to other neighborhoods. Great dining, shopping and nightlife.	None
Kenmore Square & Fenway	Close to major sights. Convenient transportation to other neighborhoods. Great dining and nightlife.	None
Seaport District & South Boston	Close to airport and waterfront. Great dining and shopping. City and harbor views.	None
Cambridge	Neighborhood charm. Close to some sights. Convenient transportation to other neighborhoods. Great dining, shopping and nightlife.	Removed from city center.
Streetcar Suburbs	Relatively affordable. Neighborhood charm. Close to some sights. Convenient transportation to other neighborhoods. Great dining, shopping and nightlife.	Removed from city center.

SLEEPING

🛏 Charlestown

Options for staying in Charlestown are very limited. But if you want to sleep on the water in Boston, this may be your only chance.

CONSTITUTION INN   HOTEL $

Map p227 (✆617-241-8400; www.constitution inn.org; 150 Third Ave; d $100-150; ▣❋🛜🏊; ▣93 from Haymarket, ⛴F4 from Long Wharf) Housed in a granite building in the historic Charlestown Navy Yard (p216), this excellent, affordable hotel accommodates active and retired military personnel, but you don't have to have a crew cut to stay. Somewhat institutional, the rooms are mostly clean, freshly painted, and furnished with cherrywood beds and desks. Some have kitchenettes. Guests gain free access to the Olympic-class fitness center (Charlestown YMCA).

GREEN TURTLE   B&B $$

Map p227 (✆617-337-0202; www.greenturtlebb. com; Pier 8, 13th St; d $290; ▣❋🛜; ⛴F4 from Long Wharf) It's not just a B&B, but a floating B&B. If you want to be lulled to sleep by the sound of waves lapping and wake up to the cry of seagulls, maybe you should be sleeping on a houseboat. The two contemporary guest rooms are surprisingly spacious, complete with kitchenettes. Hot coffee and fresh pastries are served in your room.

🛏 West End & North End

The North End's close-knit Italian community is not known for welcoming visitors – for dinner, yes, but not to spend the night. Save for one or two small places, all of the accommodation options are in the West End.

BOXER HOTEL   BOUTIQUE HOTEL $$

Map p228 (✆617-624-0202; www.theboxer boston.com; 107 Merrimac St; d from $209; ▣❋@🛜🏊; ▭North Station) 🍃 Exemplifying the up-and-coming character of this once-downtrodden district, this boutique hotel occupies a fully restored 19th-century flatiron building on the western edge of the Bulfinch Triangle. Design elements like open-frame wardrobes and plaid bedding exhibit a subtly masculine sophistication. Technology perks include Keurig coffee makers, iHomes and flatscreen TVs.

Due to the unique triangular shape of the building, the rooms vary by size and shape, and some of them are pretty cramped. If this is a concern, it's worth requesting a larger room when you make your reservation.

ONYX HOTEL   BOUTIQUE HOTEL $$

Map p228 (✆617-557-9955; www.onyxhotel. com; 155 Portland St; d from $224; ▣❋🛜🏊; ▭North Station) 🍃 Done up in muted grays and browns with bold crimson accents, the Onyx exudes contemporary sophistication. Attractive perks of the hotel (a member of the Kimpton Hotel Group) include free use of bikes and yoga mats in every room, as well as the evening wine reception. Note the $20 daily amenity fee.

★LIBERTY HOTEL   HOTEL $$$

Map p228 (✆866-961-3778, 617-224-4000; www. libertyhotel.com; 215 Charles St; r from $375; ▣♿❋🛜; ▭Charles/MGH) It is with intended irony that the notorious Charles St Jail has been converted into the classy Liberty Hotel. Today, the 90ft ceiling soars above a spectacular lobby. All 298 guest rooms come with luxurious linens and high-tech amenities, while the 18 in the original jail wing boast floor-to-ceiling windows with amazing views of the Charles River and Beacon Hill.

Over the years, the jail housed many famous residents, including the anarchists Sacco and Vanzetti, black liberationist Malcolm X and Boston's own James Michael Curley. Check out the small exhibit on the building's history, which is just off the lobby.

BRICCO SUITES   APARTMENT $$$

Map p230 (✆617-459-1293; www.briccosuites. com; 241 Hanover St; d/apt from $335/450; ❋🛜; ▭Haymarket) Immerse yourself in the Italian American Boston experience with a stay in a lovely, light-filled apartment in the heart of the North End. The local restaurateur DePasquale family rents 15 studios and apartments – all decked out with kitchens (minimally stocked), polished hardwood floors, marble bathrooms, Italian linens and gas fireplaces. There's no elevator, but it's worth the climb.

The flats are mostly unhosted (though concierge and cleaning service is available).

🛏 Beacon Hill & Boston Common

Beacon Hill is a delightful place to call 'home' during your stay in Boston. The options are few (and expensive) but delightful (and worth it).

BEACON HILL HOTEL
& BISTRO   BOUTIQUE HOTEL $$
Map p236 (📞617-723-7575; www.beaconhill hotel.com; 25 Charles St; d/ste $269/369; P❋🤧; TCharles/MGH) This upscale European-style inn blends into the neighborhood without flash or fanfare. Carved out of former residential buildings typical of Beacon Hill, the hotel has 12 very small but stylish rooms, decorated with contemporary furniture, louvered shutters and a designer's soothing palette of paint choices. Added perks include the exclusive roof deck, and complimentary breakfast at the urbane, on-site bistro.

XV BEACON   BOUTIQUE HOTEL $$$
Map p236 (📞617-670-1500; www.xvbeacon.com; 15 Beacon St; d from $349; P❋🤧❋; TPark St) Housed in a turn-of-the-20th-century beaux-arts building, XV Beacon sets the standard for Boston's boutique hotels. Guest-room decor is soothing, taking advantage of color schemes rich with taupe, espresso and cream. You'll find custom-made gas fireplaces and built-in mahogany entertainment units, alongside heated towel racks and rainforest shower heads in the bathrooms, and romantic canopy beds dressed in Frette linens.

🛏 Downtown & Waterfront

The Downtown and Waterfront area is in the middle of the action, which makes it a fantastic base for exploring Boston. But you'll pay for the privilege of sleeping here, as all of the hotels are upscale and expensive.

HARBORSIDE INN   BOUTIQUE HOTEL $$
Map p234 (📞617-723-7500; www.harborside innboston.com; 185 State St; d from $289; P❋@🤧; TAquarium) Steps from Faneuil Hall and the waterfront, this boutique hotel inhabits a respectfully renovated 19th-century mercantile warehouse. The

116 rooms are on the small side, but are comfortable and appropriately nautically themed. Note that Atrium Rooms face the atrium (ahem) and Cabin Rooms have no windows at all. Add $20 for a city view (worth it).

BOSTONIAN BOSTON   HOTEL $$
Map p234 (📞617-523-3600; www.millennium hotels.com; 26 North St; d from $279; P❋🤧; THaymarket) 🕊 The Bostonian proudly touts its roots as part of the Blackstone Block, the city's oldest block. From the moment you enter the cool, contemporary lobby, to the time you step out onto your balcony overlooking the bustle of Haymarket, you'll appreciate this hotel's singular position.

NINE ZERO   BOUTIQUE HOTEL $$$
Map p234 (📞617-772-5810; www.ninezero.com; 90 Tremont St; d from $352; P❋🤧❋; TPark St) 🕊 This chic Kimpton hotel appeals to a broad audience, courting business travelers with complimentary shoe-shine service and ergonomic workspace; active visitors with complimentary bikes and in-room yoga mats; and animal lovers with Kimpton's signature pet service. All of the above enjoy excellent customer service and marvelous views of the gold-domed Massachusetts State House (p73) and the Granary Burying Ground (p73) from the upper floors.

AMES HOTEL   BOUTIQUE HOTEL $$$
Map p234 (📞617-979-8100; www.ameshotel.com; 1 Court St; d from $369; P❋🤧; TState) It's easy to miss this understated hotel, tucked behind the granite facade of the historic Ames Building (Boston's first skyscraper). Starting in the lobby and extending to the guest rooms, the style is elegant but eclectic, artfully blending modern minimalism and old-fashioned ornamental details. The upper floors yield wonderful views over the city.

GODFREY HOTEL   HOTEL $$$
Map p234 (📞617-804-2000; www.godfreyhotel boston.com; 505 Washington St; d from $369; P❋🤧; TDowntown Crossing) In the heart of downtown Boston, the Godfrey is a welcome addition to this revitalized area. The boutique facilities are super-sleek, with lobby and rooms decked out in contemporary whites and golds. Smartphone room entry, smart TVs (with web-streaming capabilities) and Bose speakers are some of the

high-tech perks. The on-site George Howell Coffee offers a different kind of perk.

INTERCONTINENTAL HOTEL   HOTEL $$$

Map p234 (☑617-747-1000; www.intercontinentalboston.com; 510 Atlantic Ave; d from $375; P❋🛜🚲; TSouth Station) 🏊 The Inter-Continental has it going on. Service is on point. The rooms are sumptuous and sophisticated. And the location – perched on the edge of the Seaport District – is ideal. You'll pay more for a water view, but what a water view! The marble bathrooms alone are worth the price of staying in this first-class hotel.

OMNI PARKER HOUSE   HISTORIC HOTEL $$$

Map p234 (☑617-227-8600; www.omnihotels.com; 60 School St; d from $354; P❋🛜🚲; TPark St) 🏊 History and the Parker House go hand in hand like JFK and Jackie O (who got engaged here). Malcolm X was a busboy here; Ho Chi Minh was a pastry chef; and Boston cream pie, the official state dessert, was created here. Rooms are comfortable and traditional, and the hotel's location, in the heart of the Freedom Trail, is incomparable.

The elegant lobby bar was a hallowed haunt for Boston's 19th-century intelligentsia and politicians. It's now called The Last Hurrah, named for the 1956 novel about former Boston mayor James Michael Curley. Enjoy a dish of hot nuts and sip a signature martini at this throwback to Old Boston.

🛏 South End & Chinatown

Most of the accommodation options are located in the Theater District, with a few B&Bs in the South End. (But isn't it nice to have Chinatown nearby when you get the munchies at 2am?)

★HI-BOSTON   HOSTEL $

Map p240 (☑617-536-9455; www.bostonhostel.org; 19 Stuart St; dm from $47, d with bath from $230; ❋@🛜; TChinatown, Boylston) 🏊 HI-Boston sets the standard for urban hostels, with its modern, ecofriendly facility in the historic Dill Building. Purpose-built rooms are functional and clean, as are the shared bathrooms. Community spaces are numerous, from fully equipped kitchen to ground-floor cafe, and there's a whole calendar of activities on offer. The place is large, but it books out, so reserve in advance.

REVOLUTION HOTEL   HOTEL $

Map p238 (☑617-848-9200; www.therevolutionhotel.com; 40 Berkeley St; d/tr/q without bath $100/125/150, d/ste from $150/250; ❋🛜; TBack Bay) A beacon for budget travelers, the Revolution Hotel is a concept hotel with a cool, creative atmosphere. Rooms are compact, comfortable and affordable. The cheapest share bathrooms are spacious, private and well stocked with plush towels and high-end products. The place exudes innovation, especially thanks to the fantastic mural that adorns the lobby.

★ENCORE   B&B $$

Map p238 (☑617-247-3425; www.encorebandb.com; r $230-260; P❋🛜; TBack Bay) If you love the theater, or if you love innovative contemporary design, or if you just love creature comforts and warm hospitality, you will love Encore. Co-owned by an architect and a set designer, this 19th-century South End town house sets a stage for both of their passions.

CLARENDON SQUARE INN   B&B $$

Map p238 (☑617-536-2229; www.clarendonsquare.com; 198 W Brookline St; d $258-358; P❋🛜; TPrudential) Located on a quiet residential street in the South End, this fabulous brownstone is a designer's dream. Guest room details might include Italian marble wainscoting, French limestone floors, a silver-leaf barrel-vaulted ceiling or a hand-forged iron-and-porcelain washbasin. Common areas are decadent (case in point: roof-deck hot tub); continental breakfast is served in the paneled dining room and butler's pantry.

REVERE HOTEL   DESIGN HOTEL $$$

Map p240 (☑617-482-1800; www.reverehotel.com; 200 Stuart St; d from $349; P❋🛜🚲🏊; TBoylston) It's hard to enter the circular lobby without contemplating the centerpiece Serra-inspired sculpture. But that's just the beginning of the artistic flair at the Revere Hotel, as the rooms are replete with furniture, light fixtures and other contemporary design elements that marry form and function. City views are wonderful, especially from the rooftop lounge.

🛏 Back Bay

Soak up the authentic Boston atmosphere when you stay at one of Back Bay's delightful brownstone guesthouses, or opt for the comfort of the classy hotels around Copley Square (p111).

COPLEY HOUSE   APARTMENT $

Map p242 (☑617-236-8300; www.copleyhouse. com; 239 W Newton St; d/ste from $180/210; ❊☎; Ⓣ Prudential) Straddling Back Bay and the South End, Copley House offers rooms and apartments in four buildings, with significant variability between them. Generally, antique wood trim and big windows beaming with light make this Queen Anne–style inn a place of respite, while the location makes it handy for exploring Boston. Simple studio rooms are not large, but offer exceptional value.

★ NEWBURY GUEST HOUSE   GUESTHOUSE $$

Map p242 (☑617-670-6000, 800-437-7668; www.newburyguesthouse.com; 261 Newbury St; d from $249; Ⓟ❊☎; Ⓣ Hynes, Copley) Dating from 1882, these three interconnected brick and brownstone buildings offer a prime location in the heart of Newbury St. The place has preserved charming features like ceiling medallions and in-room fireplaces, but the rooms also feature clean lines, luxurious linens and modern amenities. Each morning a complimentary buffet breakfast is laid out in the attached restaurant.

COLLEGE CLUB   B&B $$

Map p242 (☑617-536-9510; www.thecollege clubofboston.com; 44 Commonwealth Ave; s without bath from $179, d $269-289; ❊☎; Ⓣ Arlington) Originally a private club for female college graduates, the College Club has 11 spacious rooms with high ceilings, now open to both sexes. Period details – typical of the area's Victorian brownstones – include claw-foot tubs, ornamental fireplaces and bay windows. Local designers have lent their skills to decorate the various rooms, with delightful results. Prices include a continental breakfast.

INN @ ST BOTOLPH   BOUTIQUE HOTEL $$

Map p242 (☑617-236-8099; www.innatst botolph.com; 99 St Botolph St; ste $289-379; Ⓟ❊☎; Ⓣ Prudential) Whimsical but wonderful, this delightful brownstone boutique

emphasizes affordable luxury. Spacious, light-filled rooms feature bold patterns and contemporary decor, fully equipped kitchens, and all the high-tech bells and whistles. Foreshadowing an increasing trend, the hotel keeps prices down by offering 'edited service,' with virtual check-in, keyless entry and 'touch-up' housekeeping. Complimentary continental breakfast.

CHARLESMARK HOTEL   BOUTIQUE HOTEL $$

Map p242 (☑617-247-1212; www.thecharles mark.com; 655 Boylston St; d from $229; Ⓟ❊☎; Ⓣ Copley) The Charlesmark's small, sleek rooms are at the crossroads of European style and functionality. The design is classic modernism, the effect urbane and relatively affordable. This hip hotel is backed by a small group of warmly efficient staff that see to every detail. The downstairs lounge spills out onto the sidewalk where the people-watching is tops. Complimentary continental breakfast.

HOTEL 140   HOTEL $$

Map p242 (☑617-585-5600; www.hotel140. com; 140 Clarendon St; d/ste from $219/269; Ⓟ❊@☎; Ⓣ Copley, Back Bay) Something of a hidden hotel bargain, Hotel 140 offers small but stylish rooms that are filled with light. The best thing about this place is the friendly, conscientious staff.

Rates can drop by as much as $100 per night in the off-season.

★ NO 284   BOUTIQUE HOTEL $$$

Map p242 (☑617-603-0084; www.no284.com; 284 Commonwealth Ave; d from $349; ❊☎; Ⓣ Hynes) This gorgeous guesthouse invites you to make yourself at home in a luxurious Back Bay brownstone. The comfort starts in the delightful common areas – an elegant library and a serene urban courtyard – and extends to the guest rooms, which are equipped with many thoughtful touches, from corkscrews and wine glasses to professionally curated artwork. Prices include a continental breakfast.

COLONNADE   HOTEL $$$

Map p242 (☑617-424-7000; www.colonnade hotel.com; 120 Huntington Ave; d from $365; Ⓟ❊☎▣; Ⓣ Prudential) 🐾 There are many reasons to stay at the Colonnade, such as its handsome guest rooms, which are well equipped with both high-tech gadgetry and simple pleasures (like a rubber duck in your bathtub). There's the VIPets program, complete with fluffy beds and walking services. And of course there's the excellent dining and the fabulous location.

LOEWS HOTEL
HOTEL $$$

Map p242 (✆617-266-7200; www.loewshotels. com; 154 Berkeley St; d from $359; P ✳ ❀ 🖥; T Back Bay) Perched on the border of Back Bay and the South End, this stunner is housed in the former Boston Police Headquarters. Luxurious rooms are done in blues and browns and beiges, furnished with pillow-top beds, high-tech gadgetry and sweet serenity. The on-site Precinct Bar is popular among locals and guests alike.

COPLEY SQUARE HOTEL
HOTEL $$$

Map p242 (✆617-536-9000, 617-225-7062; www. copleysquarehotel.com; 47 Huntington Ave; d $269-369; P ✳ ❀; T Copley) ✦ The Copley Square Hotel is downright sumptuous, with gorgeous contemporary rooms decorated in muted tones with splashes of color, complemented by subtle lines and soft fabrics. Flat-screen TVs and iPod docks are de rigueur. The morning coffee bar and afternoon 'Wine Down' are lovely perks.

LENOX HOTEL
HISTORIC HOTEL $$$

Map p242 (✆617-536-5300; www.lenoxhotel. com; 61 Exeter St; d from $349; P ✳ ❀; T Copley) ✦ For three generations, the Saunders family has run this gem in Back Bay. And while the atmosphere is a tad old-world, you don't have to forgo modern conveniences. Guest rooms are comfortably elegant (with chandeliers and crown molding), without being stuffy. If your pockets are deep enough, it's worth splurging for a junior suite, as these boast the best views.

🏨 Kenmore Square & Fenway

Kenmore Sq is home to some of the city's finest hotels, as well as a few more affordable options.

OASIS GUEST HOUSE & ADAMS B&B
GUESTHOUSE $

Map p250 (✆617-267-2262; www.oasisguesthouse.com; 22 Edgerly Rd; r $219-279, s/d without bath $139/199; P ✳ @ ❀; T Hynes; Symphony) These homey side-by-side (jointly managed) guesthouses offer a peaceful, pleasant oasis in the midst of Boston's chaotic city streets. Thirty-odd guest rooms occupy

four attractive, brick, bowfront town houses on this tree-lined lane. The modest, light-filled rooms are tastefully and traditionally decorated, most with queen beds, floral quilts and nondescript prints. Complimentary continental breakfast.

★ GRYPHON HOUSE
B&B $$

Map p250 (✆617-375-9003; www.innboston.com; 9 Bay State Rd; r $268-335; P ✳ ❀; T Kenmore) A premier example of Richardson Romanesque, this beautiful five-story brownstone is a paradigm of artistry and luxury overlooking the picturesque Charles River. Eight spacious suites have different styles, including Victorian, Gothic and arts and crafts, but they all have 19th-century period details. And they all have home-away-from-home perks such as entertainment centers, wet bars and gas fireplaces.

HOTEL BUCKMINSTER
HOTEL $$

Map p250 (✆617-727-2825; www.bostonhotelbuckminster.com; 645 Beacon St; d $249; P ✳ ❀ 🖥; T Kenmore) Designed by the architect of the Boston Public Library, the Buckminster is a convergence of Old Boston charm and affordable elegance. It offers more than 100 rooms and suites of varying shapes and sizes. The accommodations are rather dated but customer service is top-notch. South-facing rooms have Fenway views.

★ VERB HOTEL
BOUTIQUE HOTEL $$$

Map p250 (✆617-566-4500; www.theverbhotel. com; 1271 Boylston St; r $349-399; P ✳ ❀ 🏊 🖥; T Kenmore; Fenway) The Verb Hotel took a down-and-out HoJo property and turned it into Boston's most radical, retro, rock-and-roll hotel. The style is mid-century modern; the theme is music. Memorabilia is on display throughout the joint, with turntables in the guest rooms and a jukebox cranking out tunes in the lobby. Classy, clean-lined rooms face the swimming pool or Fenway Park.

HOTEL COMMONWEALTH
HOTEL $$$

Map p250 (✆617-784-4000, 617-933-5000; www. hotelcommonwealth.com; 500 Commonwealth Ave; r/ste $349/379; P ✳ ❀; T Kenmore) Set amid Commonwealth Ave's brownstones and just steps away from Fenway Park, this independent luxury hotel enjoys prime real estate. Spacious Commonwealth suites offer king-size beds and two LCD TVs. The rooms are slightly smaller, but some do offer a view onto the ballpark. All guests can enjoy the amazing amenities, which range from turn-down service to iPods and PlayStations.

ELIOT HOTEL
BOUTIQUE HOTEL $$$

Map p250 (☑617-267-1607; www.eliothotel.com; 370 Commonwealth Ave; r from $349; P ❋ 🐾 🕿 🖵; ⊤Hynes) 🐾 Akin to a small London hotel, the Eliot offers posh quarters, decked out in delicate fabrics and contemporary but classic furnishings, plus Italian marble bathrooms, plush terry robes and down duvets. Service also exceeds expectations, from the warm welcome to the complimentary shoeshines. Ken Orringer's acclaimed sushi restaurant Uni is on the 1st floor.

🛏 Seaport District & South Boston

Following the opening of the Boston Convention & Exhibition Center, the Seaport District became a hotbed of hotel development. It's a bit removed from the action unless you are actually attending an event at the convention center, but it's nirvana for nightlife lovers, seafood eaters and art connoisseurs. Bonus: it's also an easy trip from the airport.

YOTEL
HOTEL $$

Map p252 (www.yotel.com; 65 Seaport Blvd; d from $226; ❋ 🕿; 🖵SL3 to Courthouse, ⊤South Station) A new concept for Boston, Yotel offers accommodations, or 'cabins,' that are cool, comfortable and compact, complete with adjustable 'smart' beds, luxury linens, heated towel racks and rain showers. Everything you need is here – it's very cozy. If you need to spread out, make yourself at home in the chic lobby or on the rooftop deck.

While service is pleasant across the hotel, the perennial favorite staff member is YO2D2, the house robot, who is trained in the art of guest services.

ENVOY HOTEL
DESIGN HOTEL $$$

Map p252 (☑617-338-3030; www.theenvoyhotel.com; 70 Sleeper St; d $339-419; ❋ 🕿 🖵; ⊤South Station) Here's a gorgeous boutique hotel perched at the corner where the Fort Point Channel meets the sea. In the rooms, floor-to-ceiling windows optimize the vantage point, offering wonderful water views. The interior design is sophisticated and stylish, keeping it simple with colors, but playing

with textures, materials and even words. The rooftop bar (p137) is an obvious draw.

RESIDENCE INN MARRIOTT
BOUTIQUE HOTEL $$$

Map p252 (☑617-478-0840; www.marriott.com; 370 Congress St; d from $352; P ❋ 🐾 🕿 🖵; 🖵SL1, SL2, ⊤South Station) 🐾 This is not your typical Marriott. Housed in a historic, brick warehouse, this boutique hotel now features an old-style atrium and glass elevators leading up to spectacular, spacious suites. Twelve-foot ceilings and enormous windows are in every room, as is a floor-to-ceiling cityscape mural. King-size beds, fully equipped kitchens and up-to-date gadgetry ensure optimal comfort and convenience.

SEAPORT BOSTON HOTEL
HOTEL $$$

Map p252 (☑617-385-4000; www.seaportboston.com; 1 Seaport Lane; d from $369; P ❋ 🕿 🖵 🖵; 🖵SL1, SL2, ⊤South Station) 🐾 With glorious views of the Boston Harbor, this business hotel is up to snuff when it comes to high-tech amenities and creature comforts. Soothing tones, plush linens and robes, and a unique no-tipping policy guarantee a relaxing retreat.

🛏 Cambridge

Cambridge offers a fantastic range of sleeping options, from affordable guesthouses to high-end hotels. It also makes a convenient base for exploring Boston. Despite being a separate city, it's a quick T-ride over the river and into town.

A FRIENDLY INN
GUESTHOUSE $

Map p246 (☑617-547-7851; www.afinow.com; 1673 Cambridge St; d $97-197; P ❋ 🕿; ⊤Harvard) While this Victorian-era inn has its pros and cons, nobody can dispute that it is indeed 'a friendly inn.' Service is efficient, offering a clean and quiet (if a little cramped) respite for budget travelers.

A continental breakfast is included, but you might prefer to head to the cafe down the street for your morning meal.

★HARDING HOUSE
B&B $$

Map p248 (☑617-876-2888; www.harding-house.com; 288 Harvard St; d without bath $140, d $240-260; P ❋ @ 🕿; ⊤Central) This treasure blends refinement and comfort, artistry and efficiency. Old wooden floors spread with throw rugs furnish a warm glow, and antique decor completes the inviting atmosphere. Noise does travel in this old house, but the place is quite comfortable. Other perks: free parking (a rarity), a thoughtfully designed continental breakfast and complimentary museum passes.

KENDALL HOTEL
BOUTIQUE HOTEL **$$**
Map p248 (☑617-566-1300; www.kendallhotel. com; 350 Main St; r $248-317; ℙ✳🤖; ⓣKendall/MIT) Once the Engine 7 Firehouse, this city landmark is now a cool and classy all-American hotel. Its 65 guest rooms exhibit a firefighter riff, alongside the requisite creature comforts. The hotel excels with its service, style, and appetizing breakfast spread. The on-site Black Sheep restaurant is worth visiting for lunch or dinner, too.

IRVING HOUSE AT HARVARD
GUESTHOUSE **$$**
Map p246 (☑617-547-4600; www.irvinghouse. com; 24 Irving St; r with/without bath from $245/185; ℙ✳@🤖; ⓣHarvard) 🍴 Call it a big inn or a homey hotel, Irving House welcomes the world-weariest of travelers. Rooms range in size, but every bed is quilt-covered, and big windows admit plenty of light. There is a bistro-style atmosphere in the brick-lined basement, where you can browse through books or munch on a complimentary continental breakfast. Free parking is a great bonus.

PORTER SQUARE HOTEL
BOUTIQUE HOTEL **$$**
(☑617-499-3399; www.theportersquarehotel. com; 1924 Massachusetts Ave; tw/d from $259/299; ⓣPorter) About 1.5 miles north of Harvard Square, the Porter Square Hotel is a quick T-ride from central Cambridge, but there's plenty of life in the immediately surrounding streets as well. This boutique hotel has simple, fresh rooms – including 'petite' twins for the cost-conscious.

HARVARD SQUARE HOTEL
HOTEL **$$**
Map p246 (☑617-864-5200; www.harvard squarehotel.com; 110 Mt Auburn St; d from $289; ℙ✳@🤖; ⓣHarvard) Guest rooms here are small but stylish, with oversize photos of local sites adorning the walls. Large windows offer excellent views of the surrounding square. The place has undeniable potential but it lacks amenities (such as a restaurant, a gym and soundproofing) and, at the time of research, it was overdue for some serious maintenance.

After renovations in 2019, hopefully guests will see some improvements.

CHARLES HOTEL
HOTEL **$$$**
Map p246 (☑617-864-1200; www.charleshotel. com; 1 Bennett St; r from $349; ℙ✳🤖🐾; ⓣHarvard) Calling itself 'the smart place to stay,' this institution has hosted the university's most esteemed guests, ranging from Bob Barker to the Dalai Lama. Guest rooms include sleek Shaker-style furnishings, Italian marble bathrooms with TV mirrors, and all the luxuries and facilities one would expect from a highly rated hotel. Prime location overlooking the Charles River.

ROYAL SONESTA
HOTEL **$$$**
Map p248 (☑617-806-4200; www.sonesta.com; 40 Edwin Land Blvd; r $249-359; ℙ✳🤖🛥; ⓣScience Park) Following an upgrade, the Royal Sonesta offers spacious rooms with a modern, minimalist flair and up-to-date amenities. Those facing the river yield some of the most expansive city views around. The hotel also has an incredible contemporary art collection on display throughout the public spaces, including the awesome ArtBar.

HOTEL VERITAS
BOUTIQUE HOTEL **$$$**
Map p246 (☑617-520-5000; www.thehotel veritas.com; 1 Remington St; d $289-389; ℙ✳🤖; ⓣHarvard) Most guests agree that the super-chic design and top-notch service more than make up for the small size of the rooms at this Harvard Square newcomer. Rich fabrics, shimmering textures and local artwork adorn the rooms. Dressed to the nines in Brooks Brothers uniforms, the Veritas team does whatever it takes to ensure a satisfying and truly special experience.

HOTEL MARLOWE
BOUTIQUE HOTEL **$$$**
Map p248 (☑617-825-7140; www.hotelmarlowe. com; 25 Edwin Land Blvd; d $289-369; ℙ✳🤖🐾; ⓣLechmere or Science Park) 🍴 The Kimpton Hotel Group's flagship property in the Boston area, just steps from the Charles River, embodies chic and unique. Perks include down comforters, Sony PlayStations and the *New York Times* delivered to your door – enough to please everyone, from creatures of comfort to free spirits to intellectual elites.

▣ Streetcar Suburbs

The Streetcar Suburbs are a sweet retreat if the city makes you feel claustrophobic. Grand elm trees shade the wide green lawns and gracious mansions, and a short ride on the T brings you into town.

BERTRAM INN   B&B $

Map p254 (☑617-566-2234, 617-295-3822; www.
bertraminn.com; 92 Sewall Ave, Brookline; d $179-199; ☐❋☎☎; ☐St Paul) Brookline's tree-lined streets shelter this dreamy, arts-and-crafts–style inn, located only a quick jaunt from downtown Boston. A quiet elegance is accented with beautifully carved oak panels, leaded windows and, if you play your cards right, a working fireplace in your room. Amenities and services match those of high-end hotels.

The same owners run the Samuel Sewall Inn across the street, an exquisitely restored Victorian with even more rooms. Both places boast tree-shaded patios, a full gourmet breakfast and a location that's just a heartbeat from the Hub of the Universe.

BEECH TREE INN   B&B $$

Map p254 (☑857-267-1783; www.thebeechtree
inn.com; 83 Longwood Ave, Brookline; s/d with separate bath $159-189, d $199-209; ☐❋@☎; ☐Longwood) This turn-of-the-20th-century Victorian home contains 10 guest rooms, each individually decorated with period furnishings and wallpaper, ornamental fireplaces with hand-painted screens, floral quilts and lacy curtains. Common areas include a cozy parlor and a pleasant patio, where you can enjoy homemade baked goodies throughout the day. It's a romantic return to yesteryear, located on a quiet residential street. Breakfast included.

ANTHONY'S TOWN HOUSE   GUESTHOUSE $

Map p254 (☑617-566-3972; www.anthonystown
house.com; 1085 Beacon St, Brookline; d with shared bath from $110; ❋☎; ☐Hawes St) Halfway between Coolidge Corner and Kenmore Sq, this family-operated guesthouse puts the rolled 'r' in rococo. With more frills and flourishes than should be allowed in one place at one time, this Victorian-era brownstone is downright girly. The 10 spacious rooms are comfortable, filled with antiques and lacy linens. Affable owners and cheap rates attract many repeat visitors. Cash only!

LONGWOOD INN   GUESTHOUSE $

Map p254 (☑617-566-8615; www.longwood-inn.
com; 123 Longwood Ave, Brookline; d $165-185; ☐❋☎; ☐Coolidge Corner) This big old Victorian mansion is in an odd location midway between Coolidge Corner and Longwood. Affordable rates (including cheaper weekly rates) attract many long-term guests, especially folks working in the nearby medical district. Simple rooms have an old-fashioned charm, with floral bedspreads and antique furniture. The cheapest rooms have separate private bathrooms. Reception closes at 9pm.

★TAYLOR HOUSE   B&B $$

Map p255 (☑617-983-9334; www.taylorhouse.
com; 50 Burroughs St, Jamaica Plain; s $179-189, d $199-209, ste $239-349; ☐❋☎; ☐Green St) Sitting pretty pond-side in Jamaica Plain, this gracious Italianate Victorian mansion has been lovingly restored – apparent from the ornamental details throughout the house and the gorgeous gardens outside. Spacious guest rooms have dark polished-wood floors, sleigh beds, bold contemporary art and plenty of sunshine. The suites are in the carriage house behind. Dave is your decorator, designer and amazing host.

Understand
Boston

Boston Today

With its sparkling cityscape, booming economy and dynamic population, Boston is everything a city should be. While youth and diversity are among the city's strengths, these segments of the population are also the most vulnerable. Many people – especially young folks and people of color - are threatened by the same development and prosperity that make the city so attractive.

Best on Film

The Verdict (1982) Paul Newman as a Boston lawyer.
Good Will Hunting (1997) Put Southie on the Hollywood map.
Next Stop Wonderland (1997) Heartwarming independent film with a bossa-nova soundtrack.
The Departed (2006) Suspenseful mob movie that won Best Picture.
Stronger (2017) A moving portrait of a Boston Marathon bombing survivor.
John Adams (2008) TV series chronicling the life and times of the second US president.
The Town (2010) Four Charlestown thugs attempt their ultimate score.

Best in Print

The Scarlet Letter (Nathaniel Hawthorne; 1850) Hypocrisy and malice in Puritan New England.
The Given Day (Dennis Lehane; 2008) A suspense-filled historical novel, following two families through the turmoil of post-WWI Boston.
Interpreter of Maladies (Jhumpa Lahiri; 1999) A Pulitzer Prize–winner that addresses the challenges of migration and multiculturalism.
The Friends of Eddie Coyle (George V Higgins; 1972) A crime novel providing a crash course in the Boston dialect.

Boston Rising

In the past decade Boston has grown up. Literally. Since the 2007 completion of the Big Dig, a highway megaproject, the city has focused on building up, starting with the 685ft Millennial Tower. An even taller residential building (742ft) is on its way up at One Dalton. Not to mention the dozens of massive buildings crowding the Seaport District.

Many see the development as a good sign – of prosperity, investment and growth. Say what you might about big-city aesthetics, you can't argue with the economics. Unless, of course, you're getting priced out.

Property values have skyrocketed around Boston. According to real-estate site Zillow, home prices have increased by 80% since 2010, bringing the median home value up to $591,000. The median monthly rent is $2700. New construction is mostly luxury condominiums, out of reach for folks with moderate incomes.

Minorities – unlikely to own their homes – feel these economic pressures more severely. In 2015, a report by the Federal Reserve Bank of Boston claimed that the median net worth of local black households averaged $8 (compared to $247,500 for white households). This difference was attributed mainly to home equity. Due to decades of redlining – denial of access to loans based on race – many black families were unable to enter the housing market and therefore unable to increase their net worth via real estate.

As housing prices increase, many people are being displaced – forced to relocate to more affordable suburbs or even out of state. Bye bye, Boston.

Changes in Law-titude

With the promise of jobs and tax revenue, the Massachusetts legislature passed a law to establish three resort-style casinos in the Commonwealth (the state of Massachusetts), including one in Everett (4 miles north of Boston). Gambling giant Wynn Resorts cleaned up a former industrial wasteland on the Mystic River and transformed the site into a casino resort. The development was mired in controversy, most recently when owner Steve Wynn was accused by former employees of sexual misconduct and rape. (The company responded to local protests by removing Wynn's name from the resort.)

Even before #metoo, the development was criticized by surrounding communities – including Boston – which anticipate sharing the ill effects, if not the benefits, of legalized gambling. They couldn't stop progress, though. The so-called Encore Boston Harbor is expected to open in 2019.

Meanwhile, a popular referendum in Massachusetts approved the legalization of marijuana. Now, bustling shopping districts are peppered with smoke shops and recreational dispensaries. A 2018 report by the Massachusetts Department of Public Health found that 20% of resident adults are already using marijuana. So far, consumption takes place strictly in private homes, as there are legal barriers to opening cannabis cafes. But one member of the state's Cannabis Control Commission estimates that such establishments will be common within a matter of years. Needless to say, many Mass residents think that's pretty cool, dude.

Millennial Boston

Boston has always benefited from the presence of young people, who bring energy, creativity and progressive thinking to the city. Nowadays, 'millennials' (born between 1981 and 1996) constitute at least 23% of the population. A recent report by Politico indicates that Boston's up-and-comers are among the largest and most impactful such group in the country, second only to San Francisco.

Boston's millennials are a diverse lot (55% are minorities). And they are making their presence known in surprising ways.

➡ Thank millennials for the expansion of programs like Blue Bikes (Boston's bike-share program), as 52% of young folks rely on alternative forms of transportation (other than cars). Apparently millennials don't like to be stuck in traffic.

➡ Despite being well educated (45% have a bachelor's degree or higher), they often don't work in traditional jobs, as evidenced by the proliferation of shared Boston work spaces.

➡ Not surprising, Boston millennials are not buying many homes due to the high cost of housing. Real-estate research-site Adobo reported that only 27.6% of millennials own their own homes in Boston (compared to 32% nationwide).

But they are still changing the face of the city. Microbreweries, public art, legal marijuana, recycling programs, avocado toast...millennials are the main drivers and beneficiaries of these trends, which are making Boston a better place for all.

if Boston were 100 people

45 would be non-Hispanic white
25 would be African American
19 would be Latin
9 would be Asian
2 would be other

Educational Achievement
(% of population)

High school not completed — 14
High school degree — 21
Bachelor's degree — 26

Some college or associate's degree — 18
Graduate or professional degree — 21

population per sq mile

BOSTON   MASSACHUSETTS

 = 885 people

History

As one of the earliest European settlements in the New World and the birthplace of the American Revolution, Boston's ties to history are strong. A prosperous trading center, the city has long boasted fine educational and cultural institutions, influential in philosophy and literature, art and technology. Industrialization brought significant changes, especially as immigrants diversified the population, leading to conflict, co-operation and growth – a trend that has continued into the 21st century.

The Shawmut Peninsula

In 1614 English explorer Captain John Smith, at the behest of the future King Charles I, set sail to assess the New World's commercial opportunities. Braving the frigid North Atlantic, the plucky explorer reached the rocky coast of present-day Maine and made his way southward to Cape Cod, making contact with the native population, mapping the coastline and dubbing the region 'New England.'

Smith noted a tricapped hilly peninsula, connected to the mainland by a narrow neck across a shallow back bay, with an excellent harbor fed by three rivers. Valued for its freshwater spring, the region was known to local tribespeople as Shawmut.

Before the 17th century, there were as many as 100,000 native inhabitants of New England, mostly of the Algonquian nation, organized into small regional tribes that variously both cooperated and quarreled.

Before the Puritans, England's religious outcasts, showed up, local tribespeople were already acquainted with Portuguese fishers, French fur traders, Dutch merchants and Jesuit missionaries. The Europeans were welcomed as a source of valued goods, but they were also feared. In the Great Sadness of 1616–17, a smallpox epidemic devastated the native population, reducing it by three-quarters.

English colonial coastal encampments quickly spread, as seemingly unoccupied lands were claimed for king and commodity. According to John Winthrop, the first governor of the colony, 'God hath hereby cleared our title to this place.'

TIMELINE	c 1600	1614	1629
	Some 3000 Native Americans fish and farm in what will become the greater Boston region.	English explorer Captain John Smith surveys the coast of Maine and Massachusetts. Upon his return home, he recounts the journey in *Description of New England*.	Shareholders of the Massachusetts Bay Colony sign the Cambridge Agreement, allowing the emigrating shareholders – the Puritans – to govern the colony and to answer only to the king.

In 1675 Chief Metacomet, son of the famed Massasoit who befriended the starving Pilgrims, organized a desperate last stand against the ever-encroaching English. Known as King Philip to the settlers, he terrorized the frontier for more than a year before he was finally ambushed and killed. The chief's body was drawn and quartered and his heathen head perched on a pole, while his son was sold into slavery. In less than a hundred years, disease, war and forced migration had reduced the indigenous population by 90%.

Mission from God

England was torn by religious strife in the 17th century. The Puritans, austere Calvinists, wanted to purify the Anglican Church of all vestiges of pomp, pope and privilege. James I, annoyed by these nonconformists, threatened to 'harry them out of the country.'

As the fortunes of the faithful diminished, New England held out hope of renewal. The first trickle of Protestant immigrants came in 1620, when the Pilgrims established a small colony in Plymouth. Ten years later, the flagship *Arbella* led a flotilla of a thousand Puritans on the treacherous transatlantic crossing. In June 1630, their leader, country squire John Winthrop, gazed out on the Shawmut Peninsula and declared, 'we shall be as a City upon a Hill, with the eyes of all people upon us.'

They landed first near Salem and settled further south at present-day Charlestown. Across the river, the Shawmut Peninsula was at this time occupied by the Reverend William Blackstone, who had survived an earlier failed settlement. He invited Winthrop and his scurvy-ridden company to move closer to fresh water. They named their new home Boston, after the town in Lincolnshire where many of the Pilgrims had lived.

Piety, Power & Profits

The new settlement was governed by a spiritual elite – a Puritan theocracy. As such, the Church dominated early colonial life.

Divine Law was above all, and the state was put in service to the Church. The General Court, a select assembly of Church members, became the principal mechanism for lawmaking, while the governor was endowed with extensive powers to enforce the laws. Local affairs were settled at regular meetings, open to the freemen of each town. (Women were allowed to attend if they did not talk.) The tradition of town meetings became a cornerstone of American democracy.

Meanwhile, Boston became a boomtown. The first inhabitants were concentrated near the waterfront, behind the town dock. The back side of the hill served as 'common' lands. Newcomers fanned out along the rivers, looking for farmland and founding new settlements. Fortunes

HISTORY MISSION FROM GOD

Anne Hutchinson was a religious free-thinker who was banished from the Massachusetts Bay Colony. Hutchinson insisted on freedom of religion as a founding principle in the charter of Rhode Island, which would later influence the US Constitution.

1630	1636	1638	1655
Led by Governor John Winthrop, Puritan settlers flee the repressive Church of England and move to the theocratic Massachusetts Bay Colony.	Church leaders found a college to train ministers for their role in the theocracy. Three years later, the college is named for its first benefactor, the young minister John Harvard.	Anne Hutchinson is banished from the colony for encouraging dissent. She establishes an outpost near present-day Portsmouth, Rhode Island.	Wampanoag Caleb Cheeshahteaumuck becomes the first Native American to graduate from Harvard.

were made in the maritime trades – fishing, shipbuilding, and commerce with the Old World. Well into the 18th century, Boston was the richest city in the American colonies.

But population and prosperity put pressure on Puritan principles. Modesty gave way to display. Red-brick mansions appeared on Beacon Hill and women's shoulders were fashionably exposed.

The Church lost its monopoly on governing when the royal charter was revised to make property-holding the basis for political rights. Life in colonial Boston increasingly felt tension between community and individual, piety and profit.

From Empire to Independence

History Syllabus

Paul Revere's Ride (David Hackett Fischer)

Bunker Hill (Nathaniel Philbrick)

Where Death and Glory Meet (Russell Duncan)

Blood & Ivy (Paul Collins)

Common Ground (J Anthony Lukas)

The demands of empire kept England at war. Colonists were drawn into the fighting in the French–Indian War. Despite their victory, all the colonists gained was a tax bill from the king. Covetous of New England's maritime wealth, the Crown pronounced a series of Navigation Acts, restricting colonial trade. Boston merchants conducted business as usual, except now it was on the sly.

The issue of taxation brought the clash between king and colony to a head. In the 1760s, Parliament passed the *Stamp Act,* the *Townsend Acts* and the *Tea Act* – all of which placed greater financial burdens on the colonists. With each new tax and toll, colonial resentment intensified, as exhibited by vocal protests and violent mobs. The acts of defiance were defended by respectable lawyer John Adams, who cited the Magna Carta's principle of 'no taxation without representation.'

To each act of rebellion, the British throne responded with increasingly severe measures, eventually dispatching Redcoat regiments known as 'regulars' to restore order and suspending all local political power.

Under siege on the street, unrepentant Bostonians went underground. The Sons of Liberty, a clandestine network of patriots, stirred up public resistance to British policy and harassed the king's loyalists. They were led by some well-known townsmen, including esteemed surgeon Dr Joseph Warren, upper-class merchant John Hancock, skilled silversmith Paul Revere and bankrupt brewer Sam Adams. Branded as treasonous rebels by the king, the Sons of Liberty became more radical and popular as the imperial grip tightened.

The resented Redcoat presence did not extinguish, but rather inflamed, local passions. In March 1770 a motley street gang provoked British regulars with slurs and snowballs until the troops fired into the crowd, killing five and wounding six. John Adams successfully defended the British troops, who were found to be acting in self-defense. The

1675–78	1689	1700–50	1754–63
The Wampanoag and other indigenous people rebel against the settlers' expansion and evangelism in a conflict known as King Philip's War.	The Glorious Revolution overthrows the Stuart Kings. In Boston, the royal governor – who has angered colonists by his interference in local governance – is run out of town.	Immigration is spurred by the promise of land and by lucrative opportunities in fishing, shipbuilding and trade. By the middle of the century, the population of Boston reaches 15,000.	The British fight over North American territory in the French and Indian War. The war debt causes the Crown to increase colonial taxes. Further western expansion is forbidden.

BOSTON TEA PARTY

In May 1773 the British Parliament passed the *Tea Act*, granting a trade monopoly to the politically influential but financially troubled East India Company. In December three tea-bearing vessels arrived in Boston Harbor, but colonial merchants refused the shipments to protest the disadvantageous trade policy. When the ships tried to depart, Governor Hutchinson demanded their cargo be unloaded.

At a meeting in the Old South Church, the Sons of Liberty decided to take matters into their own hands. Disguised as Mohawk Indians, they descended on the waterfront, boarded the ships and dumped 90,000lb of taxable tea into the harbor.

The king's retribution was swift. Legislation was rushed through Parliament to punish Boston, 'the center of rebellious commotion in America, the ringleader in every riot.' The port was blockaded and the city placed under military rule. The Sons of Liberty spread the news of this latest outrage down the seaboard. The cause of Boston was becoming the cause of all the colonies: American independence versus British tyranny.

Sons of Liberty, however, scored a propaganda coup with their depictions of the Boston Massacre, as the incident came to be called.

Shot Heard Round the World

Until now, all but the most pugnacious of patriots would have been satisfied with colonial economic autonomy and political representation. But the king's coercive tactics aroused indignation and acrimony. Both sides were spoiling for a fight.

British General Gage was sent over with 4000 troops and a fleet of warships. Local townsfolk and yeoman farmers organized themselves into Minutemen groups, citizen militias that could mobilize in a minute. They drilled on town commons and stockpiled weapons in secret stores.

In April 1775 Gage saw the chance to break colonial resistance. Acting on a tip from a local informant, Gage dispatched 700 troops on the road west to arrest fugitives Sam Adams and John Hancock and to seize a hidden stash of gunpowder. Bostonians had their own informants, including Gage's wife, who tipped off Joseph Warren on the troop movement.

Word was then passed to the Old North Church sexton to hang two signal lanterns in the steeple. Paul Revere got the signal and quietly slipped across the river into Charlestown, where he mounted Brown Beauty and galloped into the night to alert the Minutemen.

At daybreak, the confrontation finally occurred. 'Here once the embattled farmer stood,' Ralph Waldo Emerson later wrote, 'and fired the shot heard round the world.' Imperial troops skirmished with Minutemen on the Old North Bridge in Concord and the Lexington Green. By

1770	1773	1775	1776
Provoked by a local gang throwing snowballs, British troops fire into a crowd and kill five people. The soldiers are acquitted, but the incident becomes known as the Boston Massacre.	The British Parliament levies a tax on tea, which incites an angry mob to protest by raiding a merchant ship and dumping crates of tea into Boston Harbor.	British troops heed reports that colonists are stockpiling weapons. Warned by Paul Revere and William Dawes, the Minutemen confront the Redcoats, initiating the War for Independence.	The Continental Army takes Dorchester Heights, giving them a shot at the Royal Navy ships in the harbor. The British evacuate Boston and the colonies declare independence.

midmorning, more militia had arrived and chased the bloodied Red-coats back to Boston in ignominious defeat. The inevitable had arrived: the War for Independence.

Boston figured prominently in the early phase of the American Revolution. In June 1775 Bostonians inflicted a hurtful blow on British morale at the Battle of Bunker Hill. The British took the hill after three tries, but their losses were greater than expected. Fighting on the front line, Dr Warren was killed by a musket shot to the head in the final British charge. A few weeks later, George Washington assumed command of the ragged Continental Army on the Cambridge Common.

Britain's occupation of the city continued until March 1776, when Washington mounted captured British cannons on Dorchester Heights and trained them on the British fleet in Boston Harbor. Rather than see the king's expensive warships sent to the bottom, the British evacuated the city, trashing and looting as they went; Boston was liberated.

Boston's Original Artistic Institutions

Museum of Fine Arts (Fenway)

Boston Symphony Orchestra (Fenway)

Trinity Church (Back Bay)

Boston Public Library (Back Bay)

Athens of America

In the early 19th century, Boston emerged as a center of enlightenment in the young republic. The city's second mayor, Josiah Quincy, led an effort to remake the city's underclass into a group of industrious and responsible citizens. He expanded public education and made the streets safer and cleaner. The 'Great Mayor' revitalized the decaying waterfront with a refurbished Faneuil Hall and the new Greek Revival marketplace, which bears his name.

Influenced by the idealistic legacy of Puritanism and revolution, Boston gave rise to the first uniquely American intellectual movement. Led by Unitarian minister Ralph Waldo Emerson, the transcendentalists shocked and challenged the Christian establishment with their belief in the inherent goodness of human nature and an emphasis on individual self-reliance to achieve spiritual fulfillment. Transcendental influences are exemplified in the romantic literature of Nathaniel Hawthorne and the civil disobedience of Henry David Thoreau. Besides philosophy, the city also became a vibrant cultural center for poetry, painting, architecture, science and scholarship, earning Boston a reputation as the 'Athens of America.'

From Sail to Steam

Boston thrived during the Age of Sail. In the 17th century the infamous 'triangular trade' route was developed, involving sugar, rum and slaves. Merchants who chose not to traffic in human cargo could still make large profits by illicitly undercutting European trade monopolies in the West Indies. In his East Boston shipyard, Donald McKay perfected the

1780	1789–1801	1813	1831
Massachusetts ratifies its constitution, which – written mostly by John Adams – will serve as the model for the US Constitution with its Declaration of Rights and Frame of Government.	John Adams of Quincy, MA, serves two terms as the vice president and one term as the president of the newly independent United States of America.	Francis Cabot Lowell establishes the Boston Manufacturing Company for the production of cotton textiles, accelerating the Industrial Revolution in New England.	Cofounder of the American Anti-Slavery Society, abolitionist agitator William Lloyd Garrison publishes the first issue of radical newspaper The Liberator from his office on Beacon Hill.

design of the clipper ship. The advent of the steam engine in the second half of the 19th century marked the decline of Boston seafaring.

Early on, Boston's industry was related to overseas trading: shipbuilding, fishing and rum. Besides this, the city had small-scale artisan shops. During the war, the disruption of commerce caused acute shortages of manufactured goods. In response, some merchants shifted their investments into industry, with revolutionary results.

By the middle of the 19th century, steam power and metal machines were changing the city. Boston became the railroad hub of New England. Leather works and shoemaking factories appeared on the edge of the city. Even Paul Revere abandoned his silversmith shop and set up a rolling copper mill and foundry.

Boston's Melting Pot

For nearly two centuries, the city was ruled by a select group of leading families, collectively known as the Boston Brahmins. A reference to the exclusive ruling class in India, the self-deprecating term was coined by Oliver Wendell Holmes Sr, but was readily adopted by the caste-conscious. Their elite status was claimed through lineage to the colonial founders or through wealth from the merchant heyday. They dominated city politics and business, mimicked the style and manners of the European aristocracy, and created exclusive clubs for themselves and cultural institutions for the city.

The rapid rise of industry led to social change. The industrial workforce was initially drawn from the region's young farm women, who lived in dormitories under paternalistic supervision. The 'mill girls' were replaced by cheaper immigrant Irish labor in the 1820s. Although their numbers were still modest, the effect of immigration on local attitudes was great. The world of English-descended Whig Protestants was thrown into turmoil.

Disparaged by 'proper' Bostonians, the Irish were considered an inferior race of moral delinquents, whose spoken brogue was not endearing, but rather suggested a shoe in one's mouth. They undercut workers in the job market; worse yet, the Irish brought the dreaded religion of pomp and popery that the Puritans so detested.

A potato famine spurred an upsurge in Irish immigration. Between 1846 and 1856 more than 1000 new immigrants stepped off the boat every month. It was a human flood the city was not prepared for. Anti-immigrant and anti-Catholic sentiments were shrill.

Subsequent groups of Italian, Portuguese and East European Jewish immigrants suffered similar indignities. By the end of the 19th century, the urban landscape resembled a mosaic of clannish ethnic enclaves.

In the 1830s, rumors of licentiousness led a Protestant mob to torch the Catholic Ursuline Convent in present-day Somerville. In another incident, an Irish funeral procession met a volunteer fire company along Boston's Broad St, and a melee ensued, leaving a row of Irish flats burned to the ground.

1840s	1850s	1851	1857–1900
The potato famine spurs Irish immigration to Boston. The influx sparks conflict over religious and cultural differences. By the middle of the century, the Irish population reaches 35,000.	The Fugitive Slave Law requires citizens to return runaway slaves to their owners. Enforcement of this law leads to the arrests of Boston abolitionists in 1850 and 1854.	Built in an East Boston shipyard, Donald McKay's Flying Cloud sails from New York to San Francisco with a damaged mast in just 89 days and 21 hours, shattering all records.	Boston is transformed when the marshland along Charles River's south shore is filled with landfill from the city's three hills. New neighborhoods are created: Back Bay, Kenmore and Fenway.

All Politics is Local

With social change, Brahmin dominance of Boston politics slipped away. By the end of the 19th century, ethnic-based political machines wrested control of local government from the old elite.

While the Democratic Party was initially associated with rural and radical interests, it became the political instrument of the working poor. Irish immigrant neighborhoods provided ready-made voting blocs, which empowered a new type of political boss. These flamboyant populists took an activist approach to government, trading in patronage and graft.

No Boston boss outshone James Michael Curley. He was conniving, corrupt and beloved. The Rascal King had a seemingly endless supply of holiday turkeys and city jobs for constituents, who between 1914 and 1949 elected him mayor four times and governor and congressman once.

After more than 125 years, Massachusetts once again took center stage in national politics with John F Kennedy's election to the presidency in 1960. The youthful JFK was the pride of Boston's Irish Catholics for being the one who finally made it.

In 1952, Thomas 'Tip' O'Neill inherited Kennedy's recently vacated congressional seat. O'Neill climbed to the top of the legislative ladder, becoming Speaker of the House in 1977, all the while sticking to the adage that 'All Politics is Local.' Meanwhile, in 1962, JFK's brother Ted was elected to represent Massachusetts in the US Senate – a post he held for 47 years. Irish Americans continue to dominate Boston politics today.

Black History Sites

African Meeting House (Beacon Hill)

Robert Gould Shaw Memorial (Boston Common)

Black Heritage Trail (Beacon Hill)

Copp's Hill Burying Ground (North End)

Reform & Racism

The legacy of race relations in Boston is marred by contradictions. Abolitionists and segregationists, reformers and racists have all left their mark. Massachusetts was the first colony to recognize slavery as a legal institution in 1641, and the first to abolish slavery in 1783.

In the 19th century, Boston emerged as a nucleus of the abolition movement. Newspaper publisher William Lloyd Garrison, Unitarian minister Theodore Parker and aristocratic lawyer Wendell Phillips launched the American Anti-Slavery Society to agitate public sentiment. The city provided safe houses for runaway slaves who took the Underground Railroad to freedom in Canada.

After the Civil War, many blacks rose to prominent positions in Boston society, including John S Rock, who became the first African American to practice in the US Supreme Court; John J Smith, who was elected to the Massachusetts House of Representatives; Lewis Hayden, who was elected to the Massachusetts General Court; and William DuBois, who was the first African American to receive a PhD from Harvard.

1863	1870–76	1881	1918
Local boy Robert Gould Shaw is placed in command of the 54th Massachusetts Volunteer Infantry, one of the first all-black regiments in the Union Army.	With a generous donation from the private collection of the Boston Athenaeum, the Museum of Fine Arts is established in a Gothic Revival building on Copley Sq.	Philanthropist Henry Lee Higginson founds the Boston Symphony Orchestra with the aim of 'offering the best music at low prices, such as may be found in all European cities.'	Babe Ruth leads the Boston Red Sox to their fifth World Series victory in 15 years. He is subsequently traded to the New York Yankees, which fans will remember for the rest of the century.

In the early 20th century, manufacturing jobs attracted southern blacks as part of the Great Migration, and Boston's African American population swelled to about 20,000 strong. For newcomers, the north promised refuge from racism and poverty, though that promise was rarely delivered on. Boston did not have Jim Crow laws per se, but it had its own informal patterns of racial segregation. African Americans were not integrated into the city, but instead established black enclaves in neighborhoods such as Roxbury and the South End, where a thriving jazz and dance scene emerged. At one point, the city was home to both Martin Luther King Jr, a Boston University divinity student, and Malcolm X, a pool-hall-hustling teenager.

As the city's economy declined, racial antagonism increased. In the 1970s, a judge determined that separate was not equal in the Boston public school system. The 1974 court order to integrate the schools through redistricting and busing exposed underlying racial tensions, and resulted in the same protests and violence as desegregation efforts in the South. Busing was eventually abandoned and old wounds remain.

Racial inequality in the US is a persistent issue, but Boston stands out among major cities, especially given its liberal reputation. The city's power base is almost exclusively white, and its reputation as inhospitable – even hostile – to black people in particular provides an additional barrier to recruitment of achieving people of color, according to a 2017 series by the *Boston Globe*'s Spotlight team. Despite a black population of 28%, Boston is one of only two cities among the 25 most populous in the US to have exclusively elected white, male mayors.

Making Boston Modern

In the mid-20th century, the city underwent a remarkable physical transformation. Two of the city's oldest neighborhoods were targeted: Scollay Sq, which was once an area bustling with theaters and music halls, but had since become a rundown red-light district; and the West End, where poor immigrants eked out an existence amid a grubby labyrinth of row houses and alleyways. Urban renewal came in the form of the grim bulldozer, which sent both neighborhoods into oblivion.

Next came the cement mixers that filled the modernist moldings of a new Government Center for Boston's sizable civil-servant sector.

The city's skyline reached upward with luxury condominiums and office buildings. The old customs tower on the waterfront, long the tallest building in town, was overtaken by the proud Prudential Tower and Henry Cobb's elegant John Hancock Tower. Boston was on the rebound.

1927	1960	1960s	1974
Two Italian anarchists, Nicola Sacco and Bartolomeo Vanzetti, are executed on trumped-up murder charges, revealing the persistence of class and ethnic animosities.	After six years in the House of Representatives and eight years in the Senate, Boston native John F Kennedy is elected president, ushering in the era of Camelot.	In a fit of urban renewal, the city razes Scollay Sq. Over 1000 buildings are destroyed and 20,000 residents are displaced to make way for the new Government Center.	Boston institutes mandatory busing in an attempt to desegregate schools. This sparks violence between black and white students and parents in Charlestown and South Boston.

Past Forward

Boston would not be Boston without a major redevelopment project. The Central Artery Tunnel Project (aka the Big Dig) was an unmatched marvel of civil engineering, urban planning and pork-barrel politics. The project employed the most advanced techniques of urban engineering and environmental science, in order to reroute the Central Artery underground through the center of the city. The project fell far behind schedule and went way over budget. When it finally opened in 2004, the walls leaked and a falling ceiling panel killed a motorist. This bane of Bostonian existence finally materialized as a boon for the city, as residents and visitors alike are now enjoying quicker commutes, easier access to the airport and delightful dallying along the Rose Kennedy Greenway.

In the 21st century, Boston and Massachusetts initiated cutting-edge reforms that would eventually be adopted elsewhere in the country. In 2004, Massachusetts became the first state in the union to recognize same-sex marriages, and the first gay marriage took place in Cambridge. In 2006, a health-care reform was enacted, resulting in near universal coverage for Massachusetts residents – years before this legislation passed at a federal level. In 2007, Massachusetts elected Deval Patrick, the state's first African American governor (and the country's second), foreshadowing Barack Obama's arrival in the White House. However, barriers to black representation remain deeply entrenched here: as of 2019, the state has an all-white slate of representatives in Congress.

In 1976 the city organized a triumphant bicentennial celebration, capped with fireworks and a concert by the Charles River. Half a million people attended the patriotic party, including Queen Elizabeth II, who showed no hard feelings over past misunderstandings in her salute from the balcony of the Old State House.

BOSTON STRONG

On Patriots' Day 2013, two bombs exploded near the finish line of the Boston Marathon, killing three and injuring hundreds. Several days later, an MIT police officer was shot dead. The entire city was locked down, as Boston became a battleground.'

The perpetrators were brothers Tamerlan and Dzhokhar Tsarnaev, natives of Chechnya and residents of Cambridge. Tamerlan was killed during a shootout with police. His younger brother Dzhokhar was charged with using and conspiring to use a weapon of mass destruction, resulting in death, as well as malicious destruction of property, resulting in death. In April 2015 he was found guilty on all counts.

The tragedy was devastating, but Boston claimed countless heroes, especially the many victims that inspired others with their courage and fortitude throughout their recoveries. Locals commemorated the city's resilience with the motto 'Boston Strong,' which you'll still see emblazoned on T-shirts, signs and elsewhere around the city.

1991–2007	2004	2011	2014
The Big Dig, the Central Artery/Tunnel Project keeps all of Boston under construction for 15 years and $15 billion. Behind schedule and over budget, the final product transforms the city.	Massachusetts becomes the first state in the union to legalize same-sex marriage. Cambridge becomes the first municipality to issue marriage licenses to gay and lesbian couples.	The notorious Boston crime boss Whitey Bulger is arrested in California. Charged with murder, money laundering, extortion and drug trafficking, he is sentenced to two life terms in prison.	Leaving a legacy of revived neighborhoods and bike-friendly streets, Boston's longest-serving mayor, Thomas Menino, declines to run for reelection, after five terms in office.

Arts & Architecture

The Puritans were spiritual, uninterested in small-minded pursuits like art or music. Despite this, in the 19th century Boston became an artistic center, earning the nickname 'Athens of America.' Boston can thank the Puritans, however, for founding Harvard College, establishing Boston as a learning center. Attracted by the intellectual atmosphere, other institutions followed suit; not only traditional universities, but art schools, music colleges, conservatories and more. Even today, the university culture enhances the breadth and depth of cultural offerings.

Literature

By the 19th century, the city's universities had become a magnet for writers, poets and philosophers, as well as publishers and bookstores. The local literati were expounding on social issues such as slavery, women's rights and religious reawakening. Boston, Cambridge and Concord were fertile breeding grounds for ideas, nurturing the seeds of America's literary and philosophical flowering. Ralph Waldo Emerson, Henry David Thoreau, Nathaniel Hawthorne, Louisa May Alcott and Henry Wadsworth Longfellow were born of this era. This was the Golden Age of American literature, and Boston was its nucleus.

Boston's 19th-century luminaries congregated one Saturday a month at the old Parker House. Presided over by Oliver Wendell Holmes Sr, the Saturday Club was known for its jovial atmosphere and stimulating discourse, attracting such renowned visitors as Charles Dickens. The prestigious literary magazine *Atlantic Monthly* was born out of these meetings.

In the 20th century, Boston continued to foster authors, poets and playwrights, but the Golden Age was over. The city was no longer the center of the progressive thought and social activism that had so inspired American literature. Moral crusaders and city officials promoted stringent censorship of books, films and plays that they deemed offensive or obscene. Many writers were 'banned in Boston' – a trend that contributed to the city's image as a provincial outpost instead of a cultural capital.

Boston never regained its status as the hub of the literary solar system, but its rich legacy and ever-influential universities ensure that the city continues to contribute to American literature. Many of Boston's most prominent writers are transplants from other cities or countries, drawn to its academic and creative institutions. John Updike, Ha Jin, Jhumpa Lahiri and David Foster Wallace all came to the Boston area to study or teach at local universities.

Boston artist John Singleton Copley is considered the first great American portrait painter: you can see a huge collection of his works at the Museum of Fine Arts.

Painting & Visual Arts

Boston began supporting a world-class artistic movement in the late 19th century, when new construction and cultural institutions required adornment. Boston's most celebrated artist is John Singer Sargent, whose murals decorate the staircases at the Museum of Fine Arts (p119) and the Boston Public Library (p108), both of which were built during this time. Prolific sculptors Daniel Chester French and Augustus Saint-Gaudens also left their marks in parks and public spaces all over town. During this period, Winslow Homer became famous for his paintings of the New England coast, while Childe Hassam used local cityscapes as subjects for his impressionist works.

Critics claim that Boston lost pace with the artistic world in the second half of the 20th century. But the visual arts are returning to the forefront of contemporary cultural life in the new millennium. The 2006 opening of the Institute of Contemporary Art (ICA; p131) shone the spotlight on to Boston's long-overshadowed contemporary art scene. Almost in response, the Museum of Fine Arts, the Isabella Stewart Gardner Museum (p121) and the Harvard Art Museums (p142) upgraded their facilities for contemporary art with new and expanded exhibit spaces and programming. Artists have transformed the South End and Fort Point into vibrant art districts that feed off the growing and changing art institutions.

Architecture

The Carpenter Center on the Harvard campus is the only Le Corbusier building in the country; across town, MIT boasts buildings by Eero Saarinen and Alvar Aalto – emblematic of how these academic institutions have enabled design prowess.

After the American Revolution, Boston set to work repairing and re-building the city, now the capital of the new Commonwealth of Massachusetts. Charles Bulfinch took responsibility for much of it, creating Faneuil Hall (p83) and the Massachusetts State House (p73), as well as private homes for Boston's most distinguished citizens.

As the city expanded, so did the opportunities for creative art and architecture, especially with the new construction in Back Bay. Frederick Law Olmsted designed the Charles River Esplanade (p111) and the Emerald Necklace (p159), two magnificent green spaces that snake around the city. Copley Square (p111) represents the pinnacle of 19th-century architecture, with the Romanesque Trinity Church (p110), designed by Henry Hobson Richardson, and the Renaissance Revival Boston Public Library (p108), designed by McKim, Mead and White.

The 20th century witnessed plenty of noteworthy additions. IM Pei is responsible for the much-hated City Hall Plaza (p84) and the much-beloved John F Kennedy Library (p133). His partner James Cobb designed the stunning John Hancock Tower (p112). Reflecting Trinity Church in its facade, this prominent modern tower takes its design cues from Boston's past, a recurring trope in the city.

The century closed with a remarkable project in urban planning – not building, but unbuilding – as parts of the Central Artery were re-routed underground and replaced by a network of green parks and plazas, the Rose Kennedy Greenway (p85). And where the Central Artery is not hidden, it is on display, as it soars over the Charles River on the new Zakim Bunker Hill Bridge, one of the widest cable-stayed bridges in the world.

Several new buildings on the MIT campus – particularly Frank Gehry's Stata Center (p143) – have made industrial Kendall Sq a daring neighborhood for architecture. Across town, the Harvard campus now boasts a striking Renzo Piano design, housing the new Harvard Art Museums (p142). Meanwhile, the dramatic space for the Institute of Contemporary Art (p131) has kicked off a spate of construction along the South Boston waterfront. All around Boston, there is a burgeoning interest in design as an art form that affects us all: the Design Museum Boston (p91) explores these questions with exhibits and presentations all over town.

Music

Classical Music

Possibly Boston's most venerated cultural institution, the Boston Symphony Orchestra (p127) was founded in 1881 and is rated among the world's best orchestras, thanks to the leadership of several talented conductors. It was under Serge Koussevitzky's reign that the BSO gained its world-renowned reputation, due to its radio broadcasts and noteworthy world premieres. Seiji Ozawa, the BSO's longest-tenured maestro (1973–2002), was beloved in Boston for his passionate style. James Levine (2004–11) was known for challenging Boston audiences with a less traditional repertoire, though he suffered from ill health throughout his tenure. In 2014, Boston proudly welcomed Andris Nelsons, a dynamic young maestro from Latvia, who brings unbridled emotion and energy to his conducting.

The Boston Pops (p128) was founded as an effort to offer audiences lighter fare, such as popular classics, marches and show tunes. Arthur Fiedler, who took the helm of the Pops in 1930, was responsible for realizing its goal of attracting more diverse audiences, thanks to free concerts on the Charles River Esplanade (p111). The Pops' current conductor is the young, charismatic Keith Lockhart, who has reached out to audiences in new ways – namely by bringing in pop and rock singers to perform with the orchestra.

Contemporary Music

Boston has a tradition of grooving to great music. Classic rockers remember Aerosmith, the Cars and the J Geils Band. (Peter Wolf, lead singer of the J Geils Band, is frequently sighted at celebrity events around Boston.)

The pinnacle of the Boston music scene, however, is reserved for the punk rockers of the 1980s and '90s. Bostonians still pine for the Mighty Mighty Bosstones and the Pixies, the most influential of many B-town bands from this era. Nowadays, no one makes more real, honest hardcore punk than the wildly popular Dropkick Murphys, a bunch of blue-collar Irish boys from Quincy.

Boston is also home to a thriving folk tradition, thanks to the venerable nonprofit Club Passim (p151), while the Berklee College of Music (p115) sustains a lively jazz and blues scene.

Opera & Ballet

Boston's preeminent dance company is the Boston Ballet (p90), founded by E Virginia Williams in 1965. The current director is Mikko Nissinen, veteran of the Finnish National Ballet and the Kirov Ballet in St Petersburg, Russia. The season usually includes timeless pieces by choreographers such as Rudolf Nureyev and George Balanchine, as well as more daring work by choreographers-in-residence. And it always includes the classic performance of *The Nutcracker* at Christmas. The Boston Ballet performs at the Opera House (p90).

The city's most prominent opera company, Boston Lyric Opera (www.blo.org) is currently without a permanent home (even as it recently celebrated its 40th year). Nonetheless, the innovative company stages performances in venues all around the city. In 2013 a second company was founded, Odyssey Opera (www.odysseyopera.org). Striving to present 'eclectic' and 'adventurous' works, the young company has been lauded in its debut.

ARTS & ARCHITECTURE MUSIC

In recent years Boston has developed as a destination for alternative theater. The American Repertory Theater has made a name for itself with its cutting-edge productions. The Boston Center for the Arts in the South End hosts a slew of smaller companies that stage engaging and unconventional shows.

Universities & Colleges

No single element has influenced the city so profoundly as its educational institutions. Aside from the big ones mentioned here, dozens of smaller schools are located in Fenway. The residential areas west of the center (Brighton and Allston) have been dubbed the 'student ghetto.' Academic suburban sprawl means there are also excellent schools in Medford, Waltham and Wellesley, north and west of Boston.

The Big Boys

Harvard University

A slew of superlatives accompany the name of this venerable institution in Cambridge. It is America's oldest university, founded in 1636. It still has the largest endowment, numbering $37 billion in 2017. It is often first in the list of national universities, according to *US News & World Report*. Harvard is actually comprised of 10 independent schools dedicated to the study of medicine, dentistry, law, business, divinity, design, education, public health and public policy, in addition to the traditional Faculty of Arts and Sciences.

MIT computer scientist Joseph Carl Robnett Licklider first conceived of a 'galactic network' in the early 1960s, which would later spawn the internet.

Harvard Yard (p141) is the heart and soul of the university campus, with buildings dating back to its founding. But the university continues to expand in all directions. Most recently, Harvard has acquired extensive land across the river in Allston, with plans underway to convert this working-class residential area into a satellite campus with commercial, residential and academic facilities.

Massachusetts Institute of Technology

At the opposite end of Mass Ave, the Massachusetts Institute of Technology (MIT) offers an interesting contrast (and complement) to Harvard. Excelling in sciences and engineering – pretty serious stuff, by most standards – MIT nonetheless does not take itself too seriously. The campus is dotted with whimsical sculptures and offbeat art, not to mention some of Boston's most daring and dumbfounding contemporary architecture. MIT students are notorious practical jokers, and their pranks usually leave the bemused public wondering 'How did they do that?'

Despite the atmosphere of fun and funniness, these smarty-pants are hard at work. The school has claimed some 93 Nobel Laureates and 58 recipients of the National Medal of Science since its founding in 1861. Some recent accomplishments include artificially duplicating the process of photosynthesis to store solar energy, developing computer programs to decipher ancient languages and creating an acrobatic robotic bird.

The MIT campus stretches out for about a mile along the Charles River. The university has a few museums, but it's really the art, architecture and atmosphere of innovation that make the place unique.

The Best of Boston

Boston University

Boston University (BU) is a massive urban campus sprawling west of Kenmore Sq. BU enrolls about 30,000 undergraduate and graduate students in all fields of study. The special collections of BU's Mugar Memorial Library (p124) include an outstanding 20th-century archive. Public exhibits showcase the holdings, which include the papers of Isaac Asimov, Bette Davis, Martin Luther King Jr and more. The BU Terriers excel at ice hockey, with frequent appearances in the national college championships, the Frozen Four, as well as victories in the local Beanpot tournament.

Boston College

Not to be confused with BU, Boston College (BC) could not be more different. BC is situated between Brighton in Boston and Chestnut Hill in the swanky suburb of Newton; the attractive campus is recognizable by its neo-Gothic towers. It is home to the nation's largest Jesuit community. Its Catholic influence makes it more socially conservative and more social-service oriented than other universities. Visitors to the campus will find a good art museum and excellent Irish and Catholic ephemera collections in the library. Aside from the vibrant undergraduate population, it has a strong education program and an excellent law school. Its basketball and football teams – the BC Eagles – are usually high in national rankings.

Since 1952, one of Boston's biggest annual sporting events is the Beanpot, a local hockey tournament between Harvard, BU, BC and Northeastern. It takes place on the first two Mondays in February.

UNIVERSITIES & COLLEGES THE BEST OF BOSTON

A WALK ACROSS THE HARVARD BRIDGE

The Harvard Bridge – from Back Bay in Boston to MIT in Cambridge – is the longest bridge across the Charles River. It is not too long to walk, but it is long enough to do some wondering while you walk. You might wonder, for example, why the bridge that leads into the heart of MIT is named the Harvard Bridge.

According to legend, the state offered to name the bridge after Cambridge's second university. But the brainiac engineers at MIT analyzed the plans for construction and found the bridge was structurally unsound. Not wanting the MIT moniker associated with a faulty feat of engineering, it was suggested that the bridge better be named for the neighboring university up the river. That the bridge was subsequently rebuilt validated the superior brainpower of MIT.

That is only a legend, however (one invented by an MIT student, no doubt). The fact is that the Harvard Bridge was first constructed in 1891 and MIT moved to its current location only in 1916. The bridge was rebuilt in the 1980s to modernize and expand it, but the original name has stuck, at least officially. Most Bostonians actually refer to the bridge as the 'Mass Ave bridge' because, frankly, it makes more sense.

Walking across the bridge, you may notice the graffiti reading: '50 smoots...69 smoots...100 smoots...Halfway to Hell...' and you are probably wondering, 'What is a smoot?' A smoot is an obscure unit of measurement that was used to measure the distance of the Harvard Bridge, first in 1958 and every year since. One smoot is approximately 5ft 7in, the height of Oliver R Smoot, who was a pledge of the MIT fraternity Lambda Chi Alpha in '58. He was the shortest pledge that year. And yes, his physical person was actually used for all the measurements.

By the time you reach the other side of the river, surely you will wonder exactly how long the bridge is. We can't say about the Harvard students, but certainly every MIT student knows that the Harvard Bridge is 364.4 smoots plus one ear.

DIVERSITY IN ACADEMIA

Boston's universities and colleges have long been recognized as a source of vibrancy and creativity. In recent years, the schools are also hubs of diversity, as students arrive from around the world. Unfortunately, the percentage of African American students remains relatively low (5 to 7%) and alarmingly static (practically unchanged since the 1980s), according to a 2017 spotlight series on race in the *Boston Globe*. This disparity in academia is representative of the persistence of racial inequalities in Boston at large.

Northeastern University

Located in the midst of student central, aka Fenway, Northeastern is a private regional university with programs emphasizing health, security and sustainability. Northeastern University (NU) boasts one of the country's largest work-study cooperative programs, whereby most students complete two or three semesters of full-time employment in addition to their eight semesters of studies. This integration of classroom learning with real-world experience is the university's strongest feature.

Art & Music Schools

Massachusetts College of Art & Design

The country's first and only four-year independent public art college was founded along with MIT and the Museum of Fine Arts in the late 19th century, when local leaders wanted to influence the state's development by promoting fine arts and technology. It seems safe to say that their long-term goal was successfully met. Nowadays, Massachusetts College of Art and Design (MassArt) offers a highly ranked art program, with specializations in industrial design, fashion design, illustration and animation, as well as the more traditional fine arts.

Berklee College of Music

Housed in and around Back Bay in Boston, Berklee is an internationally renowned school for contemporary music, especially jazz. The school was founded in 1945 by Lawrence Berk (the Lee came from his son's first name). Created as an alternative to the classical agenda and stuffy attitude of traditional music schools, Berk taught courses in composition and arrangement for popular music. Not big on musical theory, Berk emphasized learning by playing. His system was a big success and the school flourished. Berklee's Grammy-laden alumni include jazz musicians Gary Burton, Al Di Meola, Keith Jarrett and Diana Krall; pop/rock artists Quincy Jones, Donald Fagen and John Mayer; and filmmaker Howard Shore.

Emerson College

Founded in 1880, Emerson is a liberal arts college that specializes in communications and the performing arts. Located in the Boston theater district, the college operates the Cutler Majestic Theatre (p102) and the Paramount Center (p90), and its students run Boston's coolest radio station, WERS (www.wers.org; 88.9 FM). Emerson celebs include Norman Lear, Jay Leno, Denis Leary and Henry Winkler, aka 'the Fonz.'

Boston is a funny place, and we mean funny ha-ha. Many of Boston's famous jokesters are graduates of Emerson College, which offers scholarships and workshops specifically devoted to comedy.

Survival Guide

Transportation

ARRIVING IN BOSTON

Most travelers arrive in Boston by plane, with many national and international flights in and out of Logan International Airport. Two smaller regional airports – Manchester Airport in New Hampshire and Green Airport near Providence, RI – offer alternatives that are also accessible to Boston and are sometimes less expensive. Most trains operated by **Amtrak** (☑800-872-7245; www.amtrak.com; South Station) go in and out of South Station. Boston is the northern terminus of the Northeast Corridor, which sends frequent trains to New York (3½ to 4½ hours), Philadelphia, PA (five to six hours) and Washington, DC (6¾ to eight hours). *Lake Shore Limited* goes daily to Buffalo, NY (11 hours) and Chicago (22 hours), while the *Downeaster* goes from North Station to Portland, ME (2½ hours).

Buses are most useful for regional destinations, although Greyhound (www.greyhound.com) operates services around the country. In recent years, there has been a spate of new companies offering cheap and efficient service to New York City (four to five hours).

Flights, cars and tours can be booked online at lonelyplanet.com/bookings.

Logan International Airport

On Massachusetts Route 1A in East Boston, **Logan International Airport** (BOS; ☑800-235-6426; www.massport.com/logan) has four separate terminals (A, B, C and E) that are connected by frequent shuttle buses. Downtown Boston is just a few miles from the airport and is accessible by bus, subway, water shuttle and taxi.

Silver Line Bus

The silver line is the MBTA's 'bus rapid transit service.' It travels between Logan International Airport and South Station, with stops in the Seaport District. This is the most convenient way to get into the city if you are staying in the Seaport District or anywhere along the red line (Downtown, Beacon Hill, Cambridge).

Silver-line buses are free for passengers embarking at the airport, and they connect directly to the red-line subway at South Station, so you don't have to buy a separate ticket for the T. Returning to the airport, silver-line prices and hours are the same as for subway lines.

Subway (The T)

The T, or the MBTA subway (www.mbta.com), is a fast and cheap way to reach the city from the airport. From any terminal, take a free, well-marked shuttle bus (22 or 33) to the blue-line T station called Airport and you'll be downtown within 30 minutes. The one-way subway fare is $2.75; buy tickets at machines in the station.

Boat

Water shuttles and ferries operate between Logan and the Boston waterfront. Take the free water transportation shuttle bus 66 from the airport terminal to the ferry dock. Fares to the North End and Charlestown are more expensive than fares to downtown.

Boston Harbor Cruises Water Taxi (Map p234;☑617-227-4320; www.bostonharbor cruises.com/water-taxi; 1 Long Wharf; water taxi one-way adult/child $15/3, Provincetown round-trip $93/68, Salem round-trip adult/child $45/35; ⊙taxi 6:30am-10pm Mon-Sat, to 8pm Sun; T Aquarium) Service to Long Wharf and other waterfront destinations.

MBTA Cross Harbor Ferry (Map p234;☑617-222-3200; www.mbta.com; one-way $9.25) Less expensive (but less frequent) service from Logan to Long Wharf.

Rowes Wharf Water Taxi (Map p234;☑617-406-8584; www.roweswharfwatertransport. com; one-way/round-trip $12/20; ⊙7am-8pm Nov-Apr, to 10pm May-Oct; T Aquarium)

Serves Rowes Wharf near the Boston Harbor Hotel, the Moakley Federal Courthouse on the Fort Point Channel and the World Trade Center in the Seaport District. Taxis also go to the North End and Charlestown for a higher fare.

Car & Motorcycle
Three tunnels connect Logan Airport to I-93 and downtown Boston. If you're driving from the airport into Boston or to points north of the city, the Sumner Tunnel will lead you to Storrow Dr or over the Zakim Bridge to I-93 North. To points south of Boston, use the Ted Williams Tunnel to I-93 South. To or from points west, the Mass Pike connects directly with the Ted Williams Tunnel.

To reach the airport from downtown Boston, take the Callahan Tunnel or the Ted Williams Tunnel.

The toll is the same for all three tunnels ($2.65). Automatic pay-by-plate billing has eliminated the need for toll booths; you'll receive a bill in the mail based on an electronic scan of your license plate. (Check with

your car-rental agency about how they handle this.)

Taxi
Taxi fares from Logan are approximately $25 to downtown Boston, $30 to Kenmore Sq and $35 to Harvard Sq.

Green Airport
Just outside the city of Providence, RI, **TF Green Airport** (888-268-7222; www.pvdairport.com; 2000 Post Rd, Warwick) is serviced by major carriers. Southwest Airlines, in particular, offers very competitively priced tickets. The airport is one hour south of Boston.

The MBTA commuter rail (www.mbta.com) travels between Green Airport and South Station ($12, 90 minutes, 10 daily), with stops at Ruggles and Back Bay stations along the way.

South Station
Located in downtown Boston, **South Station** (Map p240; 617-523-1300; www.south-

station.net; 700 Atlantic Ave; TSouth Station) is the terminus for Amtrak trains to/from New York City, Philadelphia and Washington, DC. It's also a stop for silver-line buses and the red line of the T.

GETTING AROUND
Boston is geographically small and logistically manageable. The sights and activities of principal interest to travelers are contained within an area that's only about 1 mile wide by 3 miles long. This makes Boston a wonderful walking or cycling city. Otherwise, most of the main attractions are accessible by subway. Some outlying sites require a bus ride. And a few – namely the Boston Harbor Islands – require a boat ride or two.

Incidentally, Boston is a waterside city, and riding in boats is part of the fun. Water shuttles are a convenient transportation option for a few harborside destinations, including the airport.

BUS TO/FROM NEW YORK
The infamous 'Chinatown Buses' originated in the late 1990s as an affordable way for Chinese workers to travel to and from jobs. They offered supercheap tickets between Boston and New York, traveling from Chinatown to Chinatown. Young, savvy travelers caught wind of the bargain transportation, and the phenomenon began to spread. It was crowded and confusing and probably not that safe, but it sure was cheap.

In recent years, more and more companies are running buses on this route; however, they don't always start and end in Chinatown. With competition has come improved service and better safety records, and many offer free wi-fi service on board. But the prices remain blissfully low.

Lucky Star Bus (www.luckystarbus.com) Leaves from South Station 12 to 14 times daily. Tickets must be purchased at least one hour before departure time. Full fare one way costs $25 to $35, while nonrefundable last-minute tickets can go for as little as $8.

Megabus (www.megabus.com) Rates vary from $5 to $50 depending on the time of day of travel and how far in advance tickets are purchased. In addition to New York, buses go to Burlington and Montpelier, VT; Portland, ME; Philadelphia, PA; Baltimore, MD; and Washington, DC. Buses leave from South Station.

GO Buses (www.gobuses.com) Buses to New York City ($18 to $44) depart from Alewife station in Cambridge. Buses also go to Providence, RI; Hartford and New Haven, CT; and Washington DC.

Bicycle

In recent years, Boston has made vast improvements in its infrastructure for cyclists, including painting miles of bicycle lanes, upgrading bike facilities on and around public transportation, and implementing an excellent bike-share program. Boston drivers are used to sharing the roads with their two-wheeled friends (and they are used to arriving *after* their two-wheeled friends, who are less impeded by traffic snarls). Cyclists should always obey traffic rules and ride defensively.

Boston's bike-share program is Blue Bikes (www.bluebikes.com). There are 200 Blue Bikes stations around Boston, Cambridge, Brookline and Somerville, stocked with 1800 bikes available for short-term loan.

➡ Download the app or visit any bicycle kiosk to purchase your pass.

➡ Pay $2.50 per half-hour for bike use or purchase a one-day Adventure Pass for an unlimited number of two-hour bike rides in 24 hours.

➡ Return the bike(s) to any station in the vicinity of your destination.

Generally speaking, Blue Bikes pricing is designed so a Single Use ticket can substitute for a cab ride (eg to make a one-way trip or run an errand). The Adventure Pass might work for leisurely riding or long trips, as long as you keep track of your time. Check the website for a map of Blue Bikes stations.

Blue Bikes recommends that all riders wear helmets (and state law requires it for children under age 16).

Bikes on the MBTA

You can bring bikes on the T, commuter trains, and most buses (those equipped with exterior bike racks) for no additional fare. Bikes are not allowed on green-line trains, inside buses, or on any trains during rush hour (7am to 10am and 4pm to 7pm, Monday to Friday).

Bicycle Rental

Urban AdvenTours (Map p230; ✆617-670-0637; www.urbanadventours.com; 103 Atlantic Ave; tours from $55, rentals per 24hr $40-75; ☺9am-8pm Apr-Sep, to 7pm Mon-Sat & to 5pm Sun Oct & end-Mar, to 6pm Tue-Sat Nov-mid-Mar; Ⓣ Aquarium) Bikes available for rent include road bikes and mountain bikes, in addition to the standard hybrids. For an extra fee these guys will bring your bike to your doorstep in a BioBus powered by vegetable oil.

Cambridge Bicycle (✆617-876-6555; www.cambridgebicycle.com; 259 Massachusetts Ave; per 24hr $35; ☺10am-7pm Mon-Sat, noon-6pm Sun; Ⓣ Central) Convenient for cycling along the Charles River. Rentals are three-speed commuter bikes.

Papa Wheelies (Back Bay Bicycles; ✆617-247-2336; www.papa-wheelies.com; 362 Commonwealth Ave; rental per day $55-65; ☺10am-7pm Mon-Fri, to 6pm Sat, noon-5pm Sun; Ⓣ Hynes) Well-established shop convenient for the Charles River.

Bicycle Exchange (✆617-864-1300; www.cambridgebicycleexchange.com; 2067 Massachusetts Ave; rental 1 day $25, additional days $10; ☺hours vary; Ⓣ Porter) This bike shop is just north of Porter Sq, convenient to the Minuteman Bikeway.

Boat

While boats will likely not be your main means of transportation, they are useful for a few destinations, primarily the Boston Harbor Islands and Charlestown. Ferries to Provincetown and Salem provide a pleasant transportation alternative for day trips out of the city. There is also a water-shuttle service to the airport and water taxis that make stops at destinations along the waterfront.

Bus

The MBTA (www.mbta.com) operates bus routes within the city. These can be difficult to figure out for the short-term visitor, but schedules are posted on the website and at some bus stops along the routes. The standard bus fare is $2, or $1.70 with a Charlie Card. If you're transferring from the T on a Charlie Card, the bus fare is free.

The silver line, a so-called 'rapid' bus, starts at Downtown Crossing and runs along Washington St in the South End to Roxbury's Dudley Sq. Another route goes from South Station to the Seaport District, then under the harbor to Logan International Airport. This waterfront route costs $2.75 ($2.25 with a Charlie Card), instead of the normal bus fare.

The silver line is different from the regular MBTA buses because it drives in a designated lane (supposedly reducing travel time). More importantly, the silver line starts/terminates inside the South Station or Downtown Crossing subway terminal, so you can transfer to/from the T without purchasing an additional ticket.

Car & Motorcycle

It is not easy and not necessary to drive in Boston. Keep in mind that Boston is notorious for counter-intuitive traffic patterns, unexpected one-way streets, impatient drivers, impromptu U-turns and the nerve-rattling 'Boston left'. (The latter refers to the move where a driver shoots out into an intersection and turns left as soon as the light turns green, instead of yielding to oncoming traffic.) And did we mention the lack of parking?

Most importantly, it's often quicker and easier to reach your destination by public transportation or by bike than by car. Even if you drive your car to Boston, you might as well give it a rest while you are in the city (though it may come in handy for day trips out of town).

Subway (The T)

The MBTA (www.mbta. com) operates the USA's oldest subway, built in 1897 and known locally as the 'T.' There are four lines – red, blue, green and orange – that radiate from the principal downtown stations: Downtown Crossing, Government Center, Park St and State. When traveling away from any of these stations, you are heading 'outbound.'

Although the MBTA might like you to believe otherwise, the silver line is a bus line with a dedicated traffic lane – not a subway line.

Tourist passes with unlimited travel (on subway, bus or water shuttle) are available for periods of

one day ($12) or one week ($21.25). Kids 11 and under ride for free. Passes may be purchased from vending machines in most T stations and at MBTA sales outlets citywide (see www.mbta. com for a full list). For longer stays, you can buy a monthly pass allowing unlimited use of the subway and local buses ($84.50). Otherwise, buy a paper fare card ($2.75 per ride) at any station or a Charlie Card ($2.25 per ride) at designated stations.

At night, the last red-line trains pass through Park St around 12:40am, but all T stations and lines are different: check the posting at the station.

Train

The MBTA commuter rail services destinations in the metropolitan Boston area. Trains heading west and north of the city, including to Concord and Salem, leave from bustling North Station on Causeway St. Trains heading south, including to Plymouth and TF Green Airport in Providence, leave from South Station.

TOURS

Bicycle Tours

★**Urban AdvenTours**
(Map p230; ☏617-670-0637; www.urbanadventours.com; 103 Atlantic Ave; tours from $55, rentals per 24hr $40-75; ⏰9am-8pm Apr-Sep, to 7pm Mon-Sat & to 5pm Sun Oct & end-Mar, to 6pm Tue-Sat Nov-mid-Mar; Ⓣ Aquarium) The City View Ride tour provides a great overview of how to get around by bike, including ride-bys of some of Boston's best sites. Other specialty tours include Bikes at Night and the Emerald Necklace tour. Bicycles, helmets and water are all provided.

Boat Tours

See Boston from the water and gain a new perspective on this city by the sea.

Boston Green Cruises
(Map p234; ☏617-261-6620; www.bostongreencruises.com; 60 Rowes Wharf; adult/child from $28/24; ⓓ; Ⓣ Aquarium, South Station) See the sights and hear the sounds of the city from Boston's first super-quiet, zero-emissions electric boat. Spend an hour floating in the Boston Harbor or cruising on the Charles River (or upgrade to a 90-minute combo trip for $39/35 per adult/child).

Boston Harbor Cruises
(BHC; Map p234; ☏617-227-4321; www.bostonharbor cruises.com; 1 Long Wharf; cruises adult/child from $26/22, Codzilla $33/25; Ⓣ Aquarium) BHC claims to be America's oldest and largest operator of passenger boats. The options range from a basic Historic Sightseeing Tour around Boston's inner harbor to sunset cruises, weekend

---

CHARLIE ON THE MTA

The Charlie in question is a fictional character from the Kingston Trio hit *Charlie on the MTA*. Charlie's sad story was that he could not get off the Boston T (then known as the Metropolitan Transit Authority) because he did not have the exit fare.

Now Charlie has been immortalized – yet again – by the MBTA's fare system: the Charlie Card. The plastic cards are available from the attendant at designated T stations. Once you have a card, you can add money at the automated fare machines; at the turnstile you will be charged $2.25 per ride.

The system is designed to favor commuters and cardholders. If you do not request a Charlie Card, you can purchase a paper fare card from the machine, but the turnstile will charge you $2.75 per ride. Similarly, Charlie Card–holders pay $1.70 to ride the bus, but for those paying cash it's $2.

lighthouse cruises, whale-watching and more.

Boston Duck Tours (📞617-267-3825; www.bostonduck tours.com; adult/child $42/28; ♿; Ⓣ Aquarium, Science Park, Prudential) These ridiculously popular tours use WWII amphibious vehicles that cruise the downtown streets before splashing into the Charles River. The 80-minute tours depart from the Museum of Science, the Prudential Center or the New England Aquarium. Reserve in advance.

Trolley Tours

Overheard on a Duck Tour: 'Trolleys can go in the water, too...once.' Nonetheless, trolley tours offer great flexibility because you can hop off at sites along the route and hop on the next trolley that comes along. All trolleys offer discounts for online purchase.

Ghosts & Gravestones (Map p234; 📞866-754-9136; www.ghostsandgravestones. com; Long Wharf; adult/child $42/25; Ⓣ Aquarium) A hair-raising tour telling tales of Boston's darker side, hosted by a cursed gravedigger. Tickets are discounted slightly if you buy them on-line.

Old Town Trolley Tours (Map p234; 📞855-396-7433; www.trolleytours.com/bos ton; 200 Atlantic Ave, Long Wharf; adult/child $79/21; Ⓣ Aquarium) Tour around the city, hopping on and off all day long. Save up to 50% when you book online. This ticket also includes admission to the Old State House, as well as a $10 discount at the Boston Tea Party Ships & Museum.

Beantown Trolley (📞617-720-6342, 800-343-1328; www.brushhilltours.com; adult/child $40/20; ⊙ tours 10am, 12:30pm & 3pm May-Nov) Take a two-hour tour of the city on

these red-colored trolleys, with 15-minute photo breaks at Copley Sq and the USS *Constitution* – but includes no other hop-on, hop-off privileges. The price includes a harbor cruise from the New England Aquarium or admission to the Mapparium.

Walking Tours

The granddaddy of walking tours in Boston is the Freedom Trail, a 2½-mile trail that traverses the city from the Boston Common to Charlestown. Most tour companies lead tours of the Freedom Trail, as does the National Park Service (www.nps.gov/bost). Tour companies that focus on a particular neighborhood are covered in their respective neighborhood sections.

Photo Walks (📞617-851-2273; www.photowalks.com; adult/youth $40/20; ♿) A walking tour combined with a photography lesson. Different routes cover Boston's most photogenic neighborhoods.

Boston by Foot (📞617-367-2345; www.bostonbyfoot.com; adult/child $15/10; ♿) This fantastic nonprofit organization offers 90-minute walking tours, with neighborhood-specific walks and specialty theme tours such as the Hub of Literary America, the Dark Side of Boston and Boston by Little Feet – a kid-friendly version of the Freedom Trail.

Free Tours By Foot (📞617-299-0764; www.freetoursby foot.com/boston-tours) Take the tour then decide how much you think it's worth. Popular 90-minute walking tours cover the Freedom Trail, Harvard University, the North End and the Beacon Hill 'crime tour.' Tour guides are passionate and entertaining.

NPS Freedom Trail Tour (National Park Service; Map

p234; 📞617-242-5642; www. nps.gov/bost; Faneuil Hall; ⊙ 10am, 11am, 2pm & 3pm Jun-Sep; Ⓣ State) Show up at the NPS Visitor Center in Faneuil Hall at least 30 minutes early to snag a spot on one of the free, ranger-led Freedom Trail tours. Each 60-minute tour follows a portion of the Freedom Trail and is limited to 30 people. Alternatively, take a self-guided tour with the NPS Freedom Trail app (www.nps.gov/bost/ planyourvisit/app.htm).

Boston Foodie Tours (📞617-461-5772; www.boston foodietours.com; $68-88; Ⓣ North Station) Make sure you start the tour hungry, is the advice from participants in these recommended walking tours. The most popular option is a three-hour walking tour of the Boston Public Market and environs, including tastings of award-winning lobster rolls and clam chowder. Alternatively, the North End Neighborhood Tour focuses on pizza, mozzarella and Italian treats, ending with a pasta meal.

Freedom Trail Foundation (Map p236; 📞617-357-8300; www.thefreedomtrail. org; adult/child $14/8; Ⓣ Park St) This educational nonprofit group leads excellent tours of the Freedom Trail, broken up into bite-sized portions (eg Boston Common to Faneuil Hall, North End etc). Frequent departures from Boston Common and Faneuil Hall make this a convenient option. Tour guides are in period costume, for a bit of fun. Discounts available with online purchase.

On Location Tours (📞212-683-2027; www.onlocation tours.com; adult/child $27/19) It's not Hollywood, but Boston has hosted its share of famous movie scenes. More than 30 films were shot along Boston's Movie Mile, which you will see on this 90-minute walking tour.

Directory A–Z

Accessible Travel

Boston attempts to cater to residents and visitors with disabilities by providing cut curbs, accessible restrooms and ramps on public buildings; but old streets, sidewalks and buildings mean that facilities are not always up to snuff. Download Lonely Planet's free Accessible Travel guides from http://lp-travel.to/AccessibleTravel.

Sights Most major museums are accessible to wheelchairs, while the Isabella Stewart Gardner Museum (p121), the Museum of Fine Arts (p119) and the Museum of Science (p58) offer special programs and tours for travelers with disabilities.

Activities Many tours use vehicles that are wheelchair accessible, including Boston Duck Tours (p212) and New England Aquarium Whale Watch (p92). Walking tours such as the Freedom Trail (p28) and the student tour of Harvard Yard (p141) are also accessible,

though the historic buildings may not be.

Transportation MBTA buses and commuter trains are accessible, although not all subway trains and stations are. See MBTA Accessibility (www.mbta.com/accessibility) for more information. Ferries to the Boston Harbor Islands, Provincetown and Salem are all accessible.

Customs Regulations

For up-to-date information, see www.cbp.gov.

Personal Exemptions Each traveler is permitted to bring up to $800 worth of merchandise into the US without incurring any duty, assuming they have been out of the country for at least 48 hours.

Alcohol & Tobacco Each visitor is allowed to bring 1L of liquor and 200 cigarettes duty-free into the US, but they must be at least 21 and 18 years of age, respectively.

Discount Cards

Thanks to its student-heavy population, Boston offers student discounts on admission to most attractions, so bring your ID. Other programs offer discounted admission to area museums and attractions.

Explorer Pass (www.smart destinations.com) Pick a package or design your own, choosing three to five sites from the 19 included options. You have 30 days to use your pass, which may mean savings of up to 35%.

Boston City Pass (www.citypass.com) Includes admission to four popular spots: Museum of Science (p58), New England Aquarium (p83) and Skywalk Observatory (p111), and either the Boston Harbor Cruises (p211) or the Harvard Museum of Natural History (p142). You have nine days to use your tickets. It makes for a busy week, but if you use them all, you'll save $45.

Go Boston Card (www.smart destinations.com) This card allows unlimited admission to 43 Boston-area attractions, including most museums, tours and historic sites. Also offers discounts at local restaurants and shops. The card is good for any number of days (from one to seven, depending on what you pay), so squeeze in

---

PRACTICALITIES

Smoking No smoking in Boston hotels, restaurants or bars.

Weights & Measures US customary units are based on imperial units, measuring distance by mile, weight by pound and volume by pint, quart or gallon.

as much as you can to get your money's worth. In reality, you have to have a pretty ambitious itinerary to make this worthwhile.

Electricity

**Type B
120V/60Hz**

Emergency

Ambulance, fire, police	☑911

Internet Access

Most hotels and hostels offer internet access in one way or another. Usually that means wi-fi access, though some hotels also have an on-site business center or internet corner that provides computers. Aside from at hotels, wi-fi is common in cafes, on buses and even in public spaces such as shopping malls and airports.

LGBT+ Travelers

Out and active gay communities are visible all around Boston, especially in the South End and Jamaica Plain.

There is no shortage of entertainment options catering to LGBTQ+ travelers. From drag shows to dyke nights, this sexually diverse community has something for everybody.

The biggest event of the year for the Boston gay and lesbian community is June's **Boston Pride** (www.boston pride.org), a week of parades, parties, festivals and flag-raisings.

There are excellent sources of information for the gay and lesbian community.

Bay Windows (www.bay windows.com) is a weekly newspaper for LGBTQ+ readers. The print edition is distributed throughout New England, but the website is also an excellent source of news and information.

Edge Boston (www.edgebos ton.com) is the Boston branch of the nationwide network of publications offering news and entertainment for LGBTQ+ readers. Includes a nightlife section with culture and club reviews.

Money

ATMs

ATMs are great for quick cash, but watch out for ATM surcharges. Most banks in Boston charge at least $2.50 per withdrawal. Look for ATMs outside banks and in large grocery stores, shopping centers and gas stations.

Changing Money

If you are carrying foreign currency, it can be exchanged for US dollars at Logan International Airport. Bank outlets around the city are less reliable for currency exchange.

Credit Cards

Major credit cards are accepted at hotels, restaurants, gas stations, shops and car-rental agencies. In fact, you'll find it hard to perform certain transactions, such as renting cars or purchasing concert tickets, without one. Some small B&Bs and family-owned shops and restaurants may not accept credit cards. Visa and MasterCard are the most widely accepted.

Tipping

Members of the service industry depend on tips to earn a living – tips constitute their wages.

Baggage carriers $1 to $2 per bag.

Bar & restaurant staff 20% for good service, 15% for adequate service; less than 15% indicates dissatisfaction with the service.

Housekeeping $3 to $5 for one or two nights, more for longer stays.

Taxi drivers 10% to 15% of the fare.

Opening Hours

Banks 8:30am to 4pm Monday to Friday; sometimes to 6pm on Friday and/or 9am to noon on Saturday

Bars and Clubs Open to midnight daily, and often open to 1am or 2am on Friday and Saturday nights

Businesses 9am–5pm or 6pm Monday to Friday

Restaurants 11am or 11:30am to 9pm or 10pm; restaurants serving breakfast open from 7am; some places close from 2:30pm to 5:30pm

Shops From 10am or 11am to 7pm Monday to Saturday; sometimes noon to 5pm Sunday. Major shopping areas and malls keep extended hours.

Post

The US Postal Service (www. usps.com) is perfectly adequate for sending postcards, letters and packages. Only Express Service guarantees delivery in a certain time period. Post offices are located in every neighborhood.

Public Holidays

New Year's Day January 1

Martin Luther King Jr's Birthday Third Monday in January

Washington's Birthday Third Monday in February

Evacuation Day March 17

Patriot's Day Third Monday in April

Memorial Day Last Monday in May

Bunker Hill Day June 17

Independence Day July 4

Labor Day First Monday in September

Columbus Day Second Monday in October

Veterans Day November 11

Thanksgiving Day Fourth Thursday in November

Christmas Day December 25

Safe Travel

Boston is a relatively safe city and most tourists are unlikely to be targets of crime or violence.

➡ Crime rates are higher in outlying Boston neighborhoods, where tourist attractions are limited.

➡ Reports of harassment of people of color – inappropriate comments and racial slurs – are more common in Boston than other Northeastern cities.

Taxes & Refunds

Massachusetts charges a 6.5% sales tax on all items, not including food and cloth-

ing (up to $175). Additionally, hotel rooms are subject to a 14.45% tax in Boston and Cambridge (which includes a city and state hotel tax, as well as a convention-center tax). B&Bs with three rooms or fewer are exempt from this tax.

Telephone

Most US cell-phone systems work on the GSM 850/1900 standard, as opposed to the GSM 900/1800 standard used throughout Europe, Australia and Asia.

All US phone numbers consist of a three-digit area code followed by a seven-digit local number. Even if you are calling locally, you must dial all 10 digits. If you are calling long distance, dial 🗺1 + the area code + the seven-digit number.

➡ **Area codes** Boston 🗺617, suburban Boston 🗺781, North Shore 🗺978, South Shore 🗺508

➡ **Country code** 🗺1 for USA

➡ **International dialing code** 🗺011

Time

Boston is on Eastern Standard Time, five hours behind Greenwich Mean Time. When it's noon in Boston, it's:

➡ 9am in San Francisco

➡ 5pm in London

➡ 9pm in Moscow

➡ 2am in Tokyo

➡ 4am in Melbourne

This region observes daylight saving time from the second Sunday in March until the first Sunday in November.

Toilets

➡ Travelers will usually find clean individual bathroom stalls in museums, large hotels, restaurants, shopping malls and large stores.

➡ For public bathrooms, visit fire stations and libraries.

➡ The self-cleaning 'City Toilet' (which costs 25¢ to use) is found at key spots around town.

➡ The city has an interactive map of public bathrooms (www. boston.gov/departments/311/ public-restrooms-city-boston), complete with opening hours and special facilities (eg changing areas, wheelchair access etc).

Tourist Information

Boston Common Visitor Center (GBCVB Visitors Center; Map p236;🗺617-426-3115; www.bostonusa.com; Boston Common; ⊗8:30am-5pm Mon-Fri, from 9am Sat & Sun; 🆃Park St) provides maps and all kinds of tourist information, starting point for the Freedom Trail and many other walking tours.

The **Greater Boston Convention & Visitors Bureau** (www.bostonusa.com) website is packed with information on hotels, restaurants and special events, as well as LGBTQ+, family travel and more.

Boston Harbor Islands Pavilion (Map p234;🗺617-223-8666; www.bostonharbor islands.org; cnr State St & Atlantic Ave; ⊗9am-4:30pm mid-May–Jun & Sep-early Oct, to 6pm Jul & Aug; 🛜; 🆃Aquarium) is ideally located on the Rose Kennedy Greenway, this information center will tell you everything you need to know to plan your visit to the Boston Harbor Islands. Don't miss the nearby *Harbor Fog* sculpture, which immerses passersby in the sounds and sensations of the harbor.

Cambridge Visitor Information Kiosk (Map p246;🗺617-441-2884; www. cambridge-usa.org; Harvard Sq; ⊗9am-5pm Mon-Fri, to 1pm Sat & Sun; 🆃Harvard) has detailed information on current

Cambridge happenings and self-guided walking tours.

Massachusetts Office of Travel & Tourism (www.massvacation.com) has information about events and activities throughout the state, including an excellent guide to green tourism.

National Park Service Visitors Center (NPS; Map p234; 617-242-5642; www.nps.gov/bost/planyourvisit/index.htm; Faneuil Hall; 9am-6pm; State) has loads of information about the Freedom Trail sights and is the starting point for the free NPS Freedom Trail Tour (p28). There is an additional NPS Visitors Center at the Charlestown Navy Yard (p53).

Visas

➜ The US has a Visa Waiver Program in which citizens of certain countries may enter the US for stays of 90 days or less without first obtaining a US visa.

➜ For an up-to-date list of countries included in the program, see the US Department of State website (www.travel.state.gov).

➜ Under the program you must have a round-trip ticket (or onward ticket to any foreign destination) that is nonrefundable in the US and you will not be allowed to extend your stay beyond 90 days.

➜ To participate in the Visa Waiver Program, travelers are required to have a passport that is machine readable. Also, your passport should be valid for at least six months longer than your intended stay.

➜ Travel under the Visa Waiver Program requires pre-approval under the Electronic System for Travel Authorization (ESTA) at least three days before arrival. There is a $14 fee for processing and authorization (payable online). Once approved, the registration is valid for two years.

➜ Travelers entering by land do not need to file an ESTA application.

➜ Those who do need a visa should apply at the US consulate in their home country.

Behind the Scenes

SEND US YOUR FEEDBACK

We love to hear from travelers – your comments keep us on our toes and help make our books better. Our well-traveled team reads every word on what you loved or loathed about this book. Although we cannot reply individually to your submissions, we always guarantee that your feedback goes straight to the appropriate authors, in time for the next edition. Each person who sends us information is thanked in the next edition – the most useful submissions are rewarded with a selection of digital PDF chapters.

Visit **lonelyplanet.com/contact** to submit your updates and suggestions or to ask for help. Our award-winning website also features inspirational travel stories, news and discussions.

Note: We may edit, reproduce and incorporate your comments in Lonely Planet products such as guidebooks, websites and digital products, so let us know if you don't want your comments reproduced or your name acknowledged. For a copy of our privacy policy visit lonelyplanet.com/privacy.

WRITER THANKS

Mara Vorhees

To the poet-for-hire on the Boston Common. Thanks for reminding me that there is a poem for every season and every reason. At times, it's a complicated or even nonsensical poem, and forget about rhyming, but still... a poem.

ACKNOWLEDGEMENTS

Cover photograph: Buildings in Downtown Boston, John Pavlish/Getty Images ©

THIS BOOK

This 7th edition of Lonely Planet's *Boston* guidebook was researched and written by Mara Vorhees, who also wrote the previous two editions. This guidebook was produced by the following:

Destination Editors
Evan Godt, Trisha Ping
Senior Product Editors
Martine Power, Vicky Smith
Regional Senior Cartographer Alison Lyall
Product Editor
Ross Taylor
Book Designer
Lauren Egan

Assisting Editors
Katie Connolly, Samantha Cook, Kate Daly, Melanie Dankel, Janet Evans, Mani Ramaswamy, Monica Wood
Cover Researcher
Meri Blazevski
Thanks to Dan Dieck, Jot Hollenbeck, Howard Schulman, Will Turton

Index

See also separate subindexes for:

✕ EATING P221

🍷 DRINKING & NIGHTLIFE P222

☆ ENTERTAINMENT P223

🛍 SHOPPING P223

🏃 SPORTS & ACTIVITIES P224

🛏 SLEEPING P2224

✖ EATING

Boston Maps

Sights
- Beach
- Bird Sanctuary
- Buddhist
- Castle/Palace
- Christian
- Confucian
- Hindu
- Islamic
- Jain
- Jewish
- Monument
- Museum/Gallery/Historic Building
- Ruin
- Shinto
- Sikh
- Taoist
- Winery/Vineyard
- Zoo/Wildlife Sanctuary
- Other Sight

Activities, Courses & Tours
- Bodysurfing
- Diving
- Canoeing/Kayaking
- Course/Tour
- Sento Hot Baths/Onsen
- Skiing
- Snorkeling
- Surfing
- Swimming/Pool
- Walking
- Windsurfing
- Other Activity

Sleeping
- Sleeping
- Camping

Eating
- Eating

Drinking & Nightlife
- Drinking & Nightlife
- Cafe

Entertainment
- Entertainment

Shopping
- Shopping

Information
- Bank
- Embassy/Consulate
- Hospital/Medical
- Internet
- Police
- Post Office
- Telephone
- Toilet
- Tourist Information
- Other Information

Geographic
- Beach
- Gate
- Hut/Shelter
- Lighthouse
- Lookout
- Mountain/Volcano
- Oasis
- Park
- Pass
- Picnic Area
- Waterfall

Population
- Capital (National)
- Capital (State/Province)
- City/Large Town
- Town/Village

Transport
- Airport
- BART station
- Border crossing
- Boston T station
- Bus
- Cable car/Funicular
- Cycling
- Ferry
- Metro/Muni station
- Monorail
- Parking
- Petrol station
- Subway/SkyTrain station
- Taxi
- Train station/Railway
- Tram
- Underground station
- Other Transport

Routes
- Tollway
- Freeway
- Primary
- Secondary
- Tertiary
- Lane
- Unsealed road
- Road under construction
- Plaza/Mall
- Steps
- Tunnel
- Pedestrian overpass
- Walking Tour
- Walking Tour detour
- Path/Walking Trail

Boundaries
- International
- State/Province
- Disputed
- Regional/Suburb
- Marine Park
- Cliff
- Wall

Hydrography
- River, Creek
- Intermittent River
- Canal
- Water
- Dry/Salt/Intermittent Lake
- Reef

Areas
- Airport/Runway
- Beach/Desert
- Cemetery (Christian)
- Cemetery (Other)
- Glacier
- Mudflat
- Park/Forest
- Sight (Building)
- Sportsground
- Swamp/Mangrove

Note: Not all symbols displayed above appear on the maps in this book

WEST END

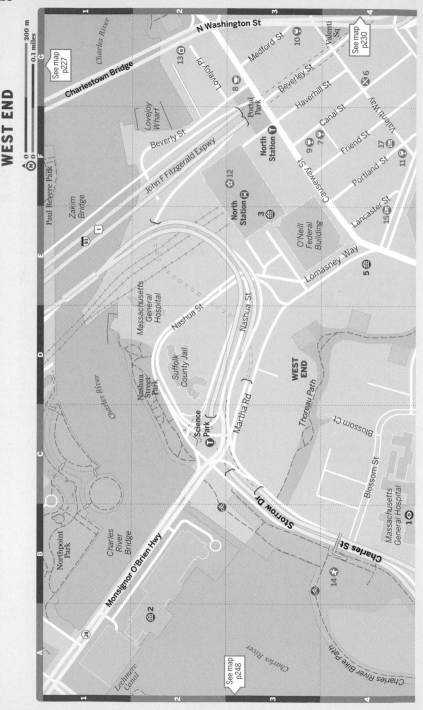

See map p227

See map p230

See map p248

Charles River

Charlestown Bridge

N Washington St

Medford St

Beverley St

Haverhill St

Canal St

Friend St

Portland St

Lancaster St

Lovejoy Pl

Portal Park

Lovejoy Wharf

Beverly St

John F Fitzgerald Expwy

North Station

Causeway St

Valenti Way

Valenti Sq

O'Neill Federal Building

Lomasney Way

Paul Revere Park

Zakim Bridge

Charles River

Massachusetts General Hospital

Nashua St

Nashua St

Nashua Street Park

Suffolk County Jail

Martha Rd

Science Park

WEST END

Thoreau Path

Blossom Ct

Blossom St

Storrow Dr

Charles St

Massachusetts General Hospital

Charles River Bike Path

Northpoint Park

Charles River Bridge

Monsignor O'Brien Hwy

Leechmere Canal

Charles River

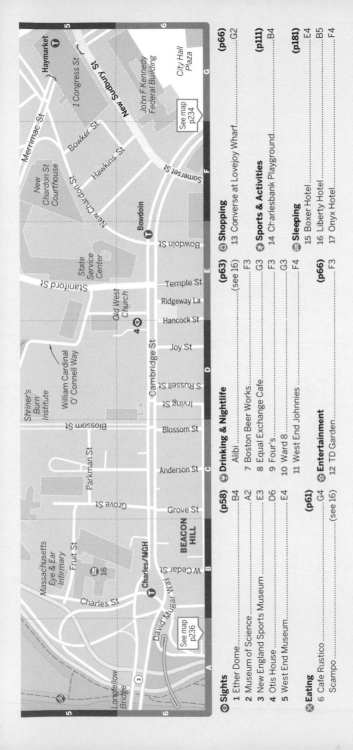

WEST END

◎ Sights (p58)
1 Ether Dome................................B4
2 Museum of Science....................A2
3 New England Sports Museum.....E3
4 Otis House.................................D6
5 West End Museum.....................E4

⊗ Eating (p61)
6 Cafe Rustico..............................G4
 Scampo..............................(see 16)

◎ Drinking & Nightlife (p63)
 Alibi....................................(see 16)
7 Boston Beer Works....................F3
8 Equal Exchange Cafe................G3
9 Four's......................................F3
10 Ward 8....................................G3
11 West End Johnnies..................F4

◎ Entertainment (p61)
12 TD Garden...............................F3

◎ Shopping (p66)
13 Converse at Lovejoy Wharf......G2

◎ Sports & Activities (p111)
14 Charlesbank Playground..........B4

◎ Sleeping (p181)
15 Boxer Hotel.............................E4
16 Liberty Hotel...........................B5
17 Onyx Hotel..............................F4

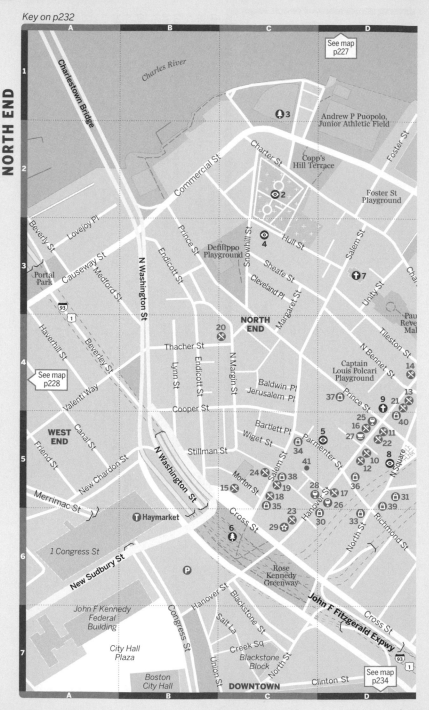

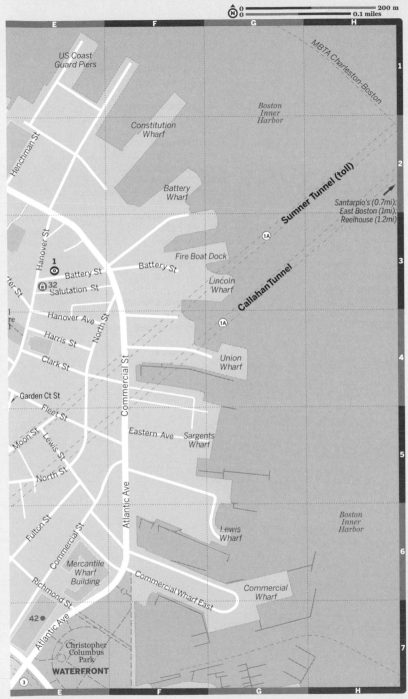

200 m
0.1 miles

MBTA Charleston-Boston

US Coast
Guard Piers

Boston
Inner
Harbor

Constitution
Wharf

Henchman St

Battery
Wharf

Sumner Tunnel (toll)

Santarpio's (0.7mi);
East Boston (1mi);
Reelhouse (1.2mi)

Hanover St

Fire Boat Dock

1

Battery St

Battery St

Lincoln
Wharf

Callahan Tunnel

32

Salutation St

Hanover Ave

North St

Harris St

Union
Wharf

Clark St

Commercial St

Garden Ct St

Fleet St

Moon St

Lewis St

Eastern Ave

Sargents
Wharf

North St

Atlantic Ave

Fulton St

Lewis
Wharf

Boston
Inner
Harbor

Commercial St

Mercantile
Wharf
Building

Commercial Wharf East

Richmond St

Commercial
Wharf

42

Atlantic Ave

Christopher
Columbus
Park

WATERFRONT

3

NORTH END *Map on p230*

DOWNTOWN & WATERFRONT *Map on p234*

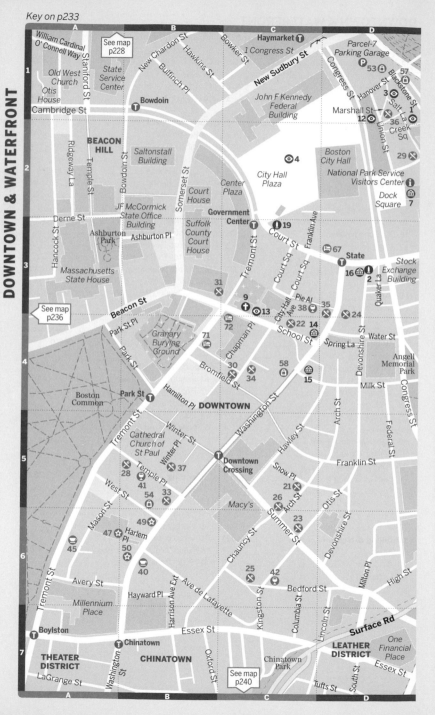

DOWNTOWN & WATERFRONT

William Cardinal O'Connell Way
Old West Church
Otis House
Cambridge St
Stanford St
Ridgeway La
Temple St
Hancock St
Derne St

New Chardon St
Hawkins St
Bulfinch Pl
State Service Center
Bowdoin

BEACON HILL
Saltonstall Building
Bowdoin St
Somerset St
JF McCormick State Office Building
Ashburton Pl
Ashburton Park
Massachusetts State House
Beacon St
Park St Pl
Granary Burying Ground
Park St

Bowker St
1 Congress St
New Sudbury St
John F Kennedy Federal Building
Center Plaza
City Hall Plaza
Court House
Government Center
Suffolk County Court House
Tremont St
Court St
Court Sq
31
72
13
Chapman Pl
Bromfield St
30
34
58
15

Haymarket
Parcel-7 Parking Garage
53
57
3
Marshall St
12
36
Union St
29
Boston City Hall
National Park Service Visitors Center
Dock Square
7
19
67
State
16
2
Stock Exchange Building
Pie Al
38
35
22
14
School St
Spring La
24
Water St
Devonshire St
Angell Memorial Park
Milk St
Congress St

DOWNTOWN
Hamilton Pl
Park St
Boston Common
Tremont St
Cathedral Church of St Paul
Winter St
Winter Pl
Washington St
Downtown Crossing
Hawley St
Arch St
Franklin St
Federal St

28
Temple Pl
41
54
33
49
47 Harlem Pl
50
45
40
West St
Mason St
Avery St
Millennium Place
Hayward Pl
Ave de Lafayette
Harrison Ave Ext

Macy's
Chauncy St
Summer St
21
26
23
25
42
Kingston St
Bedford St
Columbia St
Snow Pl
Arch St
Otis St
Devonshire St
Milton Pl
High St
Lincoln St
Surface Rd
One Financial Place
LEATHER DISTRICT

Boylston
Chinatown
THEATER DISTRICT
LaGrange St
Washington St
CHINATOWN
Oxford St
Chinatown Park
Essex St
Tufts St
South St
Essex St

See map p228
See map p236
See map p240

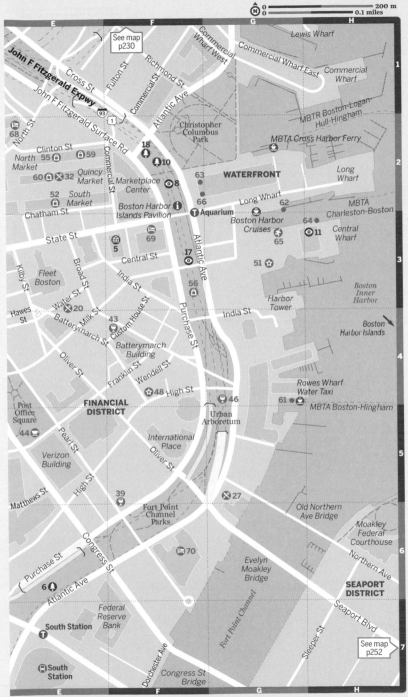

0
0
200 m
0.1 miles

See map
p230

John F Fitzgerald Expwy

Cross St

Fulton St

Richmond St

Commercial St

Commercial Wharf West

Lewis Wharf

Commercial Wharf East

Commercial Wharf

John F Fitzgerald Surface Rd

Atlantic Ave

93

1

68

North St

Clinton St

North
Market
55

59

Christopher
Columbus
Park

MBTR Boston-Logan-
Hull-Hingham

MBTA Cross Harbor Ferry

18

10

WATERFRONT

Long
Wharf

60

32

Quincy
Market

52

South
Market

Commercial St

Marketplace
Center

8

63

66

Long Wharf

62

MBTA
Charleston-Boston

Chatham St

Boston Harbor
Islands Pavilion

Aquarium

Boston Harbor
Cruises

64

11

Central
Wharf

State St

69

5

65

Central St

Fleet
Boston

India St

17

51

Kilby St

Broad St

56

Boston
Inner
Harbor

Hawes
St

Water St

20

Batterymarch St

43

Custom House St

Batterymarch
Building

India St

Harbor
Tower

Boston
Harbor Islands

Oliver St

Franklin St

Wendell St

48

High St

46

Rowes Wharf
Water Taxi

61

MBTA Boston-Hingham

Post
Office
Square

FINANCIAL
DISTRICT

Pearl St

International
Place

Oliver St

Urban
Arboretum

44

Verizon
Building

High St

39

27

Old Northern
Ave Bridge

Moakley
Federal
Courthouse

Matthews St

Fort Point
Channel Parks

Northern Ave

Purchase St

70

Evelyn
Moakley
Bridge

SEAPORT
DISTRICT

Congress St

6

Atlantic Ave

Seaport Blvd

South Station

Federal
Reserve
Bank

Dorchester Ave

Fort Point Channel

Sleeper St

South
Station

Congress St
Bridge

See map
p252

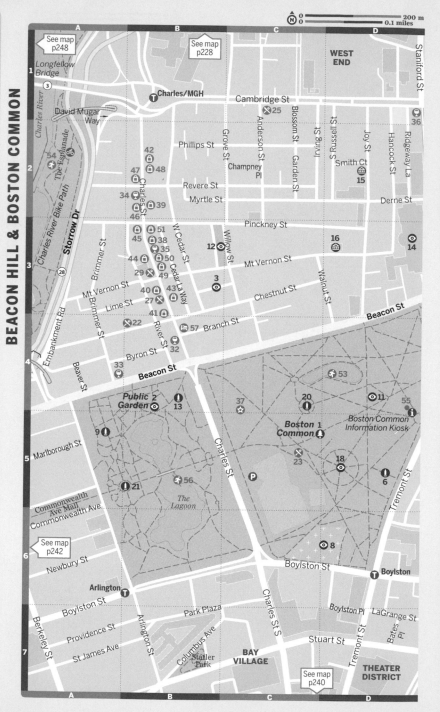

N

0   200 m
0   0.1 miles

See map
p248

Longfellow
Bridge

Charles River

David Mugar
Way

The Esplanade

Charles River Bike Path

Storrow Dr

Embankment Rd

See map
p228

Charles/MGH

Cambridge St   25

WEST
END

Staniford St

Phillips St

Champney
Pl

Revere St

Myrtle St

Grove St

Anderson St

Blossom St

Garden St

Irving St

S Russell St

Joy St

Hancock St

Smith Ct

15

36

42

47   48

34

46   39

51
45   38
35
44   50
29   49

Charles St

W Cedar St

Willow St

12

Pinckney St

Mt Vernon St

16

Derne St

14

Brimmer St

Mt Vernon St   40   43 La Way
27
41

Lime St

Brimmer St

22

33

River St

57   Branch St

32

Byron St

Beacon St

3

Chestnut St

Walnut St

Beacon St

Beaver St

Public
Garden   2
13

9

Marlborough St

21

56

The
Lagoon

Commonwealth
Ave Mall
Commonwealth Ave

See map
p242

Newbury St

Arlington

Boylston St

Berkeley St

Providence St

St James Ave

Charles St

37

20

Boston
Common   1

23

P

18

53

11   55

Boston Common
Information Kiosk

6

8

Boylston St

Boylston

Tremont St

Park Plaza

Arlington St

Columbus Ave

Statler
Park

BAY
VILLAGE

Charles St S

Stuart St

See map
p240

Boylston Pl

LaGrange St

Tremont St

Bates
Pl

THEATER
DISTRICT

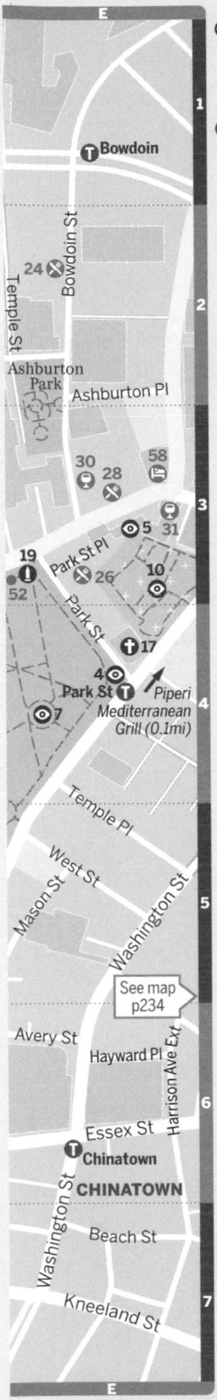

E
1
Bowdoin
Bowdoin St
24
Temple St
2
Ashburton Park
Ashburton Pl
30
28
58
3
5
31
19
52
Park St Pl
26
10
Park St
17
4
Park St
Piperi Mediterranean Grill (0.1mi)
7
Temple Pl
West St
Mason St
Washington St
5
See map p234
Avery St
Hayward Pl
Harrison Ave Ext
6
Essex St
Chinatown
Washington St
CHINATOWN
Beach St
Kneeland St
7
E

Top Sights (p70)
1 Boston Common....................C5
2 Public Garden........................B4

Sights (p73)
3 Acorn Street...........................B3
4 Blaxton Plaque......................E4
5 Boston Athenaeum................E3
6 Boston Massacre Monument..........................D5
7 Brewer Fountain...................E4
8 Central Burying Ground......D6
9 Ether Monument....................A5
10 Granary Burying Ground.....E3
11 Great Elm Site......................D4
12 Louisburg Square.................B3
13 Make Way for Ducklings Statue.................................B4
14 Massachusetts State House.................................D3
15 Museum of African American History..............D2
16 Nichols House Museum......D3
17 Park St Church......................E4
18 Parkman Bandstand............D5
19 Robert Gould Shaw Memorial..............................E3
20 Soldiers & Sailors Monument..........................C4
21 Statue of George Washington.........................B5

Eating (p74)
22 75 Chestnut..........................B4
23 Earl of Sandwich..................C5
Figs..............................(see 27)
24 Grotto.....................................E2
25 Ma Maison.............................C1
Mooo............................(see 58)
26 No 9 Park...............................E3
27 Paramount.............................B3
28 Scollay Square......................E3
29 Tatte.......................................B3

Drinking & Nightlife (p76)
30 21st Amendment..................E3
31 6B Lounge..............................E3
32 Bin 26 Enoteca.......................B4
33 Cheers.....................................A4
34 Pressed...................................B2
35 Sevens......................................B3
36 Tip Tap Room.........................D1

Entertainment (p78)
37 Shakespeare on the Common...............................C4

Shopping (p78)
38 Beacon Hill Chocolates........B3
39 Black Ink................................B2
40 Blackstone's of Beacon Hill...B3
41 Crane & Lion.........................B3
42 Crush Boutique.....................B2
43 December Thieves...............B3
44 Eugene Galleries..................B3
45 Good.......................................B3
46 Helen's Leather.....................B2
47 Marika's Antique Shop.........B2
48 Paridaez.................................B2
49 Red Wagon............................B3
50 Twentieth Century Ltd.........B3
51 Upstairs Downstairs Antiques..............................B3

Sports & Activities (p79)
52 Black Heritage Trail..............E3
53 Boston Common Frog Pond.......................................D4
54 Community Boating.............A2
55 Freedom Trail Foundation...D4
56 Swan Boats............................B5

Sleeping (p182)
57 Beacon Hill Hotel & Bistro.................................B4
58 XV Beacon.............................E3

SOUTH END

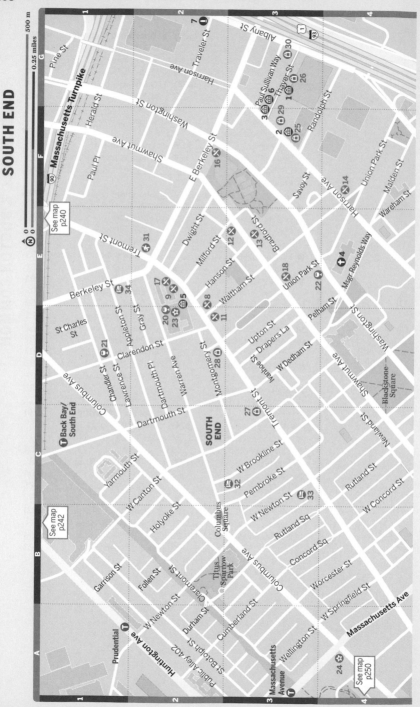

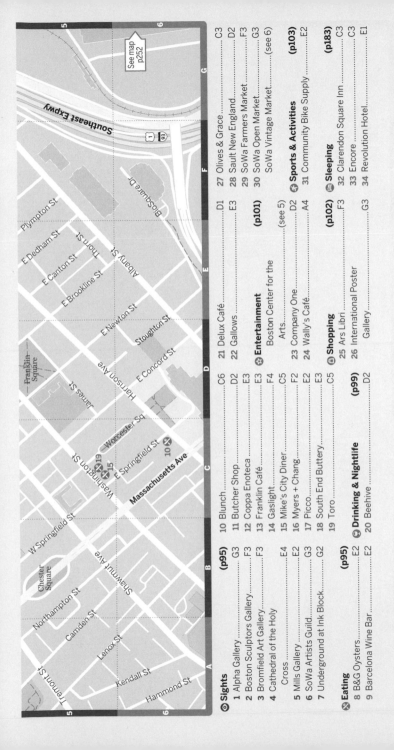

See map
p252

Southeast Expwy

◎ Sights (p95)

1 Alpha Gallery	G3
2 Boston Sculptors Gallery	F3
3 Bromfield Art Gallery	F3
4 Cathedral of the Holy Cross	E4
5 Mills Gallery	E2
6 SoWa Artists Guild	G3
7 Underground at Ink Block	G2

✕ Eating (p95)

8 B&G Oysters	E2
9 Barcelona Wine Bar	E2
10 Blunch	C6
11 Butcher Shop	D2
12 Coppa Enoteca	E3
13 Franklin Café	E3
14 Gaslight	F4
15 Mike's City Diner	C5
16 Myers + Chang	F2
17 Picco	E2
18 South End Buttery	E3
19 Toro	C5

🍷 Drinking & Nightlife (p99)

20 Beehive	D2

21 Delux Café	D1
22 Gallows	E3

★ Entertainment (p101)

Boston Center for the Arts	(see 5)
23 Company One	D2
24 Wally's Café	A4

🛍 Shopping (p102)

25 Ars Libri	F3
26 International Poster Gallery	D2

27 Olives & Grace	C3
28 Sault New England	D2
29 SoWa Farmers Market	F3
30 SoWa Open Market	G3
SoWa Vintage Market	(see 6)

⊕ Sports & Activities (p103)

31 Community Bike Supply	E2

🛏 Sleeping (p183)

32 Clarendon Square Inn	C3
33 Encore	C3
34 Revolution Hotel	E1

CHINATOWN, LEATHER DISTRICT & THEATER DISTRICT

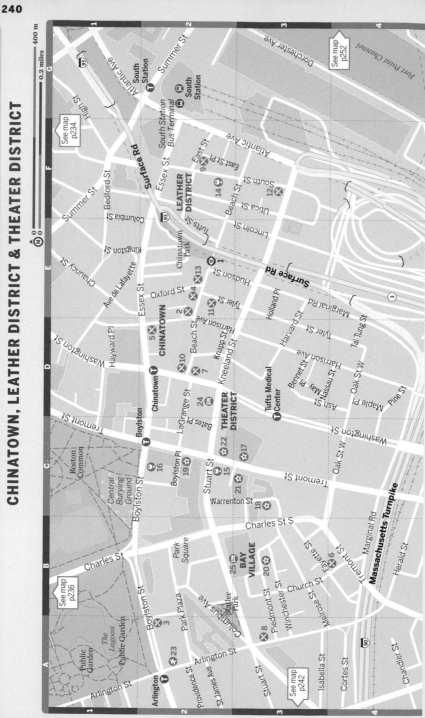

CHINATOWN, LEATHER DISTRICT & THEATER DISTRICT

⊚ **Sights** (p95)
1 Chinatown Gate E2

😋 **Eating** (p98)
2 Avana Sushi E2
3 Bistro du Midi A2
4 Gourmet Dumpling House E2
5 Kaze Shabu Shabu D2
6 Mike & Patty's B4
7 My Thai Vegan Café D2
8 Nahita A3
9 O Ya F2

10 Q Restaurant D2
11 Shōjō E2
12 South Street Diner F3
13 Taiwan Cafe E2

🍷 **Drinking & Nightlife** (p101)
14 Les Zygomates F2
15 Tunnel C2
16 Whisky Saigon C2

🎭 **Entertainment** (p101)
17 Boch Center C3

18 Charles Playhouse C3
19 Cutler Majestic Theatre C2
20 Jacques Cabaret B3
21 Shubert Theatre C3
22 Wilbur Theatre C2

🏆 **Sports & Activities** (p103)
23 Exhale Spa A2

😴 **Sleeping** (p183)
24 HI-Boston D2
25 Revere Hotel B3

Key on p244

BACK BAY

Charles River

Harvard Bridge

Storrow Dr

Storrow Dr

Back St

Charles River Bike Path

45

Beacon St

Marlborough St

Fairfield St

Exeter St

Commonwealth Ave

Massachusetts Ave

Hereford St

Gloucester St

2

35
37 36

30

Commonwealth Ave Mall

56

55

21 16

BACK BAY

14

41

Newbury St

22

13

26

53

39

Newbury St

33

25

Boylston St

Ring Rd

Massachusetts Turnpike

42

Hynes Convention Center

40

Massachusetts Turnpike

See map p250

Cambria St

28 43

12

32

Scotia St

Belvidere St

Dalton St

9

St Germain St

Prudential

48

Haviland St

Clearway St

52

Follen St

Hemenway St

Norway St

Edgerly Rd

10

W Newton St

49

Burbank St

5

Reflecting Pool

Public Alley 402

St Botolph St

Durham St

Titus Sparrow Park

Westland Ave

Massachusetts Ave

Huntington Ave

Blackwood St

Cumberland St

Claremont St

Hemenway St

Symphony Rd

St Stephens St

Symphony

Albemarle St

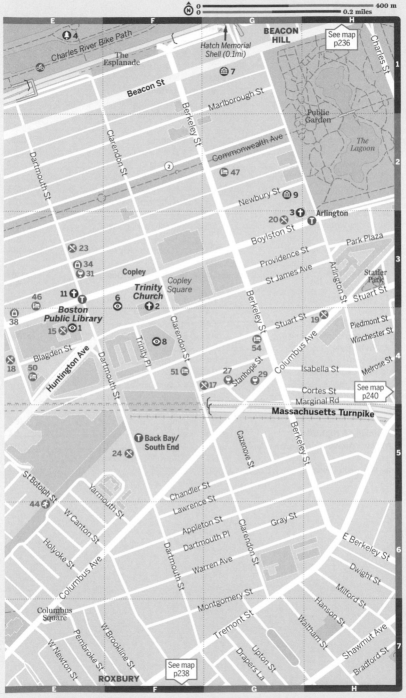

BACK BAY *Map on p242*

BACK BAY

HARVARD SQUARE Map on p246

HARVARD SQUARE

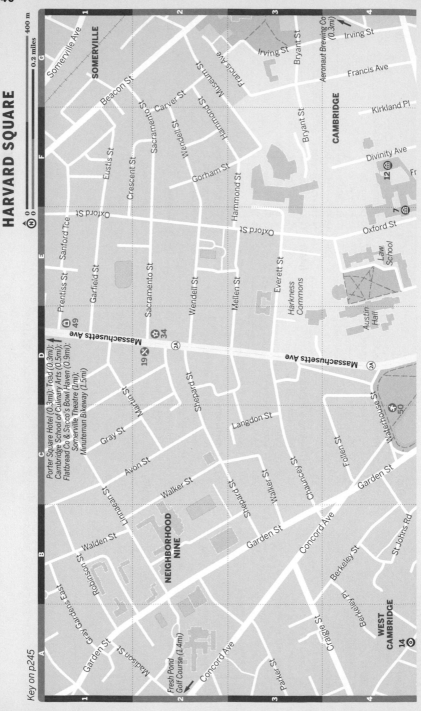

Key on p245

400 m
0.2 miles

SOMERVILLE

CAMBRIDGE

Porter Square Hotel (0.3mi); Toad (0.3mi);
Cambridge School of Culinary Arts (0.5mi);
Flatbread Co & Sacco's Bowl Haven (0.9mi);
Somerville Theatre (1mi);
Minuteman Bikeway (1.5mi)

NEIGHBORHOOD
NINE

WEST
CAMBRIDGE

Aeronaut Brewing Co (0.3mi)

Fresh Pond
Golf Course (1.4mi)

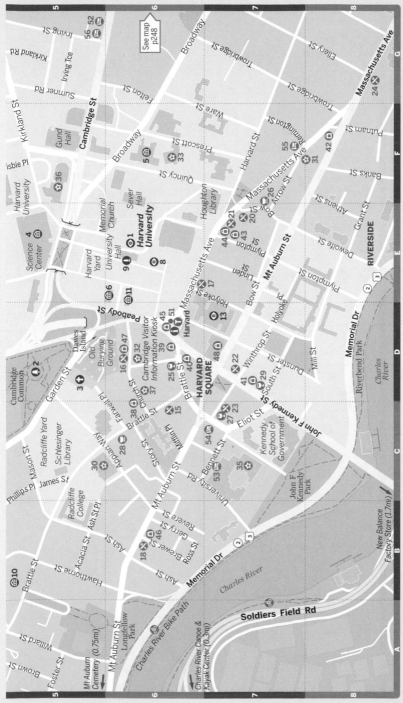

See map p248

CENTRAL, KENDALL & INMAN SQUARES

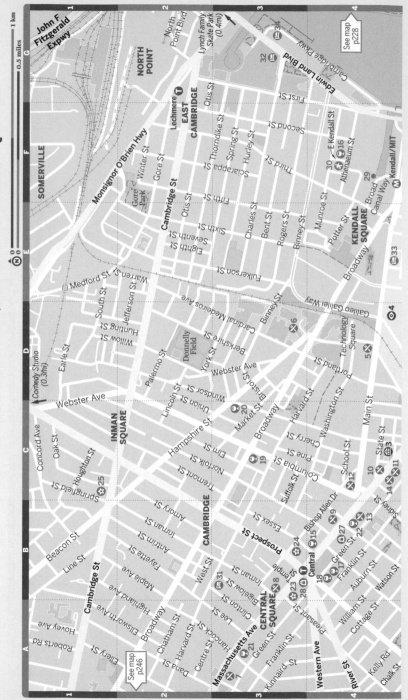

See map p228

See map p246

CENTRAL, KENDALL & INMAN SQUARES

◎ **Top Sights** (p143)
1 Massachusetts Institute of
Technology.....................................D5

◎ **Sights** (p143)
2 List Visual Arts Center.....................E5
3 MIT Museum.....................................C4
4 Ray & Maria Stata Center................D4

✕ **Eating** (p146)
5 Area Four...D4
6 Bon Me..D3
7 Dumpling House...............................A3
Friendly Toast..........................(see 6)
8 Life Alive..B3
9 Little Donkey...................................B4
10 Miracle of Science Bar & Grill..........C4
11 Roxy's Grilled Cheese.....................C4

12 Toscanini's......................................C4
13 Veggie Galaxy.................................B4
14 Whole Heart Provisions...................C4

🍷 **Drinking & Nightlife** (p150)
A4cade...................................(see 11)
15 Brick & Mortar................................B4
16 Café ArtScience...............................F4
17 Green Street....................................B4
18 Havana Club.....................................B4
19 Lamplighter Brewing Co...................C3
20 Lord Hobo..C3
21 Plough & Stars.................................A3
22 Zuzu...B4

🎭 **Entertainment** (p152)
23 Cantab Lounge.................................B3
24 Improv Boston..................................B3

25 Lily Pad...C1
Middle East............................(see 22)

🛍 **Shopping** (p154)
26 Central Flea......................................B5
27 Cheapo Records...............................B4
28 Rodney's Bookstore.........................B3

⚽ **Sports & Activities** (p154)
29 Charles River Canoe & Kayak Center...F4
30 Community Ice Skating @ Kendall Square...F4
Flat Top Johnny's.....................(see 6)

🛏 **Sleeping** (p186)
31 Harding House.................................B3
32 Hotel Marlowe.................................G3
33 Kendall Hotel...................................E4
34 Royal Sonesta..................................G3

KENMORE SQUARE & FENWAY

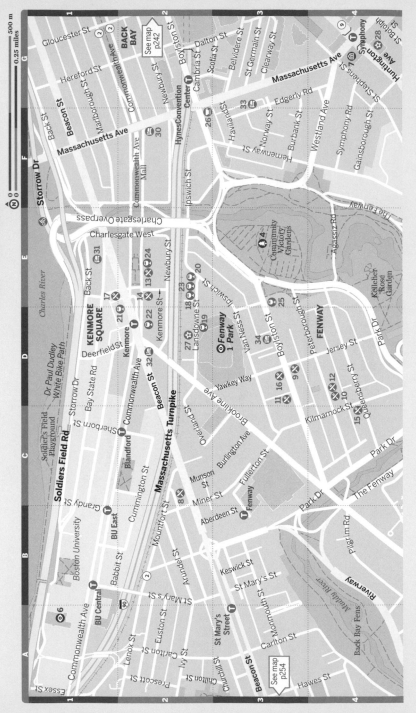

KENMORE SQUARE & FENWAY

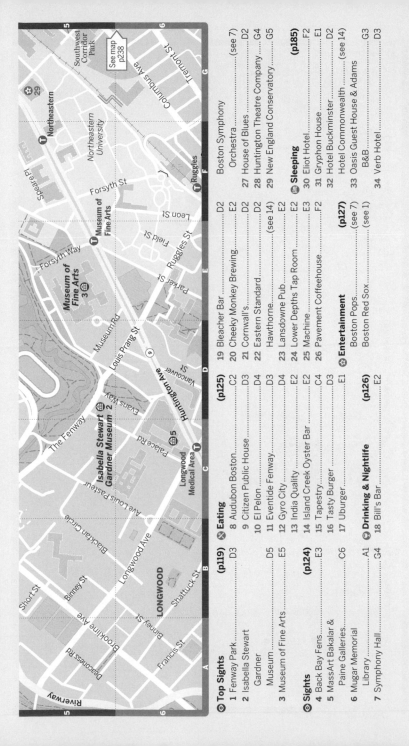

SEAPORT DISTRICT & SOUTH BOSTON

Downtown Crossing T

FINANCIAL DISTRICT

See map p234

See Enlargement

Fan Pier Park

Boston Inner Harbor

Institute of Contemporary Art 1

South Station T

Congress St Bridge

3

Seaport Blvd

P

World Trade Center

29

Fish Pier

14

LEATHER DISTRICT

See map p236

Summer St

Fort Point Channel

A St

P

33

Congress St

Northern Ave

26 20

Broadway T

FORT POINT

Boston Convention & Exhibition Center

27

22

Broadway T

31

SEAPORT DISTRICT

Dry Dock Ave

South Boston Bypass

Cypher St

D St

E St

Pappas Way

Reserved Channel

See map p240

21

W 1st St

Bolton St

Athens St

W Broadway

E 1st St

E 2nd St

Summer St

Medal of Honor Park

See map p238

D St

E St

F St

SOUTH BOSTON

Dorchester St

Old Harbor St

6

G St

E Broadway

E 4th St

E 6th St

E 8th St

K St

L St

M St

N St

O St

P St

15

Faragut Rd

Dorchester Ave

Old Colony Ave

Columbia Rd

Day Blvd

Andrew T

Old Colony Ave

Joe Moakley Park

Day Blvd

4

Old Harbour

Southeast Expwy

Boston St

1
93

Columbia Rd

JFK/ UMass T

Mt Vernon St

Dorchester Bay

Pleasant St

DORCHESTER

Dorchester Ave

Southeast Expwy

Morrissey Blvd

Boston College High School

Savin Hill Cove

COLOMBIA POINT

7

10

University of Massachusetts Boston

University Dr S

Savin Hill T

1
93

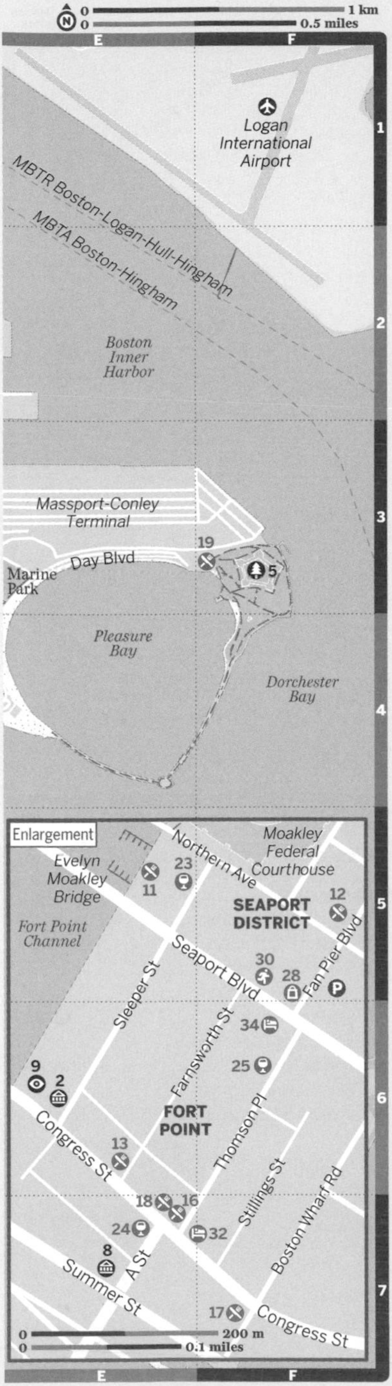

0 1 km
0 0.5 miles
E
F
Logan International Airport
MBTR Boston-Logan-Hull-Hingham
MBTA Boston-Hingham
Boston Inner Harbor
Massport-Conley Terminal
Day Blvd
Marine Park
19
5
Pleasure Bay
Dorchester Bay
1
2
3
4
5
6
7
Enlargement
Evelyn Moakley Bridge
Northern Ave
Moakley Federal Courthouse
23
11
12
SEAPORT DISTRICT
Fort Point Channel
Seaport Blvd
30
28
Fan Pier Blvd
Sleeper St
Farnsworth St
34
25
9
2
FORT POINT
Congress St
Thomson Pl
13
Stillings St
Boston Wharf Rd
18
16
24
32
8
A St
Summer St
17
Congress St
0 200 m
0 0.1 miles

Top Sights (p131)
1 Institute of Contemporary Art C1

Sights (p132)
2 Boston Children's Museum E6
3 Boston Tea Party Ships & Museum B1
4 Carson Beach B5
5 Castle Island & Fort Independence F3
6 Dorchester Heights B4
7 Edward M Kennedy Institute for the United States Senate C6
8 Fort Point Arts Community E7
9 Hood Milk Bottle E6
10 John F Kennedy Presidential Library & Museum C6

Eating (p133)
11 Barking Crab E5
12 Committee F5
13 Flour E6
14 Legal Harborside C2
15 Local 149 .....D4
16 Menton E7
17 Row 34 .....F7
18 Sportello E7
19 Sullivan's F3
20 Yankee Lobster Co C2

Drinking & Nightlife (p137)
21 Croke Park Whitey's B3
Drink .....(see 18)
22 Harpoon Brewery & Beer Hall C2
23 Lookout Rooftop Bar E5
24 Lucky's Lounge E7
25 Trillium Fort Point F6

Entertainment (p138)
Barbara Lee Family Foundation Theater .....(see 1)
26 Blue Hills Bank Pavilion C2
27 Laugh Boston B2

Shopping (p138)
28 For Now F5
29 Society of Arts & Crafts B1

Sports & Activities (p138)
30 Kings F5
31 The Lawn on D B2

Sleeping (p186)
Envoy Hotel .....(see 23)
32 Residence Inn Marriott F7
33 Seaport Boston Hotel C2
34 Yotel F6

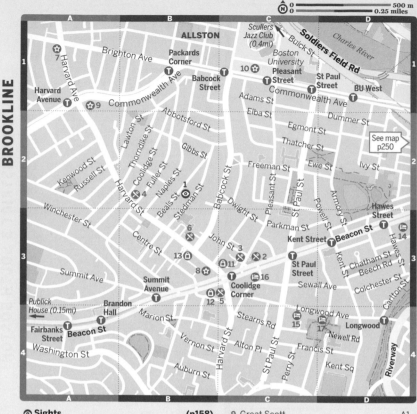

BROOKLINE

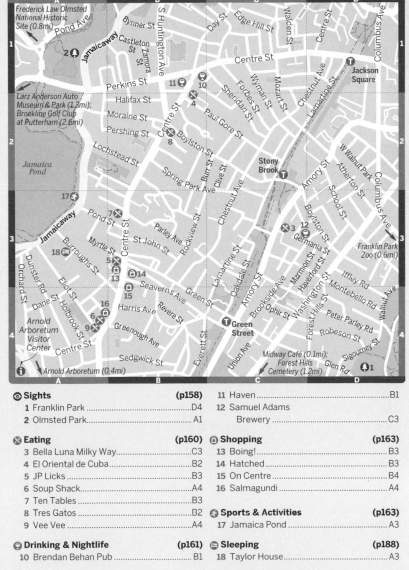

Our Story

A beat-up old car, a few dollars in the pocket and a sense of adventure. In 1972 that's all Tony and Maureen Wheeler needed for the trip of a lifetime – across Europe and Asia overland to Australia. It took several months, and at the end – broke but inspired – they sat at their kitchen table writing and stapling together their first travel guide, *Across Asia on the Cheap*. Within a week they'd sold 1500 copies. Lonely Planet was born.

Today, Lonely Planet has offices in Franklin, London, Melbourne, Oakland, Dublin, Beijing and Delhi, with more than 600 staff and writers. We share Tony's belief that 'a great guidebook should do three things: inform, educate and amuse'.

Our Writers

Mara Vorhees

Mara writes about food, travel and family fun around the world. Her work has been published by BBC Travel, *Boston Globe*, *Delta Sky*, *Vancouver Sun* and more. For Lonely Planet, she regularly writes about destinations in Central America and Eastern Europe, as well as New England, where she lives. She often travels with her twin boys in tow, earning her an expertise in family travel. Follow their adventures and misadventures at www.havetwinswilltravel.com.

Contributing writer: Robert Balkovich wrote the Provincetown section of the Day Trips chapter.

Published by Lonely Planet Global Limited
CRN 554153
7th edition – November 2019
ISBN 978 1 78657 178 6
© Lonely Planet 2019   Photographs © as indicated 2019
10 9 8 7 6 5 4 3 2 1
Printed in Malaysia